This book was purchased with
U.S. Department of Education
Title III grant funds.

A Conversational History of Modern America

A Conversational History *of* Modern America

Richard D. Heffner

Edited by Marc Jaffe

CARROLL & GRAF PUBLISHERS
NEW YORK

A CONVERSATIONAL HISTORY OF MODERN AMERICA

Carroll & Graf Publishers
An Imprint of Avalon Publishing Group Inc.
161 William St., 16th Floor
New York, NY 10038

Library of Congress Cataloging-in-Publication Data is available.

ISBN: 0-7867-1087-X

Interior design by Paul Paddock
Printed in the United States of America
Distributed by Publishers Group West

To Elaine
and
our children
and
our children's children

Table of Contents

THE MEDIA

RACE

WOMEN'S ISSUES

MEDICINE

POPULAR CULTURE & THE AMERICAN SCENE

PREFACE

by Mario M. Cuomo

For more than fifty years, Dick Heffner has provided a cornucopia of ideas and discussion that have described and elevated the political and social culture of our nation. A distinguished Professor of Communications and Public Policy at Rutgers University, his best-selling *A Documentary History of The United States,* revised continually since its original publication in 1952, is a careful selection of great documents that have helped shape the United States' formation and growth. From the Declaration of Independence to the written speeches of modern Presidents, his collection is a small library of the bright letter principles and policies that provide the fundamental framework of our democratic structure. Since 1956, Professor Heffner has complemented that written history with *The Open Mind,* hundreds of televised conversations during which Heffner invariably engages his guests in the kind of intellectually stimulating discourse which early idealists—like his hero Edward R. Murrow—envisioned for the media. His provocative but palatable questioning promotes a spontaneity in responses that adds dimension and subtlety to the discussion not possible in the eloquent but frozen words of historical documents.

I know from personal experience that even measured against other television interviewers, guests seem to converse with Professor Heffner in more depth with less reserve, producing a nuanced conversational history of our times that nourishes the intellect of its audience. You will have that experience yourself as you read this splendidly edited volume. Enjoy the feast . . . as I have for so many years.

INTRODUCTION

"I'm Richard Heffner, your host on *The Open Mind* . . . " These simple introductory words haven't changed since I began to produce and host my weekly public television series nearly a half-century ago. But, why should they change? After all, the same intentions inform *The Open Mind* and its conversations today as in May 1956, when I first put the series on the air—and as now inform this book.

What are these personal imperatives? Essentially, to bring my audiences face to face with many of the seminal thinkers of the Twentieth Century, and now of our own new times. Each week I try to make the show a compelling exploration into the world of ideas by eliciting my guests' most passionate insights into the challenges Americans face in a variety of areas. The objective of these conversations—often provocative, though neither strident nor personally intrusive—has been to provide the light of reasoned, rational discourse, rather than the heat of verbal battle.

First and foremost, after all, I am a teacher and historian, not a broadcaster (as my media colleagues have always been quick to point out). And these are the same objectives that motivated me to become a college instructor early in life and then to reach out to the ever increasing numbers of Americans who began to turn to such easily accessible means of mass education as paperback books (among them my own *A Documentary History of the United States*) and the newest electronic medium, television.

Indeed, when I sign off each week's *Open Mind*, it is with "As an old friend used to say, 'Good Night and Good Luck'", my own tribute to Edward R. Murrow, that extraordinary CBS newsman whose pioneering work convinced an entire generation that television could be as important an educational force as the printed word and perhaps as the classroom itself . . . if used as it could and should be used. It was he who inspired so many of us to find our way into television. It is my fervent hope that *The Open Mind* has been seen and used in this way, just as I hope A *Conversational History of Modern America,* derived from the show, will be read and used in the same way.

It was Murrow who so memorably said about television, "This instrument can teach, it can illuminate; yes, and it can even inspire. But it can do so only to the extent that humans are determined to use it to those ends. Otherwise, it is merely wires and lights in a box. There is a great and perhaps decisive battle to be fought against ignorance, intolerance and indifference. This weapon of television could be useful . . . The trouble with television is that it is rusting in the scabbard during a battle for survival."

Over the past near-half century, some guests joined me on *The Open Mind* several times; a few, very many times. Yet not even these could all be included in this present collection . . . let alone each and every person who has sat with me even just once at the microphone or before the camera. Hopefully, in future volumes many more of those whose words importantly reflect our history will appear as well . . . Eleanor Roosevelt, Sidney Hook, Lionel Trilling, Milton Friedman, Linda Greenhouse, Richard Helms, Sylvia Nasar, John Sexton, Margaret Mead, and hundreds of others.

As must be abundantly clear to the reader of this volume, I choose many of my broadcast guests because of the newsworthiness of their activities or their fields of interest at the moment. Yet, the very breadth and scope of their comments on the air have almost always given them a timelessness that makes them worth consulting years— quite frequently even decades—later. Perhaps that is because basic American issues worth examining at any one point in our history turn out to be worth discussing at all times. This phenomenon has given these conversations a surprisingly long shelf life and a relevance none of us would have been able to imagine at taping time . . . despite both the fact that transcriptions of the spoken word are often faulty and our own hesitancy to take liberties with the printed word.

My indebtedness to so many others for this volume is enormous . . .

and gratifying to note. Certainly to all of those who have joined me in this conversational history of our times, I extend my heartfelt thanks for being willing to interrupt busy schedules to give ever so freely and so much of their wit and wisdom to the cause of keeping an open mind on the air. Their only compensation for participation in this adventure in teaching and learning—like my own—is the certain knowledge that important ideas have been shared with untold numbers of devoted viewers and listeners, to whom I also express my gratitude.

My special thanks to Marc Jaffe as well. Marc is the distinguished publishing industry executive and talented editor of my *A Documentary History of the United States* and of my edition of Tocqueville's classic *Democracy in America* at New American Library's Mentor Books back when we, and the world, were so much younger. More relevant, it is Marc's continuing editorial skill that has now made broadcast transcripts into readable text . . . and thus made this volume his as well as mine.

Will Balliett is the inspiringly indefatigable Avalon executive and editor in charge of this project who gave it life and substance and sustains it to this very moment. In this endeavor, we have also all been expertly organized and supported by Avalon assistant editor Kristen Couse. David Halpern is my intrepid literary agent at the Robbins Office whose efforts made the project possible in the first place . . . as is his wont. And, of course, it continues to be my colleague Daphne Dwyer Doelger, the very best of friends, who always makes good on the commitments I grandly assume for programs and books and other ventures . . . to some extraordinary extent by skillfully organizing the work of such of our recent Rutgers University Interns as Sherine Aboelezz, Richard Edson, James Fabiano, Nicole Himmelman, Maribel Luna, Sonal Pandya, Christine Scheller and Kristen Van Sise, to name but a few.

Over these many years, to be sure, the programs from which the selections in this volume have been taken have owed much to a quite notable cadre of Executive, Associate and Assistant Producers, including, and most fairly accounted for alphabetically: Edith Bjornson, Kelly

Cahill, Thomas Chandler, Barbara Davidson, Janice Elsesser, Esther H. Kramer, Andrea Levin, Linda Murray, Elinor Riger, Kelly Rounds and Jan. C. Waldman. Over the years, too, continuing production of *The Open Mind*, as well as its distribution via American Public Television's broadcast satellite, has been generously made possible by grants from many public-spirited individuals, businesses, large and small foundations and various other institutions. At present, they include the Bluestein Family Foundation; Phyllis and Richard L. Gelb; The Malkin Fund; the Rosalind P. Walter Foundation; The Center for Educational Outreach and Innovation at Teachers College, Columbia University; The Commonwealth Fund; and from the corporate community, Mutual of America.

Lastly, this book, like all of my broadcast and other widely disparate endeavors, owes much to my wife, Dr. Elaine Heffner, who over more than five decades now, has herself patiently watched, listened to . . . and vastly improved upon . . . this continuing conversational history of our times.

RICHARD D. HEFFNER
Lake Oscawana, New York
August 5th, 2003

POWER & POLITICS

ROBERT CARO

There is no better way to understand history than through biography. Thomas Carlyle wrote that "The history of the world is but the biography of great men;" Ralph Waldo Emerson, that "There is properly no history, only biography." In either of these assertions, Robert Caro emerges as a unique literary figure, very likely the preeminent non-academic historian/biographer of our time. Caro's monumental biography of Robert Moses, The Power Broker, *published in the early 1970s, won both the Pulitzer Prize and the Francis Parkman prize, awarded by the Society of American Historians. His epic life of Lyndon Johnson has seen three volumes published,* The Path to Power, Means of Ascent, *and* Master of the Senate *(which also won a Pulitzer), with more still to come on Johnson's Vice-Presidential and Presidential years. Taken together, these two biographies—already classics—constitute perhaps the most important study of modern American political power ever undertaken. And in our conversations, Robert Caro and I attempted to examine the very essence of that power, and how it was achieved and exercised, in the lives of these two larger-than-life figures of the twentieth century: Robert Moses, of New York, and Lyndon Johnson, of Texas and Washington, D.C.*

Heffner: How could it possibly be, as you've said, that the history of New York City in the twentieth century is really, to an amazing extent, the story of Robert Moses?

You know, he had power in New York for 44 years, almost half that century. And with that power he shaped the city. You can see it if you fly into New York. If you fly into LaGuardia you pass the Throgs Neck Bridge—Robert Moses built it. The Bronx/Whitestone Bridge—Robert Moses built it. The Triborough Bridge, the Henry Hudson Bridge—Robert Moses built them. If you're flying in from the south, to Kennedy, you pass the Verrazano-Narrows Bridge, which Robert Moses built, the Cross Bay Bridge, the Marine Parkway Bridge—he built them all. Every major highway that you see, 14 expressways and 16 parkways. Every major road that you see cutting across the city, with the single exception of the East River Drive, was built by this one man. Every park was either created or re-created, re-shaped by him. Whole areas of public housing in New York were also built by him. He left his mark on this city.

Heffner: Is there an easy way to explain how one man could do all this?

Well, the bridges were built by his Public Authorities. He created the Public Authority in its modern form, the Triborough Bridge and Tunnel Authority. But he also was the head of seven other Authorities at the same time. You know, when he came to power we thought of a public authority as an entity that built a single bridge or tunnel, floated bonds to pay for it, collected the tolls until the bonds were paid off, and then the Authority went out of business. Moses, with his genius for bill drafting, created Authorities in a way that they would, in effect, be eternal. And as long as he was head of them he would have absolute power over their revenues. Now as to the revenues—for decades every time you paid a toll on any bridge or tunnel within the borders of New York City, you were in effect paying it directly to Robert Moses. Because he was the head of the Triborough Bridge and Tunnel Authority, which collected those tolls. And he had absolute discretion over the spending of that money. And how much was it? For decades he had more money to spend on public works in New York City and its suburbs than the city had. And no Mayor, no

Board of Estimate could tell him how to spend it. He did what he wanted.

Heffner: But we can't leave it at that. How did he get all this power?

He got it in many different ways. Before he began building bridges, he started building the parks on Long Island. Jones Beach State Park, Sunken Meadow State Park, all the parks on Long Island. He undertook that because he was a young dreamer, who from the time he came back from Oxford, started to dream of huge public works in and around New York. For many years, until he was about 30 or 32, his dreams came to nothing. And in fact, he was a reformer then. He was an idealist. He was a real thorn in the side of Tammany Hall, which had controlling political power in New York. And Tammany Hall decided that they had to crush him. And they did crush him. At the age of 30, Robert Moses was standing on line outside the City Hall in Cleveland, Ohio, looking for a rather minor municipal job, which he didn't get. Then suddenly, Al Smith became Governor of New York State. His eye had been caught by this young man. He raised Robert Moses to power and put him in charge of the State Park program on Long Island, Jones Beach and all the others, and the parkways, the Northern and Southern State Parkways, the Wantagh and the Meadowbrook. And Moses spent the next four or five years hammering out those parks. I mean, that's the wonderful side of Robert Moses. Because at the time he wanted to build these state parks and parkways there were none, not on any scale. And the masses of New York City had no place to go out on Long Island. Moses conceived of this park program—Jones Beach, Sunken Meadow, fourteen parks in all and parkways to get to them. No one had done anything like this in America before. The powers of New York State were determined that he wouldn't build this program. And the story of how he got them built, hammered out, with Smith behind him—but it seemed like everybody else against him—was just thrilling to me.

Heffner: Then why doesn't he surface in Caro's *Power Broker* as a magnificent, heroic figure?

I think in the first three or four hundred pages of *The Power Broker* he *is* a magnificent, heroic figure. He is an idealist and a dreamer. The change comes very, very slowly. You know power is a very dangerous weapon. I recall I use the image in the book that power is like a sword, and the hilt as well as the blade is razor-sharp. So while a man is using it, the sword is cutting into him as well as into the people on whom he uses it. We can see even when Moses was building these early parks and parkways, he was utterly ruthless. He would do anything to get these roads and parks built. But at least he was doing it for a noble, wonderful cause.

Heffner: Was there ever a time when "the cause," when the end, was not one that we would embrace?

Oh, by all means. When he moved from the empty landscape of Long Island into New York City and started to build his expressways right across neighborhoods, and started to build public housing, really on a philosophy of separating the poor from the rich, we would say now that the impact of Robert Moses on New York was very destructive. It is 30 years since he left power. We're only now beginning to address the problems caused by his policies.

Heffner: Yet when you write about the fall, it's *and*—Robert Moses *and* the fall of New York. You're saying that we shouldn't embrace the ends of what he achieved, let alone his means.

I used as an epigraph in this book a quote from Sophocles—"One must wait until the evening to see how splendid the day has been." Let's look at the hallmarks of Robert Moses' policy. Absolute concentration on the automobile. For forty years he used his power systematically to starve mass transit—the Long Island Railroad being the most dramatic example—while pouring the public resources into highways. More and more highways. I think I could answer your question probably by taking one road as an example—the Long Island Expressway, which he started in 1952.

When he wanted to build the Long Island Expressway, he had the money to do it. He didn't need anyone's permission. He was told that the population of Long Island was starting to grow, though it was still largely empty space. You can build a six-lane highway, which is what it was then, but if you don't make provisions for having some sort of rapid transit, light rail lines down the middle of the Expressway, the road can never work, it's just going to generate more traffic, it's always going to be congested. Moses hated the idea of rapid transit; he viewed it as a competitor for the tolls he was getting from his automobiles, so he wouldn't even consider that option. Then they said to him—this is not hindsight because they were saying it to him at the time—"If you won't build these lines, at least buy an extra 40 feet of right of way. Keep it in the middle, keep it empty now if you want, but if in the future we should need rapid transit lines down the center, we will be able to do it." Land then was so cheap that the entire cost of that right of way for the whole length of the expressway was only 20 million dollars. He was spending 500 million dollars on it already. He was told that for an additional four percent, you can ensure the road will always work better. If you don't spend this money now, it will always be congested. He wouldn't acquire that extra 40 feet. More than that, he engineered the expressway so that rapid transit can never be built down its center. Now it's impossible to do that, and the road never worked. The same thing happened with the Van Wyck Expressway and with many other of his highways.

Heffner: Thinking of my years in California, and of the automobile there as the exclusive means of transportation, we know that the story there was in part a story of corruption and in part the story of the domination of the oil people. I gather there is nothing that you would consider parallel to this in Caro's Moses.

Well, that's a complicated question. Moses was personally very honest. He didn't care about money. He never cared about money. Someone, a friend of his once said to me, you know some people want caviar, Robert Moses was happy with a ham sandwich, if he could have power on the side. He, himself, was personally honest. But this man who was himself honest was the locus of corruption in New York City for four decades. When he built a bridge or a highway, every cent of the insurance premiums went to the right insurance brokers. Public relations retainers went to the right public relations men. The contractors were the politically well-connected contractors.

Heffner: To what end?

To the end of being able to get these things built. That's why I called the book *The Power Broker*. That's a very exact title. He was taking all these forces and acting as the broker. There is a chapter in the book called "One Mile" about how he rammed the Cross Bronx Expressway *right* across a neighborhood—in one mile he had to knock down 54 six- and seven- story apartment houses, displacing 5,000 people and ruining a neighborhood. There was an alternate route that would have displaced nobody—just six small tenements—two blocks away. The Mayor, the Board of Estimate, the Bronx Borough President, every elected official, the State Assemblyman from that area, and the State Senator said, "build it over there." But when these elected officials tried to impose their will on Moses, they found that all the forces that kept them in power, the contractors who made contributions, the lawyers, the public relations men, they all said, "Do what Moses wants". It was an irresistible power that he could marshal. And of course, in addition to that he had immense popularity.

Heffner: Based upon service?

Based largely on service. In 1920, when he was fighting for Jones Beach and Sunken Meadow State Park, Heckscher State Park, he got into a major lawsuit because he was really using means that verged on illegality to get them built. But he knew he would win in the court of public opinion. And he said to one of his assistants, "You know if you're on the side of the park, you're always on the side of the angels." And his park work was always wonderful, and he created a great blessing in the city. When I was a boy, I went to Horace Mann. We had to write a junior-year paper. We all had to write on the same topic, and the topic was "Robert Moses is the example of the White Knight in literature." That's how popular he was.

Heffner: And you were the one who said, "No."

No, I thought he was a great public servant.

Heffner: That points, obviously, in the direction of asking you again about power: *The Power Broker*, then Lyndon Johnson, *Means of Ascent*, *Ascent to Power*, of course. Power is what you are interested in.

Yes. Political power.

Heffner: Political power. Why do you say political power specifically?

Political power is the force that shapes all our lives. You know, I mean with Lyndon Johnson, if you say a young black man or young woman gets to go to college because of his affirmative action policy, that's political power, isn't it? If you talk about a young man who died in Vietnam or a village that was destroyed needlessly in Vietnam, that's political power, isn't it? As for Robert Moses, I see examples of it every day driving around New York City. Both for the good and the bad. I got interested in political power because I was a newspaper reporter and I wasn't happy with the job I was doing. And I felt that something was wrong with what I was doing. I was an investigative reporter; I had won some minor awards. I thought I was explaining to people how power works. And then one day I realized I was really not doing that successfully, and for me the awakening came. I couldn't understand even exactly who Robert Moses was. Where did he get his power? He was never elected to anything, yet he seemed to be able to do pretty much whatever he wanted in the field of public works. That's why I'm interested in political power.

. . . He really ensured that democratic considerations were often set aside. Let's talk, for example, about a playground in the days before Robert Moses. Of course, there was always corruption; economic forces always played a role in the city. Tammany Hall was a very corrupt organization. But if you had an alderman from a little ward on the Lower East Side and there was a question of where were you going to build the playground. Were you going to build it on one side of a major street or another? The alderman had a lot to say because he was kept in power by the votes of the people. He had to respond to the wishes of the people in that neighborhood. If they knew that they didn't want their children to cross an avenue, let's say, then the weight of their opinion to have the playground on the other side of the avenue would be very strong. What Moses did was remove consideration of public opinion from that neighborhood consideration. In *The Power Broker* I think I identify 20 separate neighborhoods that were destroyed by his expressways. These neighborhoods were basically towns, little towns, East Tremont in the Bronx was not so little, 60,000 people lived there. These neighborhoods were really the communities that made the city a home to their people. They had nothing to say about it. The expressways rammed right across them. Moses built them where he wanted to build them.

Heffner: All in all it comes back to the question of power. Does that make you a devotee of Lord Acton, that power tends to corrupt and absolute power tends to corrupt absolutely?

Actually, I don't quite agree with that. I feel that that's only sometimes true. The thing that is true is that power reveals. What it always does is reveal. When you rise to a position of power, the higher you get the less—if you're not elected, and that's the case with Robert Moses—the less you have to conceal yourself, the more your own tendencies can shine forth. Now, with Moses you would say that to a great extent Lord Acton's axiom is true. However . . . you see with Al Smith, who's a big figure in *The Power Broker,* the opposite is true. He was a Tammany figure, always wanting to help his people, and when he got to be Governor, it's like power cleansed Al Smith.

Heffner: That, of course, was why Lord Acton was careful enough to say that power only *tends* to corrupt.

Yes, tends.

Heffner: What do you mean about how "power reveals"—in connection with Lyndon Johnson?

Well, we see this, as with everything else with Lyndon Johnson, in a very intensified way. In the first two volumes of my biography, he's trying to get power. He's desperate to have it. And he's willing to do almost anything to get it. In the beginning of the third volume, he's rising to power in the Senate. When he gets it, suddenly two things happen. But they are both summed up with what you ask, "power revealed." Because when a person is rising to power on the one side he has to try to conceal the traits that might make other men not want to give him power, if they see, for example, that he'll be too ruthless, too arbitrary in using it. But at the same time, power reveals itself. It gives Johnson an opportunity to unleash things that these same men have wanted to unleash. In his case it is the compassion he always had for poor people, particularly poor people of color. Suddenly with the power—that is revealed.

Heffner: At the same time, I wondered as I was reading the book, "Is Caro changing his mind, making a newer, kinder judgment about Lyndon Baines Johnson?"

Oh, not at all. This has always been my judgment. He's the same person. In the first volume we see him when he has compassion for poor people, empathy because he, himself, was poor. I described how he really worked when he was a teenager . . . with mules, operating a Fresno, a highway-grading machine. I said, "How could he not have empathy for these people who do this work?"

And then we see him when he becomes a Congressman at the age of 28. He knows what the people of his district need. They need electricity, because without electricity they're all just poor farmers and ranchers. They have to do every chore by hand, from ironing to pumping up the water from the well. He says, "If you elect me Congressman, I will bring you electricity." No one believes he can do it. It seems like an impossible task to bring electricity to this isolated area; there's not even a source of hydroelectric power around. But he does it.

But then we see, in the second volume, there seems to be no place for him to go, he's lost his first race for the Senate. And he loses interest in politics to a large extent. Without the promise of power, he really is not very interested any more. And he says when he runs for the Senate in '48, "If I don't win, I'm leaving politics." He was born for politics; he was a master of politics. But if he didn't have power he wasn't going to stay in it.

But now in this volume, it's the same driven, relentless, savage person who's determined to do whatever he sets out to do, with this real savagery of will. But now the ambition and the compassion come together; for both reasons, he has to pass the first Civil Rights legislation and he does it. And that, of course, is a large part of the story of this book, the first Civil Rights Act in 1957. Not the great ones he will do later, but the first one, that had to come first. And I think the story of how he did it is the same story I always wrote about earlier. Only now he's using power for something other than his own needs.

. . . One of the great aspects of democracy is that it almost requires that someone attain great heights in the political system in order to accomplish things with it. It almost requires one to act in what you call "the best of human nature." If you're a dictator, you can be a dictator for a long time just by getting power from the barrel of a gun.

But in a democracy, if you want to be a great President, you have to get power from the ballot box, and people's opinions, from people's votes. They have to approve of what you're doing. Now, with Lyndon Johnson it's certainly true that as in the earlier books, in the first part of this book, several times his compassion, his desire to do things particularly for poor people, suddenly comes into conflict with ambition.

Quite specifically, here he's being raised to power in the Senate by the Southerners. Whenever he is on the verge of going too far for civil rights he realizes he must stop. And he stops . . .

The Southerners have the power and Johnson allies himself with the Southern Caucus. He becomes one of its strategists. The leader of the Southern Caucus, of course, is a fantastic figure, Richard Russell of Georgia, who's never lost a civil rights fight in 25 years. The South calls him the greatest general since Robert E. Lee, with the difference that Russell is winning. Lee lost. Johnson so convinces Russell that he's on the same side on civil rights, that Russell raises him to power, makes him first Minority Leader, then Majority Leader, and anoints him his successor.

Now as late as 1956, after Johnson's been in the Senate for seven years, this is the situation. In 1956 the South crushes a civil rights bill, I mean they've crushed every civil rights bill for 82 years. They crush it again and Johnson plays the leading role in that, he is the guy who does it. And then all of a sudden in 1957, he completely reverses himself, decides that a civil rights bill must be passed, for both reasons, his compassion and the ambition coming together—and it is going to be passed. The story of Johnson getting this bill to passage, to me is one of the amazing political stories of all time.

Heffner: I don't see how people today possibly can believe, without your detailed recounting, what this country was like in terms of its legislative bodies just a half century ago.

Well, a major part of this book is about legislative power, it's about the history of the Senate, and how power works in the Senate. It's one reason the book is so long. Remember that before the Civil War we had in the Senate men like Webster, Clay, and Calhoun. So the Senate was a central, maybe *the* central, point in American government. In our lives, we have come to consider power only in terms of executive power. I mean, in my case, I didn't even realize I was doing that. Then you start reading all these English biographies; you have great biographies of Disraeli and Gladstone, Peel and Pitt. They are, by definition, studies of legislative or parliamentary power. We know very little of that, and in my opinion, we have very little understanding of what legislative power is and how important it is in American government. How it used to be important. Now I tried to show that the executive branch was starting to move towards civil rights. I mean up and down, but certainly in the judicial branch, the Supreme Court was moving towards civil rights—Brown v. Board of Education, etc. Even the House of Representatives was passing civil rights legislation. Not much, but some. Yet every bill that was sent over to the Senate for 82 years was killed in the Senate. It was the dam, not just for civil rights legislation, but against all attempts at social justice. All attempts to ameliorate the human condition came up against the rock hard power of the South in the Senate. I think I myself would have to say I hardly knew about it. But when you learn about it, you realize how almost impossible it was to crack. And how what Johnson did, in getting this legislation through in 1957 seemed almost impossible. But he was determined to get it through and he managed to do it.

Heffner: And yet that first legislation was so watered down—

It was almost meaningless. But of course Johnson with his gift of the phrase said, "We've got to break the virginity." He said, "You know, once we break the virginity, it'll be easier next time." And, in my opinion, he was really right about that.

Heffner: How was Johnson able to convince Russell and other Southerners that the South would rise again if and when he became President?

Well, I don't think I say in the book that the South would rise again.

Heffner: It's my expression.

. . . In fact, the overall feeling was that the South would be a lot better off with Lyndon Johnson than with, say, a Hubert Humphrey. That he would keep the pace of segregation more moderate. You see, he tailored his argument to the man. With Eastland of Mississippi, who was a truly disgusting racist—I'm not even going to repeat the way Johnson would talk in those terms.

He'd walk into the Senate Cloakroom and Paul Douglas and Hubert Humphrey would be on one side, you know, and he'd say, "You know we're going to bring up that civil rights bill now, it's high time that America did this." Then he'd walk over to the Southerners and say, "We gotta give the niggers something, you know." And he'd say, "They're uppity now, they've got this colored Baptist preacher—that's Martin Luther King." He says, "You know what a colored Baptist preacher is," he says, "We gotta give them something. You know, we've got to give them a little bit. We don't have to give them too much, but we've got to give them something." He would tailor his argument as he walked from one side of the room to the other and his accent would change. It would get deeper with the Southerners . . . So when you talk about how he appealed to the Southerners, I think he appealed to them in a tremendous variety of ways, tailored to their different personalities.

Heffner: And to Hubert Humphrey?

Well, we see the story of Hubert Humphrey here, and of course it will come to its climax in the last volume. What you see with Humphrey is the way in which Johnson was a reader of men. We don't even remember, I know I didn't remember, Hubert Humphrey's fantastic speech to that 1948 Democratic Convention. It seemed so thrilling to me that I went to a lot of trouble to get a kinescope of it. And I said to myself, "This is one of the most thrilling speeches I've ever heard." Then you realize that when he was young—and I certainly had never heard of this—when he became Mayor of Minneapolis, the city was known as the anti-Semitism capital of America. The police force was one of the most brutal towards black people in America. Years later, I think when Humphrey died, Thurgood Marshall was asked to assess him. And he said, "He did a lot of great things, but nothing he ever did was better than what he did with the police force in Minneapolis." Then in '48 he wants to make an impact. He's still very young, and he leads a fight for a strong civil rights plank at the 1948 Democratic Convention. And he is told, "You are young, you are a comer, if you make this speech, your career is finished." And he decides to make it anyway. It's one of the great addresses in American history. And it turns the Convention around. It's one of the few times in American history, that such a thing happened. The Convention passed a strong civil rights plank. Then, of course, he gets to the Senate where the Southerners have the power and they humiliate him. And they keep him from any meaningful assignments; they ostracize him; they attack him on the floor. There's a scene in the book we know about because Senate staffers at the time knew about it. Humphrey was broke and looked it. Richard Russell said once, as he walked by, "Look at that"—the distinguished, gracious, Richard Russell, I think this is the quote, the exact quote—"What do you think of the people of Minnesota sending an ass like that to the Senate?" And Humphrey is just broken-hearted. He is the outsider, and then I write that in 1951 Lyndon Johnson fixed his "restless, reckoning eye on him." The two of them were riding on the Senate subway, and Johnson began trying to make a friend of Humphrey and to bring him into the Senate leadership. And their relationship, which was to begin then, goes through ups and downs, but it is the story of two very strong men. But one is just stronger than the other.

Heffner: But what purpose did Humphrey serve Johnson? Why was Johnson willing to bring Humphrey in slowly, but surely, to leadership?

I don't know that I can answer that. . . . I mean this is the Senate in which one is not even supposed to speak during the first couple of years. And then speak very infrequently in your whole first term. Yet at the end of Lyndon Johnson's first two years, he's his party's assistant leader and at the end of four years he's the party's leader—the Democratic leader of the Senate. Then when it becomes the majority party in 1955, he becomes the Majority Leader of the Senate. Now, he is raised to power. And we don't remember this about Lyndon Johnson, but I hope people will remember now because it's important, in my opinion, to the understanding of Johnson. He is raised to power by the Southern Caucus. That is who installs him as leader. And therefore the Democratic Party is very divided. If he wants to have a unified party, a party that will be effective, so that he will be an effective leader, he has to have a bridge to the Liberals. And Humphrey is the Liberal leader. He is a charismatic, principled, idealistic leader whom the Liberals follow. More than that, he is the great Liberal voice. We may not remember this any more, but in the year that I'm writing about, Hubert Humphrey was a great voice for Liberalism. And Lyndon Johnson saw that Humphrey could therefore help him in many ways, but all based on the fact that he gave Johnson a link to the Liberals who distrusted him [Johnson].

What did Humphrey see in this? Well, we happen to know by way of a number of existing memoranda. Humphrey could not conceal his innermost thoughts and in my book I think I quote memoranda of conversations that took place in the 1950s where he says, "You know, Johnson wants"—I'm over simplifying now—"Lyndon Johnson wants to be President, but of course, he's never going to make it, because he's from the South." And then—I can't remember if Humphrey actually says this, or it's implicit—"so therefore, as long as I'm friends with Johnson, his strength is going to come to me in the end. So it's going to help me be President." At the same time Lyndon Johnson is thinking something, too. And as it turns out, he's right.

Heffner: You know, reading this volume makes me feel that LBJ is always right, that there's something almost mystical about this man's grasp of the American political process.

I don't think you're wrong. As you'll see in the next volume, there is something almost mystical going on. He's always right about human beings—up to a certain point. I say in this book that he was a great reader of men. Lyndon Johnson didn't like to read books. I mean the number of books that he read after college is really small. But when it came to reading men, he never missed. He used to tell John Connolly and Horace Busby and George Reedy and Walter Jenkins, "Watch their eyes. Watch the hands, but watch their eyes . . ."

Heffner: This is what Johnson would say?

Yes, these are Johnson's words: "What a man is saying to you is never as important as what his eyes are telling you." You know, he'd say, "Yeah, I wanna, I wanna touch 'em, I wanna smell 'em, I wanna feel 'em," and then he would say, "You know what a man tells you is never as important as what he doesn't tell you. What he isn't saying to you." And Horace Busby, I think it was, said to me, "See, that's why Lyndon would never let a conversation end. Because he didn't want it to end until he found out what the man wasn't telling him." So when he evaluated another human being, I think that he knew how to appeal to him.

Heffner: And he also knew himself, didn't he?

Yes, he did know his Lyndon Johnson. There is an unbelievable quote, which I don't have accurately in my mind, but it's something like, "I'm just like an animal, I can go for the jugular in any man, but I keep myself on a leash, just like you would an animal." And I think he had that quality.

Heffner: And what does that tell us?

There was a quality in Johnson that just drove him to win. He had to win. It's something going back to his boyhood in Johnson City. When I started these books I was young, and you know Lyndon Johnson died young, at the age of 64. So that when I started working on these books, people who had grown up with him in Johnson City, who went to high school and then went to college with him at San Marcos, were still around. You could talk to them about the young Lyndon Johnson. And one of the things that they said was, "He had to win." If you got into an argument with him, it wasn't like getting into an argument with anybody else. He would not stop arguing. He'd hang all over you, he wouldn't stop. Then when he became a Congressional Assistant— I remember talking to a woman, now deceased, named Estelle Harbin, who worked with him in a two-person office in the Capitol. She said, "The thing about Lyndon is he had to win, he could not stand not being somebody. Just could not stand it." And all through his life, he had to win. And there was a savagery in the way he would fight for it. Now in the first two volumes, that has a lot of totally unfortunate connotations. But in this third volume, we see that he decides to pass the civil rights legislation. Forget about what the motives are for just a moment. He knows he has to pass it, and one way or another, impossible as it seems, that legislation is going to be passed.

Heffner: Do you think any differently about the man now than you did when you began your work?

Yes, I think differently about him, but probably not in the way you have in mind. I see his political genius more. I see his genius in the Senate. I mean I use the word "genius" a lot in this book. We haven't had many authentic legislative geniuses in the United States. He is the authentic legislative genius. You probably mean, has my opinion of him, of his motives, or whatever, changed. I think what I always think, which is that he's the most complicated man I've ever encountered. He has emotions that are incredibly strong on one side or the other, but they could change. He had an ability to change himself. —1998, 1999, 2000

DONALD RUMSFELD

Donald Rumsfeld was the "brilliant and tough-minded young Illinois Republican Congressman" who newly chosen House Minority Leader Gerry Ford suggested take his place in the mid-1960s as a resource participant in the distinguished Aspen Institute Executive Seminars I moderated for more than a decade. Later, Ford would become President of the United States and Rumsfeld, his White House Chief of Staff, then the nation's youngest Secretary of Defense.

Highly successful in many guises—businessman, diplomat, bureaucrat— Rumsfeld is one of that cadre, a fairly large cadre to be sure, of what could be called the public elite. Not social, not academic, but one of those necessary individuals in public life without whom nothing would get done.

Retuurning as President George W. Bush's Secretary of Defense, Rumsfeld engineered the preparation of U.S. military forces for the major assault on Iraq in 2003. When we had our first conversations back in 1975, however, primarily at issue was the "management" of political life—interesting training exercises for the challenges of a country and a globe in disarray.

Heffner: I'm fascinated by the fact that as President Ford's Chief of Staff, you don't want to be characterized as the keeper of the White House gates, or of President Ford. But perhaps you would embrace the notion that in as complicated a time as our own, someone would have to watch those gates, that information glut could deluge a President and push him under just as easily as a denial of access.

Well, it seems to me that your statement presumes that the President doesn't know how to handle himself, or that a President wouldn't. And it strikes me that that's not the case. A President doesn't get there by accident—he is a person who is capable of conducting the affairs of the public, and therefore he's perfectly capable of making judgments with respect to priorities about his own time. Also, I'm kind of old-fashioned; I think that the Constitution does put the power in the President and that, to the extent possible, the President should make judgments, and people should not make judgments for the President. Now, that requires that a President not make each individual specific decision in the executive branch of the federal government. Conversely, it requires that he develop broad policy guidance so that a whole range of decisions can be made the way he would want them made under that policy guidance. And that is, in fact, how the executive branch of the federal government works. And it also works this way with respect to scheduling.

. . . What he has to give the country is time and the judgments that are made during his waking hours. There is probably nothing more important for the President to decide than how he's going to use his time. Because it's the judgments that are made, that he addresses, during the time he devotes to foreign policy, to economic policy, to energy policy, that is in fact shaping the direction and the course of the administration.

Heffner: You've said elsewhere in talking about how decisions are made in the White House, that "Form is substance, that a properly organized decision-making process does not guarantee decisions of high quality, but you are certain to have uneven decisions without an orderly process."

My recollection of what I said was that procedure can affect substance.

And this is true. It can affect it in a variety of ways. Let's say that the President is about to make a decision with respect to oil, just to take an example. Now, oil, at the same time, can be a matter that's of highest importance to the National Security Council and the Secretary of State. It can be of the highest importance to the Secretary of Treasury and the Economic Policy Board. It can be of great importance to the Congressional Relations Office, because they're dealing continuously with the committees in the Congress that have an interest in that. It's a subject that's very much in the news, therefore the Press Office is involved. It certainly is something that the Office of the Counsel has to be engaged with, from a legal standpoint. If you have a Presidential decision-making process that has reasonable integrity and discipline, one would assume that the president would want to assure himself that he had the advice of the principal people in his administration, and out, who have competence and background and/or statutory responsibility for that area.

Now, to develop this a bit more, when I say, "Procedure can affect substance," what I mean is this: If the system, the White House presidential decision-making process, and the system that sees that it moves along, lacks integrity or lacks discipline, one or more of those individuals who has a legitimate interest in seeing that he and his bureaucracy, his interest, has an opportunity to be expressed—if he's cut out of the process, then in fact you run the risk that the President of the United States will be making a decision with less than the advice of each of his principal advisors. That means that he runs the risks of being blindsided, not knowing something that he should have known in making that decision. He runs the risk of having an imbalance in the advice, not the proper weighting. He clearly runs the risks of having an unhappy Congress, because the Cabinet officers are dealing with the congressional committees continuously. And for them not to have their views reflected in the process, if he were not to take them into account, would be unfortunate. And therefore, the decision that's finally made can be dramatically affected by the procedures you have in place to determine whether or not the President is or is not getting the advice of his principal people. Now, in every instance, he need not. That is to say, it's perfectly proper for a President to say to himself, "This is a decision which requires the utmost secrecy and the utmost speed. Therefore, I am consciously not going to broaden the consultation process so that I will have the advice of every conceivable person who might have a view or legitimate interest in that subject." That's all right if he decides it. In my judgment, it's wrong if someone else decides it. In other words, my task is to make sure that the process has integrity, so that he either has the advice of those principal people, or he knows consciously that he does not, and that it's his decision not to.

Heffner: Then your responsibility, once the President has decided to put that process into motion, is an extremely important one, isn't it?

It is important, although it's not one of excluding. Quite the reverse. It's one of trying to ensure that the other elements of the government are in fact part of that decision-making process.

Heffner: Those who get into the process, of course, wield a tremendous amount of influence and power. You really don't want to deny that, do you?

I guess I don't deny or affirm it, because it's not my power, it's Presidential power. If he says to me, "Rumsfeld, this is how I want this to operate," I operate it that way . . .

Heffner: With no judgment? Just a mechanical . . .

It is his decision that that's how he wants it to operate. And if I fail to see that the appropriate people are properly included in that process, he certainly will learn about it very rapidly. And I will have failed in my job, my task, my assignment. And certainly then the correction comes very quickly. So there's discretion in seeing that it's done in the way that he advised or that he wishes. But there's not broad discretion over a period of time without fairly rapid correction, which is as it should be. . . .

I can't think of a worse job for anyone with ambition than the job I'm in. It's a graveyard. People who've served in it previously have had tremendous difficulties. It's an incredibly difficult job. It's exhausting in terms of the number of hours. It's terribly demanding. There's a great reluctance on the part of people to criticize a President. So when a President decides that he'll veto a bill instead of not vetoing the bill, those that are happy praise him, those that are unhappy claim he got bad advice from some mysterious somebody. Or if they find that he makes a judgment not to see them rather than see them, they, needless to say, don't attribute that to the President, because that would mean that they lost face. Therefore, they suggest that somebody is keeping them out, there's somebody mysterious up there in the White House who's doing something very bad. Well, that's life. And while I didn't volunteer for the job, I accepted it, and I'm happy to do it for the President because I think he's a fine person and doing a good job. But it is certainly the worst spot in Washington from the standpoint of trying to advance yourself. I mean, it's just a constant source of criticism and difficulties, because any time you try to coordinate eight or nine people and see that they're all part of that process, why, some win, some lose. And there's always some criticism of the person who's involved in that process of coordination.

Heffner: What would make it the best job in Washington might be that the person who holds it became President of the United States. Wouldn't you admit that, at least?

Well, I don't know that I've ever really spent that much time thinking about that statement. I've been around the office of the President, and I've seen several Presidents. I guess my hope and intention at some point is to leave government for a period of years, try to spend some time with my family as my children continue growing. Try to walk away from the trees so I can see the forest. I've been in Washington for the most part since 1962, with the exception of two years in Belgium as Ambassador to NATO. I've had a chance to be involved in the legislative and the executive side. I've had a chance to be involved in the domestic, the economic, and the national security side. I feel very fortunate, but I think it would probably be good for me, just as before I left for a period to go to Belgium, to leave Washington for a period and be in Illinois or some other part of this country as a member of the private sector, either in business or in the academic community, not wrestling with government problems every minute. I think that would be a helpful thing to me personally in terms of perspective, in terms of balance, in terms of knowledge. And so I would kind of point in other directions, I'm afraid.

Heffner: Another subject: Hasn't our society become so much more complicated that the possibility of being well-informed has diminished considerably?

No, indeed, just the reverse is the case. The means of communication today are so far superior to those of 21 years ago. Now, it's true that this is not ancient Greece, where the constituency could sit on a hillside and discuss and debate the affairs of the city state. We talk of future shock, the compression of events, the glut of information. But, you know, the human being is an amazing mechanism. People are able to adjust to things. And I don't question for a minute but that as the technological changes have occurred, as television has come upon us, as the velocity of world events has accelerated, I don't question for a second but that there may be periods during which people might lose their bearings, where it's more difficult than in other times. But people adjust. Their tolerance level changes. And they find that they can sift and sort. And it's not necessary for each citizen . . . in this nation of ours, to have all information on all subjects so they could act in each other's stead in government on all decisions. What is essential is that there be a rough sense of direction, that there be a point where a correction can be made, as we do have every two years when all the members of the House and a third of the senators are elected, and where a President is elected every four years or reelected. In our country, to govern successfully, an individual has to have a sense of the American people. He or she has to be in communication with them, to prove themselves and be measured against what they say and what they do. So I think that, despite the changes we've seen in the world, despite the changes we'll see, probably at an accelerated rate in the coming 21 years, my estimate is that our system of government does work, that that magnificent gamble is a good gamble, and that in fact we'll find that human beings can adjust and continue to adjust and fulfill that role of public responsibility.

Heffner: In one of your speeches that I read earlier, you said, "But what struck me and what remains in my mind was the importance of trust in the American system." I must ask you whether you meant trusting the American system, or whether you meant the importance of the element of trust, of believability, in our system.

Without question I meant the element of trust in the sense of believability. If you have a system that suggests that the people can play a role, and if you have a system in which leaders lead not by command but by consent, by agreement, that means they lead by persuasion, by communication. And without trust there is no communication. If people disbelieve, they don't listen. They don't want to listen. And if one thinks of graduating college seniors today, or thinks of any of us, we've gone through some perfectly startling events in the last 10 to 15 years, in the lifetime of these students now graduating. We've had a President assassinated in office, we've had one candidate for President wounded, another killed. We've had a President who wasn't able to run for reelection. We've had a President who, for the first time in our history, resigned. We've seen inflation, recession, war. There have been some very unusual events. And we'd all agree, I think, that we've also lived through a period where, for one reason or another, the reservoir of trust has been drained somewhat. You know if you're in a sailboat and you shift the rudder and you're not moving, the sailboat doesn't turn. It just stays there. You need steerageway to steer the sailboat, for the rudder to work. Trust is like that for our society. If everyone's going off in their own direction and doing their own thing, or doing nothing as their own thing, nothing happens in our society, because although we believe in the individual as the real source of creativity in our society, we know that for really great things to be achieved, it requires that people work together. And the only way that they can work together is if, in fact, there is a leadership and a follow-ership that comes from communication, that comes from trust, that comes from assent. That is to say that cooperation and cohesion, voluntarily achieved, is in fact the thing that has enabled our country to do some perfectly splendid things.

Heffner: There seem to have been a great many people in the last decade who have felt that that assent literally has come down from the top, and that what you had was a high degree of carelessness on the part of the government about what the people felt or what they wanted or what they meant, if indeed there was any consensus that you could identify. Do you feel that there is some sense of reversing that today?

I was out of the country for two years, and when I came back I was struck by the fact that the leadership structure of our society seemed to have flattened somewhat, that there weren't groupings of people working towards common goals, that there was a sense of anti-institutionalism and anti-leadership and anti-politician and anti-union or anti-school or anti-church feeling. This is disturbing. It tends to confirm what you're suggesting, that for one reason or another people were mistrustful or not willing to be a part of something bigger then themselves, not willing to submerge their own views into something that had the support and cooperation of a great many more people. I see it changing, personally. I think there's probably nothing more frustrating than freedom that's purposeless. And freedom is a very special thing. And when one doesn't have it, one tends to value it greater than when one does have it. But it's not a very special thing if it's for nothing. And that freedom that we have as individuals, I think, is purposeless unless we begin to recognize that it's through groupings of people and institutions and working with others that something important can be accomplished.

Heffner: And you see the role of leadership as providing that purposefulness?

Well, I guess I think the first thing that has to be done—and I personally believe it is now being done—is to refill that reservoir of trust. I don't think you have steerageway without that. Because unless you can communicate and be believed and people have a sense that is in fact where you are and what you are and who you are as a political figure or as a leader in a family or in a company or a union, there isn't any followership, there isn't any cooperation, there isn't any communication back and forth so that the direction can be voluntarily agreed upon by more than one person. We see a microcosm of this, I think, in the United States Congress today. Now, as a former congressman, I don't want to sound critical of that institution, because I think it's a great institution. But the fact of the matter is it truly represents the country. And in its most recent period, it's reflected something of what I've just described. That is to say, 435 members of the House and 100 members of the Senate tending to each go off and do their own thing. Well, that's not good enough. Simply because a person has a mimeograph machine doesn't mean we need 535 economic policies or 435 energy policies or 100 foreign policies, one to suit each senator. In fact, we need one foreign policy for the country. And that means that there has to be compromise, there has to be adjustment, there has to be a movement toward some common principles, and at some point we will see some gelling of the leadership structure in the House and the Senate, and we will, I think, probably see it at a point where we also see it in the country. —1975

HENDRIK HERTZBERG

Hendrik Hertzberg's modest byline appears almost every week in The New Yorker *Magazine, usually appended to the lead piece in the famed Talk of the Town section. He has been a presidential (Jimmy Carter) speechwriter, twice editor of the conservative/liberal, or liberal/conservative,* New Republic, *and has for some time now been the informal editorial voice of his magazine, in his capacity as Senior Editor. I asked what perspective about the nature of human nature most influences his commentary.*

There's some combination of values and sensibility that my experiences of a lifetime have bred into me and that I've come to trust. And these inform what I write. I'm very sensible of the responsibility that writing these little pieces entails. And in a way, it's a matter of tone, even though it's nothing, there's an emotional vibration that I can't really put into words but that, I hope affects the way I put words together. This is as abstract an answer, in a way, as your question.

Heffner: It's a difficult question, I know. But, you remember the old Edward R. Murrow "This I Believe" series . . .

Yes, I do.

Heffner: That really is what I'm asking. What do you believe?

Well, I believe in democracy, I believe in rule by the people, but not for its own sake. For the sake of liberty . . . my bedrock value is liberty. And democracy just happens to be the best and, indeed, the only way that liberty can be guaranteed. If there was some other way to guarantee liberty, I'd be happy to hear about it. And go along with it.

I don't know of any. And I believe in a kind of fairness. Equality is a word we don't hear much of anymore. But I believe in civic equality and I believe that, while the market is a wonderful mechanism for the ordering of economic activity and the distribution of goods, it is not a moral force. It has no morality and so we have to organize our society in a way that mitigates the inequalities that the market creates. Those are my basic politics.

Heffner: It's interesting when you talk about the marketplace because it seems to have become the singular, moral principle, or immoral principle that guides us today every where you turn. Liberals, as well as Conservatives—there is this talk about "market values." That's what destroyed the Soviet dictatorship, the triumph of our "market values." What's your own feeling about that. . . ?

I don't think that's what destroyed the Soviet Union. I think it was the triumph of democratic values, not market values.

Heffner: I meant our market values, that we were so superior in power, in our material power that it destroyed the Soviet Union. They couldn't keep up with us. No?

I don't believe it. I think that the Soviet Union collapsed because it was so out of sync with human nature. It was an unnatural arrangement. And once the pall of fear was lifted from the Soviet union by Gorbachev, the rest followed more or less, more or less automatically. And power, American power and material superiority and prosperity played a role. Certainly American power played a role in containing the Soviet Union and in preventing a catastrophic war between East and West. But that's not what brought it down. And that's not what brought South Africa's repressive regime down. And that's not what brought Mexico's one-party state down. It's a mistake to think of these developments all over the world in the late eighties and early nineties as a triumph of market capitalism. I'm convinced that one of the reasons that we tend to think that way is that our political system, for all the liberty that it gives us, doesn't work terribly well. It doesn't work as well as some other democratic systems around the world. And so we have come to think of the public sector in a democracy as inefficient and undependable and that it doesn't really work.

Heffner: And because it doesn't always work, we have come to think of government as the enemy.

Yes. And, no one ever seems to notice that there's a glaring contradiction between our pride in our Constitution and our way of life and our democracy on the one hand, and the idea that government is the problem and that politicians are all a bunch of, of selfish "no-goods." On the other, we hold these two ideas in our mind at the same time, and there's a real contradiction between them. I believe that our system needs reform, our political system needs reform. And keep in mind that most of the other countries of world in the last decade or so, most of the other advanced and semi-advanced countries of the world have undergone some fairly dramatic reform.

Heffner: Reforms? Interesting. Can you give me an example?

Well, I'd certainly like to see things like proportional representation; like instant runoff voting. Various ways to mitigate the undemocratic features of our 200-year-old political arrangements. I mean, our political arrangements were established at the dawn of democratic technology, you might say. The framers did an incredibly good job, working with what they had to work with. But they were working from essentially no basis in experience, purely from theory. They did a hell of a job considering where they started. But I think they would be the first to be appalled that we regard the outcome as immutable, that we haven't fixed up their handiwork. There's a wonderful Library of America volume, called "The Debates on the Constitution." Full of letters back and forth among the framers. And basically what they say is "Well, this Constitution that we've drawn up, you know, it's okay. It's not what any of us really wanted, but thank God we put in that part about how you can amend it. So in ten years or twenty years the mistakes, whatever mistakes we've made, they'll be fixed. So let's not worry about it too much."

Heffner: The framers really thought they were making it, I won't say, easy, but at least, more possible to amend than it has seemed to become.

They certainly underestimated how difficult amendment would be. Essentially they made it as easy as they could, while still making a deal with the slave states. Much of what's wrong with our Constitution is there because the interests of slavery had to be accommodated. And I don't mean just the three-fifths rule, just the parts that accommodated slavery. But the building in of ways in which determined minorities can thwart the will of the majority was largely done in the service of preserving slavery. Because that was the only way to get a deal. That was the only way to get the Union together and organized in something like a functioning national government. And as we saw, that national government was unable to solve the country's most basic problem, namely slavery. The Constitution essentially collapsed in 1860 and that's part of the story that's always left out. You know, when we say, "Gosh darn it, this Constitution of ours has served us well for 200 years"—well, it didn't serve us well when it came to solving the biggest problem America had. And it also didn't serve us well in solving the successor problem to that, the problem of racial segregation. I mean it's a tremendous failure of our Constitution that racial segregation, legalized racial segregation had to be abolished by a court rather than by the workings of democratic, political institutions.

Heffner: It's interesting, in Robert Caro's third volume of his biography of Lyndon Johnson, he begins with a magnificent section on the Senate of the United States. What you are saying was so true, that the impact of what initially was a question of slavery, then became a question of civil rights and race relations, tied up the Senate of the United States through the filibuster, and therefore tied up so much of our potential as a country.

And this is continued in so many ways. The great controversy over what went wrong with Clinton's health plan. We know all the standard explanations for why it failed, but the real explanation is that the Republicans, or a decisive part of the Republican Party, decided to stop it and would be willing to use the filibuster to stop it. That's what really happened. And that undemocratic feature of our Constitution has stymied us time and time again. It's one of the reasons, the main reason, really, why we're different from Europe. Why we're different in terms of equality and welfare and taking care of people.

Heffner: What do you think the consequences of that difference will be, not for the moment, but over time, a long period of time.

Well, I hope that eventually the consequences will be that we'll move in a more democratic direction. And yet when I talk to Europeans, and try to tell them about the advantages of the way they govern themselves, they say, "Oh, but we love the way you have a voluntary sector. And the way your markets are so much more vigorous than ours." Etcetera, etcetera. I think that America has to learn that it's part of the world. And one of the things that keeps us from doing that as fully as we should is the peculiarity of our institutions. We don't know anything about other people's institutions.

Heffner: Do you think that's a lesson that September 11th taught us, that such separateness is impossible?

Well, it certainly seemed that way at first. That seemed to have profoundly shaken the idea of American exceptionalism. We certainly learned that we were not protected by the oceans, that we're vulnerable, just like the rest of the world. And it seemed as if we were about to abandon the sort of "go-it-alone" unilateralism that had marked the Bush Administration's foreign policy and to some extent the foreign policy of all American administrations. Evidently that's a lesson every American generation has to learn for itself, learns the hard way, but learns incompletely and forgets quickly.

Heffner: "You say "forgets quickly," but it's only been six months . . . How could we be forgetting so soon? What are the forces that drive us to forget?

Well, our immense military power enabled us to accomplish in Afghanistan something that was really unexpected, I think, even by the Administration itself. Certainly by any political critics. . . . The rapidity with which the goal of removing the Taliban regime was accomplished, was good news, I think. But it may have strengthened some retrograde tendencies in the Administration which reflect retrograde tendencies in a large part of the nation. We may have been misled by our success.

Heffner: Were we misinformed about our success or misled?

It doesn't mean that what happened in Afghanistan, a purely military approach to the problem of terrorism, is tenable in the medium, even in the medium term. And part of the duty of people like me, and people like you, is to keep that discussion going, to remind our society that there are other ways of approaching these problems and that those ways are as important as the military way—perhaps more important. Certainly in the longer term, they're more important.

Heffner: I guess the question I was raising was whether in your estimation the military victory, the military successes were as extensive as the media seemed to paint them.

Well, given the terms through which the military action was understood, yes, I think they were as extensive as the Administration portrayed them. But there was an implication, there was an almost unstated implication behind the way the Administration presented the situation and the way the press followed them in presenting it in the media, the implication being that victory was the end of the story, and that what we have to worry about in Afghanistan ended with the fall of the Taliban. We're now seeing that that's very far from the case. Afghanistan will continue to be trouble. It's trouble now, it will be trouble in the future. And it's commonplace, I guess, the idea that Americans want a tidy end to things.

Heffner: Yes, of course.

And we're not going to get that. —2002

JAMES MACGREGOR BURNS

James MacGregor Burns, Woodrow Wilson Professor of Government Emeritus at Williams College, writer, historian, and biographer extrordinaire, has been a friend and fellow conversationalist for decades. Among his works, a personal favorite is The Lion and the Fox, *a volume of his FDR biography, followed closely by his political profile of John F. Kennedy, and his magisterial trilogy,* The American Experiment. *The subject of a recent program was the publication of* The Three Roosevelts: Theodore, Franklin, and Eleanor, *written with fellow historian Susan Dunn. I asked him what new perspective about our nation and ourselves he derives from the three Roosevelts, nearly a half century after* The Lion and the Fox.

Well, first of all, I've always been one of those who frowned on Teddy Roosevelt as just too much of a character, you know, the whole San Juan business, running up a hill and so on. But the more I got into TR, the more impressed I was with something that I think is crucial to leadership, it's one word: conviction. This man really believed in what he was doing. And he showed it in every area. Sometimes excessively. And sometimes in the wrong area. But there was that kind of conviction. And I think this also is true of FDR, who also made mistakes, but who, first of all in the New Deal, showed his absolute belief in reform. And then was able to conduct a huge transformation of his own Administration to meet the menace of Hitlerism. And there he, too, showed his dedication and conviction. And then Eleanor Roosevelt who was—for Susan Dunn and me—our hero, or heroine—she was right in there on every major issue that came up in this country. In the political realm, in the civil rights realm. And she, too, had that dedication and that consistency that I think is the essence of great leadership.

Heffner: You talk about conviction and you talk about Teddy Roosevelt and about Eleanor Roosevelt in that regard and I'm very sympathetic to those points of view. Why, then, were there so many people and so many historians who saw Franklin Roosevelt as an opportunist, rather than a man of conviction.

Well, because he was that, too. And you kindly mentioned my FDR book, *The Lion and The Fox*; he was a fox, as well as a lion. But he made his fox-like tactics serve his lion-like strategy, his lion-like vision. So, it raises the most fundamental question about leadership: to what extent do you follow the followers? To what extent are you expedient? To what extent do you keep your ear to the ground, and do what you think the people want? And to what extent, if you really believe in something . . . the way FDR, for example, was convinced that Hitler was a menace and that we would have to face up to it—this ability to bring the people along with somewhat fox-like devices in order to bring about the great strategy of defeating Hitlerism.

Heffner: When we come closer to our own times, it's true, isn't it, that you're not quite so generous with the fox and the lion qualities of Bill Clinton.

That's true. You can carry fox-like qualities too far. Not that I would say that Clinton was just a fox. I think he was a small lion. I think Clinton did lots of very good little things. But did not do the great things that I think were possible. . . .

Heffner: Do you think it may be that in time you will look back—you and I have never talked about the present President of the United States, George W. Bush, but that you might look back and find him wily enough to have become President, and that behind expediency is real concern.

I think we're finding in George Bush that he's a much better tactician, or if you wish, much better fox than we had realized. He not sort of a dumbbell out of Texas. He's a shrewd politician. But again, when it comes to the lion aspect of this, the vision aspect, its not very clear to me as he gives his speeches and talks about the broader aspects, essentially conservative—I don't have a sense of great commitment, that his heart is in it. You always had a feeling FDR's heart was in it. Eleanor's, too. Or TR's, too.

Heffner: Could Eleanor Roosevelt have been not just First Lady, but President of the United States?

I think with better timing. She was pretty elderly, of course, by the time the other two Roosevelts had had their time. I don't think we yet, at that point, were ready for a woman President. I think an Eleanor Roosevelt today would definitely have a good chance of running for President, in one of the major parties. And a good chance of winning.

Heffner: You're very generous to her. You dismiss some of those early attitudes, which you attribute, as with FDR and TR, to their backgrounds.

Yes, Eleanor had, of course, as you know, a very difficult upbringing and she inherited some of the prejudices of the class that she grew up in. There was, strange to say for this wonderful woman, a little tinge of anti-Semitism. I mean the kind of casual things that people say about Jews. And she grew out of that, of course, but she had to grow. She had to do her learning process, too, to become the kind of person, the kind of leader she did become.

Heffner: And you feel, too, that she was of enormous help to him. To FDR.

Politically. Yes. Personally. No. Politically she was backing him, she was moving ahead of him, she was supporting him, behind him, flanking him, all the way through his Presidency. And helping take on some of the tougher problems, like civil rights, that he was rather cautious about.

Heffner: But personally?

Personally, she simply was not there. And this goes back, as you know, to the revelations about his affair with Lucy Mercer and other activities of his that she might have thought were the case. Whatever the real truth. And she was really operating independently of him. Almost like a Vice President. Out in the country a lot. Away from the

White House a lot. She was not there weeks and weeks at a time to give him the kind of personal support he might have wanted.

Heffner: Now, everyone must ask you, how do you compare FDR and Eleanor with Bill Clinton and Hillary Clinton?

Well, Bill Clinton is no FDR. I think Hillary could be an Eleanor.

Heffner: Not an FDR?

Hillary as an FDR? That's a very enticing thought. I think she has to go a long way before she can do that. But I think she has the qualities of courage and imagination and vision that FDR did. Yes.

Heffner: You've written so much about all of these leaders—that I'm interested in what I would consider the tentativeness with which you approach the answer to my question about Hillary.

It's because she's not yet really proven on a national scale. She was, I think, an excellent First Lady. I had the good fortune to have had a good long talk with her and was enormously impressed. She fought, I thought, a brilliant campaign in New York State, although New Yorkers might disagree. And I think she's turning out to be a good Senator. But whether she could fill an office like the Presidency, of course, we cannot tell. And the trouble is, the more you get into the Senate mode, which again, is very much a mode of constant compromise and negotiation, the less effective you may be in the White House.

Heffner: What about LBJ?

LBJ is the great exception to that. Of course, he didn't win the office on his own. But he was quite remarkable because he had been the prime negotiator, the fox, of the U.S. Senate, who made an amazing transformation into a very strong lion.

Heffner: I want to ask you about that Senate being a bad place for the production of Presidents.

I can illustrate this by telling you how I used to talk with Jack Kennedy when he was in the Senate about when he was a Representative, and he would always be dismissive. He would say, "We were just worms there." And then when he got to be President and I talked to him about the Senate, he would say, "Ah, we were just worms there." And I've always thought that was a strange expression to use. But I think there was something in that, in that he felt the people in Congress are so much part of a vast machine of compromise and negotiation, that they don't have the leeway that a President must exercise.

Heffner: I wonder, in this year following the election of 2000, how you feel about third parties, or efforts to intrude into the two-party system.

I have very strong feelings, as you might suspect, about third parties. I say to people in third parties "join one of the major parties and make it better." Take Ralph Nader.

Heffner: No, you take Ralph Nader.

I'll take Ralph Nader. I had a long talk with him on the phone about this one time. About third parties. And inviting him, if I have the right to do so, to get into the Democratic Party, to fight in the Democratic Party primaries, to try to make the Democratic Party a more liberal, a more purposeful, a more honest party instead of sifting out there separating himself and helping produce the horrible December that we went through last year. So, they say to me, of course, "Well, these parties are too compromising, flabby and so on." And I say, "That's right. Come in and make them better."

Heffner: Are you convinced that by making them better, and by that I believe you mean taking extremely different stands on issues—

Not extremely different, but significantly different.

Heffner: Let me ask about that. What about the definition, the difference between "extremely" and "significantly." What do you think this country would tolerate?

I think an extreme position for the Democratic Party would be to become in effect or by name the Socialist Party of the country. Whereas, when I talk about being significantly different, it would mean much stronger positions than Clinton took. If I were a Republican, I would probably feel that Bush should take much stronger Conservative positions than he's presently taking. The point is to get a choice before the American people; that's what this comes down to in my view. Why are we getting this decline in the voting turnout? A number of reasons. To me the most significant reason is people say to me, and I'm sure to you, "Why vote? There's no difference between the candidates. There's no difference between the parties."

Heffner: On specific issues, how would you identify where they would stand, Social Security, minimum wage laws, tax levels—

Well, on taxes I think it's outrageous that we had a tax reduction that so much benefited the rich. I'm not the first one to say that, but it just stares me in the face at this point in time. On the minimum wage, and I'm close to a lot of people on the minimum wage, it's absurdly low, you cannot live on the minimum wage. Take . . . the Health Bill of Clinton's, where that was a case of, of the Democratic Party going significantly to my left. But the thing that struck me about that was the aftermath. It got badly treated, they did not do a good job in bringing it out, but the thing that bothered me was that once they got that initial defeat, Clinton pulled away. I don't think Hillary did, but

Clinton seemed almost embarrassed that he had presented this bill to the Congress. And to me, much of the greatness of leadership lies in persistence, which means conviction. You believe in something so much, you stick with it. And the history of reform in this country has been the history of persistence. Take one example, women's fight for the right to vote. Imagine all the decades that they failed, the way that health bill failed. They could not get the vote, all sorts of problems, but they stuck to it. It took much too long. But in a hundred years, women got the right to vote through sheer persistence and a lot of militancy. So, I think great changes take place that are needed by one party, whether it's the Conservative Party under Reagan, or a Liberal Party under an FDR-type, or a Republican Party under a TR-type, who really believe in what they're doing, stick to it, fight for it, take their defeats, come back into the battle, and hopefully, finally win out.

Heffner: What about bipartisanship and consensus in American democracy?

I think these are terrible words in a democracy because the essence of democracy is conflict. It's disagreeing, it's presenting different points of view. And I think the media don't seem to understand that. They do play up a lot of sort of trivial conflict from day to day, of course, because it makes news. But when it comes to examining the leadership of the country, any time somebody is particularly bi-partisan, negotiating with the other party, sifting around the table and making agreements, they play this up as wonderful leadership. I don't want people sitting around the table making deals, I want two parties to go to the people with different programs and to give the people a choice.

Heffner: I was very happy to hear you tick off issues, yet it seems to me that one could easily say, "But Jim Burns, on those issues, we know that the Democrats, by and large, stand here. And the Republicans, by and large, stand there." Don't we have that already?

I don't think sufficiently. I don't think Clinton made it that clear as to the differences between him and the Republic opposition. There was a great deal of negotiation during that period.

Heffner: Well, what changes would you make in the fundamental instruments of government?

Well, you've got me in kind of a corner here because I happen to be one of those who feels that the framers—

Heffner: Knew what they were doing.

It's the most brilliant feat of what I call "transformational leadership," in the history of the West by, collectively, again, working up this Constitution, which I think was very appropriate for let's say the nineteenth century, but is not appropriate for this century. What would I change in this masterwork of the framers? . . . I would do away with the two-year terms for Congressman. I ran for Congress once and I knew that if I won, as soon as I won I'd spend most of my time simply raising money for the next race. I would shorten the Senate terms from six years to four. I would have President, Congressmen, and Senators all running at the same time so we could elect a Republican government or a Democratic government and get stronger leadership in Washington. Now if that probably doesn't curl your hair enough. I could probably offer some other radical ideas.

Heffner: Should we call it parliamentary government?

Not really, because parliamentary government does not have the Presidency that we have, and the Presidency that we have, with all it's dangers is the great strengthening force. I think we could get a combination of parliamentary government and Presidential government the way the De Gaulle did, to some extent, in France.

Heffner: You think it could happen?

No, I think we consider the Constitution to be sacred. I think the Bill of Rights is sacred, but I don't think the Constitution, itself, is sacred because it's just a structure of government. And I think it should be modernized. But do I think it will happen? Too much Constitution worship in this country.

Heffner: As an alternative then, what is your "back off" position?

I think we'll continue to turn to the Presidency during crisis and put a greater and greater burden on the White House. And I worry that some time in this century there will be a Constitutional crisis that will lead to a kind of Presidential dictatorship, such as we've never known. I mean we've had quasi-Presidential dictatorship—actually under Abraham Lincoln, but to put it more simply, I think that with an old-fashioned Constitution and with what's likely to happen in the twenty-first century, we'll have a Constitutional crisis, and I'm just worried that we might do very bad things at that point. One reason I work on this whole question of Constitutional reform, like the little changes I suggested, is to have something in place in case that should ever happen.

Heffner: Why do you feel that this will happen in the twenty-first century? What are the elements that will bring about this situation.

I think it's going to happen because of the fundamental thing that's happening in this country, in my view, and perhaps in the whole world. It is the contrast between the enormous changes that are taking place in this country, let's say, in industry and finance, in the media, in science, in technology, in medicine—many other areas. Tremendous changes on the one hand, and a feeble, incrementalist government trying to catch up with, to do something about, to cope with these changes. And at a certain point, I think, in this century, as these non-governmental changes take place, the government will still be this ponderous old machine that we watch. There will be such a gap between change on the one hand and lack of change in government that there will be a crisis because the only thing you and I and the rest of the people control to some extent is the government. We can't control these great corporations, the media, nor do we really wish to. And so, my guess is that at a certain point that gap between the two will be so obvious that we'll have a Constitutional crisis. . . . And to answer your question, I say to my students, in my lifetime, this will not happen. I think it will happen in their lifetime.—2001

Mario Cuomo

Mario Cuomo is a unique politician, a man with an enormous sense of self to rely upon, as well as real loyalty to family and roots, to traditional values. Cuomo was, and remains, perhaps the most eloquent Democratic Party spokeperson for the liberal philosophy established by the New Deal of the 1930s. And yet, a politician who was, to paraphrase Rudyard Kipling, "The Man Who Wouldn't Be President." Values, always values, are at issue when we speak together, as in March, 1987, when our topic was "Governing Principles" and when Governor Cuomo had recently delivered a particularly provocative speech raising the question of teaching values in our public schools. I asked him just why he was bringing up this troubling and controversial issue at the time . . . and got the kind of thoughtful answers that over the years—to this day!—have so saddened me, as well as disappointed and angered me, that Mario Cuomo never chose to run for President of the United States.

If you look around in this society, one of the things that becomes apparent is that we appear to be having difficulty describing our values. At least that's the way it seems to me. What do you believe in, in a world where teenage suicide is so important a problem that you have to put together a task force headed by your Lieutenant Governor to look at it. What do you believe in, when you have Ivan Boesky and a whole lot of people to whom God could not have been better, who were rich early, had everything that life could afford you, had limousines beyond limousines, had strength and power at an early age and decided that they had to cheat and steal and risk it all, when they were already up into the hundreds of millions of dollars. What do you believe in, when you're piling up missiles upon missiles in a world where you can't afford to feed everybody and you know you can't use the missiles, but you're spending your wealth on them anyway. At one point you have to sit back and say, "Now wait a minute, where are we going? Why are we doing it? Why are children destroying themselves with drugs? So . . . I think you arrive at a point where you say, "No wait a minute, let's just slow down. What is it that we believe in? Where are we going. We're still the mightiest nation in the world. Do we believe in anything. Do we have a rule? Do we have a morality? Should we have?"

I just think what happened to me, and it's happened to a lot of people, is, I see the disproportion everywhere. I see the disparity. I see the incongruity. I see the stupidity. I see the absurdity of it. From Manhattan you can see the towering buildings of the affluent and, blocks away, people sleeping on grates, looking for a little heat from the vent outside Madison Square Garden. Why? What is it that we believe in? So, the question of values. And it's a fascinating question. You know a lot of us grew up taking a lot of things for granted. Momma and Papa taught us values; it was great; it was simple. You got your instruction from the hard end of the broom. You knew what was wrong because, when you did it, you got hit with a broom. That's an easy way to be instructed. You don't have that as much now. You don't have that clear a message being delivered either at home or in the schools. Should you have? Can you? Can you teach people without indoctrinating them? Can you teach them about good and evil without teaching them about sin and God? Because we wouldn't want to teach them about God; that has to be done at home, certainly not in the public school. And I regard it as the first question, before you talk about arms limitations, before you talk about the trade deficit and the debt, you ought to know why you're considering these subjects, where you want to be, what the value of things is.

Heffner: But when you talk about what has happened to this country, you lead me to ask, whose values are you going to teach? Governor Cuomo's? What about former Governor Reagan's? Which ones?

Well that is, of course, the dilemma. And I think you can respond to that one way. You can say, "Hey look, I took a quick look and it's going to be so difficult to identify these values, that I'm not even going to try." And so I'm going to instruct the people in the public pulpit . . . "Stay away from values." Don't talk about anything that sounds like values. Have indifference when it comes to moral judgments. Don't say it's right or wrong. Don't instruct the kids that having children recklessly is wrong. Don't tell them that having sex too early is wrong. Just stay away from it all, let the kids decide. Otherwise, God forbid, you'll be indoctrinating them. You can do that. I believe when you do that, what you teach them is there is no right and wrong. Do whatever you want to do. You want to pass the exam? You have to steal to pass the exam, by looking over her shoulder, to write her answer, "It's okay, don't worry about it." . . . Well, I think that's not satisfactory. And I think we went through that stage where we stepped away from the question, thinking we, at worst, would leave a vacuum. We didn't leave a vacuum, we left an instruction. And the instruction is, "There are no rules." That's chaos. So we have to find another alternative. I think there is one.

I think that at the base of every society, every well-formed society, and we've had two hundred years to form one, there's a credo, there's a rule, there's a consensus of values. We have some help. We, unlike most societies, started with our own civic Ten Commandments, called the Constitution; a lot of societies don't have that. They can't look back to a single instrument that designed them. A set of plans and specifications that was used before they were constructed. We can look at the Declaration of Independence, the Constitution, and we can find certain values. Equality, despite the amazing, stunning contradiction of the people who wrote this instrument about equality, having slaves, the truth was that we came to understand it. But one of the central truths is you and I are equal. And all of us are equal. The men are equal to the women, we understand that now. The blacks to the whites; the poor to the rich. That's an important principle.

Dignity is another one. That personhood is important. There is no such thing as an individual being less important than the totality. It took generations to come to that truth. We started with it two hundred years ago. Commonality—community is a value here. If you look at our original instruments, the one thing the Founders knew for sure is, "We're better off when we hang together." That Bruce Springsteen is right, nobody makes it, unless you all make it. Now that's another value. Accountability, responsibility, you do something wrong, you should pay. The rule of law, that it applies to everybody, Ivan Boesky and some kid who steals a pair of sneakers. The rule applies to all of them. A President who lies and breaks the law, whether it's Nixon or anyone else. The law applies to them just as it applies to you, if you evade your taxes. Or to me, if I commit some civic sin.

All of these are values. Why not teach them in the public school? I think you can teach them without getting into trouble. You don't have to be a Jew, you don't have to be a Christian, you don't even have to be a theist, you never have to mention God. And still it would be a body of principles, rules, that this country would agree on. I think we should recognize that and try teaching them.

Heffner: Governor, you remain, for me, the most eloquent person in public life. And what you say sounds so true to me. But you still somewhat avoid the basic question that I would put to you, which has to do with the kinds of values that you have attacked in the past. In your first Inaugural Address you wrote, and this is some years back, "It has become popular in some quarters to argue that the principal function of government is to make instruments of war and to clear obstacles from the way of the strong. The rest, it is said, will happen automatically. The cream will rise to the top, whether the cream be well endowed individuals or fortunate regions of the nation." Now that's a reflection of values other than yours, but values that are certainly held by a great many people in this country. What, then, will we teach about that question in the public schools?

Well, we have two categories. We have what I would say are non-controversial values. No one's really going to argue with you if you say that implicit in the documents that formed us, explicit in our conduct for 200 years, there's been a general understanding that people have responsibility for their actions. That it doesn't all come free in this society. That you have to live within an ordered society or pay the price. That the rule of law is important. That's not controversial.

Heffner. You say it's not controversial.

Yes. Exactly.

Heffner: Yet we live at a time when in the highest regions of government there have been those who have said, "Look, for the sake of national security, in order to survive, we must do these things that shave a little in the area of the law." Isn't this totally accepted?

Well, I still think it is a noncontroversial value. I think the people of this country would say that if President Reagan were clearly guilty of violating a statute, a law of this country, he should be made to pay just the way Nixon was. There is no question about that, in my opinion. They might love him for it; they might forgive him in their hearts, but I do not believe the

American people are prepared to say, "If a President violates the law, we'll let him get away with it, because his intention was good." Why not then a senator or a group of senators. A judge or a group of judges. A wise man or a wise woman. No. The people of this country said it in Watergate: "If you violate the law, you must pay." Look, if you're Martin Luther King or Mahatma Gandhi and you're a man or person of peace and you choose to violate the law to make a point, still the society will insist you pay the price for the violation. You do your time in prison. You make the point that while we're free to violate the law, we insist that the rule of law be perfected by punishing you for it. Now I think that's noncontroversial.

But let me get to a controversial value, the one you mentioned earlier. I believe this society we call the State of New York, the society we call the United States of America should posit as a value its obligation, corporately, its obligation as a people, to take care of those who are not able to take [care] of themselves. When I say government should be "family," that's what I mean. That we have an obligation to assist those who can't help themselves. I'm not talking about people who could help themselves, but choose not to out of laziness, out of whatever sin. No. They're on their own. But the child born to a wheelchair, the person grown too old to care for herself, with no relatives, no friends. We have a positive obligation in government to care for that person. Now, not everybody agrees. Jack Kemp, for example, says that my idea of family is patronizing. That my idea of family belongs at home with "Momma and Papa," that's his expression, but not with government. He regards that as too close to socialism. But what he's suggesting is another value. Which a lot of people liked enough to make the conservative ethic very strong. And the other value is, we tried helping the poor people, it didn't work. We lost ground doing it, so let's not try anymore. They made the denial of compassion respectable. They said government shouldn't even try to help all those people. What we should do is make the economy as strong as possible, let the fit get as powerful as possible, then hope that the church and the synagogue and the private foundations will do the rest.

So that is a controversial value. It has been the political issue of the last six or seven years. I believe my value structure there is better for this country, it's fairer, truer to our instinct as a people. But I would admit to you that it's controversial. I don't believe President Reagan believes what I believe. I know Jack Kemp does not believe what I believe about the idea of family. A controversial question. And I've lost the last two elections on that proposition. Not in the State of New York where it's won and won very handily, but at the national level, President Reagan represents a different value entirely. I think he's confused it. Because being surrounded with religious people, being soft of voice and manner, being apparently congenial and sweet and compassionate, I'm not sure that people understood fully the value he was representing. Which was, "We'll spend money on missiles, but have more homeless people than at any time since the Depression." Create more poor people than at any time since the Depression. Create a larger underclass than we've had in years, and squeeze the middle class. The middle class is just waking up to that. So that's controversial, that value structure is definitely controversial.

Heffner. But the only question I'm really raising is, is it ever possible to teach values in the public schools and stay away from these other splits in our society. If there weren't those splits, you wouldn't have run for Governor of New York, you wouldn't have delivered that magnificent Inaugural, you wouldn't have gone to San Francisco in '84 and electrified that Democratic gathering. So we're talking about very fundamental things.

Well, if the question is, "Will you ever be able to achieve a perfect consensus on values, that's permanent and noncontroversial from beginning to end," then the answer is "No."

Heffner: And I'm not so much of a dummy that I would ask that question.

No. Are there answers to all of the questions that I could pose? No. Should we nevertheless insist on producing a set of values that addresses these questions? Yes. Let's be precise. This a society where we have decided as a value not to allow the public places and people and instruments to teach any kind of theology. You cannot teach that there is God. When I went to public school we read from the King James version of the Bible. I happen to be a Catholic and it was some time before I realized that I was standing on a stage reading the wrong Bible. But from David, the Psalms. We read at the beginning of assembly. You can no longer do that. God is out of the classroom.

Heffner: Do you approve of that, by the way?

It's academic, but I think probably now, after living half a hundred years, I think we're better off with public schools staying away from any kind of theology. Because I'm afraid you would teach my children the wrong theology. I would prefer to deal with that myself.

Heffner: So if I were teaching values, Governor. Might I not teach them the wrong values, values you wouldn't embrace?

That's why I want you to stay with noncontroversial values. Like the sacredness of life, which I regard as noncontroversial. What might be controversial is the definition of what life is. And, well, there's nothing strange about that. That's a scientific question. Even for those who are mightily opposed to abortion, even for those in my own church, the Catholic Church, who argue against abortion. They can point to a time before Augustine when there was a different definition of life than there is today. And that's true. You see, but I think the point is that you might occasionally have some difficulty in applying these rules.

. . . I think the point is that you might occasionally have some difficulty in applying these rules. That's not an argument against structuring the value. Otherwise you're left in the position we started with. Let's stay away from the whole subject, and teach in effect that there are no values. And that, to me, is moral chaos and much worse.

Let's take another example. One that's going to get more and more real in this society. A governor in the west raised the question and paid a big price for it. "Are we allowing our people to live too long in this society, using machines? Can we afford to do it? Is the quality of their life worth it?" You remember Dick Lamm saying this.

Heffner: I do.

Boy, he paid a terrible price for that. I'm afraid, whether you like the implications of it or not, that's a question we're going to have to face. That's a question some of us have faced already. Should you unplug the machine on your parent? Now, how do you deal with that? We have a group in our state called the Life and Law Group. I've brought ethicists, religious and non-religious, from all over the country under Dr. David Axelrod, our Commissioner of Health, a brilliant, brilliant man, quite apart from his brilliance as a scientist and a doctor. And we tried addressing this question. We start with a proposition: "Life is sacred." Life is the greatest value we have, especially if you can't posit a God. If you can't posit that there's an eternal entity beyond all of us, then what is the greatest value you have to work with? Life . . .

Heffner: Why can't I posit that? Because a court tells me that I cannot?

Because there are people who don't believe it.

Heffner: And a court tells me that I cannot.

Because there is a substantial number of people who don't believe it. And because when you say God, you'll have to define God. And your God may be different than my God. Your God may come in three persons, your God may impose obligations that I don't recognize from my God. And rather than deal with that, and what it leads to, a state God, a state religion, which eventually then, because it's the ultimate truth, insists on oppressing all others who don't believe. That's where we came from. That's where the Jews came from, that's where the Europeans came from. They fled from places like that. And came to this country to have a place that was free of that kind of religious oppression.

So, our value judgment, civically, and I think it's a good one, has been, "Hey, look, we will allow you to believe in God. We will nurture your opportunity to believe in God. But the way we protect your opportunity to believe in God is not to insist on a civic God for everybody."

Heffner: Governor Cuomo, were we so much worse off in terms of the very values you're concerned about when we would say, under the mantle of our governmental apparatus, "In God we trust."

Well, we still say, "In God we trust."

Heffner: I know. Were we so much better off?

Well, I don't know that you can say that we are worse off now because of the Supreme Court decisions. I could probably make an argument that says that the challenging of the policy which allowed them to teach me at Public School 50 in South Jamaica, Queens, about a God, the challenging of it, produced a good thing. It made us think about it. It made people think about school and God and theology and maybe a lot of the people who took it for granted when you read from King James, maybe they were caused to think about it, once it was challenged. And I hope I'm not being perverse therefore, when I say, you might even have attracted more attention to God by denying him in the classroom or denying the right to teach him in the classroom, than by letting the status quo exist. There is good in everything. —1987

WILLIAM F. BUCKLEY, JR.

William F. Buckley, Jr. first gained fame, even a measure of notoriety, with the publication in 1951 of his signature work, God and Man at Yale, *written while he was still an undergraduate. He later wrote more books of nonfiction espousing a politically conservative philosophy, and several novels, and founded the* National Review, *a beacon of conservative journalism. By the time the following conversation took place, in 1996, he had become the guru, or rather the patron saint, of American conservatism. That's why I was still surprised, even shocked, when I found myself almost debating with Buckley about his then recently announced call (along with other conservatives such as George Schultz and Milton Friedman) for the legalization of drugs.*

First of all, please don't mistake my position for that of people who are indifferent to drugs. I'm not indifferent to drugs. I think I've been quoted as saying if I could turn a single latch which would make all the drugs disappear from the face of the earth, with the exception of here and there, a vineyard in Bordeaux, I would turn that latch. Now, is it inconsistent for a conservative to take my position? I don't think it is, because a conservative seeks to be grounded in reality. That which works is quantifiable; that which simply does not work, isn't. If you were to pass a law requiring people to go to church on Sunday, it wouldn't work. Under the circumstances, you would eventually simply withdraw such a law. My position on drugs is that the drug laws aren't working, and that more damage, net, is being done by their continuation on the books than would be done by withdrawing them from the books. This, as I say, should not be confused as a sanction for drugs. Drugs are a form of escapism, and the damage in taking them is not by any means self-limited. It damages other people also. For that reason, the question is: how do you diminish the net harm done by drugs? Well, suppose one were to ask the following question: How do you measure the net damage done by the existing situation? Well, you begin by assessing the damage to people who take drugs. Then you add to that the number of people who are engaged in trying to prevent them from doing that. That means 400,000 policemen. Then you add whatever dollar measurement you wish to attach to derivative losses in liberty and security. Mr. and Mrs. Jones, who can't safely cross the park at night because they would likely run into a drug marauder, have lost something tangible. Mr. and Mrs. Jones, who need to lock up at night, have lost something tangible. To the extent that you can talk about cities being imperiled, they are imperiled by what? By people who need either to sustain their own habit or who wish to profiteer from the weaknesses of others who have that habit, which means that they are robbing or stealing approximately 100 times the pharmaceutical cost of that drug. Now, I've seen varying estimates of what that cost figure is. I've never seen one that's less than 500 billion dollars. And we're spending 125 or 130 billion dollars in our war on drugs. I would infinitely prefer to reduce that net loss to the cost of looking after people who have the habit and who need care, which would take us down to 20–30 billion dollars a year, and have the relative liberty that would flow from a situation in which half of America isn't constipated by worrying about drug-takers and by drug-sellers, and by people who rob and steal in order to profiteer from the situation.

Heffner: In a recent issue of *National Review*, you summed up some of the responses from your readers. One of the questions they raised is whether this isn't, in a very real sense, a moral question, the answer to which cannot then be given in terms of hundreds of millions or billions of dollars spent, and that you, yourself, would be the first person to indicate that.

No, because the moral stigma continues, in my judgement, to attach to it. Anybody who becomes an alcoholic, which is probably the primary curse of this country, in my judgement, is morally stigmatized by permitting himself to get into that condition. That is not an argument for prohibition. Adultery is widely practiced. So is fornication. You can simultaneously say it's morally wrong, but we're not going to tell the police to open the doors of every motel to find out whether the people inside have marriage licenses.

Heffner: But in this instance we have to say to our youngsters, "This was against public policy up until yesterday." Today, it is not. That's a strange message.

Well, it's a message that we undertook to say in 1933.

Heffner: With the end of Prohibition.

That's right. And it's a message that, in my judgement, we are perfectly capable of taking when things don't work out. We pulled out of Vietnam, and we pulled away from Prohibition. We pulled away from a number of compulsory blue laws, all of them in the last few years, by the way. This doesn't mean that you encourage a defiance of the Commandment that you shall keep holy the Sabbath. It simply means that church business doesn't become state business.

Heffner: But it still seems so strange to me that—

But I don't mind developing a policy that seems strange to you if the result of it is going to make a society improved over how that society currently operates.

Heffner: I'll accept that, but is there any downside, as you see it?

Well, the downside is that almost inevitably you will find X number of people—I don't know how many there are, and there are disputes about this—X number of people who say, "Now that I can actually walk into a federal drug store and buy it, I'll go ahead and do so." Now, this is widely reflected on. How many people in that category are there? The ACLU, at least Ira Glasser, who is the head of it, doesn't think there would necessarily be any increase in drug-taking. His point is that the fact that it is illegal adds a certain allure to it that will all of a sudden dissipate if it weren't illegal. A second school of thought says, "okay, they will try it, but having tried, having had their experience, they will withdraw from it." Ninety-eight—I want to get the figures anyway—98 million people in the United States have experimented with illegal drugs. Three-and-a-half million are current addicts as defined by, "Did you take one in the last 30 days." Now, if you say, well, 95 million can pull out of it, having done it in school, in college, or whenever, there's no reason why you can't project that experience in the future by the number of people who say, "Okay, it's legal, I'll try it," and then do it once. Now it's very dangerous to do. I would certainly caution against it. But all that money that's currently spent on constraint could be spent on education. And, by the way, there's no reason not to encourage social sanctions against it, i.e., if you come to work for Mr. Heffner, you can't take drugs. And if you don't consent to have an occasional drug test, extemporaneously scheduled, then don't apply for a job. I'm all in favor of social sanctions; it's the legal sanction that I think is killing us.

Heffner: Now, as a prime debater, would you say that that was a very good summary of the downside? Seriously.

Well, I can't think what the other downside there is.

Heffner: I can. Let's ask the question about saying to our young people, "Yes, this campaign against drugs and the dangers their use involves is tough. We haven't been able to make it, as yet. And since it's so tough and it's so costly, we're simply going to abandon the effort." For some reason, I see that as a major downside. As you've said, you're not embracing drugs. You wanted to make that perfectly clear. You're just saying successful prohibition is just too damned tough to achieve. And I'm saying in turn that surrender of this is immoral and unacceptible.

Well, I would offhand guess that the majority of young people would be encouraged by a finding of that character, because it would tell them they're adults living in the real world. Let me remind you that the opposition, the illegality of drugs, does not actually affect the quantity of their consumption. As one person put it to me only last Fall, it's easier to buy marijuana in Cambridge than it is beer. Why? Because if somebody sells you illegal beer, he forfeits his license, and his license might have cost $200,000, his whole business. Whereas people who peddle marijuana can do so furtively with no overhead. I don't think anybody would maintain that if you want drugs you can't find them. The very fact that they're imported and consumed in such quantities simply defies that assertion.

Heffner: If you had become the Drug Czar with total authority at some time during the past 10–20 years, do you think you could have been more effective in solving our problem?

Okay, if I were the Drug Czar, I would say, "Okay, here are the five or six popular, illegal drugs. You can get them at the federal drug store for just one percent more than the pharmaceutical cost of producing them. Enough to sustain the overhead, but enough also to discourage a black market in them. But before you go in there you're going to have to read a description of what this drug does to you. And if you're in a mood to play Russian roulette, go ahead and take some crack cocaine, because the probability that you will be seriously affected by this is up around eight, ten percent." So therefore I would give them all the warning needed about the acceptable level of toxicity in indulging this habit, but I would not let the price rise to where Mr. Middleman decides that he's going to sell you that crack cocaine, and in order to get it he's going to fumble around in people's living rooms or steal women's purses or mug people.

Heffner: Now, you were in the Army. You remember those horrendous films—all about what's going to happen if you pick up syphilis when you go into town. And you know that the AIDS horror pictures, the horror information, has been about as effective as those old Army films, not terribly, terribly much more. Do you really feel that a warning on the dangers of drug use to consumers would be effective?

Well, first of all, let me distinguish between the two, because AIDS and syphilis are the result of passions that become ungovernable. Lust or love causes people to do things that they wouldn't do in premeditation. "Deliver us from temptation," says the Lord's Prayer, i.e., deliver you from that third drink if you have alcoholic tendencies and are going to want the tenth drink. By the same token, people who give in to unsafe sex practices are "carried away." But this would not apply to a relatively clinical decision to buy crack cocaine, because people wouldn't buy it when they were stoned. That's not the way drugs work. You have your trip and then you're over it. Then you reflect and decide whether or not to go again. So there is that distinction.

A second distinction is that there is no way ever to protect people categorically from the results of their own unruly appetites. This is obviously true of sex. It's obviously true in alcohol. And it should be obviously true in respect to drugs. . . .

Heffner: All right. Let me ask you this question: What do you think's going to happen?

We need to await the day when a politician with national prestige says, "Look, this hasn't worked." Now, I don't predict that day's around the corner, but I think there is an increasing natural sense that it hasn't worked. We got an awful lot of mail after that issue [February

1996] went out; 450 letters is a lot of mail for general opinion. And only four or five percent said, "You shouldn't have even brought the subject up." Although a half were opposed to the conclusions we arrived at, 100 percent were glad that we ventilated the controversy. So I think there's a lot of latent feeling out there, and I would like to see the politician who just risks a forward position on it. Mayor Schmoke of Baltimore is the closest, and he was reelected quite thunderously, notwithstanding that he had made his position clear just before his last election. So I think that there will be a distillation of sentiments that are already empirically widely felt.

Heffner: Now, if you were in my position, what would you say to Buckley about the potential for damage in this position?

I'd say, "I surrender."

Heffner: No, you wouldn't. Not if you were in my position. I asked you about downside before. Now, in a sense, a similar question. What damage do you see that *National Review* is doing to the war against drugs?

Oh, we can hardly damage the war against drugs, because the war against drugs is futile. —1996

GEORGE SOROS

While economics is not always the subject of a lively conversation, when one of the participants is George Soros, the result is more than likely to be provocation. In 1997, Mr. Soros was, and still is, one of the world's wealthiest men—a self-made billionaire. But he is, at the same time, a model contrarian. We talked first about his notion of the capitalist threat to society, which he had set forth in a highly controversial article in the Atlantic Monthly. *We then went on to explore the subject of philanthropy, about which George Soros, a "giver" of massive proportions, has equally controversial ideas and practices.*

Heffner: Much of the criticism levied against you in this past year has been, in relation to the *Atlantic* piece, that you were, in a sense, a traitor to capitalism. How do you respond to that?

Well, you know, I'm a human being first, and a capitalist afterwards. That would be my answer. In other words, I don't consider myself committed to the money that I have made. Money is supposed to serve a purpose; I'm not supposed to be its slave. So I can still think for myself. And I'm more interested, actually, in the truth, in understanding things as they are, than in defending my, call it class interests, or my personal interests.

Heffner: But that runs quite counter, doesn't it, to the very essence, the very being of laissez-faire capitalism?

Well, of course, I'm a critic of laissez-faire capitalism, and I think that we ought to be concerned with something more than our self-interest. The laissez-faire thesis is that the common interest is best served by everybody looking out for his personal interest. And my position it that that's not enough. It won't do. Markets can do a lot of good, but they're not as perfect as they're cracked up to be. So there is a common interest that is not served by the markets, that goes beyond markets. And we have to be concerned with those interests.

Now, that is the subject of politics. And actually I'm critical of markets, but in some ways I ought to be more critical of the political process, because it's the failure of the political process that has allowed the market mechanism to penetrate into areas of social life where it really ought not to be the dominant force.

Heffner: But why do you say "the failure?" Mightn't one say that capitalism, as it is practiced now, is a function of, in this country, the triumph of Reaganism, which is a facet of the political system? So why is it a failure?

Because we now have a global economy, and a global capitalist system. Of course, we do have political processes in the individual countries. And when things go too far out of line in the economic life, there is a political process to correct it. For instance, when the trusts came into existence, big business became very big. You then have the antitrust legislation, and you had big government to bring big business under control. Now we have a global capitalist system. The power of the states is greatly reduced. Which, incidentally, I applaud. But nevertheless, there isn't an international political process to keep pace with the internationalization of our economy.

Heffner: You say you applaud that. Why do you say that?

I say it because most states, being authoritarian institutions, tend to abuse their power. They are usually instruments of oppression. I've been, and continue to fight, against the oppressive state. I mean, Communism was basically state oppression of the people. So it was a real threat to open society, and it continues to be a real threat in many countries.

Now, we do have a rather good democratic system in this country. But if you look around the world there are many places where governments abuse their power. And here too.

Heffner: Are you then a believer in international government?

Well, no, because I don't think that we need government as such. Government goes too far. But I do think that you do need international regulation of an international economic process. We do have a few institutions—we have the International Monetary Fund, the World Bank—without which the capitalist system would have already collapsed in the last few weeks. So they are very necessary.

Heffner: Why do you say, "the last few weeks?"

Because we are in the midst of a worldwide financial crisis right now [late 1997]. It started in Thailand, and it has spread, first in Southeast Asia, then to Korea. Japan is in very dire financial straits. The system is in a very bad way. It spread south to Brazil. There's a considerable problem in Russia. Ukraine is on the ropes. There are a lot of worrisome things going on in the world.

Heffner: With what result? Potentially, that is.

Well, of course, you could have a financial meltdown. You could have a banking crisis where markets cease to function. I'm convinced, and I really sincerely believe that that is not going to occur. In other words, the financial system is going to hold together. There will not be, let's say, defaults by governments in paying their debts, and that kind of thing. However, what is happening now is imposing great strains on the economic and political life of individual countries. . . . There is a lot to be worried about. I'll give you just one example: Our trade deficit next year will probably double what it is this year. It will become a very major increase. If it is combined with a slowdown in the economy, which at the moment does not seem to be the case, you could have a great deal of protectionist sentiment. You could then have a resistance to accepting imports.

Heffner: Don't we have that sentiment now?

Yes, we have the sentiment, but you would have a lot more provocation for it. You would have a lot more to worry about, because there would be a greater imbalance.

Now, you need those imports to allow the countries that have debts that they cannot pay actually to pay the debts. They have to export. So, for instance, a country like Thailand, which is now in, heading into or is in the midst of a suddenly occurring depression—the country doesn't import anymore. People can't afford to buy cars or computers. But they'll sell everything abroad that they can. Their currency has fallen by 40 percent, so they will sell everything cheaper than they should; they'll sell at any price. So will Korea. So that's what's in the works next year. It will have some political repercussions. If the world economy is prosperous as it is, hopefully that will absorb it, and eventually the system will correct itself. But if it results in restrictions on imports, then the debtors can't pay their debts and then you have a breakdown as well.

Heffner: Do you see, in and among your capitalist colleagues, the wisdom required to accept the kind of modification of capitalism that you suggest?

I think we all have to put our heads together, because I don't exactly know what kind of modification I'm suggesting.

Heffner: What do you mean?

In the sense that I can see that the system is defective, I can see the problems, but I don't have solutions. I don't know exactly what to do about it.

Heffner: But your basic solution is attitudinal, isn't it?

Yes.

Heffner: It has to do with modifying the dog-eat-dog, Darwinian approach that we're taking now?

That is right. But then, once we've changed the attitude, we then have to put our heads together and see what kind of institutional changes we need. We'll probably need to strengthen some of the international institutions. We may have to create new ones. We have to make them work better. You have got the United Nations which has a function and is not fulfilling that function very well. So there's a lot of work to do. First, I would like to advocate a change in attitudes. And once you have changed your attitude, you then have to use it for developing new solutions, new institutions.

Heffner: Well, before we even get to that, seriously, what chance do you see that there is going to be an attitudinal change?

Well, I think one has to work at it. I, you know . . . [Laughter]

Heffner: You're hedging. You're a great hedger.

[Laughter] No, that's true. I really don't know. All I can say is that we need to change our attitude. Whether we'll have the wisdom to do it, I don't know.

Heffner: What's the alternative?

Well, we go on as we are. I think this global capitalist system is very powerful. It really is a thing that hangs together very well. It's very painful to quit, for any country to renege on its obligations. The consequences are quite disastrous. But if the conditions deteriorate, and being in the system becomes too painful, then you will have eventually some countries that will react negatively. So I think we are facing now a period of considerable political turmoil, I would say particularly in Asia, in the countries which have been hit by the financial crisis. Very interesting what's going to happen in China, which, at the moment, has not yet been affected by it, but indirectly it will be affected and it will have to respond. So I think there could be quite some changes in China also. I think the situation is very complicated, and I think you will have important political developments in the next couple of years.

Heffner: And in this country?

Well, we are in actually, in a way, the beneficiaries of what's happening in the world.

Heffner: How so?

Because the global capitalist system has a center. And we are, in effect, the center. You see? It's the dollar that is the dominant currency in the world. Of course, Europe is in similar position. They are also sort of dollar and deutschmark, the new currency, the European currency, these are the strong currencies. So, being at the center, one actually benefits from goods that are going to be supplied at lower prices. So inflation, which has been a threat, is no longer a threat; it's the other way around. Prices are very stable, and they even may decline in certain areas, particularly import prices are likely to come down. Which means that without inflation we don't need high interest rates to fight inflation, so we can lower interest rates. The lower interest rates stimulate the economy. So actually, since we are at the center, the fact that you have got a storm in the periphery is to our benefit.

Heffner: But if it is to our benefit economically, as you suggest, in those terms, do you anticipate that the benefits will include a diminution of the dichotomization in this country between rich and poor? Do you anticipate that lower interest rates will bring about a better sharing, a more equitable sharing?

No, I don't think so. Because, actually, in some ways, there will be more tension between the lower-paid, let's say, whose jobs are more easily substituted by imports from abroad, and the more skilled, say, the service industries. These are not subject to competition from abroad, and will be much better situated than the areas which have import competition. So . . . if anything, the social tensions might actually increase.

Heffner: Well, that's the point that puzzles me in terms of the reactions to what you have written and have said. And in *Soros on Soros* the same messages are there. I think it was two years ago, Lester Thurow wrote a piece raising the question: How long can a democracy sustain itself if there is a continuing division, a widening division between the "haves" and the "have-nots"? And I guess you're suggesting that that division is going to get greater.

Somewhat greater. There is a tension here, and it's something to be concerned about. But I'm much more concerned with the international setting. You see? This is where our perspectives are different. There is tension between the "haves" and "have-nots" here. But must one look at it as a global system, and there the tension between the haves and the have-nots is going to increase greatly. I'm really much more concerned about the international implications than the domestic ones. We are, in some ways, in a privileged position. There's plenty to be concerned about. I'm not minimizing it. But what I'm saying is that the international problem, the international tensions, are much greater. . . .

Heffner: But the tensions in our own country will lead, must lead inevitably to the kinds of pressures toward protectionism that you feel will push the world over into a free-fall.

Right. And if we turn protectionist, then there's a danger of replaying what happened in the war period. That is the case.

Heffner: How long do you think we can abuse the patience of those who are have-nots, and increasingly are have-nots, in our own country? Do you think there is a point at which those who are deprived see how much the rest of us have, and will say "no further?"

Look, any kind of revolution, I think, can be pretty well ruled out in this country. This is basically a healthy country. I have an international perspective. I see how rotten situations are in other countries. So I'm a great admirer of this country. I don't think that we are ripe for a revolution. Correction has to be a political process. And unfortunately money plays too big a role in politics. That has to be corrected. The people have votes, and this is a democracy. So if people are fed up with the way things are now, they can express it in the political process. I'm more concerned about the political process functioning properly. I'm concerned about the role of money in politics, which is excessive. And I'm concerned about the attitude of the elite, who are too much taken up by the laissez-faire ideology that one leaves it to the markets and everything will take care of itself. So I think there has to be a change of heart among the leadership.

Heffner: What in the world would bring about that change of heart?

Oh, I think, I think that some of the things enacted in the last few years have had an adverse consequence that people are aware of. Take, for instance, the legislation on immigration, which was very repressive, very unjust, because it effectively disqualified taxpayers from receiving the benefits to which they were entitled. Legal immigrants were denied those rights. I think that, in fact, legislators, Republicans, realized that they have made a big mistake, that it needs to be corrected. And, in fact, they have gone quite a long way towards correcting it. They haven't entirely reversed it. But a large part of the injustice has been corrected. So that shows that the process, the political process, actually works.

Heffner: Yes, but I'm talking about the thing you're most concerned with, and that is attitudes toward the role of the marketplace. We are a market-driven society. Everyplace you turn you hear, "Well, the market provides."

Well, I'll give you another example. I'm concerned about the role of the professions. The loss of professional values, and the fact that they are being superseded by the dollar mark . . . Take the medical profession, which has been very much mesmerized by the dollar sign. I see a change of attitudes, partly because of the new system of HMOs, which hurt the doctors as well as the patients. And I think the possibility of, let's say, new coalitions between patients and doctors to change the system. Because I think the doctors are not too happy with the way the system is developing. And this is a purely market system where, you know, providing healthcare becomes strictly a business. And so there is among the professionals an increasing resistance to it.

Heffner: So a nonrevolutionary revolution of a sort.

Right. You see, while I am almost a specialist in revolutions, in actual fact I prefer nonrevolutionary change. I like the political process to work.

Heffner: Let me ask what personal imperatives drive you to spend as much as you do on good causes?

I sometimes ask myself why I'm doing it. And, in a way, I really got sucked into it, because I'm a critic of philanthropy. I think it's very often a corrupting influence, or it is corrupt because there is no proper feedback mechanism, and so on. So I'm actually a critic of philanthropy. It's a bit ironic that I should be also a practitioner.

Heffner: More than a bit. A few billion dollars worth of irony.

Yes, that's about right.

Heffner: But how have you overcome your criticism? Or at least set it aside ?

Well, I would actually like to make the world a better place. This is a rather pretentious thing to say, but that is really why I'm doing it. It's not philanthropy in the traditional sense. It's certainly not charity. We're not giving money away. We are trying to make things work better. So I got involved in the Communist countries trying to change the system. And when the Soviet system collapsed, I got involved in trying to build a better system, what I call an "open society." And that requires a lot of help. So I wanted to provide whatever help I could. I was hoping that the rest of the world would join me, that there would be a Marshall Plan, as there was after the Second World War. I was hopelessly naive on that issue. But I did what I could in my personal capacity, and I can say it actually amounts to something. We have actually accomplished something.

Heffner: Why wasn't there a Marshall Plan? The opportunity was there.

Absolutely. And it was a tremendous missed opportunity. I was doing everything I could at the time to try to draw attention to this issue. But we were actually dominated by a belief in laissez-faire, that you can't interfere in other people's lives, that they have to organize, fend for themselves, and let the market mechanism take care of everything. And actually that was one of the worst, let's say, side effects of that belief. I was trying desperately to get to Margaret Thatcher, who was the one person who could have had a Thatcher Plan, because she had the respect of the United States and she had position in Europe. And she understood what was going on. But she didn't respond because she didn't believe that it is the role of the state to get engaged in any kind of aid, much less philanthropy.

Heffner: Despite the success of the Marshall Plan after World War II?

Yes. But that was different; it was a different era. And this was perhaps my biggest mistake, that I thought that the Western democracies would be motivated by a belief in their system and would want to propagate that system and would want to help the formerly Communist countries to make the transition. Since democracy and open society, which includes, of course, a market economy, is a more sophisticated system than communism, when [the latter] collapses, you can't make the transition in one step unless there is somebody from the outside giving you a helping hand. And that's what we missed. We should have done that. And I did it in my personal capacity. And what I did personally has been, I think, helpful, but it was obviously not enough.

Heffner: You frequently talk about the open society—the basis for your various foundation and philanthropic works. What do you mean by it?

Well, in a superficial sense it really is just a broader definition of democracy; not just rule of the majority, but respect for the minority, respect for the law, and so on. The concept itself is based on the recognition that our understanding of the world in which we live is imperfect, and we cannot have a blueprint, we cannot have a perfect society. Therefore, we must content ourselves with the second best, that is, an open society and a society that is open to improvement, where you recognize that things are not as good as they should be, and try to improve them.

Heffner: That's a very difficult concept for people to hold onto.

It is. It was relatively easy during the Cold War. We stood for an open society and they were clearly a closed society. So you had a dichotomy: open and closed . . . it was clear. Now Communism has collapsed and all they have is our system; but people don't have an understanding of what an open society is. And this is why I'm at loggerheads with the dominant belief in laissez-faire which says, "No, you don't need a system. You just let people fend for themselves, let the market take care of everything." That is the dominant belief today, and that belief is wrong, because we do have a society, we do have common values, we need to have some common bases and some institutions even to preserve the market mechanism. But we are unaware of that, and we have failed, in the case of the Soviet collapse. I'm afraid that we may be failing in preserving the global capitalist system.

Heffner: Explain that.

Markets are not perfect. We have a false ideology. We're supposed to have a scientific base. The scientific base is economic theory. Now, economic theory is based on certain assumptions. Those assumptions do not apply in the real world. But we believe they do. You see, economic theory tells you how the markets achieve equilibrium. Now, they do achieve equilibrium if certain conditions are given. But those conditions, in reality, are not given. And so you don't have equilibrium. Therefore, you don't have the beautiful outcome that the theory gives us. So people think, well, there's a tendency towards equilibrium. But that is false, because there is no equilibrium, and sometimes there is no tendency towards equilibrium. In fact, sometime there is tendency to get far away from equilibrium. Financial markets can collapse. They can be very, very unstable. And we have a false understanding, for instance, of how financial markets operate. The prevailing wisdom happens to be wrong.

Heffner: What are we doing? Substituting chaos, then?

Chaos is the extreme of far-from-equilibrium conditions. Actually, life is conducted at the edge of chaos. No equilibrium. Our understanding of the world is always biased, always deficient. There's always something wrong in the way we construct things. All our constructs, all our institutions have something that doesn't withstand the test of time. So we have to be constantly on the alert to correct the deficiencies, to keep the system going near equilibrium, to avoid breakdown.

Heffner: But isn't that one of the bases for the critics, even of your philanthropy, that you invest so much, there is such an overwhelming amount of money that you are putting into your various projects, that you prevent us—and now I'm thinking in terms of open-market notions, marketplace notions—from seeing what the faults are in your own thinking?

That's correct.

Heffner: And you guard against this?

No, no, because however much money I pour into a country, I cannot correct the deficiencies. And I'm not pouring the money into correcting the deficiencies; I'm empowering people to work towards correcting them. So we are not there, for instance, to substitute for the budget, the state budget. Certain things the state has to care of. We are not trying to do that. We are trying to give people better education, give them opportunities to try out new ways of doing things. To organize a civil society itself, to make itself heard. We don't have a blueprint for solving problems, because we don't know the solution. If you recognize and accept your own fallibility, you know that you don't have the final answer. Therefore you have to help people in that country to develop better solutions. And that's what we're doing.

Heffner: Well, I know from the time two years ago that Dr. Kathleen Foley, who heads your project on death and dying, was here, that there is an open-mindedness, not single solutions. But also there are people who are very, very annoyed with you, in your approach, for instance, to drug policy.

Very much so. And I'm happy to irritate some people, because I know that I'm accomplishing something. But take the Project on Death. Death is a problem that one cannot overcome. However, the way one approaches it can make it worse or better. And in our country there is, generally speaking, a denial of death. We are not willing to come to terms with it. Families are not willing to accept it. Patients themselves fight it, but can't come to terms with it. The medical profession cannot accept that their patients are dying . . . they need to learn to accept the fact that patients die. The project actually is making quite an impression.

As to drugs—a serious problem. However, the way we are handling it now is doing a lot more damage than drugs themselves. Look at the people in prison. The abuse of power that was actually involved in many of those cases. The disruption of entire communities. The racist aspect of our war on drugs. A lot more damage is done by our attempt to deal with drugs the wrong way, the war that cannot be won, instead of accepting the fact that there is a drug problem and we have to try and make it better. We have to treat people, we have to give them a chance to get out of the drug habit. People who are in the drug habit can kick it, and they do kick it after a while, if they survive. So I think that our drug policy is wrong. In this case, I happened to touch on a particularly sensitive nerve.

Heffner: Indeed, you did.

I mean, when I talk to politicians who don't dare touch it, they call it the "third rail." You touch it, and you're dead, as a politician. Now, I'm in a privileged position because I'm an independent person. I can speak my mind. And that's what I do.

Heffner: Isn't that what ticks off so many people?

Yes, yes. I think it is annoying for others, and it's a bit dangerous for me.

Heffner: Dangerous?

Yes, yes, because nobody is really independent. I mean, I am part of this society, and I'm not all-powerful, and I can easily slip up and do the wrong thing and get hurt. So I'm aware of that. But nevertheless, I think it's worthwhile to speak out. I'm actually really interested in getting closer to understanding the world in which we live.

Heffner: Because you are very much aware of the uses of power, the power of the marketplace and its powerlessness at times, are you concerned about the power that you have and that you are now exercising in your philanthropies?

I'm very concerned about it. Actually, I've got a lot more power than I ever thought I would. It has grown. Partly because I've become a public figure . . . because I'm talking to you and people are watching me and listening to me. So that's a very important part of it. And it's a tremendous responsibility. And almost for the first time in my life I feel that I can actually make an impact. I can actually change certain things. And that makes me really wonder what it is that I want to accomplish. So it makes me question myself a lot more than I used to, because before I knew exactly what I wanted to do, and I couldn't do it. Now that I can actually do it, I'm not so sure exactly what I want to do.

Heffner: From a slightly different perspective, do you think that George Soros will ever say, "I can't assume this responsibility or use this power any longer."

Well, because I have that responsibility, I can't walk away from it. I mean, I'm trying to actually give away my wealth while I'm alive, and then I'll walk away from it. I probably won't succeed actually, but I would like to do as much of it as I can while I'm alive exactly because I feel a sense of responsibility.

Heffner: In the science of your giving, you are very much involved.

Yes. But I don't call it "science"; I call it "alchemy." You see? I wrote a book called *Alchemy of Finance* because I think, while you can't change dross into gold because of the laws of chemistry, you can actually change the world in which you are a participant by making statements about it. You can, for instance, make a lot of money in financial markets by incantation, and by all kinds of promotions. So we are dealing in a different world when we are dealing in the human world.

Heffner: I like that, "making money by incantation." That's spin-control.

Absolutely. And you might as well recognize it. Of course, we deny it because we pretend to be scientific about it.

Heffner: Is that what the economists do?

There is a large element of that. Because in order to be accepted as a science, you have to have the trappings of science. But, in actual fact, the doctrine of perfect competition has had a tremendous effect on the way society is organized, because it's that theoretical abstract construct that is at the basis of this laissez-faire belief. You see? So it is a form of incantation.—1997

SIMON SCHAMA

Simon Schama is one of the growing number of eminent historians writing brilliantly in the nineteenth century narrative, subjective tradition. Our 1989 conversation was stimulated by the publication of his splendid history of the French Revolution, Citizens, *which ranged widely over a number of aspects of the nature of history and culminated in an eerily prescient insight into the emergent power of nationalism after a military conflict, and a Tocquevillian comment about American democracy. I supposed that Professor Schama dismissed as naive the assumption that any historian of the past or the present—certainly the journalist—is or truly can be dispassionate, and that American historian Charles Beard may have been right in characterizing all written history as primarily an act of faith. I asked my guest whether that is a fair statement of what he generally believes.*

I think it is. . . . There's an Italian historian, Benedetto Croce, a great historian and philosopher, who produced the quotation "all history is contemporary history." By which he meant that the historian who suffered from the delusion that he could magically, objectively reach the bedrock reality of a long, remote past was really fooling himself. At the same time it isn't to say that history is completely a shifting, protean, slippery, elusive thing. It's this morning's prejudice and lunchtime's prejudice and the evening's prejudice, each of which may cancel each other out. I don't want to be a "relativizer," God forbid, but I do think, these days, at least, for my own part, historians might own up more than they are often trained to do to the fact that very often what they write, or the things that they select to be of interest are colored by their own convictions.

Heffner: Why don't you want to be a "relativizer, God forbid"?

Well, relativizers, I take it, believe that there are no remote objects, there is no hard reality of any kind, that we're all flying about in some sort of primordial soup, bumping into random objects, and that the world is full of "speech," "acts," "states of mind," "states of perception," and there's nothing to stub your toe against. I mean, at the most preposterous level you'd say, "Well, Auschwitz is really, you know, a matter of historians talking to each other, there were no gas chambers," or, less sensationally, "There was no Battle of Hastings." Well, one knows—one would have to be an idiot not to know—really that there were such events. What I think engages me is the possibility of reinterpreting them, with all of our own immediate late twentieth-century baggage of prejudices and preconceptions, and not attempt to nail down exactly how the Battle of Hastings might have been to those who fought it. Of course this would be a horror to the great nineteenth-century historian Leopold von Ranke, whose most famous remark about history is that historians ought to tend to what really happened.I think they tried to do this for nearly a century, for the first century of the life of the profession. Now, I think more and more things intervene between being absolutely convinced you can replicate what exactly happened, and the process of storytelling or witnessing or narrating or chronicling. And I'm very happy that historians are returning to this kind of loose, but not I think, relativizing, activity.

Heffner: You've been criticized for storytelling.

Yes, I have been. Well, I'm happy to shoulder that particular criticism, and it's true that some of my peers and colleagues say, "Tut, tut, tut, you cannot make an argument and tell a story at the same time." It is, you know, Rule Number One, that was drilled into us. Not into me because I actually had a wonderful teacher at Cambridge University, who was a really incorrigible storyteller, so he in some sense, himself, harked back to that older tradition. But the rules of the profession, you know, severely embedded in the pages of the *American Historical Review*, are that analysis and argument is in effect a form of science, and you mustn't muddy it up, or color it, or twist it around like so much intellectual Playdough by narrating at the same time. I was taken to task in the august pages of the *New York Review of Books* for trying to do that. "A low attempt to seize the readers' attention" . . . "a journalistic attempt to seize the readers' attention" was the way the critic described it. Well, of course, you know, from my part this ignores all of the greatest traditions of history writing. Michelet, Macaulay, not to say Tacitus and Thucydides, both in their hapless naivete thought that you could not only argue and tell a story at the same time, but that that's actually the best history to write, and the hardest. And I must say I do think actually some of my colleagues who don't like this story-telling stuff, say, "Well, you know, narrative is a kind of second order of intellectual activity, any fool can put a fairy tale together." Let me tell them to try it and see actually that it's the most exacting and most challenging. I don't know, if I bring it off or not, but it's both a very exciting and an extremely complicated process.

Heffner: Of course, you bring it off, and that, of course, is what leads people to be concerned about Schama-the-popularizer.

Yes, well, it's a shocking problem, isn't it, actually being read? I really don't want to sound too conceited about this because I do think actually there are really a quite substantial number of "closet" narrative historians in my profession, some who may have come out of the closet. For example, James McPherson of Princeton wrote an absolutely magnificent narrative history of the Civil War, which was also a best seller. So there are not only the people who taught me, but many historians practicing now who have no sense of embarrassment, I think, about narration, and what narration means. But I think it is a problem for many departments of academic life, that have closed themselves off in a kind of guild mentality. And guilds, of course, have the masterpiece—traditionally when you were an apprentice you produced the masterpiece, the "*Meisterstuck*," you presented it to your master and you became an official, you know, woodcarver, or printer or whatever it was.

Heffner: Or historian.

That's the point. Oddly enough, at the end of the nineteenth-century the intellectual disciplines really replicated that mentality—the "*Meisterstuck*" was the monograph, the Ph.D. dissertation presented to the doctor, who then patted the apprentice on the head and said "Welcome, welcome to the profession, don't give any secrets away hereafter, you are now one of the guild." And I think, guildsmen who were there then said, "Well, enough of all this, you know— masonry—" to mix my metaphors. History is really the memory of the past, we all belong to a community which ought to be seeking its memory pretty much always. I will write for all those interested. And increasingly that was regarded as, I think, a shocking thing to do, or at least a reprehensible kind of intellectual vacation.

Heffner: Now you do so at a time when there are other professions indulging in narration, in the narrative, I should say—that is television, film, and even docudrama. I wonder as a historian, how you relate yourself to those forms of expression?

What actually bothers me about docudrama is that most are so extraordinarily dull. That may sound like a very lofty remark, but I remember seeing an absolute yawner about Napoleon. It struck me as an immense achievement on the part of a network, actually to produce a docudrama about Napoleon that sent people to sleep. I'm not against dramatic versions, or dramatizations of history. I think two things really have to be present in such dramas. Where possible, they need to recover the kind of sound and intensity of the contemporary speech, without being obscure or esoteric, and secondly, I think they somehow have to give a sense, in the same way that gripping historical writing does, of place, of the smell, of the sound, of the events. Let me give you one example of a film which I thought really worked very well, even though it was terribly long, and that was Sergei Bondarchuk's film of the Battle of Waterloo —I hope he's still around. He was regarded as a terrible Stalinist hack, but he was a wonderful filmmaker in the tradition of Eisenstein. There were problems with this film, I dare say one of them was Rod Steiger as Napoleon, who just looked as though he was suffering from acute dyspepsia through the whole film. But what was really marvelous I thought, about *Battle of Waterloo*, was that by being, as Russian directors were allowed to be, incredibly prodigal with horses and thousands of people, he did give a phenomenonally powerful and, I think, accurate sense of the chaos and disaster, the extraordinary sense of terror of what it was like to be in a battle. It wasn't all flashing sabers. There was a sense of not being able to see much, being deafened with the sound, grand strategy disappearing into blood and smoke. That was really a very extraordinary achievement, I think.

Heffner: But, aside from possible dullness, what's the down side of docudrama, or "faction," that mixture of fact and fiction?

Well, I suppose that docudrama, even if it allows itself many hours in which to show what's happening, necessarily has to compress the making of historical events into the most intense moments, and there are ways in which, really very profound historical changes come about in a kind of coral reef way. It's almost as though those great time-lapse pictures we all saw in Natural History of a kind of flower opening, taking 30 seconds to go from closed buds to open blossom. That's the way the docudrama has to work. Whereas really, in some sense, political protagonists themselves, whether we're talking about Churchill, even, or Robespierre or Napoleon, often, spent an enormous amount of time themselves thinking about their decisions, so that in docudrama you do get a kind of qualitative shift towards impulsiveness. It's the history of impulse, very often, and that, if I had to think about it just for a minute, is probably one drawback, I would suppose.

Heffner: Isn't that an enormous distortion of the historical process though?

Yes, it probably is. I don't think all history is like that. I mean, the great French historians of the 1920s through the '50s thought that all history is, indeed, like so many little animals living in a coral reef building up by immensely discrete, painstaking purposes, their own houses, combining into the great kind of structure we think of as history. However, I don't think that's always the case. There certainly are short, sharp, violent moments that blow the whole thing apart, the French Revolution being an obvious one. But it does distort, and much of history is represented by the more sedimentary process.

Heffner: But, as I understand, it is the violence of the Revolutionary period that disturbs you the most.

Yes, it is a book that both grew out of my feeling, and as I wrote it, this became rather more intense, a deep sense of dismay at what I call a kind of "narcotic" politics. That is the politics of ecstasy, which can include a kind of poetry of death. You know, it's very fine when it's in speeches, or in the "Marseillaise," all these bloody banners, you know, in the "Marseillaise" lyrics. But what of the cost in real lives? I'm not naive or jejune enough to suppose that great changes in power come without costing lives. My real problem in the French Revolution was the enormous number of lives lost, over and above the violence that seemed to me to be necessary to change sovereignty.

Heffner: You mean "so many eggs must be broken to make an omelet . . ."

Well, I don't want to suggest too that there's a horrible kind of calculus at work here. But to make it less cold-blooded and ridiculously arbitrary, let me give you one example. Paris—12th July, night of 12th July,

1789—there is in effect a civil war going on in the army. Think of it in the same way that Western journalists were speculating before the days of Tiananmen Square, and saying, "Well, the Chinese army is breaking into two parts." That's more or less what people were wondering about in mid-July, 1789, and what happened was a battle between the Royalist side of the army, many of them foreign troops, and the side that had already gone over to the National Assembly, which said, "We will only accept orders from the National Assembly, and the new municipality in Paris." They fought out this slogging, chaotic battle at midnight over the sand, and by the morning the Royalist side in effect had lost. They were unable to dislodge the troops that had really gone over to the National Assembly. Really, basically, that was it as far as the position of the Revolution in Paris. The Revolution had taken Paris. The Bastille, as you know, was not an insignificant place. It was an overwhelmingly potent symbol and there was a lot of gunpowder stored there, but it was essentially a kind of symbolic coda to what had happened two days before. Nonetheless, lives were lost at the Bastille through a series of mistakes and misapprehensions, and then after it was all done, the governor of the Bastille's head was cut off while he was being frog-marched to the City Hall, [then] stuck on a pike and paraded around the streets. It was this kind of visceral, punitive, cathartic, really very emotional violence that had already announced itself. And in some ways you could even expect that to happen because people were very mad and very hungry. But it's the kind of polite applause on the part of the politicians that disturbs me, who in some sense, I think, condoned that sort of display of blood. That's really what I had in mind when I said there is gratuitous cruelty and brutality in the revolution.

Heffner: But what have you thought of those who have applauded the acts of violence that took place as necessary to overturn the ancient regime. You debunk that notion?

Yes, that indeed, was the kind of piety which really most disconcerted me and which was, if anything, a principle target of my book. Let me just say one thing, like all good nineteenth-century chronicles, the point about the relationship, the intrinsically disastrous engagement between violence and freedom, was a theme which grew with the writing of the book. There were many other positions I took, "*pris-de-position*," as the French would say. I fully admit I came to the book with prejudices—Tocquevillian ones especially. What I took to be a much more promising kind of modernity, pre-Revolutionary modernity, was taking place in the old regime. I came to the book with those sorts of reflections and prejudices. What I really was taken aback by during the new research I did for the book, and during the writing was the centrality of violence as an empowering thing, and so it was the sense of the kind of glory of the bloodstained banner, that aspect of the Revolution, which I wanted to distance myself from, and actually make people indeed have sort of second thoughts about.

Heffner: If Charles Beard was right, Professor Schama, let's go back to ask, what's your essential act of faith?

Well, that I suppose it's that of your standard late twentieth-century liberal democrat, with a small, or possibly even a big D, actually. That is to say, I hope, intend, to take the rights of man seriously. The only point of agreement I might have, presumptuously, with François Mitterrand, is that I thought the rights of man were well worth celebrating in 1989. The difference I would have with other liberal democrats who see the Revolution as the precondition for the rights of man, the precondition for democracy, and my own view is quite opposite, it would be to say that really we have to shake ourselves out of the Revolutionary romance and that so far from the Revolution being the precondition of realizing the rights of man, it was likely to overturn them. So my own belief in the sort of parcels that I have clutched to my chest for the moment are an attempt, really, to find ways of realizing the promise of democracy, or representative freedom without violence, without a kind of ecstatic embrace of Revolutionary wholeness. —1989

DANIEL JONAH GOLDHAGEN

Books about the Holocaust and the Hitler era in Germany have been involved in serious controversy from time to time, probably none more so than Harvard Professor Daniel Jonah Goldhagen's Hitler's Willing Executioners: Ordinary Germans and the Holocaust. *The title alone may well have sparked the critical and public controversy that followed publication in 1996 in the U.S. Later that year, its publication, and the author's appearance in Germany, occasioned months of newspaper and magazine articles pro and con, and public debate. Our conversation in mid-'96 began on a quiet note inspired by Goldhagen's use of a quote from Alexis de Tocqueville as an epigraph for the book. I asked him whether it couldn't actually be used against the position that he takes. "No man can struggle with advantage against the spirit of his age and country." Couldn't that be interpreted as an apology, in a sense, an explanation, for what the Germans did?*

I must say that when I chose this for the epigraph of the book, it never occurred to me that some people might read it in this way. It comes from a section of "Democracy in America" on why great revolutions will no longer occur. And it's really about leadership. This is about Hitler. And what it says is that no man, Hitler, no matter how powerful he is, can move people against their hopes and desires. And that is part of the argument of the book, that Hitler, as powerful a figure as he was, as charismatic as he was, could never have accomplished this had there not been tens of thousands, indeed, hundreds of thousands of ordinary Germans who were willing to help him. The Toqueville quote is about Hitler's incapacity to have moved Germans against their hopes and desires. So, in no sense is it exculpatory.

Heffner: But isn't there a truth to this in terms of the larger question of whether indeed the ordinary German was an executioner?

Well, there are two issues here. If you'll notice, if we stick with Tocqueville, that it's in the singular, "No man," not "No people," but "No man can struggle against." I don't have the quotation in front of me exactly. And individual Germans, of course, in Germany, could have done little to have prevented what happened. But if millions of Germans had been opposed to the persecution of the Jews in the 1930s, a very radical persecution in which Jews were stripped of their citizenship, in which they were forbidden to marry non-Jews, in which they were subjected to the most intensive campaign of verbal violence in Western history, if ordinary Germans by the millions had been opposed to this, then they could have done something in unison. And, as I said, had they been opposed to Hitler, as they were on other issues, the regime would have been hard pressed to have carried out what it did, and may not have even attempted it.

Now, the second issue is, as to the perpetrators themselves, what individual German perpetrators could have done. And as I show in the book, they were offered the option, many of them, to exempt themselves from the killing, by their own commanders. Every individual made choices about how to treat Jews, even the individuals who were in institutions of killing. They didn't have to struggle against the spirit of the age, to stay with the Tocqueville quotation for a moment; they were just given the option, "If you're not up to this, we'll give you other duties." And very few of them accepted this option, accepted the opportunity to exempt themselves from what was gruesome slaughter. And so the question remains: Why, uncoerced, would people choose to kill men, women, and children, often shooting children at point-blank range?

Heffner: You make the point that they had free will. You make the point about choice rather strongly. Was it as simple as all that? Choice: kill or not kill, participate in those police activities or not.

I think it ultimately was. We have to remember what they're being asked to do. And if someone thought that this was wrong, if someone thought this was a crime, indeed, one of the greatest crimes of human history, the psychological and emotional impetus to exempt himself from this would have been great. Some of the descriptions in the book of what it was like to kill someone else are so hair-raising that some people have told me they have trouble reading them. Which gives some indication of how much pressure there would have been upon these individuals not to do it if they'd actually been there. They weren't just reading these descriptions; they were creating the scenes which are described in the book. Often, I should add, by the men themselves. The book uses their own testimony.

So the pressure would have been enormous to get out of it. So, in this sense, I think it really was a simple choice. But more importantly, even if I would grant you that maybe it was more complicated, there are many other things the perpetrators did, which I detail in the book, which indicates that they were engaged, that they were assenting, that they were willing executioners. . . . Whether you believe that someone should be killed or not, if you're given an order to do so, you don't have to torture the person, you don't have to beat the person, you don't have to mock the person first. And this was a constituency of the Holocaust. So this shows that there weren't merely executioners who somehow couldn't remove themselves from the killing because they were in the unit, but that they liked what they did in some sense, that they believed it was right, that they were, as I said, engaged in what they were doing.

Heffner: Having done the research, the massive research that you have, what are the implications, for your own thinking, about Germany and Germans after 1945?

Germany is a markedly changed country. Germany, as we know, has had an economic miracle. The Federal Republic of Germany I'm speaking of. It has also had a political-cultural miracle as well.

It's been the great success story of the postwar period. In the last 50 years, Germans have remade their society according to democratic values, have remade their political culture. And with generational replacement, with new generations being taught new, universalistic values, essentially all people are created equal, instead of the previous values which divided the world into a hierarchy of races differently abled and differently valued, we've seen a sea change in values and beliefs in Germany to the point where Germans today are, by and large, genuine democrats, and share the same general orientation and cultural ethos that others in Western countries do, with all the exceptions in Germany and exceptions elsewhere. I should add also that anti-Semitism has also declined enormously in Germany and been transformed in nature. There are few in Germany today who look upon Jews and see devils in human form instead of human beings.

Heffner: What do you mean, "transformed in nature"?

. . . Well, we only have one term, "anti-Semitism," to describe an enormously wide range of complexes of beliefs about Jews. So the term "anti-Semitism" applies to those who harbor the garden-variety stereotypes that we know from American culture, that Jews are stingy and they're clannish and that kind of thing, too, and the term also applies to someone like Hitler, who believed that the Jews needed to be exterminated. And so, while many Germans shared a Hitlerian image of Jews in the 30s and 40s, today, to the extent that Germans are antisemitic, they, by and large, share views that are more akin to the garden-variety stereotypes that we know from American society.

Heffner: You'll forgive me, but I find that such a strange position to take. First, you take me through these many hundreds of pages of documenting for me that ordinary Germans participated in enormous numbers, without being forced to, in the most horrendous brutalizing extermination that we've experienced. And then what happened? 1945—a transformation?

Yes. This transformation is reflected, first of all, in the survey data. Surveys of German attitudes toward Jews in 1946 done by the American Occupation Authority show that they were rabidly anti-Semitic. And there have been consistent surveys done. And we have seen a demonstrable decline in anti-Semitism. So the data reflect this. But it's not just the data that suggest this. When you think about the ways in which people's values and beliefs are developed, young people's, you can see how this makes sense.

The beliefs that Germans had about Jews were completely artificial: Jews are not human beings, Jews are responsible for all the evil in the world, etcetera, etcetera. What you read in *Mein Kampf.* Without social and institutional support of the kind that existed in the 30s and before, it was very hard for Germans to retain views that had no accord with reality, particularly when the whole world was saying to a conquered, pulverized, and occupied Germany, "What you have done is the greatest evil in human history, and the beliefs that you had are evil." And so this was the beginning of a reexamination and a stripping-away of these hallucinatory views about Jews.

Heffner: But then you yourself are putting emphasis upon the support system for anti-Semitism that was Adolf Hitler and his cronies.

And that existed before Hitler ever came to power as well. I mean, as I show in the book, already in the nineteenth-century major institutions put forward and propagated notions of Jews which were very similar to what the Nazis believed.

Heffner: And I have the sense now that you don't want to feel that way about postwar ordinary Germans. How could such a sea change take place given the incredible exterministic—

It's very simple. Take a young German born in 1960, let's say, brought up in the Federal Republic of Germany, a democratic society, taught in an educational system which teaches democratic, universalist values, part now, really part of a Western community that has a certain shared view of the Holocaust, Jews, etcetera, and this person is brought up never exposed to anti-Semitism in a public forum. You know, anti-Semitic utterances have been illegal in Germany since the founding of the Federal Republic. You cannot make an anti-Semitic statement in public. You can be prosecuted for it. Is it surprising that in such a transformed society with this educational system that young people in Germany would grow up without harboring the demonic views of Jews which, as I said, had no accord with reality, but which were common in Germany before?

Heffner: This is a wonderful statement then, of the malleability of human nature.

That is, of course, true. Some critics have said that I'm making an argument about German national character, or some critics have even said I'm making a racist argument about Germans, a genetic, biological argument, which is nonsense. Anybody who reads the book will see that the argument is about political cultures, beliefs, and values, which can be transformed. Not overnight, but gradually. Fifty years is a long time. And so, yes, this is an optimistic, an optimistic development. And we should all note this, that we can remake ourselves individually and as communities in a society, the things that we, the beliefs that we share, which, of course, will inform very much how we act.

Heffner: What have you considered your primary responsibility in researching and writing *Hitler's Willing Executioners?*

My job is to unearth the facts and to explain the actions of these people, to explain what happened. And that is the thrust of the book. I make this point particularly forcefully because some critics, particularly in Germany, have charged me with saying that the Germans are collectively guilty, that I am charging the Germans with collective guilt, which is something that raises a red flag in Germany. And, in fact, I never say any such thing. I don't talk about guilt or innocence, moral guilt or moral innocence; I leave it for every reader to judge as he or she sees fit. And I think that's really the right approach to this material. Of course, I condemn the deeds. And, of course, most people do. But the complex evaluations of different people positioned and doing different things during this period is left for each person to decide for him or herself.

Heffner: That's difficult for me to accept. Surely you've sat down and reread large sections of the book, long after the writing. Do you not come away from this extraordinary volume with thoughts of collective guilt?

No. Collective guilt is, I think, an indefensible notion. When we talk about guilt here, we mean it in a legal sense: they are guilty only for deeds which they themselves committed. For the deeds. For the actions. For the things that would bring charges against people. What people thought or believed, what they, in their hearts, supported, or what they might have done if they had been in another position, is to be evaluated by each person individually, just as we would evaluate neighbors of ours who have thoughts that we believe to be reprehensible, but who have not themselves committed crimes. I'm saying in the book that in Germany far more individuals are guilty of crimes, or were guilty of crimes, both in the slaughter of Jews, and also in the many other crimes that were committed against non-Jews during this period. Millions of non-Jews were enslaved, and the German economy, with millions of Germans participating in the enslavement and exploitation and often brutalization of these non-Jewish slaves. I'm saying individual guilt is far more widespread than people have recognized. But the only people who are guilty are those who committed crimes. It has nothing to do with collective guilt.

Heffner: And as you tote up the crimes that were committed, the executions that were carried out, are you saying, "Gee, these executioners, these particular individuals, were just ordinary people?"

They were ordinary people. As I show, when you look at their backgrounds, they came from all walks of life, all social classes, all educational backgrounds, different religious denominations, all parts of Germany, and a very large number of them were not in the SS; and of the policemen I've studied, 96 percent of them in one unit were not in the SS, and the vast majority were not in the Nazi Party. So they were ordinary in the sense that they came from all walks of German life, that they formed some representative sample of German society. That's all I mean by it.

Heffner: And you want to say that, that's all you mean by it. Because for me, who applauds your book, and for those who condemn it, equally, the concept of "ordinary Germans," I think, carries a much greater weight along other lines. Not just that those 100,000, 200,000, however many you may list in terms of the police, in the citizen police, whom you describe so well here in their actions, it wasn't just that they were ordinary Germans, but there is an implication—at least as I read it, and, I think, as many of your critics do—that you're saying, "Scratch a German, and this is what you will ordinarily find."

There's no attempt at mere implication in this book. I say quite clearly that the views which motivated the Nazi leadership to exterminate European Jewry were generally shared in German society in the 1930s. There's no implication here. I say it quite clearly, I demonstrate it in the book, that these views, a kind of virulent, eliminationist anti-Semitism which suggests that Jewish people in power had to be eliminated even in the most radical of ways if Germany were to be secure and prosper, that this was the common sense of German society. So I'm not implying anything. That's clear.

Heffner: All right. Then, if you say that and say it as clearly as you've said it and as clearly as I've read it, why do you back away from the notion of national guilt?

Because, as I said a moment ago, you have to commit an act to be guilty. If you want to look back at people who were anti-Semites but who committed no crimes, and condemn them for their views, that's your privilege. Just as you might look upon someone in American society today who has racist views, and condemn the person for his views. But what is a person guilty of? Are you going to say he's guilty?

Heffner: Perhaps you can't do that for the entire nation, but there is a sense that Germany is an unindicted coconspirator as a nation. Unfair?

Two different responses. One is, as I said, you're a reader, you can draw your own judgments. It's fine with me. And we can have long discussions about how to evaluate, how you or I or anyone else might evaluate people of the kind that we just described, who never did anything. The second point is that there were exceptions in Germany. This is why we can't talk about Germans in toto or Germany as a nation without qualification, because there were Germans who resisted, there were Germans who departed from the standard views of Jews, and we have to recognize that. And so the vast majority of Germans shared these views. Many, many individual Germans committed crimes against Jews and non-Jews. They should all be condemned. They are all guilty of the crimes they committed if, indeed, they committed them.

Heffner: That takes us a giant step beyond where I think you want to leave it at this particular moment. Your book certainly, at least for this reader, carries with it the notion of national guilt, the guilt that comes with applauding that feeling that we must exterminate the Jews.

I condemn, as you do, the anti-Semitism that exists in Germany, but the book does not put forward the notion of national guilt. And I don't, as I just said, believe in it. And I don't think that it can be defended conceptually, at least in the way that you've put it.

Heffner: There was something that I quoted earlier in our conversation, "The conclusion of this book is that anti-Semitism moved many thousands of ordinary Germans, and would have moved millions more had they been appropriately positioned, to slaughter Jews."

It's just a conclusion. There are two conclusions there that anti-Semitism moved the killers, and since the killers, as I show in the book, form a representative sample of German society, at least of adult males and their age cohort, that we can generalize to other Germans and know what, in all likelihood, they would have done in the same position. It's a social-scientific inference based on the same principle that all public opinion polling is based on. If you have a representative sample, you can generalize to the larger population.

Heffner: I'll accept that. Now, what do you see as the central issue?

The central issue is: How do we explain how this regime could induce Germans by the tens of thousand, by the hundreds of thousands, to participate in the persecution and then even in the extermination of the Jews? This is the central issue. Why did ordinary people lend themselves to brutal persecution and systematic killing of other people? They did so because they shared a view of the world which led them to believe that the killing of the Jews was right and necessary. Just as historically in many other societies ideas, beliefs have moved people to commit deeds which we abhor. This happened in Germany in the thirties and the forties. But these are the issues. And there are many other issues attendant to this central question which can be discussed at great length, and, you know, and people, reasonable people can disagree about how to interpret some of the facts. But to the extent that others are talking about collective guilt, are saying that, well, there's really nothing new in the book, are diverting attention away from everything but the core historical issue, they're doing a disservice.

Heffner: There's no way in the world, it seems to me, that anyone can say there's nothing new in the book. There is so much that's new here. But you seem now to be backing away from the consequences, the intellectual consequences of what you have uncovered.

I don't think so at all. I simply take issue with the notion that the book is about moral evaluation. . . . It's not. It's about historical explanation. I attempt to uncover many new things about the perpetrators, to tell it as it was, often from their own perspective, and then to explain why they acted as they did, and then to set their actions within a broader interpretation both of the Holocaust and of Nazi Germany. I'm a social scientist; my job is to explain, not to judge.

Heffner: Extermination. Would you say that what you have uncovered would indicate to you that most Germans would, if not participate in (though so many did), would not decry the extermination of the Jews?

Most Germans in 1942 did not decry the extermination. Most Germans, some reluctantly, to the extent that they knew about it, gave their support to the extermination of the Jews, as far as we know. I mean, most people didn't speak out on the subject. What we do know is that there was an enormous amount of dissent expressed in Nazi Germany against a whole range, a wide range of governmental policies. The image of German society as a totalitarian society like the Stalinist Soviet Union is false. There was an enormous amount of dissent expressed, openly expressed by Germans, which the regime did not punish. Despite this vast record of dissent, which the regime itself collected and has been published, we have virtually no principal dissent against the persecutions of the thirties, which were utterly radical, known to everyone, and based upon the same anti-Semitic model of Jews that led to the exterminations of the forties, or against the exterminations themselves, which millions of Germans knew about. It's a myth that nobody in Germany knew about it. Millions knew. So the question is: Why do we have a vast record of dissent against a whole range of policies, religious policies, economic, even the treatment of non-Jewish slave laborers, but not against the persecution or extermination of the Jews? The obvious answer, and the right answer, is that Germans didn't disapprove of what was happening.

Heffner: And yet you say that that has nothing to do with collective guilt?

You know, we've already talked about this issue.

Heffner: I know.

I use the term "guilt" in a legal sense. Only for crimes.

Heffner: What other word could we use? Let's say, I understand, guilt means you're judged guilty—

For a crime that you as an individual have committed.

Heffner: Right.

Or have abetted.

Heffner: What word would you replace it with? You know what I mean.

How about responsibility?

Heffner: Okay, responsibility.

Responsibility. Again, I would shy—You know, we're having a semantic discussion here.

Heffner: I don't think so.

I would shy away from the term "collective." Widespread individual responsibility.

Heffner: Okay. Widespread. You don't mean—

I mean widespread. Millions and millions of Germans have some kind of responsibility for either what they did or for what they didn't do. Every individual is responsible for his own acts.

Heffner: We're not just talking about Hitler and his group; we're talking about millions upon millions upon millions of ordinary Germans.

Who lived during that period who could have done otherwise, could have spoken out, could have organized themselves in defense of their Jewish neighbors. They organized themselves in defense of other things they valued, but not in defense of their Jewish neighbors. And we're talking about the perpetrators in particular, the killers and the others who contributed directly to the killing of Jews . . . many of whom could have refused. You know, in the history of the Holocaust, there never was a single German perpetrator himself ever killed, sent to a concentration camp, jailed or punished in any serious way for refusing to kill Jews, and many knew they didn't have to kill. Every person made choices. We first need to uncover the patterns of choices, explain them. And then, if we want to, we can evaluate them however we want to.

Heffner: What did that research do to you?

In some sense, I think—Let me get at your question in this way:

sometimes I think that my conclusions are really very unstartling. I'm really, in some sense, surprised that so many people find them to be such a revelation. What I've written is common sense. The common sense that one should have, knowing what the history of humanity—which, in some ways, is a tale of brutality and slaughter—and common sense knowing just superficially what was done to Jews by Germans and others during the Nazi period. What I'm saying here is that, in doing the specific research for this book and writing it, [it] didn't really change my view of human beings. If you know human history, most societies have been slave societies. Slaves in many societies have been treated abysmally. Not necessarily killed, but treated abysmally. There have been many mass slaughters historically. The Holocaust is different, has important differences, is singular in some ways. But everything that was done, or at least most things that were done in the Holocaust, have been done in other societies at other times. So it's not a great revelation in this sense. What I've written is only a great revelation against the backdrop of how this period has been written about and how it's been portrayed, both in the popular media and by other scholars.

Heffner: What you just said, how does that position you in relation to Hannah Arendt's approach to the Holocaust, the banality of it?

Hannah Arendt said that Eichmann was not an anti-Semite, and that he acted as a good bureaucrat would, carrying out his duties as good bureaucrats do, with no particular attitude towards them. And that's simply nonsense. It's not true about Eichmann; Eichmann was clearly an anti-Semite. After the war he boasted about his killing of the Jews. And Hannah Arendt leaves this out of her book. And it's clearly also false about at least the vast majority of the perpetrators, who were anything but bureaucrats; they were ordinary guys, often, who were drafted into these police units and told to shoot people at point-blank range, and who, in their every action, in their own testimony after the war, have indicated that they believed that what they were doing was right. One of the perpetrators said, after the war, in his testimony, speaking for himself and all of his brethren, "The Jew was not acknowledged by us to be a human being." This is why they killed; not because they were bureaucrats carrying out their duties, but because they had views of Jews and views of the world which moved them. This is the event . . . that people look upon as being perhaps the greatest evil, as many will call it, the greatest evil of Western history. So clearly it focuses our attention in ways that other events haven't. And it rightly should. I mean, there are many things that are different about it. And because we know so much about it, because we have such detailed records, it really can bring to light the great brutality that people are capable of, that they willingly perpetrate upon others. —1996

Arthur M. Schlesinger, Jr.

Arthur M. Schlesinger, Jr. is America's most noted historian. He won his first Pulitzer Prize for The Age of Jackson *while still in his twenties, and he continues to write voluminously and teaches enthusiastically, having taken time off these pursuits only to serve in Washington as an advisor to Presidents Kennedy and Johnson. His books include biographies of FDR, John F. and Robert Kennedy,* The Imperial Presidency, The Cycles of History, The Vital Center, *and many others. One of my many broadcast conversations with Arthur Schlesinger took place soon after publication of the first volume of his autobiography,* A Life in the Twentieth Century, *as the year 2000 came to a close. He was wearing his signature polka-dotted bow tie at the time.*

Heffner: I would begin by asking just why, when you sum up *The Vital Center*, your great liberal credo of 1948–49, in your autobiography you write, "It is, I suppose, evidence of lack of imagination or of some other infirmity of character, but I am somewhat embarrassed to confess that I have not radically altered my general outlook in the more than half-century since *The Vital Center*'s publication. "Perhaps I should apologize," you continue, "for not being able to claim disillusions, revelations, conversions. But in fact I have not been 'born-again,' and there it is." Why do you write that?

Well . . . because so many people have changed their views. I am totally unapologetic about the fact that my views were formed under the New Deal of Franklin Roosevelt, and during the Second World War, the War for the Four Freedoms. And that still seems to me the general outlook which is most profitable for democracy.

Heffner: I had the feeling as I read *A Life in the Twentieth Century*, that our generation is very fortunate, not really to have had to shift and change our positions.

Well, I do think we were very fortunate. I'm not sure that we deserve Tom Brokaw's generous definition as "The Greatest Generation." I would reserve that for the generations that won the War for Independence and wrote the Constitution. But we have been lucky, we've survived desperate times: the worst depression in American history, the greatest war in American history. We survived it partly because of the potentialities of democratic leadership as embodied in Franklin Roosevelt. And that gave us a sense of being a participant in historic times, under historic leadership. I often wonder about the contrast between those Americans whose conception of democratic leadership was formed by Roosevelt, Truman, Eisenhower, and Kennedy, with those whose idea of Presidential leadership was formed by Nixon, Ford, Carter, Reagan, Bush, Clinton. I think we had a much more exalted view of the possibilities of democracy.

Heffner: So you think that those traumas—the war, then Depression—were, in a sense, our good fortune.

Well, they were, in a sense. . . . Those who were not killed or maimed in the war, for them it was the most exhilarating experience they ever had. And it changed the whole direction of many people's lives. But it was a tragic time. I don't think tragic times are necessary for Presidents to achieve greatness or semi-greatness. I don't think a crisis is essential for that. There have been Presidents who've imposed their own sense of priorities, or persuaded the American people that the direction they wanted to take the country was the right direction to go, without a major crisis. Andrew Jackson was one, Theodore Roosevelt was another, Ronald Reagan was another. These were Presidents who pointed the country in one or another direction without benefit of crisis.

Heffner: What do you think it takes though?

Well, Henry Adams, our most brilliant historian, said the President of the United States resembles the commander of a ship at sea. He must have a helm to grasp, a course to steer, and a port to seek. Now I think the Presidents who made a difference have been mostly the Presidents with a course to steer and a port to seek, even if in Ronald Reagan's case that port seemed to be back in the late nineteenth century.

Heffner: There's always been the practice among historians such as yourself to sum up and list our greatest Presidents. Have you changed you mind about who those were and those who weren't?

Well, I think, there's a general consensus that the three greatest Presidents were Lincoln, Washington, and FDR. There is much more discussion as to the near-great Presidents, but on the whole Jefferson, Wilson, Theodore Roosevelt, and oddly, James K. Polk, are on that list. Then there are proponents on the right for Reagan and on the left for Kennedy and Johnson. Also, I would rank Eisenhower higher than I did some years ago because at the time we thought he was an "out-to-lunch" President who played golf and read Westerns and associated with millionaires. The documents now show that he was much more of a "hands-on" President, and that his syntax, his muddled, murky syntax in press conferences was sometimes put on deliberately in order to mask his intentions. I think he was a much more purposeful President—I wouldn't call him an activist President, but he was more purposeful than we thought earlier. And as his Vice President, Richard M. Nixon once said, he was a very devious man, in the best sense of the word. Which is a perfect Nixon qualification [laughter].

Heffner: Well, how did he manage to be "in the best sense of the word"—devious?

He would seem very self-protective as a President. And it was generally supposed, at least on the Left in the 1950s, that Dulles was the untrammeled Secretary of State, and that Eisenhower just delegated foreign policy to Dulles. We now know that Eisenhower kept Dulles on a leash, and one political scientist, Fred Greenstein of Princeton, describes Eisenhower as a "hidden hand" President. Meaning that he put on an act, but behind the scenes was really running everything. I think Fred Greenstein may exaggerate. The whole concept of a "hidden hand" President abandons the notion of Presidential leadership in a certain sense. I mean politics is at bottom an educational process. It's a process of persuasion and consent. And Eisenhower wasn't very good at persuasion and consent. And the whole concept of a "hidden hand" President means the President who does well by stealth. Whereas the really great Presidents have been the people who rather have had the capacity to stir people by their words, pointing out why the direction they want to take the county is the right direction to go.

Heffner: But, Arthur, when you talk about "revisionism," about revising your own estimate of Eisenhower, what does that do to your present day judgments about people in high office? What does it do to your own sense of wisdom and correctness and rightness, as you make judgments about contemporaries?

Well, I think if one revises one's thoughts, it shows an open mind. Naturally people feel virtuous when they revise their opinions. As I say, I haven't revised my general approach. I'm a New Dealer, unreconstructed and unrepentant. But as new documents become available, as perspectives lengthen, one sometimes alters one's judgment of people.

Heffner: When you talk about slavery and the Civil War, and the differences among historians in judging the causes of the coming of the war, you write, "All this raised the question of the place of moral judgment in the work of the historian. There seem to be certain profound issues that demand a moral recognition by historians it they are to understand the great movements of history. Such issues are relatively few because there aren't many historical phenomena that we can confidently identify as 'evil.' " And you make the connection here with the trouble you got into when you wrote, so many years ago, "The unhappy fact is that man occasionally works himself into a logjam and that the logjam must be burst by violence." There were fellow historians who took great exception to that notion. I gather that your feeling about it now is that you were right?

Yes. I think that the great question, the great argument then was over the causes of the Civil War. And a number of revisionists regarded it as a needless war. Reversing W. H. Seward's conception of the war as "an irrepressible conflict," the revisionists described it as a "repressible conflict." And I thought in so doing they totally underestimated the moral urgency which was generated by the fact of human slavery—one person holding another as personal property.

And I think there was a minimization of slavery. Even Charles Beard, for example, did not regard slavery as a major cause of the Civil War. He thought it was a conflict between an agrarian civilization and an industrial civilization. Others felt that the abolitionists were a bunch of gratuitous agitators, raising the level of discourse to such a degree that war became inevitable. What I tried to do was to ask in this essay—how else would slavery ever have been abolished? And the revisionist historians have to suggest some alternative to war, as a means of getting rid of slavery. And they'd never worked out in their own minds, as far as I can see, how slavery was going to disappear, when by this time it had been so firmly embedded in the South that people were saying, "Slavery is a positive good." And that it's the only basis for a democratic society, following the example of Athens, in the Classical days.

Heffner: The logjam that you saw in the conflict between the ideals of abolitionism and the property interest in slavery resulted in a great, bloody conflict. And later on in our war, the Second World War, you saw the same kind of logjam.

Yes. And I think historians, like everyone else, are prisoners of their own experience. The revisionist historians were of an older generation. They were part of the disillusionment following American participation in the First World War. They thought we'd been conned into that war and they were skeptical of wars in general as providing solutions for anything. The disillusionment following the First World War is reflected in the disillusionment about the necessity of the Civil War. Whereas those of us who were in the generation that fought in the Second World War felt it was a necessary war. Not a good war, because no wars are any good. But it was a necessary war and we had the same sense that the Civil War was a necessary war, not a needless war.

Heffner: Arthur, what will that do for future young historians, who look back and read Schlesinger and say, "Well, he was simply a product, not of World War I, but of World War II, and now we move on to our generation's interpretation." What does that do to the validity of any interpretations.

Well, again, as I say, historians are prisoners of their own experience. The generation that was screwed up during the Vietnam War was very cynical about the Cold War and even perhaps about the Second World War. William Appleman Williams, for example, who had a moment of influence as a revisionist historian, said we got into the Second World War because we were afraid of German economic commercial successes in South America, which seemed to be a really loony theory. But, you see historians aren't exempt from the tides of change. As Oscar Wilde once wrote, "The one duty we owe to history is to revise it."

Heffner: A man you admired greatly, Charles A. Beard, wrote that all recorded history is an act of faith. Is that essentially what you're saying, and that the particular faith is a product of one's own times?

Beard felt that written history is an act of faith, and that meant some decision about the future. And his act of faith was a belief that the world was moving toward democratic collectivism. I don't think historians are required, as Beard was arguing then, to make up their minds about the direction in which humanity is moving. But I think they must become aware of the extent to which they are affected by the pre-occupations of their own day. As you and I know, American history has been revolutionized in the last couple of generations by the Women's Rights Movement and the Civil Rights Movement. So that American historians today pay much more attention to the role of women and to the role of minorities. The women and minorities were always there, but we historians had our attention directed elsewhere. Now it's almost over done. It's impossible, or very difficult to establish a new course in political history and diplomatic history because there are so many courses on the history of women or the history of minorities. But, as a great Dutch historian once said, "History is an argument without end."

Heffner: And what does that mean to you—"an argument without end"?

You don't argue necessarily about facts. I mean, the Declaration of Independence was signed on July 4, 1776. But you argue about the significance and the interpretations of the facts. Of course the very selection of facts implies an interpretative scheme of some sort. And some of the arguments seem to be settled. For example, we were talking about the argument about the causes of the Civil War. I think practically all the historians today accept the fact that slavery was the cause of the Civil War. But 30 or 40 years ago this was a heated question for heated debate.

Heffner: You basically write that *The Vital Center* is very much where you are. How do you define it today?

The Vital Center, was a book published in 1949, and "The Vital Center," as I used the term, described liberal democracy as against fascism on the Right and Communism on the Left. It was a whole conception of a global context of the fate of democracy. We now think that democracy is triumphant, but in fact, for the first half of the century democracy had it's back to the wall, fighting for its life, severely wounded in the First World War, resulting in the two great anti-democratic movements, Bolshevism, and Fascism. Then it appeared to be morally wounded by the Great Depression, which showed the incompetence of democracy to provide full employment. And then the Second World War came and, Anne Morrow Lindbergh, you remember, wrote a book called *The Wave of the Future,* in which she essentially said, "democracy is doomed . . . totalitarianism is the wave of the future, and you can't resist it." A bestselling book in America in 1940. By 1941 there were about a dozen democracies left in the world. So that democracy seemed a much more precarious thing when *The Vital Center* appeared than it seems today when all countries aspire, or are supposed to aspire, to democracy.

Heffner: And you remain at the "Vital Center."

Yes, but it is not the middle of the road. That seems to me the *dead* center. "The Vital Center" is a continuing struggle to spread as widely as possible the benefits of liberal democracy. —2001

DEREK BOK

In the late fifties, I talked with James B. Conant, then a former President of Harvard University, about major issues in American education. As the Millennium drew to a close, I talked with a successor at Harvard, Derek Bok, about the nature of democracy in America. And I led with a question about Ronald Reagan's oft-quoted proclamation that "government is not the solution to our problems; government is the problem," and Bill Clinton's rejoinder some years later, "government isn't the solution, yet it isn't the problem either."

"What does it mean that government has to be the solution?" If you look at what Americans think about their society, despite differences about methods, there's a remarkable unanimity about what the goals of our society ought to be. And as you look at those goals, it's impossible to find any country of the world that has come close to achieving them without the government playing a very, very substantial role in the process. That's true of health care, it's true of safety on the streets, it's true of so many other things that Americans consider important. And so I would guess, based on that experience, if we are to achieve the society we want, government will have to continue to be the solution, as it has been, for all successful societies up until now.

Heffner: But you seem to point out that "a" trouble, if not "the" trouble, is that while we want government to do so many things, we also protest, as Reagan did, as so many others do—that government is the problem.

Yes, and I spent a lot of time trying to figure out whether or not this judgment was fair. And I think it probably is a little extreme . . . Because in reality over the last thirty or forty years our society has made progress toward the goals that Americans hold dear in a remarkably high proportion of the cases. And in almost all of those cases the government has played a substantial and positive role. Unfortunately, if you compare our progress with that of other leading democracies, you find that though we have progressed, we haven't progressed as fast as most of these others in a very disturbing number of cases. And you can't help being concerned when you look at problems such as the fact that our health care system is the most expensive by far in the world, and yet is the only one among advanced democracies that doesn't cover millions of citizens. As you look at those kinds of problems, you can't help feeling that the government has not been performing as well as it might, or should.

Heffner: But isn't the answer to that that government has not been permitted to act by the propaganda of those who keep insisting that government is the problem.

Well, it's true that Americans are quite divided about what to do about health care even though they are very united on what the ultimate goals ought to be. But we had difficulties in achieving what we wanted through government even at a time, in the fifties and sixties, when government was looked at much more positively than it is today. So, even when the atmosphere's been much more favorable, we've still run into problems. We still haven't been able to achieve things that some other governments have been able to achieve. . . .

Heffner: Then the question has to be "why?"—or "why not?"

There are many reasons for that. One is the disturbing fact that although Americans want to have more and more influence over their government, they're willing to spend less and less time at the work of being informed and participating citizens. And, contrary to a number of people, the more I look at it, the more I come to the conclusion that the apathy that Americans have been displaying for the last thirty years or so really has a lot to do with many of the things that we dislike the most about the way government and politics perform here.

Heffner: And, what do you do with that? Do you have hope, or do you despair?

Before I despair, I look at some other things which I think are helpful. One is, of course, that there are other societies in which people aren't very different from ourselves, yet the citizens are much more active in their government. They vote much more, they're more participating, they're more informed. I look at periods in the past where Americans have been much more inclined at least to cast a ballot at election time than they are today. And some of those times were not so very long ago. And I look at places in this country where citizens are far more active and participating than they are in the country as a whole. And if they can be active and participating there, I don't see why it's impossible for them to be more active and participating in the country as a whole.

Heffner: And your analysis of why it's "Yes" in some places, but "No" in most other places in this country?

It's a difference, in some cases, of education. It's a difference in how seriously civic education is taken in the public schools. It's a difference in all kinds of intangible cultural factors about the obligations one has in a democratic society towards one's government. But most of those things can be worked at by conscious effort. And what disturbs me is that, if you look at what's gone on in America over the last 30 or 40 years, the effort that we put into trying to develop really concerned, informed, participating citizens has pretty steadily gone down. For example, civic education used to receive considerably more emphasis than it does today. It's been eclipsed almost entirely in the public schools by an emphasis on training the workforce for the next century. Which is certainly an important endeavor, but not to the point that it obscures the role of the public schools in preparing citizens. Colleges, including Harvard, I regret to say, which used to regard the preparation of active, informed citizens as the most important goal of liberal education, now scarcely mention that as an explicit aim of undergraduate education. Newspapers are devoting less time and space and attention to public affairs. So throughout the society, there's been a real lag of energy and effort going into the very crucial task of teaching people that they really have an obligation as citizens if they expect democracy to work and live up to their hopes and ideals.

Heffner: Then why don't you at the end of your book, *The Trouble with Government*, simply throw up your hands in despair?

Because I think many of the points that I've just made could easily be reversed as a matter of public policy. We could put much more emphasis in the schools on civic education and a better kind of civic education that we've had in the past. There's no reason why colleges can't begin to pay explicit attention to the role of liberal education in preparing citizens. And more and more colleges are now waking up to the fact that they need to do that. We could spend much more money on public affairs programming than we do. We spend far less on this than any other advanced democracy. The whole series of changes of that kind could have, over time, a real effect on the participation of citizens.

Heffner: But what about "would," instead of "could?" What changes will be likely to take place?

I think if we set about trying to overcome this problem through the variety of measures I've described in my book, we would see over time substantial increases in voting participation and other forms of political participation. I have no doubt about that. What I am doubtful about is whether the will is there. There are lots of people who are very ambivalent about more participation by ordinary people in government. There are some who for partisan reasons feel this is going to hurt them or interfere with their own political fortunes. There are others who feel that, as you implied, it's hopeless. There are still others who feel it's a very good thing that relatively few people vote because they assume that the ones who don't vote are ignorant and even dangerous, less concerned about civil liberties and other important aspects of American life and that if everybody voted we would run into all sorts of trouble. Now I think all of those points are dead wrong. But they are widely shared, so I think the important point is to recognize that we're paying quite a price for diminished participation in government. And that price is almost bound to increase because the one thing we know is that people in my generation, in which even high school dropouts voted at a rate of 60 percent or more, are going to pass from the scene and they're going to be replaced by younger people who vote—and I'm speaking not just of high school dropouts, but even everyone, including college graduates—vote at the rate of about 33 percent. And as more of them come in and more of us leave the stage, the rates of participation are going to continue to go down and the ill effects of that on our democracy are going to continue to increase.

Heffner: What has to be done to change that direction?

You've got to do all the things that I have pointed out in the book, starting with civic education, and going right up into making it easier to vote, and easing some of the registration requirements. But if all of those things are done so that they are self-reinforcing, I think you can overcome the cumulative downward spiral, this vicious circle, that's diminishing our attention to government, and begin to push it in the other direction so that good things will happen. I firmly believe it can be done. It has never really been tried. We've never recognized that this is a major objective for the society, and gotten behind doing the various things that need to be done.

Heffner: But what really did happen? Was it the media? Was it the institution of the lie, perhaps of public relations? What did happen here that seemingly has not happened elsewhere in the world?

You mean what happened to increase the level of distrust and disaffection and disengagement with government? Well, there's no doubt that there was a series of shocks in the 1960s, which pushed the public very rapidly from having a very high degree of confidence in government, not necessarily in political leaders, into much diminished confidence. Certainly the war in Vietnam and the sense that the government was not entirely forthcoming with us about the way that war was going. The assassination of a number of leading Americans, beginning with President Kennedy, and of course, Watergate. Those shocks cumulatively reinforced one another and pushed the level of confidence very rapidly from one in which 76 percent of the American public said they trusted the Federal government to do the right thing all or most of the time, a very high number, down to the point where less than a third had that degree of confidence.

That's a complete turnaround. And once it began, then a whole set of other forces began to kick in as the public grew more distrustful of government. And, of course, the media, which is very sensitive to the market, began to reinforce that. You can see that negative stories in the media and in television became steadily more prominent from one decade to the next. Less and less time and space began to be devoted to public affairs so that lots of cultural forces moved in to reinforce the shock that had occurred during the sixties and early seventies and perpetuated the low degree of trust. And, of course, that was then reinforced, by politicians who have run against the government instead of for it. And who denigrate government very frequently. There are, as well, a lot of people who believe that government should be inherently limited. Indeed, it is dangerous in some ways. But the remedy is not necessarily to weaken it further. Finally, in the nineties, you began to get a little bit of a revival because things were so well off economically in the country. Even crime and teenage pregnancy were going down. Finally, toward the end of the decade, you began to get some restoring of confidence. But it's still only a mild recovery and we are very far from where we were in the early sixties.

Heffner: What about the individual institutions and procedures that many people identify with, that could be corrected?

I think they're very difficult because many of the institutional features that get in the way of efficient government respond to very strong desires among the American people. Reforming them in a significant way would be very difficult. For example, many of our policies, such as our health policy, seem incoherent, fragmented, into many different pieces that don't fit together very well. That certainly is caused, in large part, by the fact that our institutions are fragmented. We have separate branches of government, each with its own independent input into policy. We have no overall coordinating agency to smooth the rough edges and make sure the pieces fit together. And ours is not a very accountable government because there are so many moving parts. There are so many different elements—Congress, the courts, the Executive branch, the states—which share the implementation of most programs. Even increasingly, many programs are implemented by private entities, with government funding and supervision. So you've got so many

people participating that it is very difficult to hold anyone accountable when the programs don't go well. . . . All of that produces
rather incoherent legislation, but is very much in tune with very
deep values and feelings about government in the United States.
Remember we were born in rebellion against government, so that a
lot of this fragmentation is an effort to make sure that government
is not too powerful, that different pieces will check one another.
Now, one isn't going to change that, one probably shouldn't change
that. It's part of our culture and in many ways it's served us well.
But it's not a particularly apt framework for creating coherent,
well-coordinated policy solutions to very complicated problems of
a kind that the Founding Fathers didn't face. They didn't think of
government as providing a health care system, or a higher education system, or doing something about the multiple problems of
the city. Although the structure of government that they devised is
very good at preventing abuse and arbitrary power, and that's terribly important, it's not very good at coming up with coordinated
policy solutions to complicated, multifaceted problems of the kind
so common today.

Heffner: So you would not spend much time talking about institutional or structural changes.

No, but I would certainly look at institutions and structures, because
there are certain changes that could make the whole thing work a bit
better without sacrificing those virtues of fragmented government
that we all believe in.

Heffner: What are some of those?

I think, for example there could be more communication between the
Congress and the Judicial branch, for example. There could be, and there
is beginning to be more emphasis on accountability by the so-called
Performance and Accountability Act that forces the Executive branch to

be more precise about the goals of its program and try to measure the effectiveness of a government in implementing programs. All of these things will have a modestly good effect if they are implemented properly. Vice President Al Gore's "Reinvention of Government," in which he's tried to make substantial changes in the way the federal bureaucracy works, is certainly the kind of thing that needs to be done to try to improve the quality of people going into the bureaucracy, to try to get them to focus more on performance and results and be more accountable for what results they achieve. All of those things are helpful.

Heffner: Let's move on to another subject—lobbyists. What the problem is and what to do.

The problem, which has always been there in democracy, has really become quite severe. And by the problem, I mean the role that money, particularly money from special interests, plays in the whole process of government and politics. In recent years, various loopholes have been found in the law. So that individuals and interest groups can give virtually any amount that they want to specific parties, to specific election races. The involvement of money in politics has begun to spread into judicial elections, even into local elections, where in the past it played a much less prominent role. And so we really have a very serious problem. The difficulty, as always, is in figuring out what to do about it. Because in the first place the people who give money to influence policy have very high stakes and therefore, a very great interest in doing something to have some influence over decisions that are going to matter a great deal to their lives. So that you can think up very artful legislation. But just like the tax laws, after a certain period of time, people find ways around that. So, probably there's no perfect solution. It's a process of continuous adjustment. But we've let that go for sufficiently long that the need for adjustment has become major and the loopholes have become great, glaring holes in the dike, allowing a lot of money and influence to creep into the system.

Now there are many things that can be done. The heartening thing is that at the state level a lot of experimentation has gone on in the best spirit of Justice Brandeis, who talked about the laboratory of democracy in which different states try different things and eventually we citizens can learn from experience what will work best. But you have three or four states that have moved to something that was thought to be impossible a few years ago, and that is full public financing of state elections, where all the money that is spent by candidates who opt into the system comes from the government. . . . There are other states which have partial public financing to a substantial extent. There are still others that are actually playing with something akin to a voucher system, where everybody gets a tax credit, which in effect says, "You can give money free." Anyone could give money free via a tax credit to the candidates of their choice. So I think we have the chance of allowing this experimental process to go forward, watching very carefully to see what works, and eventually arriving at a better solution than we have had in the past. The problem is that we can't wait for the states to work this process out before doing something . . . to keep the current system in better order while we wait for this process of experimentation at the state level to go forward.

Heffner: . . . but you also say, "That's not something we can wait upon."

Yes. Well, we've come very close to getting substantial reform at the federal level. . . . But, of course, there's always a big problem, and I think at the root of our difficulties lies something that we haven't really faced up to. Whether we're talking about redistricting or whether we're talking about campaign finance reform, or anything that bears on the rules of the game for electing candidates, we suffer from the fact that the rules are being set by those people who have the greatest individual personal stake in the outcome. It's a little as though we said that in baseball from now on, when the New York Yankees win the World Series, we will ask the New York Yankees to make the rules of baseball for the following years. We would all regard that as ludicrous. But that is very much what we're up against in campaign finance reform. So I think what we ought to do, especially because, as I say, you're not going to solve this problem in one great final perpetual solution, is require continuous adjustment. And you need some more impartial way of doing that. I would be searching for some way of finding an impartial group of very great prestige involving former federal judges, even retired Presidents, who become much more statesmanlike after leaving office than they may have been before. And other leading citizens could participate on some regular basis in reviewing our campaign finance and other election rules and making recommendations that would carry enough prestige so that it would be much more difficult for Congress to refuse to accept them.

Heffner: So many of the problems that you deal with seem to me to stem, in part, at least from profit motive, the free-market system. And I wondered what your sense of the appropriateness of that involvement is?

Again, it's like so much else in the book. It's really mixed. Our reliance on competition, which is pervasive in America, and on the market, has some wonderful results. Particularly in the economy, but even in other spheres of life, as well. Competition, for example, in the media, produces a lot of healthy energy, in innovation, in digging out better stories than other newspapers and so forth. But competition, if it is not carefully regulated in some fashion is likely to produce bad results. That's why we have antitrust laws, for example. That's why we have laws about truth in advertising, and product safety. And similarly, in the field of government I think one glaring problem with unrestrained competition is that competing newspapers and television stations cannot recapture as profit the value of an informed citizenry. So that on strict and classic economic principles, you will underinvest in public affairs programming and newsgathering. Other countries recognize that by putting a healthy subsidy into various forms of public affairs programming. The United States does far less. We need to accept the virtues of the marketplace, but supplement it where it doesn't work quite well enough. And one of those places is in the absence of sufficient public affairs programming to adequately inform the citizenry.

Heffner: You know, I have the feeling that if you have your way, a lot of things in this nation would be turned upside down.

I've tried to look at this in a quite hardheaded way because I'm really very skeptical about vast Utopian reforms. I think what I'm suggesting are a series of adjustments which I think would make the government function better, not in bringing about my policies or your policies. I'm trying to figure out how can we make the government function better to achieve the things that large majorities of Americans say they want to happen in this country. I think you could significantly improve the government's performance, not by any one big thing, but by a whole series of things. Underlying all that, the biggest single thing I think would be trying to increase participation. And I think one change that that would [create], is that it would mean that the welfare of, not just poor people, but the welfare of the bottom 40 or 50 percent of the American people would be taken more seriously than it is now. Because quite apart from the fact that we have the highest poverty rates, by the far the largest number of children in poverty, we do less to get people out of poverty. All of those things are true and often remarked on. What isn't always looked at is the kind of legislation that serves the interests of working people, that makes it possible to hold a job and look after your family, that gives you child care, that gives you preschool, that gives you security from the basic hazards of life. Consistently in the comparisons that I make between the United States and other leading democracies we fall behind. And the most obvious reason for that is that Americans in the bottom 50 percent of the income scale simply vote at very much lower rates that the rest of Americans, and very much lower rates than their counterparts in other industrial democracies. So that would be one big change that would have substantial beneficial results in the quality of our government. —2000

OTHER VOICES

Daniel Patrick Moynihan on Being a "Conservative"
U.S. Senator, former American Ambassador to the United Nations

Heffner: Are you a Conservative, Senator?

Well, you know that word, conservative, is always a relative one. Conservatives conserve . . .

I was sitting in the General Assembly one afternoon, trying to pay attention to the speaker, having difficulty, and started playing some word games with the names of the UN members who were up there listed on, in effect, a scoreboard on either side of the podium. There were then 148 members of the United Nations. I asked myself, how many had both existed as countries in 1914 and had not had their form of government changed by violence since 1914. Of the 148 the answer: seven. We live as Americans in a world of such stability. I'm serving in the 199th Congress. Next year will be the 200th Congress. Oldest constitution on earth. Oldest constitution in the history of the earth. You know, a stable society, well, that can give you the illusion that stability is something granted by God even though it's made by man and very few have it. Hence, am I in that sense conservative? Yes. I'd like to conserve the society. —1985

Averell Harriman and Sam Rosenman on the Character of President Franklin D. Roosevelt
Respectively, former Governor of New York and former counsel to President Franklin D. Roosevelt

Heffner: Gentlemen, I would begin our program, knowing that I am with two men who knew the late President intimately, by asking about a phrase that Franklin Delano Roosevelt used and that many people thought was rather peculiar. It has come up time and time again.

It was Frances Perkins, FDR's Secretary of Labor, who wrote that at a press conference a young reporter asked President Roosevelt whether he was a radical, a capitalist, a communist, or what? And the President drew himself up in some surprise and said, "I'm a Christian and a Democrat." What do you think he meant?

Rosenman: Well, that answer by the President doesn't surprise me. I think that what the President meant was not a Christian in the strict religious sense, and I am sure that what he meant by "Democrat" was a democrat with a small d. And I think in many ways the President thought that those two terms were synonymous.

He was a very religious man in the sense of believing very firmly in the brotherhood of man and the fatherhood of God, and I think that his whole concept of social justice and the emphasis which he laid on social legislation bespoke his deep belief in Christianity. And I think that he felt that being a democrat, believing in democracy, was a modern political method of carrying out what he conceived as the brotherhood of man.

I think his social legislation was directed at removing social inequalities, economic inequalities, promoting opportunities for all; and I think that in many ways, and in fact in some of his speeches, he expounded on the fact that he thought that this was another way of saying Christian.

Harriman: Well, Sam, don't you think one of the strengths of Franklin Roosevelt was the fact that he was not dogmatic? He was pragmatic in his approach to government. He recognized that we had a dynamic society and there were changes which would come in a natural way, but he had this very definite objective as you have described it, that our country should carry forward the principles on which it was founded and make it a finer place for everybody to live in on a truly democratic basis. And he tried so many different experiments to achieve that, and he was always ready to admit when he was wrong. —1959

David Halberstam on American Power
Pulitzer-Prize-winning journalist, author of The Reckoning

Heffner: I remember that Walter Lippmann's "American Foreign Policy Shield of the Republic" back in the Second World War made the point that we mustn't as a nation let our promises outstrip our resources, our ability to deliver.

One of the things we found out in Vietnam is the limits of our power. We are a very rich, powerful nation and part of that power rests upon a great economy. Compared to the Russians, we are just wonderful. I mean they have an economy that doesn't work. They are a failed nation in terms of the basic human premise of a government's ability to deliver minimal acceptable services to its people. It can't house its people, it can't really deliver food. It's a soured, failed bureaucracy. The one thing they can do is build large missiles and they can supply a lot of troops. For us to waste too much of our economic energy going one-on-one with them is a disaster. We have got to keep our economy viable because that's a source of our overall social political strength. In addition we have. . . the lesson of Vietnam, not to apply power where power cannot be applied. —1986

John Oakes on Individuals and Foreign Policy
Editorial Board, New York Times

Heffner: Can and should an individual affect foreign policy?

Foreign policy really is more directly related to the individual today, I think, than it was in Colonial days . . . So it becomes much more important for the individual to have some knowledge and concept of his own effect on foreign policy, even than it was in simpler times.

Heffner: Why do you say "more closely related"?

Because in the kind of complex society that we're living in, every action of government has an effect on the individual, and every action of other governments has its effect on ourselves, and every action of our government has its effect throughout the world—particularly in our case because we're such an important country. And therefore it seems to me it's extremely important that individual people in the United States don't get this cynical idea that they can have no effect on foreign or, for that matter, on domestic policy. I think they can. —1958

Brian Urquhart on the United Nations
Undersecretary General of the UN for Special Public Affairs

Heffner: You use an interesting metaphor. We don't demand the disbandment of a police force because it hasn't succeeded in protecting us totally from crime. Are you referring to the United Nation's capacity to use police power?

No, I'm referring to it more in its primary role, which is an organization which is supposed to keep the peace, and to prevent war. That was its initial main function. And I think it has been more successful in that role than people are prepared to admit. But in stopping smaller wars, of which there are a number going on at the moment, it has been far less successful than it should have been. And I think that the reason for that is that people, as they draw away from the shadow of World War II, forget that really large wars come very often out of the clear blue sky, with very little warning. And the object of the United Nations was to protect the world against a recurrence of that disaster, this time with nuclear weapons. And the organization has performed a good deal better than people think . . . I mean, where did the United States go, for example, when the Soviet Union went into Hungary in 1956? It didn't go into a nuclear war with the Soviet Union, which was the other alternative. It came to the United Nations Security Council, and passed the responsibility for the Hungarian situation to the United Nations, which finally passed it to the Secretary General. Now, I don't say this was necessarily the most glorious moment in history, but that is what happened. —1952

Richard Viguerie on the Genesis of the New Right
Leader of "the New Right"

Heffner: Who makes up the New Right?

Who are we? Dick, the New Right is conservatives who have been here for many years, who are no different than the conservatives of the '50s or '60s, except six, seven, eight years ago they began, some of them, to meet and talk about how we're always losing. We were getting 35 percent of the votes on election day, or 40 percent, 45; seldom getting 51 percent. And we just got tired of losing. We began to analyze the Left: How was the Left successful? Why were they winning elections? And so we developed an aggressiveness about our attitudes. We began to duplicate the institutions, the organizations, the structures of the Left, and apply them. And we've been so successful that now the Left is duplicating us.

Heffner: Aren't you a bit afraid when you imitate so many of the tactics and strategies of the Left that you may yourself become enmeshed in them?

Technology is neutral; it's morally neutral. It works for anybody. And setting up single-issue groups is very proper. In fact, the liberals have the power that they have now and have had for many, many years because they went out there and organized special-interest groups. In the '50s it was the civil rights groups. In the '60s, Vietnam. In the '70s, ecology. And about the middle of the '70s the conservatives realized that we had a lot of people out there who were concerned about various interests, but there was nobody to represent these people. The political parties didn't represent people who were concerned about abortion, giving away the Panama Canal, prayer in school, busing. Neither of the two major parties was speaking out on these issues. So we began to look for people who were leaders in these areas and bring them into a kind of cohesive movement. —1981

Anthony Lewis on the Tone of Political Discourse
Columnist for the New York Times

Heffner: I swear there has to be something to the feeling that I have had, as I've read you in the last year or so, that your patience is being more sorely tried now than ever before.

Well, I think probably what you have in mind is my revulsion at the meanness of political discourse in this country today. It's not that I'm trying to stop it; it's just that I regret it. And, you know, regretting it is something we can do. We can, as I say, we can answer back, comment, criticize. I think the attacks on President Clinton and Mrs. Clinton, even Chelsea Clinton, and then the preachments from the television evangelists, it's pretty nasty stuff, and it's lowered the level of political dialogue. So that I, as I say, I regret it. And I think it evokes in the public a cynicism that I regard as profoundly dangerous in the democracy. We're in a very cynical time when people really, I think, hate government, don't want government, and they've lost their sense of the necessity of government to do things. Of course it makes many mistakes, it has many faults, government. But we need it. We have to try to make it as good as we can.

Heffner: How do you account for what you seem to think of as the lowest of the low points that we've reached in hate speech? And this is a kind of hate speech.

Well, I'm not speaking of hate speech in terms of racist speech, for example, but of just nastiness toward political figures and the kind of personal attacks we see.

Heffner: Worse than ever before?

No, because I won't surprise you when I say that I have in mind the McCarthy era. That was pretty bad, in a different way, and very cruel and unjust. But it's a pervasiveness now, kind of lowest common denominator of public feeling that I find distasteful, and I think dangerous in a democracy, as I say. —1994

Rudolph Giuliani on American Cities
Mayor of New York

I think the most important thing is to try, when you're dealing with very difficult problems, to find the positive things that are happening, and use them to push forward. We've spent 40 or 50 years thinking about cities from the point of view of their problems, of which there are many—social, criminal, economic, educational. They're all significant. They all need a great deal more attention. They need a lot more creativity. So, in all that, what we fail to look at are the assets that cities have. How they are the biggest contributors to the wealth of America. Without America's great cities: New York and Chicago and Philadelphia and Los Angeles and Boston, Miami, Houston, Dallas, the American economy would be in shambles. These are the centers of wealth. Bigger contributors to the federal government than they are receivers of dollars from that source. We think of cities as a drain on federal tax dollars because of the problems of urban society. What we don't think about is that, in the balance of payments in this country, cities contribute more to Washington than Washington gives back to cities. New York City's deficit with the federal government is about 9 billion dollars. We contribute, from New York City, 9 billion dollars more to Washington DC than we receive back in return. And that's true of most of the major cities in the United States. We are the engines of America's wealth. Therefore, our being able to handle our problems more effectively is going to mean a real net gain for the American economy.

Heffner: It's interesting, in a recent speech, you talk about other countries, and you make reference to the fact that, in France, they treasure Paris as more than their capital city, as something very wonderful, something that provides the rest of the nation a great deal of profit and good. Why don't we do that?

Maybe because we developed differently. Italy, France, Germany, England, the European nations, by and large, developed from their cities into countries. The Italian city-states predate the nation of Italy. Rome predates the Italian city-states. Europe was built around cities. Then they became nations. America was an agrarian society. And I don't think we've ever properly understood the role of cities in the development of a nation.

But, if you think about it this way, you can understand that the same thing is happening in America. Many, many more people develop their notion of America while thinking about its cities, New York being at the top of the list. New York is probably better known to many people than America. So it shapes the sense that people have of America. And as the economy becomes more international, as

America has to deal more in the international economy, the role of cities becomes even more important to us. If our cities succeed, America gets a larger share of the international economy. If our cities fail, America tends to fall behind. So cities do shape a lot of the fate of the American economy, even for suburban areas and for rural areas. And that's something that we don't properly appreciate in the political dialogue when we talk about how to deal with our cities. —1995

THE LAW

ALAN DERSHOWITZ

As a member of the faculty of the Harvard Law School and a highly public legal gadfly, Alan Dershowitz has been a regular presence on television news and talk shows, been portrayed by Ron Silver in the movies (Reversal of Fortune), *celebrated—and sometimes excoriated—in hundreds of newspaper and magazine articles, and written best-selling books on subjects as varied as the O. J. Simpson case and the importance of "chutzpah" in the Jewish character. With all this, he has also served as appeals attorney in a range of major cases. My first conversation with Mr. Dershowitz took place during the time when an infamous libel case was under review by the U.S. Supreme Court: A noted psychoanalyst, Jeffrey Masson, had sued journalist Janet Malcolm for certain statements she had attributed to him, seemingly as direct quotations, in a* New Yorker *magazine article. I asked my guest to sum up the issue before the High Court.*

Ms. Malcolm . . . at least this is according to the allegations, took some statements that Jeffrey Masson had made, paraphrased them—there's a dispute about whether they're actual paraphrases, or greater liberties were taken—and put them in quotation marks. That is, sent a message to the reader of the article that these were the actual words of the subject of the interview. He then sued, claiming that not only were they not his own words, but they didn't actually reflect the intention and the meaning of what he said. The Supreme Court has now taken this case, on the very important issue of whether or not, when a quotation mark is used around a statement, whether or not that's a certification to the public that those are the actual words of the subject or whether a writer has some liberty to put in quotes the meaning, the paraphrase; and whether or not, if the person is a public figure, as Masson certainly is, whether he can sue alleging that there was malice because his own words were put in quotes and they weren't quite his own words. Those are the issues that the Court will have to deal with.

Heffner: They pose quite an ethical dilemma for the court, don't they?

. . . . It would be a mistake for the Supreme Court to impose its or our own view of ethics on journalists. I think the best service the Supreme Court could actually do in a case like this, is to send a clear announcement to the public that "when you see quotes, don't you be fooled into thinking that always means that it's an accurate quotation of the subject. From now on, be aware that . . . we are told by distinguished journalists . . . that when journalists use quotation marks they don't really mean it. So the public beware." And that may be the best service the Court could perform.

I think that the average reader of the daily press certainly thinks a quotation mark means that the person said it. By the way, the American public doesn't have such high regard for journalists as a profession, and so it's not clear to me whether they always believe what they read in the newspaper. Surely they should not. But I do think that we're at a crossroads. And when I think about what the effect would be if the Supreme Court set down a categorical rule saying, "Quote means quote and if you don't have the words exactly right, you're going to be held liable, maybe even bankrupted." . . . I compare that against the evil of saying, "Look, we've lived in an area of ambiguity; from now on the public ought to know a quote doesn't mean a quote." As a supporter of the First Amendment and also as a reader of the press, I would err on the side of more breathing room for the First Amendment, and to let journalism deal with its own ethics. The Supreme Court doesn't do very well, by the way, when it gets into ethical problems. When they've tried to get into legal ethics on a few ocassions, they've really made a mess of it. . . .

I think, on balance (though it's a hard question for me) that journalists ought to be held to account by other journalists, and not by people wearing robes and people who work for the United States government.

Heffner: And how do you see that happening?

. . . I'm not talking about licensing or disbarment, but much more vigorous ethics committees, which will at least be able to inform the public that when there is a journalist who does the wrong thing, when a journalist, for example, reveals a confidence that was given to him, or reveals the name of a source . . . we very rarely hear about it. We hear journalists talking about the privilege all the time, about how important it is; we very rarely hear about journalists who breach the privilege. We very rarely hear journalists called to account for violating their own ethical norms, and I think one of the messages is, "If you don't do it, the Supreme Court may do it to you . . . so beat them to the punch."

Heffner: You seem to want to stay as far away as possible from the highest court. Does this reflect a lack of high regard?

I would love to operate in a system where the nine justices were the nine most brilliant lawyers in America, and I could argue abstract legal theory to them and understand that I was going to win or lose on the merits of my argument. There are few courts in the world where that is true, but they use a very different selection mechanism. That's not the United States Supreme Court. The United States Supreme Court not only does not contain the nine best lawyers in America; it's not even a close question. If you listed the thousand best lawyers in America, you might find, at most one or two of them on the United States Supreme Court. Maybe, at it's best three or four on the United States Supreme Court. The Supreme Court has been a place where very mediocre lawyers have spent long periods of time having enormous influence on the American public. And so it's important not simply to make abstract arguments to the courts.

Heffner: And your evaluation of the American press?

I still think that we need to have an independent fourth estate, an independent group of people, who just don't have to account for what they do to the government, who have to live and die by their words. By the way, that's why I'm opposed, very much opposed, to schools and universities subsidizing the press. I don't like government subsidizing the press. I really believe that capitalism and the marketplace of ideas should work in newspapers and the media. It doesn't work perfectly, obviously. But I think that they should only be accountable to their journalistic peers and to their readers. Now, obviously I'm not a total absolutist who believes that a journalist should be able to make up stories about public or private figures that could destroy careers. There is something left for the law of libel and slander. Yet . . . the right of a free press, is the right to be unfair. There's no question about that. It's the right to be wrong. Every society gives its press the right to be right; not every society, certainly not Iraq and certainly not the Soviet Union, gives it the right to be wrong. But the right to be wrong, and the right to be unfair is certainly a very important aspect of journalistic freedom. If it were only the right to be fair, we wouldn't have these great struggles.

Heffner: But apart from libel and slander, isn't there such a thing as media that have grown too powerful for the nation's well-being?

. . . if the power of the press has increased dramatically, as it has over time, so has the power of government. The power of the central government in the United States, the power of the Presidency . . . if you compare the Presidency today with the Presidency back in George Washington's time, the power of *every* branch of government has increased. We are a country that has centralized power in government, centralized power in the media, and I see greatly increased, powerful media as a counterplay to the power of the government.

I think when given a choice between whether the proper role of a court is to protect the individual in relation to government or to protect the individual in relation to a powerful, but still private force, the primary concern has to be government. Remember that newspapers can do terrible damage, they can even start wars. We know that. But in the end they can't imprison anyone. In the end they can't deny anyone liberty, the way government can, and that's why a free press, even an irresponsible free press, and again, just coming back to the Soviet Union . . . what kind of press do you think is emerging in Eastern Europe? A very irresponsible press, a press that is competing for readers, and for power, and yet the last thing I would want would be to see the newly free governments of Eastern Europe starting to impose restrictions on the press. It's going to have to work itself out . . . and there's no free lunch.

Heffner: You like the way the press can go after government and just about all other institutions, don't you?

My favorite T-shirt, one that my kids gave me several years ago, said, "Question authority, but raise your hand first." I don't ask my students even to raise their hands. Given a choice between too much respect for institutions and too little, I much prefer to have too little respect for institutions.

Heffner: But why do you make it a choice between too much and too little? Is there no balance?

Well, I think . . . the balance should be struck in favor of everybody being critical of institutions, being critical of churches, being critical of governments, being critical of the press, being critical, period. In a democracy I think a certain degree of cynicism, a certain degree of distrust, is probably a good thing. When it comes to government, we're talking about the most powerful force that we have unleashed on this planet. Governments have done much good and much harm, and I think the idea of citizens being skeptical of institutions, particularly the government, is a very, very healthy thing. If more citizens had been skeptical of Nazi Germany, if more citizens had been able to be skeptical of Stalin's Soviet Union, I think we'd have been better off. The idea of skepticism of institutions is a very healthy thing in a democracy. I teach at the Harvard Law School, which is in itself an institution, whose integrity—not integrity—but whose power I like to undermine with my students. When you think of my students going into a profession where they adore judges, where they adore the Constitution, where there is a sense of the tradition of Harvard, teaching them a little bit of skepticism is a very healthy thing. In my private life I have a lot of faith. In fact I'm a religious person. In fact, I do love the pledge of allegiance. In my own personal life I sometimes suspend my disbeliefs. But when I'm teaching and when I'm in my more public situation, I really think that instilling a sense of distrust, instilling doubt is a very important role for a teacher to play.

The role of philosophers and teachers, from the beginning of time has been to challenge institutions, and we who challenge always understand that the institutions will always have their cadres of support. There will always be those who stand up for institutions. There will always be those who say, "But the church can't be questioned." Or "The State can't be questioned," or "The media can't be questioned." And then there are those of us who will always say, "Question. Question. Question. Question."

Heffner: That puzzles me, because certainly the drive to question authority in every respect must have been the same in your personal, private life as in your public life.

But it doesn't have to follow through in the same way. For example, I have myself chosen family values. My children are very important to me, I have a very happy marriage and a very nice family and a little baby and I personally strongly believe in the values of family in my own life. On the other hand, I'm out there every day defending the rights of gays, defending the rights of people with alternate lifestyles. I challenge the concept of family when I hear it from Republicans. I challenge conventional values, though I myself live with conventional values. I don't have difficulty separating out my own choice. For example, I have real doubts about abortion. On the other hand, I'm out there defending any woman's right to choose to have an abortion. So, I can separate out the public skepticism and criticism because I think I understand, I hope I understand the role of individuals in the larger society.

Heffner: How do you balance concerns about crime and personal safety with concern for civil liberties?

I think the greatest dangers to American society still don't come from individuals who commit crimes. I think it still comes from the potential of big government to take our liberties away from us. But we may be close to the point at which the increase in crime is out of control. We may be getting there, and there may come a time when we have to say to ourselves, "Are we really prepared to continue to free ten or a hundred guilty people for fear that one innocent may be wrongly convicted?" I don't think we're there yet, and I'm certainly not going to give into the hysteria about crime . . . if we ever say "We're there," we'll never get out of it. It's one of these things you can't ever reverse. You go back and you read the newspapers in the 1850s and '60s and they're talking about crime waves. You go back in the 1920s and '30s and they're talking about crime waves. Every time we see a few criminals commit crimes, it's a crime wave. I think that we can do a great deal about crime that we're not doing. We have to have a policy relating to drugs that's a lot more rational than the one we now have, a policy relating to guns that's more rational than we now have. And until we start dealing with those fundamental causes as well as other, more traditional causes, such as unemployment, and the difference between wealth and poverty in our society, the last thing I want to do is compromise on civil liberties.

Heffner: You've been severely criticized for arguing as much before the court of public opinion as before judge and jury. How do you respond to critics of your consistently public posture?

Well, I think one of the points that I like to make is whether you can really stand out there and defend the Bill of Rights without exposing yourself to the kind of criticism that you rightly say I've been exposed to. My own feeling is that lawyers have been far too elitist, that we talk a strange, funny language . . . that the legacy of the Warren Court was a message to liberals that if you can persuade nine men in robes that your point is right, you don't have to persuade the American public. And I've always taken the opposite view. I think if the Bill of Rights is going to survive somebody has to be out there persuading everyone in this country that it's for them, and that's why I don't turn down opportunities to be on television shows that reach a general audience. That's why I don't turn down opportunities to write in the popular media. That's why I don't limit myself to law journals and to only the *New York Times,* because I think you've got to be out there persuading everybody the Bill of Rights is for them. And so my question is, can you do that in this society without being accused of kind of pandering and being a self-promoter. —1990

A. Leon Higginbotham, Jr.

With the electoral crisis of the year 2000, the U.S. Supreme Court once again emerged as an enormously potent political force in our nation's history. We may never know what role the religion, race, and gender of the members of the Court played in that episode, but those matters were very much on the surface in my conversations with A. Leon Higginbotham in the mid-1990s. Judge Higginbotham, then recently retired from the federal bench as Chief Judge of the U.S. Court of Appeals for the Third Circuit, spoke provocatively on the subject. An intriguing recent Supreme Court Historical Society publication had listed "The Jewish Justices of the Supreme Court Revisited: Brandeis to Fortas," giving me the opportunity to ask my guest whether he could actually identify special qualities with the high court's Jewish justices.

If you look at the type of justices who were on the court from the time Justice Brandeis went on in 1916, you have the Jewish justices demonstrating that . . . as a group, they were extraordinarily competent. The Presidents of the United States, when they chose each one of them, seemed to have had clearly in mind that we're putting a minority justice on the court and that we want that person to be stellar in every way. That's what happened when you go all the way from Brandeis to Breyer, in every instance. When they put other justices on the court, the Presidents were not thinking necessarily of the person being extraordinarily competent. Take, for instance, Justice McReynolds, who went on the court, and I believe was appointed by President Wilson. McReynolds is the one who, you may recall from my articles, referred to Howard University as a "nigger university." When McReynolds was appointed, for whatever reason, he did not go in the court with some perception that he was a member of a "minority," and that he had to be better than any of the others. I could pick a whole series of other justices who, on balance, were pretty mediocre. But each one of the Jewish justices was extremely competent as lawyers, as craftsmen, and they had demonstrated that before they got on the court.

Heffner: In addition to competence, would we expect from these Jewish justices, that they would be overwhelmingly concerned, to a person, with fairness? Because Jews had been mistreated? Because Jews had been singled out throughout history?

I think that has to be a factor. Oliver Wendell Holmes once said, in his famous Holmes Lectures more than a hundred years ago, that "A page of history is worth a volume of logic." And anyone who is familiar with the nature of history can deal with certain logical arguments and put them in an appropriate perspective. Earl Warren, for example, understood this, and you saw it in a whole series of events. There's a story a black judge told me about Earl Warren, who played on the University of California Los Angeles football team. (And, by the way, I don't think he was as great a tackle as some people suggest he was.) In any case, when the UCLA team played against another school, which I will not name, there was a black fullback named Gordon. A couple of the players on the other team said, "Nigger, we're going to get you on the next run." And Earl Warren stood up and said, "You've got to get the rest of us first." And that just came out. And that same Gordon, who became a judge, talked to me time and time again about what Earl Warren demonstrated on the football field by saying to him, in effect, "Listen, I'm not going to let anyone hurt you if I've got a chance." I think, therefore, that a person like Warren seems to understand these things instinctively. There are other individuals who, either because they have not had the experience, or because they've lived a particular type of sheltered or isolated life, have more difficulty in coming to grips with it. But anyone who's Jewish, anyone who understands the history of the Holocaust, anyone who understands all of the injustices that Jews have sustained, does not have to walk as long a distance to understand why treating injustice differently is essential to the society.

Heffner: In a comment concerning Supreme Court Justice Clarence Thomas, you said that you cannot accept the notion that someone separates himself, or herself, from life's experience. Does that mean that you would expect Clarence Thomas to reflect the fact that he is an African-American as you would expect Felix Frankfurter and these other justices to reflect the fact that they were Jewish?

Yes. But let me refine it a little bit. I'm not saying that there's only one African-American position, nor is there one Jewish position. But let me give you an example of Justice Thomas' approach. There was a case that came before the United States Supreme Court, in which a prisoner was beaten, lips burst, teeth loosened, bruised under the eye, dental plate broken. The question was: Was that a violation of the cruel and unusual punishment clause in the Constitution? An opinion by Justice O'Connor says, "Of course, in a civilized society, you cannot shackle a prisoner as they did, and without justification beat them, without violating the cruel and unusual punishment clause." And seven justices saw that without any question. I mean, justices who are as conservative as Justice Rehnquist, moderates like Justice Kennedy. Everyone said you can't allow that in a civilized society. And who writes the only dissent? It was Justice Thomas, joined by Justice Scalia. It seems to me that it is incredible that anyone who sees that police power has been so abused could join in writing that dissent. When he did it, the *New York Times* said that he was the cruelest, youngest justice on the court. And I think that statement was an understatement.

Heffner: So, you're ticked off by the fact that an African-American could be that conservative. Is that fair to say?

Yes, it disturbs me, particularly when that African-American has been the beneficiary of federal constitutional benefits. Let me go for the jugular vein. Clarence Thomas is married to, obviously, a thoughtful woman, who happens to be white. In Virginia, under the laws, under the racial integrity statute, that marriage was illegal. And in the case called Loving v. Virginia, a person was sentenced to 25 years in prison just because there was an interracial marriage. The sentence was modified. But the Supreme Court of the United States went further and said that it was unconstitutional. That one court opinion, which says it is legal for him to be married to his wife, preserves his privacy. [But] if you follow the states rights view, which was the unanimous opinion of the state court, Clarence Thomas today would not be on the United States Supreme Court, but could be in the penitentiary. So how someone who's been the beneficiary of the protection of federal constitutional rights can now, after he's made it and after he's gotten the benefits, close his eyes to the importance of that to the weak and the poor and the powerless, is incomprehensible to me.

Heffner: Why do you make the demands you make upon Clarence Thomas?

That's true. I do make demands. Read my articles. I also talk about pluralism. I talk about its importance. I talk about its values. But Clarence Thomas, I must confess, is to me more salt in the wound when I see him take a position, not occasionally, but consistently, time and time and time again. We should remember that he got where he is solely because of Justice Marshall. If Justice Marshall had not given up his seat, do you think that there's any possibility that Justice Thomas, with his slim credentials, could have been nominated to the Supreme Court? I guess the best example of that is what Judge Calabrese, former dean of Yale Law School, had to say. Here he is, dean of Yale Law School, called down to testify about Clarence Thomas.

Heffner: And he went.

And he went. But what did he say? Read the record. Look at my footnotes. What does he say? He says, "The best thing you could say about Justice Thomas is that he's got the potential." Now, since when do you put someone on the United States Supreme Court because they've got, theoretically, the potential? And the tragedy of it is that Justice Thomas has not lived up to the potential which Judge Calabrese hoped he would. . . . When black people have struggled all of these years to try to get into the door—we end up with Thomas. Brandeis went on the court in 1916, Cardozo in the 1920s, Frankfurter in the 1930s. You've had this magnificent half-century of great judges from a minority. And Thurgood goes on, I think, in '66, '67. Fine justice. And after the two decades we've had with Justice Marshall, then we go to the bottom. The difference between Justice Thomas and Justice Marshall is like what physicists would call the difference between zero and infinity.

Heffner: You know, Thurgood Marshall was here at this table long before he went on the bench. As you do, I remember him with both great fondness and enormous admiration. And I don't think you'll ever forgive Justice Thomas for his attack on Thurgood Marshall at the time of the Bicentennial.

Well, I'll tell you what, I certainly will if he becomes as enlightened as Justice Souter, if he becomes as thoughtful as Justice Blackmun. I will not only forgive him, I will write him a letter of apology. But until that day arises, I'm not prone to forgiveness.

Heffner: Do you make the same demands on the women who sit upon the high court?

Well . . .

Heffner: That they vote as women?

No. No. But I want them to vote with a sensitivity to that. I would hope that women who go on the court would have some sensitivity to the whole issue of what's occurred to women in this country. What we're always dealing with is that magnificent phrase Justice Cardozo used in *The Nature of the Judicial Process*. He talks about the "interstitial spaces of the law." And what he meant by the "interstitial spaces" is that you get to a point very, very often where there is no clear, undisputed answer as to whether one must go one way or another. At that point values have everything to do with it. And I would hope that women would bring into their adjudication some understanding of the plight that women have sustained, and evaluate the legal issue within that context. I think I saw some of that in Justice O'Connor in Casey v. Planned Parenthood.

Heffner: And if she hadn't voted the way she did?

Well, I tell you, if she hadn't voted the way she did in that case, I wouldn't be unduly harsh. I would only be harsh if every time a case came up involving a woman, when there's a rational compelling argument which could be made on either side, that she voted consistently against women.

Heffner: I understand. But let's get to the heart of the matter of pluralism. How do you feel about a Jewish seat, an African-American seat, a woman's seat on the Supreme Court?

Good question. I think you need pluralism, and over a period of time you want a substantial number of people of different groups . . . And it is in that context that I'm delighted that there have been Jewish justices. It is in that context that I'm delighted that there has been some diversity. And it is in that context in which I'm delighted that women have gone on.

What we've got to do is to say, "Why has it taken so long?" Let me give you a classic example concerning Harry Truman, for whom I have a lot of admiration. There was a woman who was a judge on the Court of Appeals for the Sixth Circuit. Her name came up as a possible candidate for the United States Supreme Court. And the story is that Truman thought about it, and some justices on the Supreme Court said no, you know, that there are plumbing problems, and all of that nonsense. Well, the tragedy in this country is that we started as a nation only with Forefathers. We had no Foremothers in this country. But if we had Foremothers, we might have had women in power with the sensitivity of an Abigail Adams, who wrote a letter to her husband in 1776 raising the issue of slavery, and the issue of women. She said, "Men are natural tyrants. And unless you do something about it, we will ultimately take over." Well, it was a threat in 1776, and yet it took 200 years before there was one woman on the Supreme Court. . . . We've got a great country, and much to be proud of. But I think that we have not done what we should have done. —1995

Louis Nizer

His paintings were quite beautiful, his sketches of friends and acquaintances simply superb. But of course Louis Nizer will be remembered most as, arguably, the best-known trial lawyer of his time, and certainly one of the most successful. His great bestseller, My Life in Court, *an in-depth recounting of several of his most important cases, still reads like a series of suspense novels. His views on lawyers and lawyering remain as wise and penetrating as when first spoken. Chief Justice Warren Burger stirred up an impressive segment of the legal profession by charging that in the opinion of judges with whom he had discussed the issue, the share of American lawyers competent in trial work—at courtroom procedures—is only "somewhere near the middle number between 25 and 75 percent." Strike the average, and it seems that only 50 percent of American trial lawyers are competent . . . a pretty frightening estimate! I asked Louis Nizer how he evaluated the Chief Justice's charge.*

I think in part what Chief Justice Burger said was correct. And in another part terribly exaggerated. It is true that the parchment of a diploma is hardly an adequate weapon for the iron and steel combat of the courtroom. And it is true that a diploma from a law school doesn't necessarily fit a man to engage in trial tactics, because a trial is not a science. It's an art. And there must be thorough preparation not only in the technical aspects of evidence and procedures, but in those psychological insights during the struggle in a courtroom which do not come easily to the novitiate. On the whole, the lawyer practices the most noble of all professions, the dedication to justice.

I find lawyers honorably dedicated to that cause, giving great service, giving free service. Every important law firm assigns leading partners to give free service to indigent clients. They serve honorably, and it is a shame that because a few are dishonest, as there are a few doctors, engineers, priests, and rabbis that are dishonest and businessmen, of course, that there should be a general cloud over the profession . . . and therefore I regret that Chief Justice Burger added to that burden.

Heffner: But, you're talking about intentions and good will. If I asked you about the way those intentions and that good will are translated into effective legal representation, what would your own estimate be in the area that the Chief Justice has ventured?

You see, if there were a right or wrong way to try a case I would answer that.

Heffner: Isn't there?

Not any more than there is a right or wrong way to write a poem or a book or to paint a painting. The right way to try a case is the one that expresses to the utmost the talents of the individual lawyer. And each lawyer approaches his task differently. It isn't something that one can be taught. The psychological approach to a resistant witness the sensitivity to realize whether or not a judge resents being told he is wrong or is the kind of a man confident enough of himself to withstand criticism. There's an old jest: A lawyer says to the judge, "Your Honor can't give an injunction in this case. Only last night the Court of Appeals, the highest court in this state, said in a case exactly like this that you cannot grant any injunction." And this defiance is met by the judge who says, "Well, I hereby grant an injunction. Have you anything more recent than that?" Such is the psychological crossing of swords with a judge. Then there is sarcasm against an adversary, or the luring of a jury with all of its biases and prejudices. It's an art, and each lawyer approaches the challenge differently. And to talk of all this as if it were like building a table or manufacturing a car ignores the complexity, the innovation, the imagination that goes into every art. And there are thousands of competent lawyers. Sometimes even in their sincerity and lack of skill they make an impression upon the jury. The art of persuasion is the very illusory and uncertain art of how to win over a human being. And it sometimes can be done even by fumbling. I've seen lawyers who aroused the sympathy of the jury simply because they're not as confident as they might be and haven't the white carnation in the buttonhole or put on striped pants.

The art of persuasion, in the end, involves a combination of imagination, felicity, facility on one's feet, and the ability to withstand sudden blows. The trial lawyer balances like a gyroscope on a string, because in every trial one is hit over the head by a surprise. As to the matter of preparation, I must say that, unfortunately, many lawyers who are ready to work their hands to the bone don't know just how to do it. It isn't merely a determination to work hard. It's the skills with which to excavate the past. To understand the problem, you must realize that in every case there are facts to be adduced which may be five years old, ten years old, twenty years old. The lawyer is an archaeologist who must dig into the past and bring up the relic. And the art of doing that is reading every piece of paper, even the seemingly irrelevant letters, and then reaching for the witness's trust. That's the only way you can get at the truth. People think that when a lawyer says he prepares his client, that he is engaged in some kind of black magic. He is not. The only way you get the truth is by digging into all of the facts and reminding him of it. "You're wrong, Mr. Witness, when you say so-and-so. Here's a letter dated July 16, 1962. That couldn't have happened if you wrote that letter, could it?" Now that's endless, patient preparation. Sometimes 20, 30 hours of preparation for one hour of testimony. But it's the only way you get the truth. The truth never flies into the courtroom through the window. It must be dragged in by the heels.

Heffner: Would you accept the picture that so many of us outside the legal profession have of a lawyer manipulating rather than constructing or reconstructing?

No. The lawyer who manipulates is bound to lose his case. That's a flat statement and I stand by it. I am never as confident and any other able trial lawyer is never as confident of winning a case as when he has a witness before him who has lied. Because if the lawyer is properly prepared, that witness must fall. It so happens that ethical conduct and success in the law are parallel. If a lawyer practices with fanatical zeal and scrupulousness, his client will entrust him with his worldly goods before death and after death. But if the client finds out that the lawyer cuts corners even in little things, if he calls him up and the secretary says he's out and somebody else calls him and he's in, I don't know if I can trust that man. The same in the courtroom. The lawyer who misquotes or picks a quotation out of context, sooner or later the judge finds out he quotes wrongly and dishonestly. And that lawyer is under a terrible disadvantage thereafter. Whereas, if the judge asks him an embarrassing question, and he says, "I must admit that's true, Your Honor," the judge has respect for him. There is no case in which all the facts are on one side, or we wouldn't have a contest. And in every case if you admit that which is adverse but insist that you have preponderance of evidence—that's the test, preponderance of evidence—the scale just tips. Therefore, you can admit the wrong things in your client's side.

In a criminal case, it's much worse. What is required is not preponderance of evidence. It's much stricter. One must prove a case beyond a reasonable doubt. That's why it isn't any great achievement for a lawyer to say that he's gotten 28 people off who've been charged with murder. Because to prove to a jury that a man is guilty beyond a reasonable doubt is very difficult. And this is deliberate on the part of constitutional prerogatives. We throw a cordon of rights around the accused because all the government forces, the FBI, the U.S. Attorney, and all the detectives they need are against him. And the position of the defense lawyer is that here is this one individual who's got to hire a lawyer and fight all this. We'll protect him. There must be a unanimous verdict. Eleven against one, he walks out. And he mustn't testify. You can't force him to testify against himself. He may have to admit all the evil facts. He sits back and says, "You prove it, Mr. District Attorney." Why do we do that? We do it deliberately because under our system of law, which I believe is wise in this respect, we throw our weight in favor of the individual and against the oppression of government. That's the theory. So therefore, a lawyer can well afford to admit the unpleasant facts in a particular case and still win.

Heffner: Can you identify the essence of the law?

I once wrote, and I put it epigrammatically: "Perfect justice, impossible; approximate justice, satisfactory; efforts to make justice more perfect, always." So I always think that there's room. It was Justice Cardozo who once said that as long as the facts keep changing, the law must keep changing. Our facts of life change every day. We used to worry about pollution of the atmosphere. There's also pollution of politics. There's pollution in the law. It is by no means a perfect instrument and we must change it all the time.

The law, as Cardozo said, is not a statue. It is a living organism that changes as we change. You know that joke: You're never married to a man for 25 years; he's not the same man after 25 years. The law is not the same after 25 years. Because the facts have changed. —1978

RUDOLPH GIULIANI

My first conversations with Rudy Giuliani took place in the 1980s. Crime—blue collar, white collar, in our nation's streets, on Wall Street— had become Americans' principle preoccupation, and Giuliani, perhaps was the nation's most visible crime-buster, first as the number-three man in President Reagan's Department of Justice, then as the U.S. Attorney for the Southern District of New York. Futhermore, the U.S. Congress had recently passed a Comprehensive Crime Control Act, which had been in the making for a decade. All this gave rise to a dialogue in which Giuliani gave us a preview of his independence of mind on subjects ranging from judical reform to the death penalty. I asked him about our changing ideas concerning crime and punishment.

I think we've moved away from the model of America that many of us grew up with, which is one in which we emphasized individual responsibility, both for innocent citizens, decent citizens, as well as those who might be caught in criminal problems.

Then we moved on to emphasize social responsibility . . . looking for the causes of crime, looking for individual reasons why people commit crime. We began describing them as excuses. And I think we did create some of the sickness ourselves in the kind of philosophy that we were applying.

Heffner: About this newer "medical" model—that's what it has been called—what would you do with it now?

Well, I think that is an excellent model for a psychologist or a psychiatrist or a doctor or a social worker, in trying to deal with an individual person. I think it's terrific in trying to move people away from criminal behavior. . . . But I don't think that is a healthy model for the criminal justice system or for government. I think a much healthier model is to hold people responsible for their criminal actions, and to elevate the rights of innocent people as the highest objective of government and of the criminal justice system.

Heffner: Would you keep the medical model for diagnostic purposes and the model of responsibility for social purposes?

In the long run, it doesn't really matter, if you are mugged, whether the person who mugs you is an insane person or a responsible person. The same damage is done to you by either. Our first goal has to be to protect innocent people in society. That has to be our first goal.

A criminal justice system that is overly permissive, and is willing to accept any excuse that is presented, and is willing to delay any time a lawyer asks for a delay, the overall social effect over time is that, in the street, people don't respect the criminal justice system. Those people who would consider mugging you, those who would consider engaging in white-collar crime, those who would consider engaging in bribery, those who would consider engaging in theft and burglary and robbery, say to themselves, "This is something we can do with relative safety," rather than say to themselves—as I think they did at times in our past—"If I engage in this kind of conduct, there's a good likelihood I'm going to have to pay a very heavy price." Now, you're not going to deter everyone. There are still going to be irresponsible people you can't reach; and there are still going to be people who take a chance on paying a price. But my belief is—and I think every objective study of this has demonstrated its correctness—that if you create in society the impression and the reality that you must pay consequences for misbehavior, you're going to bring down the level of criminal activity. And you're going to do a better job of protecting decent citizens.

Heffner: I'd like to go to the question of capital punishment. Obviously, it is the ultimate deterrent for the person who is punished. Do you really feel that it does deter others?

Capital punishment, I believe, is a deterrent. But I also believe that capital punishment has been used very, very poorly by politicians and sometimes, even by criminologists, as an answer to the crime problem. And because there's such emotion attached to it on both sides—people in favor of it, people against it—it can become your entire crime program. You can run for mayor, governor, senator, or whatever, and your answer to crime is capital punishment. I happen to believe that capital punishment is important, and does have a role in our system of criminal justice, but I don't like to talk about it a great deal because I think it sends people in the wrong direction. There's no doubt that capital punishment can deter certain kinds of crimes. It can have an effect on the level of murder that we have in our society, one that is alarmingly high in comparison to other nations. And I think it can have an impact, for example, on someone who commits robberies as a way of living. If capital punishment were part of the law in a particular state, I believe it would be less likely that individuals might plan a robbery with a loaded gun, or put themselves in the position of possibly killing someone. But I don't think that it is an answer, any kind of a general answer, to the problem of crime. And, no matter how we construct the law of capital punishment in our society, it should be very, very limited. It should be limited to certain very egregious cases, and it should be limited to those cases where we're absolutely certain of the defendant's guilt. So, the number of times that we would impose capital punishment would be so small that it couldn't possible be some kind of general, across-the-board deterrent.

Heffner: Why don't you embrace instead the notion that the ultimate punishment is simply removal, total removal from society? The life equivalent of death. Imprisonment. Throw the key away.

Well, because I don't know that we can do that.

Heffner: Why can't we?

As a practical matter, I don't know that we can do that on a broad scale . . .

Heffner: Why not?

A number of correctional officials tell me that the worst kind of prison to administer is a prison filled with people without hope, without any possibility of returning to society. Because there is absolutely no deterrent to their misbehavior. In fact, you really get into a circle here. The only deterrent to their misbehavior becomes capital punishment. If you're going to spend the rest of your life in prison, then, I guess, you can slightly alter the conditions of confinement. But we have a federal prison, for example, in Marion, Illinois, where we have 500 or 600 of the worst criminals in America, including those from the states that the states can't handle. These are essentially people who are committed to prison for life. When I was Associate Attorney General, we had one individual who, during the short time that I was in office, two years and a couple of months, committed murder twice while confined. And when asked why he did it, he said, "Why not? Why shouldn't I? It gets me a trial if I do this." So he gets out of the boredom of his day-to-day existence. And we could not impose capital punishment on him because it was a federal facility, and the House of Representatives has failed to pass a Constitutional capital punishment bill for the federal government. So this person is just a living source of danger, not only to other inmates, but also to the prison officials who have to deal with him. And this is not one isolated individual. There are a number of people in Marion, Illinois, where there are three times more correctional officers than there are [inmates], and it's a tremendously tense situation.

Heffner: Of course, if that is the case, then what you're saying, we simply have no alternative to capital punishment.

In an ideal society I would be against capital punishment, but in an ideal society we probably wouldn't need government—I think in some situations you have to come to the unfortunate choice that the only thing available is capital punishment. And I don't think you could have a system where you used life in prison without possibility of release, if you didn't also have as a fall-back deterrent, capital punishment. And that's why I think it's false hope that's offered by politicians who don't want to bite the bullet and say, "In some situations, capital punishment is necessary."

Heffner: Do you think we're likely to run into abuses, whatever that means, of capital punishment?

I think we could run into abuses of it. And I think there are people that are too zealously committed to capital punishment, either as a deterrent, and they over-promise it as a deterrent, or even people who frighten me because they'd want to use it more generally than I think is healthy for our society. And I think we're going to have to be very careful now that we're moving again in the direction of utilizing capital punishment, at least in most of the states, that it only be reserved for a situation in which there is absolutely no other alternative. And I don't see any reason why you couldn't have both. I don't think they're mutually exclusive. I don't see any reason why you couldn't have both capital punishment in your system as well as life without possibility of release.

Heffner: Can I move on to the question of courtroom procedures and how much of what you have deplored about our criminal justice system has been attributable to these procedural failures?

I think a good deal of it has. I think I'd have to join together two groups, although they probably are part of the same group. Lawyers and judges, are probably most responsible for it. And I think if you could isolate the single most important problem faced, particularly in our urban criminal justice system, it's the problem of delay. The tremendous amount of time that goes by between the time a person is arrested and the person is finally held to answer for that crime. That has so many devastating effects, including diminishing the deterrent effect of punishment. We could probably impose lighter penalties if we imposed them more surely and more swiftly than we impose them a year or two years later. And that delay is primarily caused by lawyers who abuse the system by asking for endless delays because they are handling more cases than they should be handling, because it is generally in the interest of a criminal defendant to delay a trial and to put it off for as long as possible. And then, very importantly, there is the failing of judges in not being harsh enough with lawyers, in not taking control of their calendars and making it necessary that cases be tried quickly and elevating that to a very, very important concern. After all, if you look at the issue societally, when you add up all of these cases, it's one of the things that is bankrupting the criminal justice system a making it impossible for it to function.

Heffner: Why, if this issue is so clear to you as it is, is it not as clear to the judges who permit these delays?

When you're inside a profession, whether you're a lawyer or a judge or a doctor or newspaperperson or whatever . . . you become terribly defensive about any suggestions that more accountability should be required of you. I think many people in each of these professions and others that we haven't mentioned feel that maybe too much is being asked of them already. And it's very difficult for them to say that there are standards we should impose on ourselves in order to make ourselves more accountable. I really believe that the single most devastating thing in the criminal justice system is the delay that we permit. And I do not think that we need more judges, or that we need more police, necessarily, or that we even have to spend more money on the system. In fact, I'm not sure that spending more money on the system right now would achieve very much. We'd just be spending more money on a system that continued to fail. I think we have to take a look at modernizing our court system. Computerizing it. Putting cases on schedules the judges are required to adhere to. And having judges with individual calendars such as they have in most of the federal courts. In those courts a judge has a case assigned to him; that becomes his case, and he's accountable for disposing of that case within a fixed period of time. Most state and local judges would get very upset at that, because they would say that it's unrealistic, you're asking too much; you already ask us to do too much. That was the reaction of many federal judges when the individual calendar system was imposed on the federal court 12, 13 years ago. They all now live under it. It's the reason why in the federal courts we can prosecute someone, try them, from beginning to end, in 30, 60, 90 days. Whereas, in the state system, sometimes it will take as much as two years to do what we can do in 60 or 90 days . . .

Heffner: Well, you know, in all the years that I've talked with attorneys and others related to the criminal justice system, no one has ever said before—"I'm not talking about more police; I'm not talking about more money, I'm not talking about more judges; I'm talking about an efficient use of the resources we have."—Why is it that Rudolph Giuliani is the only one to have said this?

Well, I don't know that people haven't said it before. It really is almost obvious if you observe the system, and you observe the amount of money that we spend on it—which is considerable—the numbers of people that are involved in it, and the fact that it just is not moving along the way it should. The justice system, if it's going to work at all, has to adjudicate someone's innocence or guilt quickly. That is very, very important. And I felt as strongly about that in my old role as a defense lawyer as I do now in my role as a prosecutor. You have to get a quick answer to the question, "Is this person innocent or guilty?" Now, quick doesn't mean immediate. It doesn't mean within days. But it should mean, at least, within several months. And, therefore, those people that are being incorrectly charged (and there are always some of those) are taken out of the system and the burden is lifted from them. And those people that are guilty would then be held to punishment; and punishment within a shorter period of time. And I think, if you did that, you wouldn't have to impose penalties as large as we impose now. One of the reasons why we sometimes have to impose a very large penalty is that we take so long to deliver the message, so that you have to make it a more dramatic message when you deliver it. Now, I'm not just talking about the individual. I'm talking about general deterrents for the rest of society.

Heffner: Is that why you were saying that even as a defense attorney, not just as a prosecutor, you felt that delay was bad for your clients?

Yes, I think we have to divide up two sets of clients. Delay is very bad for an innocent client, because you want to get it over with, and you want to prove your innocence. You want his problem gone. From the point of view of a client that's guilty, sometimes delay isn't so bad because you're just delaying the inevitable and hopefully witnesses will forget, they'll become discouraged, and they won't testify. But in no event does delay help society as a whole. It harms us greatly. —1984

HAROLD J. ROTHWAX

Harold J. Rothwax was a tough, smart, learned, and eminently fair trial judge. I loved and respected him enormously, but still argued with him both on and off the air concerning the fact that as the New York State Supreme Court Judge who presided over the notorious Joel Steinberg/Hedda Nussbaum child abuse trial, he had permitted television cameras in his courtroom . . . and enjoyed having them there! He also firmly believed that a judge must be a full participant in all judicial proceedings rather than sitting quietly like a "potted plant." And after a quarter century of distinguished service on the bench, Judge Rothwax had an urgent sense of concern about the health and viability of the American court system, which shortly before his untimely death he reflected on in a characteristically frank and abrasive volume, Guilty: The Collapse of Criminal Justice.

Heffner: Precisely what charges do you think our criminal justice system is guilty of, and why.

Well, it's guilty of not being rational, it's guilty of not being knowable, it's guilty in the sense that it's not subject to review. Almost alone among our democratic institutions, the law, as pronounced by the Supreme Court, is not subject to review and rethinking. As a result of that, we tend to be somewhat passive and accepting in relation to it. The Supreme Court is reluctant to review its own rulings because of the power of precedent. State legislatures are inhibited in passing bills because of the constitutionalization of our criminal law. And over the years . . . since the Warren revolution in the early 1960s, I think our law has become encrusted with rulings and with precedents and with statutes and procedures that have increasingly become irrational, increasingly hard to understand and know about, and which have burdened the search for truth in meaningful ways, so that very often what our criminal justice system represents is an obstacle course, rather than a search for truth.

Heffner: You say "search for truth." But I remember doing a program with the distinguished Harvard law professor Paul Freund, in which he laughed at the fact that I had titled our program together, "Search for Truth." He said that has nothing to do with the law.

Well, I hope it shocked you then, and I hope it shocks you now.

Heffner: It did. And it does.

I mean, what is the purpose of a trial, what is the purpose of a hearing, if it is not a search for the truth? In a way, Paul Freund, who was an eminent legal scholar . . . and a widely known and highly regarded professor, expressed, I think, the cynicism that lawyers feel about the inability of our system to ascertain the truth under these circumstances. But it's certainly true that a primary objective of criminal procedure is to search for the truth. I mean, when you go to trial, the issue is: Did he do it? Can the people prove the guilt of this defendant beyond a reasonable doubt? And you have to know what the truth is in order to make that judgment. And if we're not seeking for the truth, what in God's name are we doing? . . .

Heffner: Well, I think the cynics are saying that one is looking for a verdict of guilty or not guilty rather than looking for the truth. Is that unfair?

The word "verdict" means "to speak the truth." That is its basis. I think probably one of the problems we have is that we have a system that is run entirely by lawyers in their own interests and for their own benefit, and that very few other people take an interest in

it or believe they can effectively act upon it. And the lawyers themselves have significant self-interest in this area so that they're not
interested in changing the system.

Heffner: Is that as true generally for prosecutors as for defense
counsel?

The prosecutors are certainly seeking for the truth. Their goal is to
seek the truth. Their job definition is to seek the truth. And, indeed,
if they don't believe that they can prove guilt beyond a reasonable
doubt, they are ethically obliged to dismiss the charge. The defense
attorneys have no such equal obligation. Their job is to be a cham-
pion for the accused person and to say everything for them, for that
accused person, that can be said under the raw by way of bringing
doubt upon the issue of the defendant's guilt. So the defense attorney
and the prosecutor are different. And over time. it seems to me, the
defense attorneys have a disproportionate authority within the profession. And they have tended to make themselves more central and
more dominant within the profession, to their own self-interest. Yes.
I mean, I think it's quite clear that the defense bar is the dominant
force in criminal justice in the United States today, and that their purpose is not to seek the truth.

Heffner: But here at this table, William Kunstler, Alan Dershowitz,
and others, have maintained, not their own pristine purity, but the
notion that prosecutors in our country too, rather than looking for the
truth, are looking to win. Now, I gather that that hasn't been your
experience over these many decades on the bench. And you were a
defense attorney to start with.

I was a defense attorney, yes. Obviously there are immature prosecutors. Obviously there are untrained prosecutors. Obviously there are
bad prosecutors. Obviously there are those who have an investment
and an interest in seeing that their side wins. Although I tend to

think that would be only in situations where they believe that me person was, in fact, guilty. I mean. on the occasions when I. as a defense attorney, would go to a prosecutor and say, "I believe that my client is innocent"—I wouldn't do that too often because it wasn't true too often—but on those occasions when I did, and there were a number of them, I found the prosecutors responded intensely and with great energy to resolve their own doubts that I had created in their minds by what I had said. So, yes, it was overwhelmingly my impression that prosecutors are seeking to do the right thing, and when they have a doubt about whether a person is guilty that they will not go on with the prosecution. And while there are obviously mis-creants within that group, as with any other, that overwhelmingly the prosecutor is seeking the truth, yes. And that, of course, is not the definition of a defense attorney. I'm not criticizing the defense attorney for not seeking the truth.

Heffner: You're not?

No. Because that is not his task. No, I'm not criticizing them for that. Their job is to say for the defendant everything that can be said for that defendant under the law with a view to seeing whether or not he can either mitigate the sentence or the punishment or the conviction that will come down, or avoid it altogether. So long as the defense attorney does that properly, so long as he does it ethically, so long as he does it within the bounds of law. then he serves our community. He serves it by challenging authority to act with integrity, to act responsibly, to act with sufficient evidence, and so on. So the role he plays is a very meaningful and important one if the adversary system is to work.

The problem is that most defendants are guilty. Under our system of probability screens we have made it important that we don't bring people to trial who have not been determined previously on a number of occasions to be probably guilty. Everybody who goes to trial has been found to be probably guilty. That doesn't mean that everybody who goes to trial is guilty. There are undoubtedly some people who are not. But it does mean that defense attorneys, 90 percent or more of the time, are representing guilty people. Guilty of something, not necessarily the top charge. And that puts a pressure upon defense attorneys to push the envelope, to use excessive zeal, to engage in tactics that may distort or may mislead juries or judges in the interests of their clients. Not all defense attorneys do that. But those who do are not controlled or punished or disciplined by the legal profession or by the judges or by any other agency in our society.

Heffner: So, where are we, Judge? How can we get out of this morass? You talk about the Warren revolution. What are you blaming on the Warren revolution? If "blame" is the word.

Well, the Warren court accurately perceived many abuses that existed at that time, and acted sometimes, I think, appropriately, and sometimes inappropriately, to correct those abuses. Some of them, it seems to me, were not theirs to correct. It should have been for state legislatures to have corrected that. Some of them, it was within their province to correct.

I think what has happened is that they have gone too far with that. The pendulum, which favored the police excessively and allowed for these abuses, has now swung all the other way. And so now the defendants are advantaged. And it's very hard to change that. Once we set a higher floor below defendants' rights, it's very hard to modify it. The Supreme Court itself is reluctant to modify it because of the power of precedent. It wants the law to he perceived as stable and lasting and enduring, and solid and noble. And so the Supreme Court is reluctant to overrule the precedent, even if it has come to the conclusion that it was a bad precedent. They'll try to modify it, they'll try to undercut it, but it's very hard for them to reverse it entirely. So that's one problem. The Supreme Court itself is reluctant to change the law.

The other problem is that the effect of the Warren court's rulings was to constitutionalize much of American criminal procedure Once you say that these are matters of constitutional law, you effectively deprive the state legislatures, and the people, from doing anything, from writing anything, from passing anything that will modify or over-rule or curtail what the Supreme Court has done. The result of that has been, unfortunately, I think, that criminal law tends to become very rigid over time. And it makes it very hard for the pendulum to swing back, however modestly or moderately or incrementally, because once you say that this advance is constitutionally required, the only way you can undo it is by a constitutional amendment.

The effect of it, also, is to leave a feeling of passivity within the public itself, a feeling that there's very little that they can do to modify this or to change it, or even, at some level, given the complexity of the Supreme Court's rulings, to understand it. I mean, one of my complaints is that so much of law is unknowable. It's unknowable by the judges, it's unknowable by the police, and it's unknowable by the public. And as a result, the public tends to leave this just as a matter for the Supreme Court, which, in a democracy, I don't think is especially healthy.

Heffner: Well, you write, in *Guilty,* and I was so taken with this, "If a chief judge of a state rides in a police car, he or she might be just as unknowing, just as puzzled as to what search and what seizure is per-mitted, as to what one can do when you're called on the police phone and told that there's a man with a gun . . ."

The Supreme Court itself has said that the law of search and seizure is intolerably confusing. Not only the chief judge of the state, it's the chief judge of the United States. We recently had a case in New York which sort of symbolized that for me. There were two people who were arrested in the same apartment. They were brought to trial together. The evidence against them was identical. The jury found both of them guilty. They had previously moved to suppress the evidence that was obtained from the apartment, and they had lost at the trial level. So now they both appeal to the appellate court. The case went up to the appellate court, and ordinarily those appeals are consolidated and heard at the same time, but as luck would have it, through some oversight, the two appeals went before two separate banks of judges. Now, these men had been sentenced to life imprisonment. And one panel of five judges, hearing the same evidence, said, "Well, this search was clearly good. The motion to suppress is properly denied, and he may go to jail for life." And the other panel, also unanimously, said, "This search is clearly bad." Okay. They all cited the same law and the same rules. I mean, the law has literally become unknowable.

Heffner: How could that be?

Well, I think it happens because the way of making the law is for the Supreme Court to decide it. That's not a desirable way to do it. The Supreme Court was never intended to be a legislature. How can the Supreme Court make intelligible the whole law of search and seizure? It only hears one case on search and seizure every other year, or one case or two cases a particular year. The parameters of search and seizure law are unusually wide. They deal with every contact between the citizen and the police officer. And those have thousands of permutations and thousands of combinations. So how can the Supreme Court elucidate that in any kind of a clear fashion by its sporadic, intermittent, unprogrammed way of passing upon search and seizure law? There's no way that they can do it in a clear way. It would be far better for legislatures to set up a code of conduct for police officers and so on. But they're dissuaded from doing that because they don't feel that they know whether or not the Supreme Court will endorse it, approve it, whether it'll be lawful. And so the legislatures are rendered passive, and the lawyers are basically rendered passive. And we all wait for the great god in the sky, the Supreme Court, to render its decisions.

I mean, one other example of the unknowability of search and seizure laws: the leading treatise on search and seizure law is now four volumes and close to 4,000 pages. Now, no police officer can know all of that. And most of the judges don't know all of that. I cite some cases where the Supreme Court came down with some decisions where appellate judges I was lecturing to disagreed almost unanimously with what the Supreme Court had done. I mean, you just don't know what the Supreme Court is going to do in the area of search and seizure laws.

Heffner: What would your recommendation be then, in terms of what position the Supreme Court should take?

Well, what we do now is, when the Supreme Court or any other court finds that the police officer has made some kind of a mistake, there is a requirement of mandatory exclusion, that is relevant and probative and reliable evidence is suppressed, and the jury never hears it. And therefore we suppress evidence, we suppress truth, we burden the search for truth.

Now, if it is true that the law is unknowable, then it seems to me foolish to require the exclusion of evidence when an officer may have acted with objective reasonableness and subjective good faith. That, it seems to me, is self-destructive and foolish. So I think that the first thing we have to do, is do away with the mandatory exclusionary rule. That is not found in the Fourth Amendment. That is a judicial construct. It's not required, and no other Western country has that. Not Western Europe, not England, not Canada, not the British Commonwealth, not Scandanavia. We're the only country in the world that has a mandatory exclusionary rule.

Heffner: In fact, it seems to me that you make the point again and again that many of the outs that the law now provides for criminals are not based upon clear and present constitutional provisions.

No. They're not found in the documents themselves. The Fourth Amendment, the Fifth Amendment, and the Sixth Amendment are fairly clear in what they say. What we're talking about and what

I'm complaining about are recent interpretations by the U.S. Supreme Court.

And for the first 170-some-odd years of our Constitution there was no requirement that any of the states of the United States suppress evidence on the grounds that it was illegally obtained. So that was a judicial construct. And though we now tend to accept it as part of our legal landscape, and many people would argue that it should not be questioned, there's every reason in the world why it should be questioned.

Heffner: If you reject the notion that if the constable blunders somehow or someway the accused must benefit, if you reject that, where do you go, what do you put in its place?

Well, one thing I would do would be to substitute a discretionary exclusionary rule for a mandatory exclusionary rule. There are two kinds of violations of the Fourth Amendment. One kind of violation would be a knowing and deliberate and willful violation by the police of a person's rights. They don't know anything, they don't suspect any crime, they kick a door down in the middle of the night, and they ransack an apartment. It's inexcusable and frightening conduct in a democracy, and it must be dealt with in a clear and forceful fashion. And the police can be told in clear and unmistakable terms that that is a no-no: they must not behave that way. So I would have no problem with excluding that kind of evidence.

But most of the infractions that the police officers are engaged in are in areas where they cannot know what the law is. It's absurd to reward a serious, guilty defendant with his freedom because the officer has made a good-faith mistake under the law as he understood it.

Heffner: And I gather, too, that you're saying that these burdens are making the criminal justice system a game in which the odds are heavily against the prosecution.

Absolutely. The burden on the prosecution is a high one, deservedly, properly so, to prove guilt beyond a reasonable doubt. But the more we interfere irrationally, illogically, foolishly with their ability to do their job—I don't mean that we shouldn't interfere with it where other important values are concerned—but when we do it with no good, corresponding, countervailing reason, then we make it harder to protect our society, we make it harder for this process to be a meaningful and useful process. —1995

LINDA FAIRSTEIN

Early in the 1990s, Linda Fairstein, who at the time headed Manhattan District Attorney Robert Morgenthau's Sex Crimes Prosecution Unit, stated that "sexual assaults remain the most underreported cases within the criminal justice system." Now, early in the twenty-first century, I'm not sure much has changed. Which is why my conversation with Linda Fairstein, who has become a best-selling author as well as a practicing attorney, and something of a celebrity, still resonates with force and meaning. I asked her to carry on from a statement she had made several years before about efforts to explain the motivation for rape: "It is the only crime, I think, that we can't understand. I've read everything about anger and power and hatred of women, all of which might play some part in every rape, but I can no better answer the question."

Rape has always been the least talked about crime. It has always been something to which, unfortunately, a stigma has been attached to the survivor of the crime—the victim, not the perpetrator. It's the only crime I know of that is often called "victim precipitated." People tend to blame the victim for some aspect of what has occurred—why she was where she was, or wearing what she was wearing. Or why did she talk to her assailant or have a drink with him. And I think that for a very long time this society dealt with it as a problem that didn't happen to "women we knew, our sisters, our mothers, our wives." And so, it is only very recently, sadly, that we have come to focus attention on this crime, and we're only now learning to begin to understand why it occurs.

Heffner: Do you have any thoughts about what the numbers would be if sex crimes were not the most underrated and/or most underreported of all crimes?

I think that in large urban centers . . . the reporting has increased. And I think that's because there are a lot more services responding to women now. I think a lot of the "good" media attention to this problem has brought women forward. So, I think while national statistics say that only one in ten report this crime, I agree with those figures that say that as many as three or four in ten now report regularly, particularly in metropolitan areas. But it's still terrifically underreported.

Heffner: But, do you think that the actual level of crimes against women is any higher today than it was a half century ago?

Oh, yes, I do. Yes, I think it is far greater today, and I think, while it doesn't explain everything, some of it, for example, has a lot to do with the drug problem in the city. . . .

Heffner: Is there a particular legal perspective on rape?

Rape was the only crime, until a decade or so ago, that, in some states, had a corroboration requirement—more than the victim's word was needed to take an offender into court. This is unlike any other crime in the penal law. It was legislated in this country in the 1800s, coming out of centuries of British law, which stated that it was easier for a woman to accuse a man of a charge as inflammatory as rape than for a man to defend himself against such a charge. And so certain provisions were written into the laws to assert that the victim's word was not enough to bring an indictment. One of the ways those laws were always justified was to say that women could falsely, *would* falsely report and would falsely charge. But let's face it, it's not an easy charge to make and anybody who has ever been through the process of reporting and prosecuting a crime (although I like to think we've made it easier in this day and age), knows that it is not undertaken lightly. In rape cases, the victim is put through quite an ordeal in the process, most of the time. And so I really reject the argument that there is a lot of false reporting and mistaken IDs. IDs, I think, and those of us who work in the field agree with me, are much better than in any other category of crime. The victim and offender have been together under much more contact circumstances and for a longer period of time than in muggings, bank robberies, or other crimes that only take a few minutes to commit. I mean sexual assaults take a long time to occur, from minutes to hours. And so the identification is, I think, generally, much more accurate in these cases.

Heffner: Do you find that the public is more perceptive and understanding in thinking about rape now? Is there a sea change in our national thinking about the subject?

Well, change is beginning to take place, but I think it's dramatically different in two kinds of cases. In what we in law enforcement call "stranger" cases, when a victim is attacked by someone she has never seen or met before, the general public tends to be understanding, sympathetic, and compassionate. After all, it's everybody's worst nightmare about someone they love, and so people do now tend to believe that the crime actually occurred. The lawyers then have to limit the case really to the issue of whether the right person is on trial, which is an easy task for me as a prosecutor. On the other hand, the category that we call "acquaintance" cases or "date" rapes, are the cases that still present the most problems to a survivor in a courtroom and therefore, to the prosecutors arguing the case. They are the cases in which public attitudes have lagged far behind the changes in the law. And whatever people talk about at a dinner table these are the cases in which, when people reach the jury box, they still tend to look for ways to blame the victim for what occurred and to excuse the defendant. They look for ways to find that he is not a rapist, that he is not a career criminal. He's more likely to be, in an acquaintance case, a middle class guy with no criminal record and often a wife and children, or from a "good" family, with a middle class background. So jurors tend to say to themselves, "Well I don't consider him a rapist."

Heffner: Given your concern for this particular type of crime, what would you have us do as a society?

There are a number of things to be done. I think it's really only very recently that the media, both print and electronic, have focused their great powers to educate society on this problem. I mean, very little has been written and understood about it. For years, when I started on these cases in the mid-seventies, the *New York Times* reporter who covered the courthouse told me that, unlike the tabloids, he wasn't writing about our sex crimes cases because his paper's readers weren't interested in the topic. And so I was interested and pleased to see that in the last year, in the A Section, the national section of the *Times,* there were, finally, many issues relating to these crimes that were addressed on a national level in a series of articles. Women's magazines for a long time were the only media covering these things, but television programs are now covering the subject. I think that educating the public about these issues is the only way even to begin to change attitudes. My colleagues and I lecture, we'll go anywhere to speak about the subject of violence against women.

We do this because members of the public all across this country end up on the juries that will be making the decisions in these cases. The only way we're going to remove the stigma from victims who have been, up to this time, unwilling to identify themselves, is to get people to talk about this kind of crime and understand that it doesn't happen because of something the victim does, but because of what the offender does. Unless we're willing to devote some resources to studying the problems—identifying them at an earlier point — we're not going to be able to curb the growth of violence.

Heffner: Are we talking about sexuality or about violence?

We're talking about very violent crimes. I am one of the people, however, who thinks that these crimes are not sexual acts, not sexuality as we normally think of it. It is violence that the criminal has chosen to express through a sexual act, not through hitting someone over the head with a baseball bat. I mean the perpetrator has choices in most cases, and he or she has chosen the sexual act as the instrument of that violence. It is extreme violence channeled through a sexual outlet.

Heffner: What would you do, as a judge, with the person who has been convicted?

I think that if someone has been fairly convicted by a jury of these crimes, the person should be sentenced to state prison. And I think it should be a very hefty sentence. I can't think of any crime, short of homicide—in which the victim survives—that so completely alters a life. It is clearly and obviously the most personal intrusion that someone can sustain. And so I think that the punishment has to be very severe. And I think because of the recidivist nature unless we isolate these offenders for as long as the law allows, and until we understand how to do something that may improve their ability to function again in society, they've got to be isolated for as long as possible, or they will repeat.

Heffner: Talking again about so-called "date" rape, do you feel, as many people have said, that really what we're talking about is a failure to understand, on the part of many of our young male college students, that what they are doing is close to the worst possible intrusion upon another individual?

Well, I think that one of the difficulties is that we can't talk about acquaintance rape as if all the cases are the same. They're very, very different. We see cases in which there is a lot of sexual foreplay and activity that's consensual on both parts and the offender thinks he's getting a certain signal and then pushes a little harder. Those acts are different, that circumstance may be different from an occasion in which a person who has seemed perfectly normal throughout the course of an evening then becomes violent, throws a woman to the ground, and threatens to kill her unless she complies with his demands. There are ranges and many different kinds of conduct within what we call acquaintance rape, which is not the least of the many problems that confront us. There are certainly some instances in which the defendant is not at all aware of what line he has crossed. Maybe rightly, maybe wrongly, but he's less culpable in some cases and those are quite often the cases in which he's not prosecuted. They're often the cases in which the victim expresses to me or to one of my colleagues that she's not exactly sure what happened. That she's not sure what signals she communicated and whether or not she said "no." Some of those cases don't belong in the criminal justice system.

Heffner: We're talking about a lot, or a few?

I think a few. The lines are generally quite clear. In most cases the women who report and present themselves are able to make it clear at what point the conduct became forcible and at what point consent was either withdrawn or never given. In very few cases is the area so gray that one can excuse the young man for this sort of "boys will be boys" conduct. I don't think that's what rape is about. —1991

WILLIAM KUNSTLER

William Kunstler gained a reputation in the 1960s as a defender of clients who espoused unpopular causes—mainly political. He was a colorful presence, with his signature glasses over his forehead, in courtrooms (and the media) all over the country, representing clients in the antiwar movement, the fight for civil rights and others struggling against the mainstream of American society. In the 1990s a Vanity Fair *article called him "The Most Hated Lawyer in America." This may or may not be journalistic hyperbole, but he was certainly one-of-a-kind, a unique personality, with a unique perspective on righting wrongs.*

Many times before we talked, I had discussed the subject of lawyers and unpopular cases with Edward Bennett Williams, Thurgood Marshall, Morris Ernst, and Louis Waldman. I realized, however, that their unpopular clients never quite tainted them as my guest's clients seem to have tainted him. I asked Kunstler why.

I guess, Dick, because they didn't represent really the damned of society. Thurgood Marshall was representing, for example, the school cases, Brown against the Board of Ed, and was representing school children who were black and who were forced to go to segregated schools. Morris Ernst, who lived with my parents for a long time after his parents died, never really had what I call pariahs to represent. And neither did Edward Bennett Williams, who was once a junior to me in a case involving a reporter, Bill Worthy, whose passport was taken away for going to what was then Red China. And Louis Waldman, I never had anything to do with. But I know that they were not representing real pariahs, people that could be totally hated by most of the population of this country.

Heffner: Then, what makes Kunstler pariah-bound?

Well, I guess I have found that it is the pariahs for whom the law changes.

Heffner: Is your concern the law, or your clients?

The client is my primary concern. But I'm also interested in illustrating how these clients get treated differently than other clients with other lawyers, how the system rears back and devours them in an illegitimate fashion, compared to other clients. I want to expose this. And I think it's always good to expose this.

Heffner: What do you mean by, "in an illegitimate fashion"?

Well, such treatment is not really legal. It has the imprint of the law, but the law is not always legal, as we know. For example, when you take away a criminal defendant's trusted lawyer. Under the Sixth Amendment, you're supposed to be entitled to have a lawyer of your choice. In the 1993 World Trade Center bombing case, they kept all of the lawyers desired by the clients out of the picture by refusing to appoint them, normally a routine matter . . . Ergo, they all had inexperienced counsel. And when they asked me to represent them at sentencing, along with Ronald Kuby, my partner, the judge locked the door in our face. Judge Duffy wouldn't even let us in the courtroom. These defendants were sentenced without counsel. Something I always thought violated the law as laid down by the Supreme Court. But that can be done with individuals society deems hateful.

Heffner: In court, what is your objective?

I think the end, for lawyers like me, always has to be opposing the system. All systems are corrupt. That's what Lord Acton said— "Power corrupts, and absolute power corrupts absolutely." All systems become corrupt. Once you have a governmental system, you give up a great many of your rights to that system. You're supposed to get something in return. And we do get something in return. But the system tends to harden. I don't care if it's the old Soviet system, the American system, the British system, any other system. Those who hold power want to stay in power. Therefore there have to be people who always fight the system. There must be burrs under the cow's tail, which I guess is maybe a good description of me.

Heffner: But, Lord Acton said, "Power *tends* to corrupt." I don't think he meant that all power always corrupts. Or is that what you're saying?

I don't remember the words "tends to corrupt."

Heffner: They're there.

. . . I think that, if you look at government today and you see what happens to people like Mike Espy, for example, a man I knew in Mississippi, the first black congressman elected since Reconstruction, who gets sucked into the situation of accepting a few very tiny favors, a little bit of tuition for his girlfriend, for example, a few plane rides, a few motel rooms. All of a sudden, here's a man who has struggled to get into power and after a while becomes just like all the rest. Bernie Sanders, an old-line Socialist, voting for the crime bill with its myriad of death-penalty provisions and war-on-drugs hoopla. It happens to men like Sanders and Espy. They want to stay in power. The only thing that is really a check on them is the people, the voters. If the people act, if the people rise up, they can control their congressmen, their congresswomen, their senators, and so on. That was proven in the 1960s. President Kennedy said in his inauguration address, "I'm going to propose a Civil Rights Act, first one since Reconstruction." For two years Kennedy never took action, until Birmingham went up in flames; and then, of course, he had to act.

Heffner: And so your opinions about Kennedy are very negative.

Because he was just like all the rest. It was the pressure of the people that made him propose [what became] the Civil Rights Act of 1964.

Heffner: Are you saying that Kunstler's sense of the nature of human nature is so totally negative that there should be no governmental structure at all?

Well, there is a structure. And we accept the structure. But what we forget, frequently, is that the people are the real repositories of power. But it has to be exerted against those they elect to office; the representatives they elect have to know there is pressure, not just in writing letters to the editor or making a few speeches in a school auditorium. Out in the streets, that's where you have to be sometimes. And unfortunately, average citizens have forgotten that. They say, "If we elect this congressman or that congressman, it's all going to change." But it doesn't change. The only change comes from the outside, from the people who have the power, who have ceded the power for certain benefits, but who always have the power to stand there and say, "You're doing wrong. I want this or that instead." And to do it in a very positive way, whether by chaining themselves to the White House, as the Suffragettes did, or by the peace marches in the sixties. Whatever the method, power has to be utilized.

Heffner: You talk about the people. And yet, by and large, throughout your career, I think it would be fair to say that the majority of people were opposed to your causes and those you were defending. If there is anything clear about your career, it's that you stood against the crowd. And yet now you express this democratic majoritarian notion.

Dick, have any intelligent people ever really been with the crowd? The crowd believed that the earth was flat, and that you'd fall off it if you sailed too far to the East or West or North or South. The crowd is not the governing factor, the majority; it is the minority people who set the pace for all morality.

Heffner: But you have always sounded as though you were saying, "In the people there is great wisdom."

It's that minority of people who think straight, who are intelligent, who understand the nature of political life in this country. Those are the people I mean. During the sixties, did we have a million out there, two million against the war in Vietnam, who were willing to risk their lives, their liberty, their school careers? We only had a very few who really did that. It's always the few who move the many; never the many who move the few.

Heffner: Then how do you make your judgments about what authority to make use of? Not the authority of majorities. Nor the authority of elected officials. But by the authority of some wisdom, inner wisdom that Kunstler and a few others have. You're talking in elitist terms that I never thought I'd hear from you.

Well, I don't think the word "elitist" is right. I think I understand the political nature of my environment. And I think I've learned it through fifty years of banging around courtrooms north, south, east, and west. I learned how you have to operate in order to move things in this country. So it's realism, not elitism. For example, in the O. J. Simpson case, when I saw that a Japanese-American judge had been assigned to the case, I knew inherently that that was a choice made between a white judge and a black judge. They couldn't appoint a white judge, and they couldn't appoint a black judge, because that would look too bad to segments of the population. So they took a third-world judge, but a careful one, one whose wife was a police officer in the LAPD. And that was done deliberately. Most people would say, 'Well, they must have drawn it out of a hat or a drum." But I know that isn't so. That's just one example of the political maneuvering that goes on. I think if you understand it, you're not an elitist; maybe you're just a realist and you understand the situation. —1994

SOL LINOWITZ

As the twentieth century drew to a close, there was a good deal of "summing up" to be heard from many quarters: "What have we done right? Where have we gone wrong? In the legal profession in particular, many distinguished practitioners felt that the Rule of Law had itself been undermined, that lawyers had many flaws in their conduct to answer for, and that the need for change was great. When we spoke, attorney Sol Linowitz—former chairman of Xerox, U.S. Ambassador to the Organization of American States, conegotiator of the Panama Canal treaties, and President Carter's Ambassador-at-large for Middle East negotiations—had written a book with Martin Mayer entitled The Betrayed Profession. *I began by asking: Who betrayed it? And how? And can it ever again rediscover and reassert its old sense of professionalism?*

The betrayal I talk about is a betrayal from within. That is to say, we lawyers inherited a noble profession, one that represented the apex of community and civic achievement, and we made it into a business.

Increasingly, it has turned into a product-selling operation, where all the nobility of the profession has been lost. And mostly we find ourselves striving for the usual bucks and the bottom line and all these things which have hitherto distinguished a profession from a business. Is there a way we can go back and do the things as were intended to? Yes. I believe we can if we first recognize that things have gone wrong and we need to do something about them. Two, that we recognize that it's a job for the whole profession. And three, that we understand that the practice of law has to do with people, and make it a human profession again . . .

Lawyers are given certain rights; to impose, to summon, to direct, not because we call ourselves lawyers, but because society grants them to us with the understanding that we will accept as well certain responsibilities, certain obligations to that broader society. One of those very great obligations is to serve the people, to be helpful, to undertake to adjust matters that need adjusting, because we uniquely have been given this authority. If we are true to ourselves and to our profession and to our calling, then this will mean a change from many of the things we have been doing. For example, the assumption that we are there to serve clients, period. That's not the fact, and it never has been. The great accomplishments that so many lawyers have had in our history have been, in large part, in dealing with their community, their state, their nation, and helping to deal with problems that are real and that need some kind of solution. Lawyers have seen that as their charge. And therefore we have so many lawyers active in the history of our country, even in the Congress of the United States today. If we believe that that is the true calling of the lawyer, then it's not a matter of saying, "Who says we have to do it?"; it's a matter of saying, "How soon can we get back to doing it?" Because there is no question but that every lawyer will acknowledge that we have a special responsibility.

A lawyer must not only be an advocate for his client; he must be an advocate for law and lawfulness. That's the charge we have . . .

If you practice law the way you should practice law, you must consider the law and lawfulness as your client, and your client as client. In other words, I think you can do both, and must do both, if you're to fulfill your responsibility. And I don't see conflict here. It means that you have to turn away some clients who will want you to do things that your interests in serving law and lawfulness would say you should not do. It means, "The law lets you do it, but don't. It's a rotten thing to do." We must learn how to say, "It's a rotten thing to do, and I won't do it."

Heffner: Yes, but then the question comes up: Doesn't everyone deserve the best representation?

Of course. Edward Bennett Williams, a very distinguished trial lawyer, once told me that he was at a reception and a lady came up to him and said, "Why do you represent someone like Frank Costello?" And he said, "Everyone is entitled to a lawyer." And she said, "But they're not entitled to you." The answer is that lawyers do have a right to discriminate among potential clients, to decide whom to represent or not represent. The lawyer must say to himself, "Maybe I don't believe you. If I don't believe you, I'm not going to represent you well. Maybe I don't like what it is you stand for and the things you're undertaking." There is no question there are enough lawyers who are ready to undertake that kind of representation. Lawyers will be assigned by the courts. When you're assigned you don't have to come in saying, "This is a man I want to represent"; you do it as part of your responsibility. But I'm saying that you have the obligation to select and to do things in a manner that will honor your responsibility to the law and lawfulness.

Paul Freund once said that the three tests for the legal profession are its independence, its accessibility, and its learning. . . . I believe that when lawyers say, "We've got to do it because my client wants me to do it, and I gotta represent him," they are immediately forfeiting their right to be called independent. They are depriving the client of the thing he is most apt to need and to want, and that is the best judgment of the lawyer as to whether what the client wants done should be done. Lawyers have been quick to give that away.

I believe lawyers really are no longer happy with what has happened to their calling, to the way they are regarded and where they come out on the list of the most admired or most despised professions. And it doesn't call for a tremendous change in order to do the things that we know are right. For example, to say that lawyers shouldn't lie does not require a thunderbolt from heaven, you know. Lawyers shouldn't lie. If there are cases where lawyers are arguing for lying, as there are, then they are affecting the way their profession is practiced. It rubs off on all the rest of us. I think the bar associations need to take some action. The American Bar Association, for example, is on an image-building program right now that is costing money. They hope it will do some good. More important by far is what goes on in the actual practice of the law. How many of the lawyers involved in this image-building contribute pro bono work, set an example in their offices for the younger lawyers? They should be showing the way the law is practiced with dignity and nobility. They should do the things that remind the young people, as well as the community at large of these qualities. This is what the practice of law has always meant, and we should go back and start it up again. I think that it could happen. It's a matter of reminding ourselves and insisting, through bar associations and elsewhere, that we've got to get back to earning the respect of the American people.

Heffner: And you believe you can do it, don't you?

And I'll tell you why—I see it as a charge to the profession, to our profession, to lead. See, I believe that we lawyers have a special responsibility, not only for law, but for morals, for ethical standards. No one else has that. You would hope it would come from the church. You would hope it would come from elsewhere. It doesn't. And we lawyers have assumed that as part of our profession. We have, in our charge, the basis for our credo. Other countries have as their totems a piece of land, a building, a crown, something. We have a piece of paper called the Constitution. It's in the National Archives under glass. And who are we? We're the lawyers who are supposed to protect and defend that piece of paper. Therefore, I find that if we're going to have a change of the kind I would like to see and you would like to see, I hope it will be because lawyers have led the way. And I do think it's possible. —1995

OTHER VOICES

Edward Bennett Williams on Defending Unpopular Clients
Board member, ACLU, and attorney for James Hoffa and Senator Joseph McCarthy

My feeling is that almost all human trouble breaks down into trouble that doctors handle, trouble that lawyers handle, and trouble that clergymen handle. Doctors handle physical trouble, lawyers handle trouble of people who are in bad relationships with society, and clergymen handle the field of morals and relationships with God.

Now, nobody would criticize a doctor for taking a patient who was too sick, or it would be a strange doctor indeed who would turn a patient out because he was suffering from some loathsome disease. Nobody would criticize a clergyman because he gave counsel to the worst sinner; as a matter of fact we would be shocked if he turned the worst and most wicked sinner away. They operate in private because what they do is not in the public arena. But when a lawyer gives his counsel to someone who has had the condemnation of society, immediately [the lawyer] needs a defense, because people point at him and say what a shocking thing, that this lawyer should be giving his services and his counsel to this man who is so scorned and degraded.

I think it is a fantastic commentary that we have to defend lawyers for giving their professional services to people who are most in need of them. —1958

Sol Wachtler on Penal Systems

Former Chief Judge of the State of New York, author of After the Madness: A Judge's Own Prison Memoir

Heffner: You write, "If the prisoner is made to feel like garbage when he is in prison, he will for certain act like garbage when he is released."

Well, I make that point in the book, and I illustrate it by telling case histories of various people with whom I came in contact in prison. I felt that way before [going to prison]. I had no sense, though, of the reality of the premise. When you go into prison you are dehumanized. Your self-esteem is taken away from you. There is a philosophy of management which says that if you treat a person like garbage, the person starts thinking of himself as garbage, and then he will be docile and be able to be treated like garbage . . . And so the prison guards have a mentality, some of them—not all of them, but some of them—that they are there to punish. They don't realize that the person is in prison, and that's the punishment. The guards feel that they are there to punish the prisoner. And so they dehumanize the prisoner. They don't look upon the prisoner as a person. They treat him with great indifference. They try their best to lower that person's self-esteem, in a conscious effort to make that person feel like garbage. And then what happens is when the prisoner gets out of prison, he still has that feeling of low esteem, he still feels himself as being garbage, and he acts like garbage. Whereas if you treated these people like people . . . And I'm not saying give them perks and I'm not saying give them luxuries. That's the extreme that people talk about. They say either you treat them like dogs and animals, or else you're treating them as if they're some kind of royalty. I'm not talking about either one of those extremes; I'm talking about treating them as people, with decency. They have to respect the prison discipline, they have to adhere to the rules, they have to recognize the fact that they're there to be punished and will be punished. But not punished by being dehumanized and humiliated. —1997

Stephen G. Breyer on Mandatory Sentencing

Former Chief Judge, U.S. Court of Appeals for the First District, currently Associate Justice, Supreme Court of the United States

Heffner: One of my favorite epigrams—Henry Wriston's insightful "Rules make decision easy, but they rob it of wisdom"—applies here. Do the present sentencing guidelines set by Congress for the Federal Courts rob decision of wisdom?

Yes, of course.

Heffner: Then why should we follow them?

Well, there's a federal district judge I work with every day who goes over cases with me. He knows, by looking at the record and the background of the individual what an appropriate sentence is for a particular crime, say bank robbery, in which $50,000 is stolen with a gun. And I've also met outstanding judges in Texas and in California, and they, too, absolutely know or have a fairly good idea from the record and the background, how a bank robber in similar circumstances should be sentenced. And all three of those judges, Texas, California, and Massachusetts, use wisdom in deciding that sentence, and all three come to totally different results.

Heffner: So?

So, do you think its fair that a person, if he's in California or Texas or Massachusetts, who has the same background and the same crime, gets totally different sentences depending on what judge he happens to face? In New York, you know how they assign judges in cases in the Federal Court? With a wheel. And the defense attorneys insisted on that because they were afraid that the sentence would depend not upon the conduct, or upon the background of the case, but upon the judge. And a system that treats people so differently depending upon what judge you get is a system that isn't terribly fair. And that was Congress's reason for instituting the guidelines.

Heffner: Couldn't a much more knowledgeable critic of the guidelines than I am say to you, "I know a judge in California, a judge in Texas, a judge in Massachusetts, and despite the differences between and among the crimes committed, thanks to these guidelines, they fit into a situation where each defendant or criminal who is convicted has to be sentenced exactly the same way." Is that totally fair?

I can only answer this way—The greatest problems for law are in resolving two basic, conflicting principles. Justice tells us to treat like cases alike. Justice also tells us to treat different cases differently. Treating like cases alike means having rules. Treating different cases differently means having exceptions. Any legal system has to have both. The decision of Congress was that we'd gone way too far in the direction of treating the same cases differently. And therefore we should have rules. Of course there's a risk that those rules will be too rigid. But the way the guidelines operate is this: there are categories, hundreds of categories, and they say to you, the judge, "Judge, if you find a defendant and a crime that fits within this category, you apply it. But if you think that's unfair, you may depart from the guidelines. All you have to do if you depart is to give the reason for your departure from the guidelines." So you either apply the category or you depart. And if you depart, you give your reason. And an appellate court will review your reason for reasonableness. You see, there's an escape hatch built right into the guidelines.

Now, it doesn't work perfectly. And there are lots of complicated reasons why it doesn't. The major one being that Congress has passed a whole lot of different laws which say, irrespective of what the guidelines say, you have to have certain mandatory minimum sentences. That's sort of eroded the system. So it's not perfect by any means, but I think it's a step in the right direction. I think it helps, on balance. —1993

THE MEDIA

BILL MOYERS

Bill Moyers represents the ultimate public spirit in journalism, especially as a chronicler and interpreter of ideas on television. From the Bible and mythology to homelessness and the media, Bill Moyers has been probing, fearless, and just plain interesting, ever since he left Washington and the White House as President Lyndon Johnson's Press Secretary. We touched on a number of hot-button issues, ethical, political, and otherwise, during our conversation in April 2000. I asked him first about his recent comments about "the media giants who treat the conversation of democracy as their private property."

A. J. Liebling, the press critic, once said that freedom of the press belongs to those who own one. And with money dominating our political culture today and with the concentration of media power in fewer and fewer hands, freedom of speech is guaranteed only to those who can afford it. It is very expensive to be heard today. Increasingly, the control over who gets heard, who can speak, who can get on television, who can be heard on the radio, is driven by a few, a handful of key executives at a small number of large corporations. And by the commercial and entertainment value that they put on their programs, their broadcasts, and who gets heard. You know, I'm a fundamentalist when it comes to freedom of speech, to the freedom of assembly, to the First Amendment. I really believe it means what it says in very simple words. And yet, you can have all the free speech you want without its meaning anything if you don't have a forum in which to be heard. And the forums today are increasingly determined by commercial and entertainment values that are set by a growing conglomeration of media giants.

Heffner: What does that do then, to your fundamentalist belief in the First Amendment, in notions of free speech?

I believe that the government should be a mediator in the balance of power in this country. And that one role of all of us acting together, that's what the government is. The government's not some entity out there that exists apart from our process and apart from us. I believe the role of government is to protect the public interest, to make sure that the seesaw of power in America is constantly adjusted so that it doesn't tilt altogether and permanently in one direction. So that organized economic interests, which have a legitimate right to be heard in the democratic process, don't become so dominant that the seesaw is stuck in one position. That it's stuck in a permanent position in which the "haves" are always dominant over those who "have not." There have been two basic powers, two basic sources of contest in American history. One is organized power, the power of organized people—the Labor Movement, the Suffragette Movement, the Civil Rights movement, the movements of people going all the way back to the Shays Rebellion, that try to keep the interest of the "have-nots," the interest of the small people in our society on the stage and in contention with the other dominant interest in our history, which is the power of organized economic interests. And that's seesawed back and forth. Essentially we are a society in which economic interests dominate. That makes us a very conservative society. It took 250 years for slavery to be abolished in this country, and then it required a Civil War because the powers that be would not yield but reluctantly to the evil of slavery. After that it took 100 years to overcome the economic interests that continued to treat the liberated slaves as an economic chattel. It took 200 and some odd years for women to gain the right to vote. The rights of equal citizenship. It took years for the Civil Rights Movement, culminating in the 1960s, to accomplish what the Civil War couldn't accomplish. Look how long it took labor unions, working people to get the right to organize. Every time we have an advance like that, then the forces of reaction set in and try to take it away. No sooner had we reached the triumphs of the Civil Rights Movement in the sixties, the profit interests, the economic interests, the organized interests begin to try to take it back, beginning with an all-out effort in the 1970s, by corporate and business interests and conservative political forces, to create a strategy that has paid off in their world view prevailing today in this country. So that, you know, wages are kept down because it's better for profits, and racism persists because we won't use the government to try to address it. So today it's unbalanced, and to me a symptom of that imbalance is in the domination of the political discourse by commercial media whose main interest is their own bottom line and not the public interest.

Heffner: What to do?

The single most important step we need to take is to reduce the power of private money over public policy. Some call this campaign finance reform. I call it democratic renewal. Politics has become an arms race with money doing the work of missiles. One side escalates, the other side escalates. So that today as everyone knows, it's so obvious it's banal today, most politicians go to the relative handful of people in this country who provide most of the money. There are only 170,000 people in this country who give above $1,000 a year, in an election cycle. So they really do determine the agenda for society. Bill Greider, in his best-selling book a few years ago, *Who Will Tell the People*, says, you know we'll never really have a vital democracy again until the public gets the chance to ask the very same questions that the politicians ask in private—who gets heard, who doesn't get heard? Who is paid, who doesn't get paid? Whose interests are really at stake in this particular issue? So until we own the politicians ourselves, until we have public funding of elections from primaries to the election, we're not going to solve the issue of free speech and even of a free press, because it's going to be those who pay who really play. And I believe most politicians are honorable people who go into public life because they want to make a difference. But they wind up being beholden to those who pay for the elections. And as long as elections are paid for by private interests, then public officials who are elected in those contests are going to be obliged first and foremost to provide access to those who paid for the election.

For example, when the Pakistanis want to have a meeting with Mrs. Clinton who's running for the Senate, they have to put up $50,000 to get some of her time in Staten Island. Roger Tamaraz, the oil man, who paid $300,000 to get a few minutes of Bill Clinton's ear in the White House, when he was called before Senator Fred Thompson's committee on the hearings of the excess of the 1996 campaign, he was asked by an irate, hypocritically irate United States senator, if he voted. And Tamaraz said, "why should I vote, money's more important than voting." Now, until we address that issue . . . we cannot find alternatives to the present system which is driven by monied interests.

Heffner: Then I gather your way of addressing this question is not simply by full disclosure of who contributes, or even in terms of limiting what can be contributed, but rather public funding of our political process.

There are a variety of ways we can address this. One is public funding of our public elections. The other is full disclosure. We've got now the means on the Internet so that, when you give $100,000 to a particular candidate, it can go right on the Internet. Instant disclosure should be a part of this. And yes, I believe in limitations on campaign contributions. The Supreme Court has upheld that. In a recent decision, a very important decision, based on a Missouri case, the Supreme Court said that money is not speech, money is property. So that if a lawyer argues before the Supreme Court, that lawyer gets only 30 minutes of time. Even in the House of Representatives, there are five minute limits put on debate. We limit free speech all the time in the interest of a larger objective. So speech can be limited, contributions can be limited, the courts—the Supreme Court has said—a thousand-dollar limit is Constitutional and it could be that even lesser amounts are Constitutional.

Heffner: Then what are people talking about when they say that the Supreme Court has said that money is speech.

Well the Supreme Court has a divided, schizophrenic approach. It did say that money is speech in the Buckley v. Vallejo decision back in the 1970s. But recently it's been saying unlimited speech is not necessarily healthy or Constitutional. So it's begun to try to see how it can seesaw again, how it can balance the interest of free speech with the interest of the public.

Heffner: What chance do you think there is for us in our present political situation to get the very people who benefit from the excesses of financial contributions to politicians to vote to limit them?

Every poll I have seen, and there is other evidence as well, shows that the majority of the American people want to change the system. So you have in fact a real revolt by the elites in this country. The political elites are in revolt against the will of the people and are using their exalted position to hold on to their power in defiance of the people, hoping to wear down the patience of the people. It's an astonishing moment in American life, in which a handful of political elites, the leaders of both parties, the leaders of both houses in the Congress and the White House are aligned in a cabal of self-interest against the interest of the public. It's astonishing. In every state where public funding of political campaigns has been on the ballot in the last several years, in every state where people have had a chance to vote, to express their opinion, public funding and campaign finance reform have succeeded. In Independent Maine they passed public funding of campaigns. In Liberal Massachussetts they passed public funding of state campaigns. Senator McCain, who is from Arizona, did not just reach up into the sky one day and bring a holy writ down that said "campaign finance reform." He watched what happened in the state of Arizona, where it was presented to the voters. They opted for public funding of state campaigns. Now, he got the message. Would you believe, in the last years of his life, Barry Goldwater, who was not a Liberal Socialist Democrat by any means, said that the single most important issue to the health of our republic, a republic he cared a great deal about, was campaign finance reform. So every time the people have had a chance to act on this, and in every poll that is open and honest, people say, "We want to change the way we finance our elections." But the people running the political process at the top don't want to.

Heffner: Thirty years ago, what was then called The Twentieth Century Fund, established a commission on "Money, Television, and Politics." We weren't concerned about the politicians, we were concerned about the voter. The voter should have time, on broadcasting, to see the candidates. And Tommy Corcoran, who was one of the members of that commission, took me aside and said, "Young man, you think something's going to happen now. Nothing is going to happen. But wait and see, if you're lucky enough to live to be old enough, you will see, not in five years or ten years, but perhaps twenty, thirty, certainly forty years you will see public financing of American politics." You think that's true?

I said to a friend down on Wall Street one day, "What do you think about the market?" he said, "I'm optimistic." And I said, "Well then, why do you look so worried?" And he said, "Because I'm not sure my optimism is justified." I'm an optimist at heart. I have to wake up every morning believing in a confident future and then working to bring it about. Otherwise I think I would sink into cynicism. And I would just resign and go pursue my private and parochial interests. I think most of us are that way. We have to believe in an optimistic future. But I'm also a realist, and I know the forces and powers that are arrayed against what we're talking about. I do believe in the long run it will happen. Because if it doesn't we have lost our democracy. The rich should be free to buy as many homes as they want, as many cars as they want, as many vacations as they want, as many gizmos as they want. But the rich should not be free to buy more democracy than anyone else. George Will, the Conservative columnist, recently wrote an article which goes to the heart of the establishment thinking today. He says, "Where does this idea come from that citizens are supposed to be politically equal?" You know that's not a Conservative position, that's a Reactionary position, that's a Tory position. That's the position of the propertied, economic muscular class of society. And it's wrong. If we don't change it, if we don't root it out, it's going to destroy America and make us into two nations. This issue of who owns the politicians, who owns the country, is the moral equivalent of slavery and abolition, women's suffrage, the Civil Rights Movement and the right of people to organize. In time it has to happen or we won't be living in the same country.

I run a foundation that several years ago decided that campaign finance reform, democratic renewal, was our major priority. And we set out to achieve this in three ways. One, we fund grass-roots activity to try to change the system at the local level. Then we fund investigative reporting because people need to know the connection, need to see what the pattern is. And we fund legal strategies. And a lot of progress has been made. But the more progress that's been made, the more entrenched and defiant the political elites become. But I have to believe it will happen, just as the slaves had to believe they would one day be free. That women had to believe they would one day vote and be politically equal. And as workers believe they could one day have a decent life with a steady income, pensions and health insurance. I just have to believe that or I would give up.

Heffner: You're also very much concerned about fairness in the media, aren't you?

The Fairness Doctrine, as you know from your own days as a pioneer in this field, essentially said that if you used the public airways, if the network or a broadcaster gives you time to make your point, or on the other hand attacks you, you should have time to get your own point across, to answer, to get your word out.

Heffner: Pretty elementary, isn't it?

It's very elementary. First, because it's right for democracy, and second, it seems a logical concession to ask of a commodity, air time, that belongs to all of us theoretically. How can you take this section of air time and sell it to CBS, or take this amount of air time and sell it to Disney. In a sense these people who own the airways are mere renters of public space. The people are the landlords, and the networks are the tenants. And so when they take this public space and use it only for their own interests, only for their own value system, with no sense of the public interest, then they're not being fair. And the Fairness Doctrine worked pretty well for something that was intended, as you know, to try to keep the balance, to prevent a monopoly of opinion in this country. But in the 1980s, under pressure from the National Association of Broadcasters and the ideological Right Wing that came to power with Ronald Reagan and under the influence of campaign contributions to members of Congress in both parties, the Fairness Doctrine disappeared. It was revoked in effect, and the odds of getting it back are less today than I thought ten years ago. But it's still a good notion and people should be held to it even if there's no law requiring it.

Heffner: But what about our friend Fred Friendly, who said it had a chilling effect on the freedom of the broadcaster.

I never agreed with Fred on that. I believe that it made the broadcaster wary of arrogance. I believe it made the broadcaster think twice about having only one view. I mean, you can go to ABC News today. ABC News, ABC radio, is essentially just a Right-Wing organ. Should free speech be determined by the fact that Right-Wingers can get sponsors, corporate sponsors for their views when people who have dissenting opinions cannot? I don't think that's right. Fred never really addressed that issue. In my opinion, he never really addressed the issue beyond the fact that broadcasters would be chilled. But remember also that broadcasters could be frozen in their own ideological conformity if there weren't some means of challenging them, of holding them to a different standard.

Heffner: But let's go back to the notion that we both want to see the Fairness Doctrine in place, although I suspect that you, like myself, would prefer that it be an FCC rule rather than a law.

Oh, yes. I think the FCC should take the initiative in this.

Heffner: Okay, but there were those who said, "Look, you fellows are free-speechers, you supposedly believe in free speech, but you now want to make us put someone on the air, 'our' air (I'll admit you will deny that it's 'their' air). You're going to make us 'speak' in a way that we don't want to speak. That's not free speech."

The Chairman of the FCC could say, "Well, we're not going to make you say anything. We're just going to require that in, in response to making so much money from renting this public property, you have to make sure that the voices that do get heard represent a wider array of opinion." What's wrong with that? You seem to be holding out the argument, supporting the argument that because organized money can buy the method of delivering the information they have the right to determine, exclusively, what messages get heard. I just can't accept that.

Heffner: Don't misunderstand me. I don't agree with that for a moment. What I'm saying is that's precisely what the broadcaster says. He says, "I want to do this broadcast, I want to reveal this evil in our society. But I'm afraid to do so, the Fairness Doctrine has chilled my willingness and my ability to do that. So rather than be an investigative reporter but then have a demand made that I give time to someone else and then someone else and then someone else in the name of fairness, I'm just not going to conduct this investigation on the air at all."

I wish that journalists in that case would say it's not even a question of fairness, it's a question of defining the news. To define the news so that it isn't just one side of things, you know. You get today an ideological world view in which, for example, business journalism reports the news only as stockholders and corporate executives define the news. You rarely get anything on the news about how this affects working people. I mean, it looks to me every day as if the newspapers and the broadcasters are saying that the only news that counts is the news of what happens to a stock, what happens to an investor. Never the news of what happens to the worker, what happens to the family affected by downsizing, or the person who loses health insurance. You know, on Bill Clinton's watch, one million people every year lost their health insurance. Today, over 43 million people don't have it. But you almost never see stories about these people on commercial television. You get the statistics quoted in the *New York Times*. Why shouldn't journalism hold itself to a higher standard than the government could ever require it to do.

Heffner: Suppose the journalist's answer is, or at least the broad-caster's answer is, "Look, there is such a thing as cultural democracy. Moyers, don't you believe in democracy? This is what the people vote for. This is what they want to see. We give the people what they want to hear and to see."

A child growing up gets to eat what's put on the table. And in our culture, in which the table is set by very powerful organized economic interests whose main, whose only concern is their own well-being, the table is set to define the choices very narrowly. Now, I agree with you, it would be very hard for government to say, "Put more food on the table, or put different food on the table." But popular pressure, organized consumers—I call it "citizen activity"—could try to bring changes into being, and I think ultimately that's what it has to be. It is going to take organized political and citizen activity in order to say to these interests, "What's on the table is not what ought to be there. We need a more balanced diet."

Heffner: Bill, what evidence do you have that indeed most people in this country feel that way? Aren't most people saying "Oh, Moyers, go away, don't bother us, we don't want to see those things that you think would be good for us. Well, maybe it's not that we don't want to see them, it's just that we'd rather be entertained."

I don't argue against the fact that people want television to entertain them. Look even PBS did a survey a few years ago which said that most people, when they come home, don't want to be bothered with the real toils of the day that have exacted such a price. They want escape. They want to be distracted from the woes and wails of the world for that time. I don't argue with that. I, myself, like entertainment. I like football on television. I like good drama on television. I like certain sitcoms on television. I'm not saying that other material ought to be mandated. I'm saying that simply there ought to be a wider offering to the public than what we get, when human beings are defined only as consumers. If you start thinking of people as citizens as well as consumers, then you provide the kind of information that helps those who take their citizenship seriously with the means of acting in a way that is informed and enables them to make better choices.

Heffner: But haven't we created from the beginning a broadcast system for consumers? Not for students. And isn't our basic problem that we've made this magnificent instrument simply and for the most part an instrument for making profit?

Yes. Broadcasting long ago set itself firmly within the rules of the economic game, and made its peace with the little (although they're not so little anymore) lies of merchandising and selling. And that set the course. It wasn't intended to be that way. Early on, as you know, even Herbert Hoover extolled the airways as a force for education, as a force for civic knowledge and civic action. He didn't want them to become commercial property. But the nature of human beings being what it is, broadcasting was turned into a commercial entity.

Heffner: Then how do we possibly make changes?

I don't think we'll change broadcasting. Oh, there may occasionally arise, although it's hard to see who they are, some voices within the networks, some journalists who rise as Edward R. Murrow did and challenge the owners to a greater standard of stewardship. I think the most important lesson to learn from the past is not to let happen to the Internet what happened to broadcasting. As you know, the fight is on right now in America to determine whether the Internet is going to be free-access or it's going to be decided by corporate and business monopolies alone. That's a big issue of public policy that is rarely debated because the powers-that-be don't want you to know about it.

Heffner: Don't you think that, by and large, it has already been decided?

By and large, yes, but it's not altogether too late. And I think there's truth in the cliché that the Internet has made all of us actors and players and journalists. So that I think, I hope, that people watching, people who are Libertarians and others who care about this, Liberals and Conservatives and others who care about free speech for citizens, send a message to the powers-that-be, that we don't want it to go the way that commercial broadcasting has gone.

Heffner: You've said that essentially you're an optimist, essentially you're not down, you're up. But I'm not that kind of optimist and I wonder whether we don't have to prepare ourselves for more and more and more bad news, so to speak. I don't know how we protect ourselves against it. But there is no sign that I see that we're going to reverse the consumerism that dominates American life.

Nor are we going to reverse the conglomeration that dominates American life. Increasingly fewer and fewer megacorporations will own the means of commercial broadcasting, the means of commercial information, this new nation of information. But we have to constantly keep finding ways to kill the censor. That's what democracy is all about. That theoretically, the First Amendment gives us the right to climb up on the deck of the ship and grab the pilot by the elbow and shake him and say, "That's an iceberg out there, that's an iceberg out there." Now the *Titanic* struck and went down. And democracy can do that, too. But you have to keep talking about this, you have to keep agitating, you have to keep doing whatever one can in one's own sphere to find ways to kill the censor. Government becomes a censor, you've got to kill that. Corporations become censors, you've got to kill that. You have to find ways to infect the system with an antibody against the uniformity, the conformity and the orthodoxy that prevails any time any given group of people have too much power in society. Whether they're in Congress or the White House, or sitting in Black Rock at CBS here in New York, or at Yahoo or Time Warner. You've got to keep finding, and fighting for, ways to keep the system as open as possible so that somebody can rise up someday with just enough truth to kill the censor and change the public perception.

Heffner: I like that traditional American approach you have, which is one of seeking balance, always of checking and balancing. And I wonder what role your colleagues, the journalists could possibly play when so many of them say, "We don't have any power, there's no one in here but us chickens. Don't impose responsibilities upon us, we're just reporting it as it is." What are you going to do with your fellow professionals?

I admire them as friends, and as colleagues. But they do have a certain power, the anchors of the three networks. The three network evening newscasts (there are four now, with Fox). They are watched by a lot of people. Relatively not as many people as used to, but still a lot of people. Ten million people, let's say, watch each of those evening broadcasts. And the anchors, all of whom have titles such as "Managing Editors," have power over those 22 minutes of turf. They can decide what signs get posted on that turf, every night. Is it the sign that displays real people, out in the country doing real things. Or is it, are the signs pointing to a lead opinion, business interest, etc. They determine that agenda every night. I would say to Dan and Tom and Peter, "You determine . . . you have the power either to say, 'Look this is my show in a sense and I'm a journalist and I want only what I want.' " Or to say, "Find somebody else to do it, and I'll do something else."

Heffner: Bill Moyers is a pretty good example of that, isn't he? In a very real sense you opted not to continue in commercial television. You opted to do the work you do in public television for the most part.

I couldn't do the work on commercial television that I want to do and I wouldn't stay around and do the work just because I could do it. I mean I've got a six-hour series that looks at end-of-life care, death and dying. My producers [did] a marvelous job, six hours on a subject that people don't want to discuss, except they talk about it all the time. I would never have gotten that on commercial television. The two-hour documentary we took ten years to film on the working class family was watched by something like three or four million people. Could have been seen by 12 or 13 million people if it was on commercial television. But I would never have gotten it there. So I'd settle for the three million people who watch it and who are now aware of what's happening to working families in this country. . . . But that's a personal choice, that comes out of one's nature. It's not any kind of moral stance that says "Aha, if you'd only do it my way, you'd be a better person." I mean this is the only way I could have done it. There are moments when I wish I could have stayed within the commercial system and nudged it in the direction of the kind of journalism I believe in. But I couldn't do it. Fortunately, I was able to go out and raise the funds. I raise every penny of every production we put on public broadcasting, take no money from public broadcasting to do what I do. I raise it from a very good corporation, Mutual of America, that has been with me for ten years, and from foundations that believe in this kind of journalism. And I'm awfully glad I've done it. I've had a good life. Do I think it's changed anything? No, I don't know how you change things, you just keep doing what you do and hope that sooner or later . . .

Heffner: What do you mean you don't know whether it's changed anything?

Well, here we're talking about all the things it hasn't changed.

Heffner: Yes, but you must believe, since you're the optimist, you must believe that there is always that potential for change.

I do. I believe that. This is a traditional American view. Whitman said, "Be radical, be radical, but not too damned radical." And by being radical he simply means try to keep the record straight. I think in time if you do keep the record straight, somebody acts on it. I come from a part of the country that suffered miserably, as did the whole country, because we killed the truth. We drove the truthsayers out of the pulpits, drove the truthsayers out of the editorial offices, drove the truthsayers out of the classrooms, those who tried to tell the truth about slavery. And as a consequence of that the South, living in its official view of reality, living in its closed world of justification of slavery, went to war with the rest of the nation. We're still suffering from that failure of politics, failure of journalism, failure of the church and failure of education, to deal with the truth about slavery.

I was part of an administration, the Johnson Administration—I was Press Secretary for the last two years of my stay there—that closed the wagons around ourselves in response to Vietnam. The truth didn't get in very easily and finally, when it didn't get in, we all shared the same view of the world, the same view of Vietnam. As a consequence of that, terrible things happened, and the Administration failed. Lyndon Johnson died a tragic former President, and the country and the Vietnamese went through a horrible thing. Why? Because the contrarian voices, the alternative view of reality, never really penetrated to the consciousness of the decision-makers. In no small part, it isn't some high moral principle that drives me to want to believe that setting the record straight is the best thing a journalist can do. It is simply the practical reality of what happens when a society, a culture, an organization, a mind, a school, a community, a family, just lives by its own law, and lives by its own reality, not aware that there are many realities out there that have to be accommodated and addressed and acted upon if we're going to have a healthy, human society. And so it's a very practical consequence of a Civil War that almost destroyed the nation, and of a Vietnam War that destroyed an Administration and tore the country apart, that makes me think you have to be hopeful about this, you have to keep agitating for this, you have to be radical, although in my own case, not too damn radical. —2000

DAN RATHER

As the emcee on the rubber-chicken circuit says, "Here is a man who needs no introduction."

Dan Rather has been a fixture on network television and one of America's notable broadcast journalists for many decades—still going strong, and still aspiring to follow in the Edward R. Murrow tradition. When we talked in late 1994, issues of media policy and responsibility, and the increasing "Hollywoodization" of television, were very much in the forefront. Rather's intimations of a somewhat positive future are yet to be fully realized, but remain a necessary reminder for every thoughtful citizen. I had asked him a question about his motives for a speech he had recently given to the Radio and Television News Directors Association that closely paralleled one our mutual role model had given to the same group back in 1955.

I think it is one of the three or four most important things that Ed Murrow accomplished in a life of accomplishment. What that speech to the Radio and Television News Directors Association did was to keep the flame alive. Yes, the flame has flickered, and I think now flickers dangerously close to being extinguished. Without Murrow's speech, I'm not sure that the flame would've survived the four or five years that followed. It was a critical time in the history of American television. And so I think that's what it accomplished. And I have no reluctance to say that, with myself, as with so many other people who were at that time entering television news, an unknown world, all uncharted water, and is still uncharted in many important ways, what Murrow gave us was a polar star. When you lose your way, you want to know, "Where am I? Who am I? Whither the voyage?" You can always look to the polar star of Murrow's great speech. Which is what

I tried to do in my own small and, I fear, ineffectual way. I tried to return to that navigational star, and to, I hope, gently suggest to others that we need to take a new bearing on that polar star.

Heffner: But you know, it's interesting, Mr. Rather, when you yourself addressed the RTNDA, there was silence when you finished, then shortly after, a standing ovation. What about the fear that you had addressed? You said, "The fear factor freezes us. The greatest shortage on every beat and at every newsroom in America is courage." Now, they got up and cheered. What good do you think that will do?

I'm not sure it will do any, over the long pull. In the short run, I think it did do at least some good. For at least a short period of time, in that it may have encouraged a few. Next to courage is the habit of just stopping to think, even for a few seconds, which is in short supply in every newsroom, particularly those who deal with daily news. And my hope at the time was, and it has been realized to at least a small degree, that at least some few would begin to stop and think and say, as they did that night, "Gosh, how do we respond to this? It's a truth." We all knew it to be truth, and I tried to pick, as Ed Murrow did, the right place at the right time. These were peers of mine. These were people who do, in one way or another, what I do. And I think they recognized, "Whew, he's speaking the truth, and we all know it. It's a tough truth, but it's the truth." But there was silence, saying, "How should we react to this?" And then, I thought the applause was not for me, but for the ideas and the ideals that had been restated basically from Murrow's original talk. Now, not everybody walked out of the room rededicated to stop, think, make a little noise about what we know is untrue. But some did. And I can see it in some places. . . .

Heffner: A few years, two years after his 1958 address, Ed was out.

Yes. As I said in my speech, they cut him out, they cut him down, and they cut him up.

Heffner: How can you balance out the inequities here? He spoke as a newsman. You speak as a newsman. But you're speaking about the masters of the media. You're speaking about the conclusions drawn, the decisions made, not by fellow newsmen, but by the people who own the franchises.

Well, there's no reconciling this.

Heffner: They weren't the ones who stood up and applauded, I imagine.

No. Some of them, had they been there, I think, would have. I'm chided by colleagues of mine who say, "Dan, you're really kidding yourself now." But some of them would have. But many would not. And this is the problem. There is, as Ed Murrow said, a struggle between doing right and doing well, in the business sense. The trying-to-do-right reporter in the newsroom sees that through one prism. Those who own the local television station, or, for that matter, own the network, see it through yet another prism. And this, in some ways, is where the two worlds collide. We all want to do right and do well. This was Ed Murrow's point. It gets out of balance, and can get out of balance very quickly when you're dealing with the huge sums of money that are involved in the profits of any commercial television enterprise in this country. Pick one. The worst commercial television makes a lot of money. The worst-run operation. It's almost impossible to lose money in commercial television. Nobody really likes to talk about this very much. The problem isn't, well, we have to make money. That's not the problem. . . . The problem—I see this from, admittedly, the prism of my own prejudices, which is a newsroom prejudice—is that the pressure's always on to make increasing sums of money each quarter and each year. The profits have to be better every time around. I have been there. These stories are not apocryphal. You walk in to a manager—not necessarily a leader; there's a difference between a leader and a manager—and say, "We'd like to do this program. We must do this program, because the public needs to understand what's happening in"—pick a place; Bosnia right now would be a good example—the manager will look you in the eye, and has looked me in the eye, "Dan, you're right. I'd love to do this program. It needs to be done. But let me tell you, my back's to the wall here. Our ratings are not as good this quarter as they were last quarter. And if the ratings are not better next quarter, I'm out of here. And you're talking about a program that is going to play next quarter or maybe the quarter after that. So get out of here and don't talk this madness."

Now, here's the point of taking you through that. I'm not sure that viewers understand that that's the reality. It's the reality, yes, for the Dan Rathers of the world, but even more so for the local station news director, or the local anchor who does read, study, and really wants to do right. You're constantly running up against wanting to do well, financially.

Heffner: Well, let me ask you then whether there was a kind of copping-out when you read with approval from Ed's address, and what he said, to begin with, was, "There is no suggestion here that networks or individual stations should operate philanthropies." But in fact, perhaps it's only philanthropies in which you will not find the question, "What did you do for me this fiscal week or month or year? Did you do better?" I remember very well, in my CBS days, the point was, if you weren't increasing the profit each year, then you were well on your way out.

True.

Heffner: So, isn't it a copout to say that it's possible within the context of the present system to do what you think, as a premier newsman, should be done?

No, I don't think so. And you and I may disagree about this. I do believe in the marketplace. I do believe that competition even, yes, even for ratings and for profit, can, and in some important ways, makes us all better. Here's why I don't think it's a copout. There was a time, and it hasn't been that long ago, when there was a much stronger element of this kind of thinking. "Yes, I own a commercial television operation, whether it be small station or a huge network. And yes, I'm constantly trying to get the ratings up, and constantly getting the profit up. But I do have a public responsibility to deliver public service." Now, let's not kid ourselves. Part of that was because, at the time, there was government regulation. The federal government, the FCC. There was a threat. If you don't do that, your license to operate your station might be suspended. While no network was licensed, as we know, the core business of networks are the owned and operated stations that they have in very large markets—New York, Philadelphia, Chicago, and so on—well, there was always this threat, sometimes only implied, that if you didn't subscribe to that notion, which is to say, yes, you're supposed to make profits, yes, you're supposed to drive for higher ratings, but you do have a responsibility to perform public service, you'd run the risk of license suspension. And news was seen as the core of that public-service component. Here's the point: I don't think it's a copout to say that the best of people in commercial broadcasting can yet be brought back around to the idea that, of course we drive for profits, of course we drive to deliver them to our stockholders, of course we want ever-increasing ratings. But when it comes to two percent, five percent, ten percent, fifteen percent of our schedule, we have an obligation to perform public service. Part of what I got out of Ed Murrow—and I say without apology that I hold him to this day in tremendous awe—is Murrow had the idea, I think he got it out of newspapering, that a public journal is a public trust, and that what everybody in broadcasting holds, some in larger measure than others, is a public trust. So if you're going to meet the responsibilities of that public trust, then you have to deliver a certain amount of public service.

Now, say, somewhere in the early-to-mid-1980s, you could go in to the worst of television station managers and get their attention, at least their attention, by saying, "I'm here to talk about public service. We need to perform this public service." Now, we are very close, very close, to having entertainment values so overwhelming everything in television that nobody will even listen to you when you talk public service. That's one reason I want to speak out . . . This is not original with me . . . I got most of it from Ed Murrow. This is what I talk about with the flame.

Heffner: What rekindles it?

Well, I'm pausing only because of some fear, speaking of fear, that this could be misunderstood. It comes from, first of all, a love of country. I still believe that there are enough people around, even among what used to be called the "captains of industry," who are beginning to understand that in a way the whole country is falling victim to Hollywoodization. Not just news, not just what's on television. But something's happening in the country. And each of us within ourselves must start saying, "Listen, part of my life has to be dedicated to something larger than just ever-greater profits or ever-greater ratings." That's where it will come from. And about that you can say, well, you're overly idealistic about it and, "Dan Rather, I wish it were true. But it isn't going to happen." Yet I think I can see and hear and feel some of it happening in my own business. They are small indicators. I see them myself. . . . I'm beginning to see some people who not very many years ago—I'm talking about in the late '80s, early '90s—said, "Listen, Dan," in effect, "get out of the way. What we're about are ratings and profits." And I was saying, "Well, you know, the country really does need for people to understand what happens in places like China." There's a tremendous story in China. You very seldom see it on television, because there is a school of thought that says it's a long way from Broadway, and foreign news doesn't sell, international coverage is passe, all of those things. I see the pendulum not swinging back, but just barely nudging back to enough people. And it only takes a few good people—a few good people can make a decisive difference—who say, "Listen, for this time, ratings won't matter. For this time, profits won't matter. It's too important to put it only through the Hollywood consideration, the entertainment values. There's too much at stake." Now, if I'm wrong about that, than all is lost. But I don't think all is lost.

Heffner: So, in a sense, you're saying there are more and more individuals in the news business who are rethinking current trends.

Yes. I see that. I wouldn't kid anybody. And I try very hard not to kid myself. We're not talking about a lot of people. Part of what I tried to talk about in Miami, at one point I said, "Listen, I'm not talking about some hero who is willing to take the spear in the chest. I understand, and I want almost desperately for viewers to understand this reality. I want people to understand what it's like, what it's really like on the inside as opposed to what they may perceive it to be." And there is a great deal of difference. Your average local station news director—we're not talking about people who operate at the network level, who have it better, bad as people such as myself may think it is on any given day—your average local station news director is a person who got into journalism because he or she was idealistic. That person, metaphorically, almost every day has their back to the wall, their shirttails on fire, the bill collectors at the door, and there's somebody with a straight razor right at their throat. And, yes, little droplets of blood are beginning to come down the straight razor. What I mean by that is the pressures on them are enormous. It's the overnights. "I've seen last night's overnights, and I'm going to tell you our newscast last night was down three-tenths of one percent." This is the reality for news directors all over the country.

Now I do find there are increasing numbers of people—it's not a wave, it's not a whole counterrevolution—but one by one there are people who are saying, "I'm going to say no. I'm going to say, 'Okay, our overnights were down last night, but I'm asking you sir, or madam, to understand that what we led with last night was important. And while it may have taken us down on the overnights, over the long pull, if we keep our credibility up, I'll be able to deliver ratings for you.' "

Heffner: All in all, have mass media in this country served the American people well?

Overall and in the main, I think the answer is yes. I suppose that's the expected answer from me. Yes, I think the American public has been well served by mass media. But I'm very worried about some current trends, including those of the effect of what I've called the Hollywoodization of the news on my craft, which is journalism.

Heffner: But has the public been served by mass media well enough?

No.

Heffner: Okay. Then what would you add?

Well, it certainly has not served our people well enough. Let's face it, journalism does in many ways exist to produce profit for owners and stockholders. And I think the public-service part of the formula, has been reduced tremendously. . . . And increasingly so. Let me put it this way, if it was true in, let's say, 1957, just before Edward R. Murrow made his never-to-be-forgotten address to the radio and television news directors in Chicago, that, say, 15 percent of the overall schedule at most radio and television stations was given over to what we might describe as public service—that, by the way, does not mean it didn't make money; I would include news broadcasts in there—if it was 15 percent in 1957, it's no more than one and a half or two percent now, in my judgment. And soon to disappear unless we begin to talk about it, debate it. The most important thing is to get a consensus among the American viewing and listening publics that they will not stand for what's happening, which is that the only standard by which anybody's work is measured is whether or not it increases circulation or ratings and profits.

Heffner: But just a second. You say, "The American people will not stand . . ." If they weren't standing for it, they'd be turning it off. In fact, the broadcasters frequently say they're simply meeting the expressed interests—maybe not the public interest—of the American public.

. . . One of the principal critics at the *New York Times* has written of me, in effect, "Rather is Don Quixote here." And this is amost a direct quote. "The public is demanding what it is getting. And who is Mr. Rather or anybody else to say that the public wants anything else?" Well, I don't agree with that. First of all, there's a mistake to talk about the public as one. Listen, this is the United States of America. This is a country made up of individuals, a lot of individual thought, so even if you take—and I do not—[that] most people would rather watch something about the Bobbitts or the Menendezes or the O. J. Simpsons, than they would about Bosnia or Somalia or Haiti. . . . there is a very large segment of the American public that wants to know, that doesn't simply want to be titillated. They may at any given hour want to be titillated. They may love to read gossip. But they also want something of real substance. Increasingly, I think, anybody in commercial television, is going to have to choose what audience to appeal to as a core audience. The *New York Times* is a very profitable enterprise. So it will become with broadcasting, in my opinion.

But we've strayed from your point. You say, "Listen, if the public wants all this other stuff, why not just give it to them?" And the answer is, you know, it is important what you think of yourself.

Heffner: Yes, but it's not so much "Why not just give it to them?" It's—"Why be critical when what the broadcaster is doing, seemingly, is responding to the needs of what mutual friends of ours once called "cultural democracy"? We go in and we vote. And we don't say that there are some people who don't want Richard Nixon, or there are some people who don't want Lyndon Johnson. The majorities have voted as they have. So with cultural democracy. Switch the dial.

Ah. But we know that the key to a viable democracy is respect for the minority. And while it is true that you say, "Okay, people vote, and we're going to have Richard Nixon or Bill Clinton as President," that's true; but you don't say, "That's the only thing that the country thinks about. That's the only way the country operates over the next four years in the case of a Presidential election." Now, this is exactly my point about what I'd call a "quality journalism," or integrity-based journalism. Simply because at any given moment someone says, "Well, most people don't want this," doesn't mean that you eliminate it. This is my argument with people who make this very flawed argument.

There is another thing. It's that sometimes people don't know what they want until they're given an opportunity to sample it. Sometimes people don't know what they're interested in until and unless they're shown why they should be interested. And I'll give you a very good example. Before the events of Tiananmen Square in China at the end of the 1980s, if you went out and used the cultural democracy argument, you sent out to the malls and said, "Here are a list of 35 stories. Tell me which ones you're interested in." China would have been 33 or 34. So, if you took the view, if you carry this to its ultimate, and said, "Well, okay, people are not interested in China. Therefore, the CBS Evening News shouldn't do anything about China. CBS News shouldn't be in China. We have a cultural democracy here. We've gone out, we've taken a survey, we've taken a poll, people say they aren't interested in China. So don't cover China." But when we thought we smelled a story in China and we went and we said to people, "Listen, in a country of well over a billion people, a country that may be a major power in the twenty-first century, a great volcano of change is bubbling up from the bottom." You know what? China went then from number 33 and number 34 on the list of stories people were interested in, right up to the top. Because, why? Because they were shown why they should be interested in it.

Now, follow the thought through. Taken to its ultimate, this business of, well, ask people what they want, and if they say they want the O. J. Simpson case, then give them that and give them only that, is very flawed thinking, and, I think, quite dangerous thinking for a democracy such as ours.

Heffner: Let me ask you about something else, about the Fairness Doctrine. I know broadcasters have always spoken about the chilling effect of the Fairness Doctrine, the idea that opposing views must be given a hearing on the air. As a longtime newsman, what's your own feeling about that?

I've changed my opinion about this . . . since the effort to . . . demolish the Fairness Doctrine. Some version of it may be necessary if you're going to have anywhere close to a level playing field for debate. The best evidence is what's happening now with so-called talk radio. If you tune in so-called talk radio—which I try to do, because I do think it's one way to stay in touch—you will hear, in some cases, hour after hour of the most racially divisive talk, the most incendiary racial talk that you can imagine, with nothing to balance it off, nothing that says, "Wait a minute." You hear hour after hour of it. So I find myself saying, I say, "There has to be somebody who says, 'Listen, you can't do this hour after hour all day long without putting, at least giving a little bit of daylight to another side.'" So I'm troubled. I think we may have been too quick to do away with the Fairness Doctrine.

Heffner: But what about the reasons why so many broadcasters were in favor of doing away with it? The chilling effect?

I subscribed to that argument at the time. Listen, you need to have unfettered debate. But now we get back to who controls the medium. My concern, the chilling effect argument was, well, listen, if you have a requirement, this Fairness Doctrine, then this encourages people not to put on controversial subjects, not to have people speak their mind because they're afraid they're going to have to put on somebody from the other side. We went from that, if that was too far in one direction, and I think it probably was, we're now very rapidly reaching the point when we're too far in the other direction, because we have only one point of view. I use racism because I'm very deeply concerned about some of the things that are said about race now on radio. Those who were in favor of doing away with the Fairness Doctrine would say, "Well, that's the way people talk, and that's what's out there." But, I get back to the point that if you have four or five hours a day of only one point of view at base being, "Listen, they—" whomever they may be, black people, Hispanic people, women, or whatever—"are causing all the problems," and you don't have somebody else who says, "Wait a minute, this is very flawed thinking," I begin to worry about discourse in a democracy such as ours.

Heffner: Do you think there are others, a substantial number of others in the field who are beginning to feel that way, too?

No, I don't. I'd have to be candid with you and say that I'm in a distinct minority. Indeed, I find most of the people in the field who say, "Dan, you're dead wrong about this. Doing away with the Fairness Doctrine was one of the best things that happened to broadcasting."

Heffner: Well, let's get at the issue another way. At times I've asked newspeople whether they aren't historians, and whether they don't have the professional obligations of the historian for measure, for balance, for fairness. I get a very negative answer usually when I ask that question, I get the answer, "We're not educators, we're not historians; we're newsmen." What's your response?

I don't want to give you a negative answer. I think we have an obligation for fairness. I think what you'll find with most journalists, including this one, is a little reluctance to describe ourselves as anything but a journalist. I'm a reporter.

Heffner: Why are you unwilling to be regarded as an historian of the present, even if not of the past?

Well, a lot of reasons, not the least of which is that, you know, the worst thing one can say about a reporter is he has pretensions. So if you start talking about being a historian, we're a long way from seeing a reporter as yet another whiskey-breathed, nicotine-stained, stubble-bearded fellow with his shirttail out. We're a long way from that. But still—and I include myself in this—there's a reluctance to say we're anything as fancy as historian. What we do is to make that proverbial first draft of history. There is a component of the historian in what we do. But journalism is something separate and apart, but, there is a requirement for fairness. I don't like the word "balance"—too long to go into—but if you say "balance," "balance" to me says, "Well, okay, if you run 14 inches in your newspaper about one side, then you must run 14 inches on the other side. Or if you give 14 minutes of a broadcast"—that'd be a long time in today's television—"to one subject, then you must give it . . ." Look, not every story has two sides. Some stories only have one side. Some stories have 14 sides. So "balance," I think, is a dangerous word for us. But "fairness," absolutely. The twin pillars of journalism of integrity are accuracy and fairness.

Now, your point. When we are making this first draft of history, I do think that we have an obligation to be as fair as possible. And one of the great failings—and I include myself in this—is too often we forget that.

Heffner: Don't you feel that the first draft is, in a very real sense, the most important draft? Isn't it the most memorable draft?

Well, in many ways and many times it is the most memorable. I'm reluctant to say it is the most important, because I think this is one difference between historians and journalists. Certainly a first impression is a very important impression, and in some ways is the most important impression. If you go to a new country, sometimes your first impressions are the most vivid and the most important. But historians have an obligation to go back and look at things with perspective. A tough word for any journalist. Particularly with television—I said before and I say again—we have difficulty with perspective. And when you're writing history on the fly, when we're making this first draft, it's very difficult to give context, perspective, and background. That's what the historian, with the benefit of hindsight and the benefit of documents, [can give] which, to take one example, your average journalist never gets a chance to see as he's writing this history on the fly. I think the historian has a better shot at true accuracy than writing the first draft as journalists do. —1994

FRED FRIENDLY

Though little known to the general public, Fred W. Friendly was a truly Olympian figure in the last half-century of the history of American journalism. For many years a partner, coproducer, and collaborator with Edward R. Murrow in numerous distinguished broadcast ventures, he went on to preside over the CBS News Division during its glory years. Leaving commercial television at the height of his powers, he devoted enormous energy to teaching, foundation work, and a variety of ventures in public television. When we spoke in 1990 about "the power of the media," I described Fred Friendly as forever "demanding, cajoling, insisting, pushing and pulling—and always achieving—in the cause of broadcast journalism excellence." I asked my guest about how often he quoted Mr. Justice Potter Stewart as saying that the trouble with broadcasters is that they focus on what they have the right to do, rather than what the right thing to do is.

The circumstances under which he said that are interesting and relevant. We were at Independence Hall, doing a television series on the Constitution, and at a point he stopped and he said to me, "Fred, the trouble with your profession—journalism—is that you fellows are all mixed up about the difference between what you have a right to do under the Constitution, under the First Amendment, and the right thing to do." And, of course, he was absolutely right that because a court can't stop us from publishing something, doesn't make it right to reveal it if it invades somebody's privacy, or if it's going to hurt somebody terribly, or if it's not true, or if it's gossip, or if it's irrelevant and just in the name of gossip. Potter was absolutely right.

Heffner: He was right, too, in what he had to say about obscenity.

He always used to say he would be remembered and it would be on his tombstone . . . it isn't, actually, but the line which he said in an opinion was, "I can't define vulgarism, or obscenity, but I know it when I see it." And, of course, it is true that no court has ever been able to define those things. Well, Justice Stewart was a remarkable man. You know one reason he was so interested in helping us with our television series on the Constitution was that when he was at Yale, many years before, he was Editor of the *Yale Daily News,* so although he went on to become a great lawyer and a great justice, his heart was still in journalism.

Heffner: Let's go back, Fred, to the bothersome question of what has happened to journalism, let's say, broadcast journalism in particular, since the time Justice Stewart said that to you.

Well, let's take it back to when your friend and my colleague, Murrow, was around. Television now makes so much money, commercial television that is, doing its worst, it can't afford to do its best.

It's an irony that an organization can make more money doing its worst, than doing its best. That's because air time has become so expensive, that commercials sell for a million dollars a minute. At Super Bowl time, more than that. The networks today, and I left much of my youth and much of my heart in one network—the networks would rather have a lousy program with high ratings than a great program, such as Murrow did, with low ratings. There's something wrong with that.

Heffner: You're talking about CBS; but you could have said the same thing about . . .

NBC and ABC and independent stations. Here's a station story I love to tell, about a station in Boston that went on the air 30 years ago for about a half a million dollars. Eventually that station lost its license and some do-gooders, Harvard professors, MIT professors, applied for that license and got it. And they ran a pretty good station. Then somebody came along . . . and bought that station for 350 million dollars. Two years later another company . . . bought it for 530 million dollars. Now what were they buying? They were buying a license, a license that gives you exclusivity on one of the seven UHF channels in a city like New York, or . . . Boston, gives you one of five or seven bullhorns. You have abridged freedom of the press, because no one can broadcast on that station without your permission. . . . So the First Amendment and television have nothing to do with each other because television by its very nature gives some people, and no one else, this enormous power.

I can remember not only when there was no television, but when there was no radio here in New York, and I've seen radio grow, and I've seen television grow, like a giant, and I believe that television will determine what kind of people we are. It does already. It's the greatest distraction ever made. Kids today watch six, seven hours of television a day. For most of them, that's more time than they spend in school, more time than they spend sleeping. They don't learn to read because they say, "Why do I have to read, television reads to me," it's a great distraction, it's changing America. And if we don't get some responsibility in there, it's going to change America in a very negative way.

Heffner: Is it enough to talk about responsibility? Or do you have a specific agenda?

Well my agenda is certainly not to get the government involved. I mean the government is involved in the wrong way because the court says, "There can be no prior restraints, no gagging, no gag orders," and the broadcasters and the newspaper men take that and say, "You see, nobody can stop us." Nobody can stop them, but that doesn't mean they have to put crap on the air. The government is going to stay out of it, as they should, as the Founding Fathers wanted them to, as Murrow wanted them to, but that doesn't mean that we can't elevate this blessed miracle to be an educational tool in this country. The biggest problem this country has today is our education system . . . you don't need me to tell you that 40 percent to 50 percent of the children in some big cities drop out of school, you don't need me to tell you that people can't learn to read today. Television could help with this—what did Ed say in his last, great speech—he said, "This instrument, television, can entertain, can illuminate, yes it can even inspire, but it can only do that to the ends that men and women are determined to use it for that purpose. Otherwise it's just lights and wires in a box."

I did a seminar the other day at the Bar Association of the City of New York with lawyers, about takeovers and lawyers, but we had some investment bankers there, too, and some journalists.

Heffner: You gave them hell, I guess.

Well, I just asked questions, but what emerged is the basic fact that these deals for takeovers of billion-dollar corporations are engineered by investment bankers. They target the company that can be taken over, they may go out and find somebody with some money to say, "Hey, you could take over this company," and then they make it happen and they get their fees, which are sometimes fifty, eighty, a hundred million dollars only if the deal takes place. So . . . with this great capitalistic society, with the best form of government in the world, we play a game of money. It's not money because one can make a better product, it's not money because one is smarter than someone else. It's money making money. And the moneymakers, the money changers, if you want to go back to the Bible, make these deals, with larger companies taking over smaller companies, because the investment bankers and the lawyers and eventually the corporate executives have this enormous appetite to grow and to grow and to grow. That's now ending because junk bonds have done them all in. We may be seeing the end of the hostile takeover, but it's done irreperable damage here. The change in management at CBS began when Senator Helms and then Ted Turner said they were going to take over CBS. They scared CBS so that a decent man, Larry Tisch, entered the arena and collected enough stock and stockholders' proxies to take over the company. Nothing wrong with that; Mr. Tisch is a friend of mine, a longtime friend of mine. He doesn't know anything about the broadcast business, just as I don't know anything about his business—the cigarette business and the insurance business and the banking business. I would not presume to run a bank, certainly not a cigarette company. But the people running NBC, which is now owned by General Electric, and Mr. Tisch at CBS, don't know anything about broadcasting. Why should they? And why does anybody think that anybody can run anything? I mean somebody now wants to take over United Airlines who doesn't know anything about flying an airplane. I wouldn't fly in an airplane owned by a company run by a guy who didn't know anything about aviation.

Heffner: Are you saying that you don't want to see the broadcast industry, or this form of information or education subject to the profit motive? Do I understand you correctly?

I wouldn't want Berkeley, the University of California, run on a profit basis. I can remember Paley [William S. Paley, former Chairman of CBS] saying to me in the presence of others, 25 years ago, that "if news ever becomes a profit center, we'll be in trouble."

Heffner: Is news now a profit center?

It is. And they are in trouble. But you see there was—I certainly had my quarrels with Paley and with CBS President Frank Stanton, but as I look back to the early years, the forties, the fifties, even before my time, in the thirties—there was a nobility of purpose in the industry. They knew that they owed something back because they had this great franchise. There was something then called "a sustaining program," which meant a program without sponsors.

Heffner: Like mine.

Like yours. But there really is no such thing as a sustaining program. Everything on the air now has to make money. The documentary which Murrow and I helped to pioneer—there are very few documentaries left because they don't achieve ratings compared to a sitcom, they don't have ratings compared to sports, so there's no place for the documentary. In Paley's better days that nobility said, "We gotta do this 'cause we owe something back to the system." Now why don't we demand more? We, the people. Why don't we say, "This situation in which you see this parade of mediocre dross night after night, one program after another, separated by one commercial after another, is unacceptable. Just like the homeless. I was in India during World War Two, I was in Calcutta. I saw tens of thousands of homeless people lying in the street, sleeping on a blanket, with their children and little girls coming up and saying to Sergeant Friendly and others, "you want to jig-jig with my sister?" And I can, 20 annas, which was just a few cents, and I can remember thinking to myself, "My God, people live on the streets like this, it's unacceptable. I know that that will never happen in my country." I was 21 years old then. Here I am in the springtime of my senility and I see homeless in New York, at Columbia University, begging. In St. Louis, begging. In California, Los Angeles, begging. I would like to think that a President like Franklin Roosevelt or Harry Truman would say, "This situation is unacceptable" and the American people would say, "It's unacceptable," and I've always believed that they would eventually say that about television. I think television has so changed the American people, they don't have it in them to say, "Unacceptable."

Heffner: But, Fred, isn't that the point? That we frequently say it is unacceptable, about the homeless, about televison, etc., but we are not willing to do anything.

But we accept it, that's right, because we're greedy, all of us.

Heffner: So you're talking about a profit-driven society, right?

Yes, but it does not have to be imposed on everything. It isn't on our great universities, it's not on our high schools, it's not on our—let's leave it at that, our universities. Why do we let this happen? Why do we let an instrument of limited access, television, why do we let that get into the hands of profiteers?

Heffner: Because we didn't listen, by God, to Herbert Hoover, who was shocked at the very thought of advertising in a university. And television is a university. You say, "I just don't believe it has to be that way," when the evidence is so clear before us that within the context of what you describe as commercial television today, as you say, "It goes down the drain."

Well, Herbert Hoover said it would be terrible if we let this great instrument get out of hand. But we have . . . I'm very worried about it. But I still—I'm an optimist. All I know is I've been better in my life at asking questions than answering them. I have a motto I repeat at all the seminars I'm involved in. I say that my job is not to make up anybody's mind, but to make the agony of decision-making so intense that you can escape only by thinking. I want you and your viewers to think about this awesome dilemma and what we are going to do about the magic of television, which has turned into something that we should be ashamed of. It's a harvest. Television is a harvest of greed. Period.

Heffner: Fred, let's talk a bit now not about the media moguls, but about the practicing journalists themselves. If you were giving advice to a friend, to someone just coming into the world of public affairs broadcasting, wouldn't you leaven your advice just a little bit with the warning, "Beware of the journalist because he or she has a personal agenda and selfish motives far beyond a noble search for the truth."

I think that what I would tell a journalist today is that your job is to portray a picture of reality on which the citizen can act. That's a quote from Walter Lippmann, in a marvelous book called *Public Opinion*. A picture of reality on which the citizen can act. The reason there's a First Amendment, the first item in the Constitution's Bill of Rights, is that the Founding Fathers knew that a democracy without a well-informed public was a tragedy or farce, or both. Along with Madison, I believe that. My mother told me only one false thing in her whole life. She said "Son, what you don't know can't hurt you." She was wrong. What we don't know as a nation and a citizen could kill us. What we don't know about the environment and the greenhouse effect and arms control, what we don't know about potholes, or the bridges in New York, can kill us. We need to have a well-informed America. The reason that the Murrows and the Lippmanns have a place in history is that they helped democracy work, they helped make people be better informed. Let's take Public Health. Three centuries ago there was no such thing as public health, and then Jenner, a doctor in London, discovered that smallpox, or some disease was passed around by people drinking out of unsanitary water pumps, so he cleaned up the water pumps. Now he didn't just do that for the rich people who could afford it. They had to have something called "public health" so that the poorest of the people of London would be protected from whatever the disease was. That's how the whole philosophy of public health in our society works; move that to journalism and public information. Everybody's vote is equal to mine and yours . . . but if 80 percent of the people don't read a newspaper or watch a decent television program, that's an upsetting thing to democracy because their vote counts the same as mine does. I want everybody to be informed, and the way you inform people today is in newspapers, and in television and radio. And if we fail to do that job, either because we're lazy or we don't want to spend the money or we think they want to read more about some celebrity than they do about nuclear arms control, then we put the nation at risk.

Heffner: Do you, Fred, think they want to read more about celebrities than about nuclear arms control?

I think gossip has always been around. People say to me, "Fred, aren't you an elitist?" Yes. I am guilty of being an elitist. But I would also say that if you let the people just eat junk food, that's what they're going to want. If you teach them that nutritional, healthy food is better for you, they'll eat the better food. I think you can sell junk news, just like you sell junk food, but it's dangerous to the health of the American democracy, and to the extent that I can do anything about it, I'm going to try to educate students at Columbia and other places where I teach, journalists capable of explaining complex issues. What do journalists do? They explain complicated issues. You can't explain something you don't understand. We need to understand these complicated issues much better. We need to know about Eastern Europe, for example. I hear radio and television reports from Poland, from

Czechoslovakia, from Romania, and I want to weep because half of them don't know what they're talking about, there's no sense of history. I was educated in the late 1930s, much of it on radio, when Edward R. Murrow, whom I didn't know in those days, and Raymond Swing, and Bill Shirer and Eric Severeid were broadcasting from London during the Blitz, from Czechoslovakia when Thomas Masaryk was the President, and Benes was there. I remember the Anschluss, I remember the fall of Poland, I remember all those details, and I remember what the Third Reich did to civilization. That's why I want people who are broadcasting today, and writing for newspapers, to explain how World War II came about, how the Treaty of Versailles 1919 created Adolf Hitler, how the Third Reich grew out of the discontent of those people. I don't hear any of this because the news is told to me in 40-second sound bites. —1990

DON HEWITT

I can normally limit myself to one-adjective praise in introducing a companion-in-conversation. Not possible, however, with Don Hewitt, the creator and producer of 60 Minutes, *the CBS News show of shows for decades now. Indomitable, indefatigable, infuriating, influential are just a few of the words which might describe the man who changed TV and politics forever with his direction of the first 1960 Kennedy-Nixon "debate." In an untypically modest mode, Don has said to me at one point that he's simply in the business of informing people about what's going on. I think otherwise: that he, like the other major broadcasters has, and exercises, great power. I asked him about that in one of our programs together.*

There is power in giving anything, or anybody, that big a soap box. What you do is, you have taken what is the dinner table conversation in this little tiny arena, and all of a sudden, you've knocked the walls out and now you're having a conversation, you know, with 30 million people listening in. Sure there's power in that. Today I think there's probably as much power with Oprah Winfrey and . . . and Larry King . . .

Heffner: Does it make you uneasy?

No.

Heffner: No?

No. No.

Heffner: Would you be made uneasy by power concentrated in government, in labor, in big business?

Am I uncomfortable with that? No, those are facts of life. I've lived through times when labor had an awful lot of power in this country. When business had a lot of power in this country. When government had too much power in this country. You know, I don't want to sound like some pedantic damn fool about it. Jefferson said, "If you have a choice between a government with no newspapers and a newspaper with no government, which would you take," and he said, more or less, "It's no contest." Somebody responsible has to be a watchdog in a democratic society. Maybe I overstated when I said . . . Oprah Winfreys . . . maybe they're not exactly the people who should be the watchdogs. You know, you practice this craft a lot of years and you begin to learn where the pitfalls are. You know what is fair and unfair. You know it in your bones, you feel it, you get it in your fingertips.

Heffner: Conceding that the nation needs a watchdog and you think of the watchdog as the press, print and electronic, I thought maybe you were also about to concede that the watchdog needs a watchdog.

Yes, but first let me comment on something—

Heffner: Sure.

If I didn't get you hot under the collar once in a while, I wouldn't be doing my job. You should get hot under the collar. I mean, I remember my father used to sit home and fume at Westbrook Pegler. You know, you need that, you need a place to vent your emotions. Everything is not black and white. And I'm sure there are things that drive people up the wall. Now, does the watchdog need a watchdog? I think if government weren't involved in Iran-gates, and Iraq-gates, and Watergates, maybe elected officials would be the preferred watchdog. But I don't think the country feels that they can trust the government to be a watchdog in anything. And I'm not just talking about Republican things. I think the worst scandal of my lifetime was not Watergate, it was not Iran-Contra, and it was not Iraq-gate, it wasn't even Teapot Dome—it was the Gulf of Tonkin. Lyndon Johnson pulled a fast one on this country, and got us to go to war in Vietnam which maybe came as close as anything ever happened to being the undoing of this country. I mean we survived Watergate, we survived Iran, we survived Iraq-gate, but we almost didn't survive the Gulf of Tonkin. Never happened. If you go back and you read the cable traffic, you find we probably were never attacked that night in the Gulf of Tonkin. We were looking for an excuse to bomb North Vietnam, and a lot of Americans have been screwed up ever since.

Heffner: So you're being nonpartisan or bipartisan, in your approach to the evils of government.

By all means. Listen, I think Lyndon Johnson perpetrated the worst scandal of my lifetime. I mean I think that makes the rest of them look like nothing. But, if those things didn't happen in government, the government would be the watchdog. I mean if half the members of Congress weren't beholden to lobbies and PACs—I mean we say this country's never been invaded. That's not true; of course, we've been invaded. We've been invaded by lobbyists. They sit and they occupy Capitol Hill. We do a lot of stupid things in this country. You know, we sent troops to Panama to kidnap Manuel Noriega and bring him back and try him. That was not where we should have gone. We should have sent troops to California to capture Alan Cranston and bring him back to Washington and try him. He did more harm to this country with his S&L connections than Noriega ever did with his drug connections. Noriega worked for us. I mean I can't say, you know, for a fact, but from stories we've done, I am almost certain that Noriega was telling us the truth when he told us that Ollie North and Poindexter came to see him, and asked him if they could use Panama as a staging ground for an invasion of Nicaragua. And when he told them "no," that's when his troubles began. Up to that point, he was our pal. I'll show you letters of commendation to Noriega from the DEA! So that you can't trust them to be a watchdog. If I have to trust somebody, I'd trust us.

Heffner: All kidding aside, who is the custodian, where are the custodians when it comes to us—when it comes to this beady red eye?

Well, I think that the problem is that there are no Bill Paleys or David Sarnoffs, and Leonard Goldensons around anymore, or Frank Stantons, or Bob Kintners—who believed very strongly that this was a public trust, and that the Ed Murrows and the Eric Sevareids were given the job, and the Howard Smiths, and the Charles Collingwoods—and the Walter Cronkites—of being the public watchdog because these guys felt like they had an obligation in return for the airwaves they used. I think the problem is that the people up top may be not as interested in having an

Ed Murrow, an Eric Sevareid, a Walter Cronkite as their watchdog as the guys we all knew and loved did.

Heffner: Speaking of the Smiths and Cronkites, what do you see happening to the venerable network evening news?

Having helped to create the evening news as a tradition, a staple of television, I think it may be on its last legs for this reason. One of these days some local station is going to say to itself, "Look, they feed us this stuff all day long because they have to feed it to us so we can stay competitive with CNN and MSNBC. Why are we giving away a half hour every night to the network. Why don't we do the national news?" And they won't do it very well, but they'll keep the revenue. That's going to happen. I fear. The first time one major market does that the rest of them are going to fold.

Heffner: So what's your "modest proposal" to save the network news problem?

Here's the way to solve it. If the three networks can pool a White House news conference, if they can pool a Presidential debate, if they can pool the coverage of a space shot somewhere, pool the evening news. The highest rated show in television, over the years, has been the evening news. Some people watch it on NBC, some people watch it on ABC, some people watch it on CBS. It is the same broadcast with three different faces. Now, if they got together and they ran an organization where they said, "We're going to use Rather, Brokaw, and Jennings. One at the desk in the studio. One in the studio, two out on stories. Next week, one comes in and the other guys go out. Now, because it's one-third the cost, but the same revenue coming in, you can reopen all those bureaus you closed. You can become both the service and business that you're not now. You're a business now. And then people say to me, "But you're taking the competition out of it." I know one vital fact about television. Competition makes you worse, not better. Competition in television is where you go for the lowest common denominator.

Perfect example is election night—usually a debacle. Three anchormen, all sitting in front of ostensibly the same map, with the same figures, calling elections they shouldn't have been calling. Why? Because God forbid, Dan Rather should call an election before Jennings and Jennings is competing with Brokaw. And they're all in competition to see who's going to make this call first. First of all, it's nervy of television to "call" elections. They shouldn't "call" elections anyway. They should tell you, "Our reporting indicates that—thus and so." Who are they to "call" an election? You take the competition out of it and you'll be better.

Now you can say, "We're going to do the story of the AIDS epidemic in Africa, and we're not going to worry about our competition doing a Hollywood story at the same moment. Because there is nothing going to be competing with us. We are it. The three of us are it at this hour and we can now do what we think is right. We can exercise the news judgment that you can't exercise when you're under the gun and you have to keep a rating going against somebody else."

Heffner: What's your fix on the so-called Presidential debates?

Let me tell you what I think about their debates. I did the first debate, but I really didn't. It never has been a debate. They've never debated. These have been joint news conferences, masquerading as debates. And they go nowhere. Mostly because I know all the guys who participate in them. And every night, or the night before they're going on, they sit down and they say to themselves, "What can I say that's going to make me look smart, but not make me look partisan?" That's the problem, nobody who's nonpartisan, should be in the debate. Debate is about partisan[ship]. It's not a joint news conference.

Teddy White, the late Theodore White, who wrote *The Making of the President*, Teddy and I once came up with an idea and we couldn't sell it to anybody. Said we think these debates should be a real debate.

Each guy—hypothetically Bush and Gore—each bring two great debaters with them from their party. And they go before a joint session of Congress for two hours. And for the first hour, it's a real debate with a moderator, the same rules, the Oxford Debating Society. Proposition. Proposed that George Bush be the next President of the United States—pro and con. And they debate that issue. Real debate, no stupid news guy's questions. Second hour, you do what they do in Britain on the back bench in Parliament—question time. The Republicans in Congress have at Al Gore and the Democrats in Congress have at George Bush. And they ask the kind of questions that really make sense. You'd have a real night of political debate and not this. What happened in 1960, when I did the Nixon/Kennedy debate, in hindsight turns out to be, maybe, the worst night television ever had. Or the American people ever had. That's the night that television and politics realized they couldn't live without each other. They looked at us as the way to campaign. We don't need whistle-stop trains. We don't need campaign buttons. We don't need bumper stickers. We don't need the speech on the courthouse steps. Television is the way we'll reach the American people. —1990

MAX FRANKEL

It would be difficult, if not impossible, to match the incisiveness and clarity of Max Frankel's comments on the principles and practice of print journalism. The most important thing about Frankel's view of the news, perhaps, is the bright spotlight it shines on the state of the nation as well. By way of credibility, his vita includes two Pulitzer Prizes and a long career at the New York Times, *culminating in a stint as its Executive Editor, arguably the single most prestigious post in U.S. print journalism. I asked him whether it would it be fair to say that in time probably just about anything that's called "news" becomes "fit to print" because somehow or other it becomes part of the public's concerns.*

Yes. And especially when people who know how to play the system are throwing oil on the flames.

Heffner: What does that tell us about the newspaper of the future?

A newspaper has to hold its wits about it and its bearings. I mean, a good example, the most dramatic example—and we practice the same thing, but people may not notice it so readily—but take the *Wall Street Journal*. It only publishes Monday to Friday. The world doesn't stop on Saturdays and Sundays, but the *Journal* says, "Our readers, they take the weekend off." The *Journal* does not deal with most news on its front page. It is examining important trends in business, in finance, in society. It does witty articles. It's a very good newspaper. But its front page is, by and large, quiet. It doesn't use photographs. It says, "We know our readers. We have trained our readers to enjoy what we have to offer. And that is what's fit to print elsewhere doesn't necessarily belong in the *Wall Street Journal*." We do the same thing. We don't look like the *New York Post*.

Heffner: But you sure as hell don't look like the *New York Times* I read as a boy.

No, because we are serving a vastly more curious, vastly more educated audience than when you and I were boys, and coming out of World War II, concerned mostly about governmental and official action. Now we're interested in what causes prostate cancer, and how do you deal with your doctor if you have a misdiagnosis, and what is the origin of the universe, and what do I do with my few savings, and who is stealing my bonds because they're speculating on the stock market. Many more complicated aspects of society are governing our lives. And the job of the newspaper, at least as we have defined it for our kind of readership, is to try to understand and explain. And all of official government, and all the military, and the Pentagon, and the White House, all of that is only a small facet of what we regard as now fit and necessary to print.

Heffner: There's no secret about the fact that the *Times* has been pilloried in the last decade for becoming less the newspaper of record and more a popular journal. I've sympathized with those concerns, and yet I know full well that you, of all people, have your good reasons for this. But I remain disturbed by the fact that now the *Times'* front page follows the crowd, if you will. In a sense, you've said that you've got to be there where the crowd is. Give me a better response that I can give to those who say, "Look what's happened to your *Times*."

No problem. First of all, you're dealing, all of us who deal with the past, are dealing in fictions. If you read the *New York Times* of 1930 and of 1925 and 1920, you would be shocked at how opinionated and how wild it is, shocked at its lead stories on bizarre local crime cases, highly opinionated dispatches from all around the world, correspondents writing what today would be unacceptable even as editorials. But let's leave that in the past. Our memories are clouded because World War II, when the entire country was devoted to a single, unified mission of defeating the enemy, and when we were covering our good government, and it was waging our battle on our behalf, the newspapers that recorded the maps and the battles and the speeches and the glories and the medals took on a nostalgic and sentimental notion of what the press was like. Also, as a paper of record, when I joined the *New York Times*, late '40s, early '50s, we were already breaking down the notion that everything that happened of an official nature had to be "recorded." We've strayed further and further from that, because that's not where the readers are, and that's not where their curiosities are.

But let me go to the current situation. I very deliberately changed the front page of the *New York Times* in my years as editor.

Heffner: God, it burned me up when you did that.

Not the content of the newspaper. I merely reshuffled the deck. For instance, I did not take the most official kind of story one day— "Congress is going to come into session next week. They are assembling." The next day, "They are going to meet on Tuesday, and they are going to do this." All front-page stories. On Tuesday, "They met and they did this." On Wednesday, "Having met, they have now done it." One serial installment of insignificant, small steps, or a major piece of legislation, every day, it is in committee, it is being discussed in committee, it is being acted on in committee, it has been amended in committee, it has come to the floor, it is being discussed on the floor, it has been debated on the floor. The routinized governmental, step-by-step business was the front-page diet of too many governmental stories, not what's in this thing, not so much of what significance does it have for my life, not what forces are behind various portions of this bill. We carried some of that information, but we put it where it belonged, inside the paper, and we took it out at what we called "the moment." Is this the moment when the reader should be paying attention because this bill is coming to a climax? Is this the moment because we have suddenly learned who's really behind this bill and its hidden paragraph and what it will accomplish? That's the moment when you pull it out. That's one level of treating official government stories.

Inside this paper, we had wonderful articles. One day, it discovered that all the skirts were going to come up on women's clothes. And I said, "Why isn't that front-page news? If you're sure that it's really happening, that all the long skirts are being burned, that all the designers, whether by conspiracy to sell more clothes, or whether by some magical seizure of the public mind and taste, every woman in America is going to have to either run to the tailor and change the wardrobe or throw out every thing that's hanging in the closet and start spending a lot of money changing fashions. In return, the stores will or will not respond, they will or will not die or live by this new trend in fashions." It is a moment. It is a trend. It sounds soft and weird and crazy, but it goes to the heart of our lives and the heart of our economy. It is a story worth calling attention to. So that, whether it is a trend in the way we eat and in the way we dress, in the way we think, in the bigotry we practice, why isn't that news as much to contend with as whether this or that bill is coming out of a committee in Congress.

So, the whole point was to turn the front page into a richer reflection of what was already in the paper, but to advertise it in poster-like fashion so that the front page is not just the slave of the government, of the president, and the mayor and the governor.

Heffner: You know, it's funny, despite my ancient prejudices, my response to that, my reaction to that, is: God, that's persuasive. But what has been the public reaction?

Well, the circulation has shot up. And anecdotally, I know, the people didn't know why. They came and said, "Gee, I'm reading more. It's a more interesting paper." It wasn't radically different from what we offered before, but we dressed it up a little differently, and we advertised. We removed the more boring stuff to the inside, and we took out other subjects. And we said, "A great piece of theater opening on Broadway." It was never on the front page before. And we had trouble figuring it out, because we don't want to put a negative or positive criticism on page one. But it is a major cultural event. If the opera redoes Wagner's Ring Cycle, for a portion of our readership that's an important cultural development. It happens once every 50 years. Why isn't that news?

Heffner: What happened in terms of the presentation of other news . . . and to its audiences? Is there now as much involvement with hard news? You've explained why "soft" news comes up front and has its proper place. What happened to the hard news in a society that is becoming softer and softer?

I have to change your vocabulary.

Heffner: Okay.

At the beginning, I, too, talked about "hard" and "soft." What journalists mean by "hard news," if you think hard about it, is that which happened yesterday. An event. Half the time staged for us. A news conference, a meeting, a summit meeting, a bill signing. That used to be called "hard news." And "soft" was something where, as I say, we discovered an important trend in the lives of our society, where suddenly we discovered that people were or were not turning away from the Democrats, people were or were not turning against the idea of busing to schools. If you've discovered a trend, and at that moment kind of put the knife into the cake and opened it up and said, "This is what it's made of," that was soft. Why? Because nothing happened. That's been the only difference between the "soft" and the "hard" news. And I submit that what happened yesterday—along with the word "yesterday"—appears still in about half the stories on the front page of the *New York Times*. But it used to be on every story, and there used to be 15 of them. And most of them were what have been rightly called pseudo-events. Events largely staged either to fool the people that things were happening, or to lure the press into forcing attention onto some event. They were not real events. And why what is happening should be less important than what happened, I've never understood.

Heffner: Yes, but that's your definition of "hard" and "soft," and I respect it. Others, however, would define "soft" as materials that really don't have an impact on life and death. Maybe hemlines, etcetera, and you can stretch them out to the economy, to the impact upon people's jobs, etcetera. I grant that. But I think what most of us have felt is that "soft" stuff is not just day-before-yesterday rather than yesterday, is not just tomorrow's social trends; rather it is the inconsequential as opposed to the very, very consequential. Is that unfair?

Yes, it is unfair. First of all, we don't know consequence. The one thing we don't do in the newsroom, believe it or not, is sit around and say, "What will be the consequence of our publishing this or of our putting it on page one or putting it on the inside?" Because, one, we don't know; two, if we think we know—sometimes we whisper about that—we're usually wrong . . .

Heffner: Oh, I didn't mean the consequence of where you put it. I meant is this an important item for the people of the United States? Consequential in that sense.

Oh, I daresay that the front page of the *New York Times,* for well-educated readers who are willing to give us a half-hour or 45 minutes a day, is overwhelmingly devoted to things of consequence, in world, national, business, social, cultural affairs. Overwhelmingly.

Heffner: Well, you see, that was my other question. That question has to do with whether, in your analysis of what your readers do with the *New York Times,* there is as much interest, there is as much attention paid now to political matters—what I would call the "hard" stuff.

But you see, the "hard" stuff itself, what's happened, can't be divorced from what's happened to society. My editorship happened to coincide with the end of the Cold War. And I had devoted my entire life to reporting the Cold War, both in Moscow, abroad, in Cuba, and in Washington. The fear of war was drained from America's psyche in these last ten years [1984–1994 -Ed.]. A profound event, first of all, that has to be reported and analyzed. The dangers of isolation on the one hand, and the shift to economic concerns, as opposed to military, was dramatic in those ten years. And that was the mission of a conscientious newspaper. We literally wrote memos to one another and to our foreign correspondents. And we said, "As this happened, what is important now in France is not whether their Communist Party is still going to be revived, because the giant seat of communism has collapsed. And therefore, whether some Communist is elected mayor in some city, and therefore possibly the French government is going to go weak on NATO, is hardly of great moment. But how the French are dealing with nuclear power in their society and whether they are building reactors safely, and whether they have anything to teach us, how they treat the elderly, and whether wine, I daresay, ruins your health or is good for you, as doctors are suddenly claiming, those are important things in the lives of Americans. And therefore, the nature of the news of France is going to change." We have as many, indeed, we have more *Times* people in France than we had at the height of the Cold War. We've got a cultural correspondent in Europe who's looking to see what's going on on the stages and in the institutions of the opera houses and the theaters all across the continent. That's news. There was no room for that when we were all busy fighting for Berlin. But the nature of society, the nature of events has changed, and we've got to respond. Our foreign correspondents have to learn economics. We're dumb about international trade. We really don't understand how the Japanese evolved . . . and what the Chinese are going to do with their economy and what that's going to mean for jobs in America. Those are the things that are now news. And they're slow-burning trends. And no one in Beijing is calling a press conference to say, "We will bury you." But they might, if we don't report those things.

Heffner: You've said here in different ways, "We've got to respond, and we can't separate out the 'hard' news from what's happening to society." Do you think a fair description of what's happening, to some extent, is that there's been a dumbing-down of American society?

There has been a multiplication of the broadcasting of the dumb things that always existed in our communications, yes. But there has been a multiplication of everything. The nature of communications is exploding in such a way, there are so many hours to be filled by people who prattle and claim to have something to tell us. Whereas what it is they have to tell us has not grown nearly by that amount. The dumber things keep reverberating, that is true. And certainly, if you turn on television from morning 'til night, the proportion of dumbness to anything of consequence and meaning is considerable. But it wasn't any different back in the days when you and I were scoffing at the *Daily Mirror* or the *Journal American,* the yellow press.

Heffner: Yes, but Max, that was different. We could scoff at the *Mirror* and the *News* and the *Journal,* the yellow journals, and a lot of those papers; but certainly not at the *New York Times.* We could never scoff at anything that appeared there. So the question that I'm really putting to you: Does the dumbing-down have to be reflected, too, in your paper and mine?

Oh, I don't think the *New York Times* can be fairly accused of having dumbed down. Not at all. On the contrary.

Heffner: Are you saying instead that it has smarted up?

It smarted up. Absolutely. It is engaged in a perpetual chase with the nature of knowledge in our society. It is, as an editor, the single most frustrating thing that, every time we hired three smart people to go and learn about microbiology, we quickly find out that astrophysics is the next frontier, and who knows from astrophysics? And the same is true in business, and the same is true in international relations, because I said, it's gone economic from diplomatic. And we're well-stocked with people who know all about missiles and who finally have learned how to cover the Pentagon and who finally know how to get the truth about a military operation. And the next thing you know, we're really dealing in the

American content underneath the hood in some automobile, and whether it should be allowed in with this much tariff or that much tariff. That's the war of today. And are we well-staffed? The nature of what's important to know. We are forever chasing it. Because, after all, we don't just change staffs every day. We try to keep people for a career. And knowledge and news are exploding away from us, and we're in a perpetual race. So, to the extent that we are dumb, it's because we aren't smart enough to understand the difficult and intellectual subjects that we need to master and somehow turn into understandable news. If that's what you mean by "dumb," we are often wrong and infantile in that sense. But not in the sense that we're going tabloid or soft or weak in our curiosities.

Heffner: Let me switch our focus. One question that has surfaced often enough has to do with the fairness of the media. Professionals asked about the fairness of the media frequently come up with very negative responses. And I wonder what your own sense about fairness is, in the print and electronic media alike.

My first problem is with the term "the media."

Heffner: You don't like that term?

No. Yet there's no substitute. I find myself using it after long resisting it. The problem is that it's plural. And it's so fast that people's impressions are blurred, it's no different than "the crowd, the mob." "I can't stand the traffic in New York." Well, there are lots of places in New York where you can walk quietly. The media are, in the aggregate, quite responsible. That is to say, my colleagues in television, whatever the limitations of the medium, and however insufficient the amount of good reporting that goes on in television, Rather, Jennings, Brokaw . . . they're fair-minded people, they're honest, hardworking people, they understand the issues. But along can come a Geraldo, and appear to be doing a news interview with some sleazebag, and that also is considered "the media." And all of us become tarred with this brush of irresponsibility or triviality or whatever else we're being accused of. That's one answer to the question of fairness.

The other is, "What do people really mean by 'fairness?'" When I was growing up, we all could very quickly, on a newsstand, pick out the newspaper that best reflected our prejudices, or the limits of our own understanding and education. There was *PM* or the *Star* in New York City for the lefties; and the *Journal American* and the *World Telegram* and *Sun* for the righties; and the *Herald Tribune* for the suburban businessman; and the *New York Times* for the Columbia University professor. And we all had our spectrum to choose from. And we all felt that we were being well served. The fact is that most of these newspapers were looking at the world through different glasses. And as long as readers felt his or her outlook was being reflected, they saw fairness. What has happened in the printed press is that, as competition has done its work, as much of the news interest and much of the entertainment value of newspapers has gone to radio and then to television, we're left—New York City is the exception; we've still got four or give vibrant newspapers, and we've got a wonderful ethnic press in the wings—we're left in most American cities with one local newspaper trying to march down the middle of the road. It has to suit the lefties and it has to suit the righties; and it has to suit the less well-educated, and it has to meet the needs of the elite. And the result is that no one finds it satisfying, and no one finds it fair enough, because his or her own point of view and outlook on life are not well enough represented.

So, when you take that sentence and try to parse it, what are you talking about when you say "the media"? Which ones? And are they fair? What do you mean by "fairness"? Do we look at the world the way you do, or the way a blue-collar, unemployed fellow does? Those people have radically different outlooks. And their sense of fairness is different.

Heffner: Well, what's your own sense of fairness, Max?

My sense of fairness is that all that journalism can accomplish is cumulatively to peel the onion of understanding, and to keep correcting, day by day, our sense of what is going on and why it is happening, as it affects our lives and our understanding of the world around us. The most important word in what I'm saying is "cumulative." On any given night, the best of, most brilliant of our reporters, and the best that ever lived, at five P.M., when that reporter is through running around town and reading books and looking up things in a hurry and interviewing people, that reporter sits down, and doesn't know the half of what he is writing about. All he can say, in effect, is, "As of this hour, dear reader, it seems to be that this and this is happening. And it seems to be this is why it's happening. And it may be that so-and-so is not entirely happy with what is happening." And then tomorrow we learn that six more people are unhappy with what's happening, and that the consequences of that situation are evolving. And we go on and on and on. And some days all of this turns out to be trivial, because nothing happens. We have written, say, about health insurance, for 30 years, and it somehow doesn't get into the hearts and minds of the population or into the political debate, and so all that newsprint and all that energy is largely wasted because the receptivity isn't there. Communication is a two-way act. Most people say, "You're telling me," the media that is, "You are doing this to me." But in fact, we, in the media, can't do anything until you're willing, really, to listen. Just buying the paper or turning on the TV isn't enough. You've got to be ready for that particular issue at that particular moment as explained by that particular writer or commentator or reporter. The best example in our lifetime was Vietnam. A lot of the reporting that we can look back on, which was quite brilliant, about how we weren't winning the war and what were we doing there anyway, fell on very limited number of ears. It was all in the paper. It was all on page one. David Halberstam and others later became heroes because of what they did, or Homer Bigart. Most people don't even remember that Homer Bigart was in Vietnam for the *New York Times.* Because those were the early stages. Why? No one was being drafted. The ground forces weren't being sent. The body bags weren't coming back. The receptivity of the audience was radically different. . . .

So what the audience demands—they may not believe it, and I know that I would be pilloried for this point of view—but I'm, say, arguing, that the nature of fairness or unfairness, and the perception of fairness, depends in very large degree whom you are addressing and how that audience is perceived by the medium that is addressing them. It's a very complicated, interactive system, even though people don't see it as interactive.

Heffner: Would you argue for some kind of professionalization of the individual journalist's responsibilities?

I would challenge every newspaper and every news medium to try to define their own standards for themselves, but to articulate them and try to make them public. We've never done that.

Heffner: Why haven't you, at the *Times,* by the way? All we read is "All the news that's fit to print."

One, because it's constantly changing; and two, because it is a very difficult thing to do, except by the case method. I mean, 20 years ago our reporters were taking favors from the people they write about. Trivial. They were accepting an extra seat in the theater if they were covering the theater, they were taking their brother-in-law to the basketball game if they were covering the basketball game. At a certain moment it dawned on us, or through various incidents it might have dawned on some other newspaper, that this was not only very compromising, but it exposed a complicated relationship, a symbiotic relationship, where we need the people who run the enterprises that we cover for information, but on the other hand, we need independence from them to be perceived of as writing about them fairly. So the whole issue of how we relate, at the most trivial level, to a sports team. Nobody ten years ago would have sat down and written about that complicated relationship in a way that satisfied our standards. And if they had, it would have changed within two, three years as something else happened.

The problem is, you can't anticipate. What do we do now? You know, the President of the United States calls up and says, "I hear you've got a story about a submarine that we found, a Russian submarine that we found near Hawaii. I want you to hold up printing that." What are our standards? Our standards are to sit down and examine that request. Usually in great urgency and with much excitement and tension as to how valid it is and why and what, where, what do we live by and how much do we owe our government and how much do we owe our readers and how do we know at any given moment what is the right thing to print. Very hard to codify that in advance. You can codify simple things, and those we've done. We will not go through the world, you know, pretending to be who we're not. We will not disguise ourselves to get the news. But if another newspaper wants to put on a costume and disguise itself and come up with an interesting story, that's their standard. Who are we to give definition or limitation to the First Amendment.

Heffner: Tell me about circulation and its role, about dollars, their role in running this great newspaper, in calculating the future of the *New York Times*.

We are, fortunately, running a very good and successful business. But it keeps getting more and more expensive. And the nature of business, the nature of technology, is changing. After all, what is a newspaper? It takes trees in Canada and chops them down and ships them to Times Square and pours words over them and puts them on the backs of trucks and starts chasing readers that keep moving farther and farther away from us. That's a very expensive process. Our future, I hope, is that all of the delivery of the news will become cheaper and more electronic, and we will reach our readers by much less expensive ways, and that more and more money can be devoted to the gathering of information, to the hiring of talent, and to the more intelligent presentation of news.

Heffner: Electronic from the reporter to the paper, to go into print, or electronic from the *Times* to the reader?

To the reader, I would think in the next few decades methods will evolve by which you will get some kind of a wonderful newspaper— it may not look much like the present one—in your home, or even to take with you on the bus, that will be essentially electronic. That isn't for a long time. The *New York Times* is a way of looking at the world intelligently, and it does not and will not always depend upon the trucks racing around Times Square. —1994

NAT HENTOFF

Nat Hentoff made his reputation early on as a jazz critic, but went on from there to become a wide-ranging journalistic commentator on society, culture, and politics—and especially freedom of speech. When we spoke together in the late 1980s, I wanted to pin him down on something he had said earlier, "We in the business of journalism—one of our besetting sins is 'preset'—you come into a standard story, most reporters do and most editors do, too, with a preset." I asked him whether this wasn't a rather strange indictment of those many of us who work so hard to protect the First Amendment and whether we might not expect more in return by way of fairness and balance.

If you don't come into any story, and this is true of anybody in everyday life, let alone reporters, if you don't approach a story with a preset based on who you are, who your parents were, whom your married to, and who you used to be married to, all [those] factors that give us our prejudices, which we call our opinions, or our certainties, then you're not alive. What a reporter is supposed to do is to be aware of this preset, and then if the facts that he uncovers go against that, to change the preset. Recently, I saw a marvelous example of this, at my own paper. A young reporter, guy named Barry Cooper—Barry Michael Cooper—his assignment was to look into those kids who allegedly raped and strangled and beat unmercifully that young woman in Central Park. He did, indeed, go around the neighborhood, talked to people, and he came back with facts that indicated, contrary to what was printed in the *New York Times* and most of the other places, that these were not good kids. Their parents certainly had tried hard to make them into good kids, but they were terrors in the neighborhood, and had been for a long time, particularly against some Hispanic people [who] lived across the street. I don't think Cooper expected to find that. It was especially hard for him as a young black reporter to write what he found, but as he said to me, he said "I had no choice. I mean that's what I'm supposed to do, is tell what the facts are." . . . If you don't go into a story with a preset then where have you been? I go into stories with them all the time. I had a preset, for example, that, let us say, Judge Bork was, for various reasons in my preset, because my idols are Brennan and Douglas (whom I think is vastly underrated these days) and Black, whom I disagreed with in many things, but—and I thought that Bork, because of my preset, was really unfit to be on the Court, and now that I see who his successor was, I wish I had thought more carefully when I wrote about Bork. Because, at least, although I do still think that Bork is essentially a majoritarian, which makes him less sensitive to individual rights and liberties than a Supreme Court Justice should be, at least he's an independent thinker, and his successor, Justice Kennedy, is quite clearly not.

Heffner: Now, wait a minute. A lot of things, as usual, crammed into one of the Hentoff paragraphs. Majoritarian. Are you saying that Hentoff is not a majoritarian?

No. Good Lord, no. I wouldn't be such a heretic and I wouldn't be so maligned, and receive death threats occasionally if I were. Much of the time I write against the tide, including the majoritarian, that is the majority views, prejudices, whatever, of the community. I wrote against the invasion of Lebanon by Israel in 1982. Never received so many letters inviting me, showing me various ways, to commit suicide expeditiously, on anything I've ever written. I am opposed to what's going on now on college campuses around the country, I think it's the most dangerous trend in the country. At some of the prestige schools, University of Wisconsin, University of Michigan, the University of California at Berkeley, and various other places, because there have been, some very ugly incidents of racist, sexist behavior on campus, the reaction is not more speech, more attempts to show people what all this leads to and where it came from. The reaction to that among Liberals, including faculty members, administrators, and the students themselves, with very few exceptions, is to set up a new set of rules that will punish speech, that will punish racist, sexist speech. This is wholly violative of both the letter and the spirit of the First Amendment. Potter Stewart, the late Supreme Court Justice, said that whenever you see censorship in a society, it shows that it has lost confidence in itself. Boy, isn't that true now of the campuses?

Heffner: You're anti-majoritarian?

In some respects you have to be.

Heffner: In some respects—?

I mean James Madison made it very clear. I will paraphrase rather liberally here, he said at one point, I guess it was in 1789 or in 1790 . . . "You know, George the Third is no longer the enemy. We've beaten

George the Third. The enemy is us. And the reason for the courts, and the reason for the Bill of Rights is that the majority is often wrong, and there has to be a place where the individual dissident, the individual minority view is heard and strengthened and allowed to continue to say what he or she wants to."

Heffner: But I'm sure that your definition of majority rule includes majority rule and minority rights. Isn't that how we put them together?

But the majority often has no respect for, to say the least, minority rights, and that's when you have to watch out. That's when you have to watch out for legislators, I mean the obvious being Joe McCarthy who, for a time, was riding a majority tide. I can give you a less, less well-known example. There was a time, in the 1920s before the First Amendment through the Fourteenth Amendment were incorporated to apply to the individual states—it was just a Federal First Amendment then . . . when the majority was so afraid of the Red Scare, that I forget how many states, maybe 17, had statutes that said if you flew a flag that was red, that's all it had to be, nothing on it, then you could go to jail. And people went to jail. That's majoritarianism. Now that couldn't happen, I hope, because the First Amendment would intervene.

Heffner: Yet, the people who are protesting on the campus obviously must remind you of the people who were protesting on the campuses in the 1960s.

Yes, but it is a legacy that rides on emotion and calls it policy. So, what bothers me now is, and this sounds very old-timey, is that many of the faculty members now . . . are products of the '60s. They were in the demonstrations. And that's fine . . . But I would have hoped that by now they would realize that they have some kind of, if not a legacy at least, they have some kind of responsibility to the students that they now have to point out the consequences of suppressing speech, for example. About five years ago at the New Paltz campus, State University of New York, a professor of political science who was opposed to apartheid, as all the kids were—he invited one of the members of the South African delegation to the United Nations to come visit. He said, to the kids, he said, "Better you should hear it first hand, then read about it. Hear what the guy has to say, maybe it will illuminate what's going on there." The guy from the South African delegation was not allowed to speak. He got on the campus, he was surrounded, big boos, all that stuff and he finally, essentially, ran away. And at the time I knew a guy who was at the UN, a correspondent for one of the big chains in South Africa, and he was delighted to hear about this. He said, "Don't you think I'm going to lead with this tonight?" because it showed the people in South Africa and the government that here are these people moralizing at us about how we don't have freedoms, they won't let our person speak. It was a good lesson, but nobody learned it.

Heffner: I have the feeling that what you're talking about on the campuses today once again, in some instances, is a rejection of our heritage.

Yes, and it's a rejection that I think comes out of ignorance. I spend a fair amount of time every year in middle schools, junior high schools, and high schools around the country. Most kids, whether at fast track schools, or schools where the kids aren't going to go anywhere, not through their fault, those kids are denotatively ignorant of their own rights, and therefore of anybody else's rights and liberties. The teachers teach the Bill of Rights like they were teaching the mean average temperature in Duluth, and it's no wonder that they come on campus and do what they do, even the bright ones. They don't know. They literally don't know. I think—sure, there are many fundamental flaws in teaching today, like reading and writing and math, but we also do not teach who we are. Why is this country different from others? What—you know—why do we have a Bill of Rights? Kids don't know that.

Heffner: Yes, you might remember, was it right after the Korean War, and a scholar did a study of how many turncoats there had been, how many American soldiers had turned coat when captured, indicating if you studied them, you found out that their minds were empty as far as the American past, the American heritage, was concerned, was a vacuum.

Right.

Heffner:. So I guess nothing very much has changed.

No. And increasingly . . . most people get their news, their sense of what's going on, their continuity, to use the term very loosely . . . from television. And television doesn't cover this stuff. The Supreme Court cases, the most important cases, you see it all in a blur of about 90 seconds unless you stay up late, and maybe you'll get it on Ted Koppel, and maybe you'll get it on MacNeil/Lehrer. Mike Gartner, who became President of NBC News, Mike is a Constitutionalist, he's passionate about that stuff. So I told him when he got in there, "Mike I assume now we're going to get more stuff on the Supreme Court." Then nothing.

Heffner: Because NBC is not exactly an educational instrument.

No, but you can still do this stuff. I mean if you tell the stories . . . start it at the beginning, tell who these people are. People don't know who the people are in these cases. If you told that on television, do about four of these a year. Take the case of DeShaney, the poor kid, Joshua DeShaney, who was beaten again and again and again by his father when he was four years old until he is now profoundly retarded, he'll be institutionalized for life. This case went to the court on the basis that the social worker in the county in Wisconsin knew what was going on, dutifully, responsibly put down everything in her notebook and did nothing. Did nothing whatever. The case was on "Does this kid have a federal constitutional right, when there is gross negligence, to get at least some damages"? Not that that'll help him. The Supreme Court said "no" because it always says "no" in these cases—because after all, he wasn't beaten by the social worker, he was beaten by the father, therefore the state has no responsibility. People ought to know about that case.

Heffner: But Nat, you're saying that story, dramatic as it is, would find, could, should find a place within our commercial-media structure.

Listen. Murrow did it, didn't he?

Heffner: Murrow did it, God bless him, but why aren't these things done? They're not done because you're asking that they be done within the context of a commercial medium.

I know. I have this absolutely unfounded illusion that eventually some people, at least one of the networks will say, "Hey, you know, we've got some time we're not selling so much of, maybe we ought to do something for [laughter], for the— here's majoritarian—for the good of the public in terms of telling them something." You can't preach, but if you tell the stories, that's something, isn't it? —1989

WILLIAM SAFIRE

I have had a number of conversations with William Safire, beginning as far back as the late 1970s. To borrow from Native American mythology, Safire has always been a shape-shifter as a writer, political essayist, novelist, reporter, speechwriter, language expert—but always with same color: Republican. Currently an Op-Ed page columnist for the New York Times, *his prose is consistently acerbic, informative, combative—he reads a lot younger than his chronological age would suggest. Safire has a unique way of speaking in solid paragraphs of commentary, a number of which here follow:*

On Standards: In Politics and English

I think there should be single standards in politics, and I think there should be high standards in English usage. And when you swing a little, when you depart from high standards, you should know what you're doing. You shouldn't intersperse everything you say with, "you know." You shouldn't talk pompously about meaningful dialogues when you're talking about two people understanding each other. You shouldn't use either childlike expressions or academic jargon. You should try to speak clearly and you should try to think clearly. You should try to adopt a political attitude. Now, I've adopted a fairly conservative political attitude. I hope it's consistent. Same thing in language.

On Conservatism, Libertarianism, and Privacy

I started in politics working in the 1952 Eisenhower campaign. I was a modern Republican, a Rockefeller Republican. I carried as banner that said, "Stay in the mainstream," in the 1964 Republican convention out at the Cow Palace. And then since I've become, I guess, a less modern Republican. I am more conservative as I've gotten older. But frankly, I've had a chance to think through things and now I'm a libertarian conservative. And that seems inconsistent. But there are two roots really to conservatism as I see it. One is the traditionalist, protect society, uphold society's values root. And the second is the libertarian root, which is, get the government out of the business of making moral decisions for individuals, and let people make the decisions for themselves. So that's why I, as a professed, avowed Conservative, say abortion should be an individual decision not dictated by the state; prostitution should be legal, although it should be perhaps licensed; and a great many other things that people will say, "Gee, that sounds like a Liberal." It's libertarian, and I'm for privacy, for personal freedom of the individual. Now, I didn't just come to this full-blown. It's been years in the making, and I've taken a few lumps along the way.

I got incensed when I discovered that my phone was tapped in the Nixon administration. I had written speeches for Richard Nixon upholding the right of privacy. And then to find out that the phone was tapped in the Nixon administration was a dash of cold water in the face. I don't think the government should listen in on its citizens. I think the government should be closely circumscribed. Now, when it comes to those outside the government, when you have the government versus the press, in the adversary relationship which should exist and the tension which should exist, government has the edge. There's no getting around it. Government has the subpoena power, it has the power of intimidating its own people to keep quiet. The press should then have the right to poke its nose in, take a few chances. That anti-privacy privacy is what I'm talking about. That right to poke our nose into the doings in government. I don't think that's an invasion of privacy. I think that's the protection of the individual.

On Watergate: The Chill Effect

They tapped my phone . . . I found out later. You come out of an experience like that, and you begin saying "What was the essential lesson of Watergate?" It was the abuse of power, and we mustn't let any center of power dominate our lives. And particularly not the White House. So, here I am a member of the media establishment, not reveling in the power of the establishment, but trying to use the power that I have in it as a countervailing force to the power of government. Government operates largely secretly. Which is wrong. The amount of secrecy in government is totally unnecessary. There are some national secrets, like how to build a hydrogen bomb, which we ought to keep, but most of the other secrets are embarrassments. And it's my job, and the job of the press to create a tension that will strike a balance, and unfold more. Now when the head of the Criminal Division of the United States Department of Justice picks up the phone to call somebody, he sends a chill across that line into whoever he speaks to because he can indict you. And the wonderful thing about our system is when he picks up the phone and *I'm* calling, or somebody like me, he feels the chill. And there should be somebody, some countervailing force reminding people in power that their power is not all powerful.

On the Art of the Leak

Well, there's leaking, and there's leaking. There's sitting there sucking your thumb staring at a wall when the phone rings and somebody says, "Hey, I've got a story for you from inside the government." And it may be someone is trying to sell you something without taking responsibility for it; it may be a whistle-blower's leak, which is somebody saying, "Hey, I don't like it around here. Let me tell you what's going on." Then there is something that frankly reporters and pundits aren't given credit for, there's the story you dig out, where you put two and two together, where you see this letter to the Senate about Burt Lance [a high official in the Carter administration] that doesn't ring true, or this story that Billy Carter is telling, it just doesn't add up. And at that point you start calling and start putting out the lines and saying, "If you hear anything about this, give me a call." And that's not a leak; that's digging out a story. And that is, I think, in the great tradition. That's what we should be doing.

On the Republican Party: Circa Early '90s

I'm certain that a rigidly moralistic view is held by the majority of Republicans. I think the majority of Republicans are reasonable Right, rather than self-righteous Right. Or Far Right. The Religious Right has a right to its view, has a right to assert its view, and quite frankly whipped the tails of the rest of the Party in primaries and in getting active and electing delegates and, and taking over that Convention. That's politics. They played it fair. And I think the rest of the party's got to wake up to the fact that in the Convention of 1996 we're going to have to put together a platform and a party that would appeal to the whole country. I felt that Iraq-gate was a scandal three years ago. And I saw those same characteristics of Watergate that I ignored then, 20 years ago. Well, I can't ignore them now. The abuse of power and then cover-up and trying to keep it away from being exposed. And so I inveighed against it. And the fact that they're Republicans—that doesn't enter my mind. I'm a good Republican, and I think a good Conservative, and I think we have to purify our own.

On the Book of Job: Part I

God was looking down on Earth and observing the perfect man—pious, upright, lived a good life, powerful man, major chieftain. And he says to Satan, "Observe my servant Job—how terrific he is, good." And Satan says, "Well, no wonder—he's rich and powerful and happy. No wonder he's pious. Does Job fear God for naught? Is he doing this for nothing? He's getting something from it." And God, in order to prove that the worship of man was not for material things, said, "Okay, you test him." Then that portion of Job ends. And the poetry begins where Job is tested, and he's afflicted. Out of the clear blue sky with these terrible misfortunes—all his children are killed, his property is taken away, and he's afflicted with terrible boils and he's sitting there on a dung heap, then contrary to the popular belief, he doesn't just sit there piously and say, "Well, this is the way the world is, and I'll stay resigned. On the contrary, he says, "Damn the day that I was born," and he's furious. He's irreverent to the point of blasphemy. Because when he says, "Damn the day that I was born, let there be darkness," that's his way of saying as in Genesis where it is said, "Let there be light," he was challenging God's justice. And essentially he said, "God is mismanaging the morality of the world" because, as the reader knows, he's a good man . . . he didn't do anything wrong, and he's being treated unjustly. And so, instead of just taking it on the chin, he challenges God and essentially says, "I'm being treated unjustly, there's no reason for this." And his friends come and sit there to commiserate with him, and they say, "Look, you must have sinned because you wouldn't be suffering otherwise." And he said, "No, I haven't sinned. And I'm suffering for no reason." Now, what was the poet who was writing this, getting at? I think he was getting at reality. Here in the first five books of the Bible, Deuteronomy particularly, you learn about retribution. You do good and God will take care of you; and you do bad and you'll be punished. But that's not the way the world always works. I mean, the good die young, the wicked prosper. There's something wrong. And there must have been a crisis in the faith back 500 years B.C.E. because people were beginning to say, "Hey, this isn't the way the world really is." So the poet who wrote Job, came up with this idea that in the real world, there wasn't morality enforced by God, and that it was for us to work it out. And we couldn't lean on God and expect him to give us perfect order. Now this was kind of blasphemous. And I think that the end of the book of Job, in order to get it into the Bible, to get into the canon, he had to tack on a Hollywood ending. He had to say, "Okay, at the end God lectures Job and Job submits and then he gives him back his family, his money, everything." Which does not really make the point of the book. The point of the book is that it's okay to object to injustice, and it's okay to assert yourself against even the highest authority if the highest authority is wrong.

On the Book of Job: Part II

We know from the Book of Job that God treated him unjustly. We who read the Bible, or any reader of the Bible, can see that this injustice was God's way of testing Job. But from Job's point of view, or from mankind's point of view, which doesn't have this opportunity to see what's going on in Heaven, it's unjust. And when we see this abuse of authority, and abuse of power, what should we do? What Job suggests is that we shouldn't just sit there and take it. That we should object at the top of our lungs, as Job did, "Damn the day that I was born," and then insist on accountability. What Job did was said, "I wish I had a lawyer, a redeemer, some intermediary, so that I could take God to court and argue with him in court to say 'you've treated me unjustly.'" And then he kind of rejects that by saying "How can you argue with the supreme judge?" And that, of course, has a political meaning for us today, i.e., how do we argue with authority when it's at the center of power? And the answer is, we should argue, we should contest and what the Book of Job teaches is that God approves of that contest. Now in *The Voice from the Whirlwind,* Job's God comes in and essentially puts down Job rather sharply, as if to say "Who are you to ask these questions?". And Job is indeed intimidated by this theophany, this appearance of God. But when you think about it, what this man has done has caused God to become accountable. He's called him down and said, "All right, face me and explain to me why injustice exists." And what I go into in [Safire's then current book] *The First Dissident* is how God symbolically explains that there may be more things on heaven and earth than mankind knows, and that it may be a grand design, that what seems like injustice may be part of a grander design of justice. But, in political terms, in confronting authority, in what we learned in Watergate, is that it's right to challenge authority, it's right to hold authority accountable and we find justification for that right in the Bible.

On the Book of Job: Part III

Deconstructionists, you know, love to take apart text. And so do I. And so do most people who write. But the purpose of taking apart and closely examining these textual things is not to say, "Aha, the meaning of this word was that," but to back off and ask, "What was this Book of Job created for? What does it do in the Bible?" What I say it does is interject a note of realism into moral thinking. Most moralists, most Bible readers will say "God runs a moral universe, and you do good and you are rewarded, and you do badly and you are punished." Well now 2,500 years ago people came to look at that and say, "That's not the way the world works. A lot of people who are good don't make it, and the wicked prosper. That's the way it really is. And how can that fit in with a just God? How can earthquakes and children born with AIDS and you know, these terrible things that happen, happen to good people. How can there be a just God?"

Anybody who's gone through a terrible experience (and I haven't suffered the way most people have suffered, but anybody that has suffered at all) has to ask himself, "Why? Why am I suffering? What have I done? What sins have I created?". And what the Book of Job teaches is that suffering is not evidence of sin. It irritates me, for example, when some people say that AIDS is some kind of scourge or punishment for homosexuality. That goes right against the teaching of Job, who says that suffering is not evidence of sin. The key point of the way Job operates is that he was not a patient man. He exploded when they did him dirty. And when he damned the day he was born, and when he cursed God's light—that's pretty blasphemous, that must have really shook them up, you know, when they were putting together a Bible.

On The Book of Job: Part IV

We can't afford not to have the Jobs. We can't afford not to have the Gandhis who go up against Colonial Empire, the Sharanskys who were the first crack in the order of the Soviet Empire, the "refuseniks."

We can't afford not to have the Sakharovs and those who were prisoners of conscience, who could have gotten out, but chose to take their suffering because they knew there was power being abused. That spirit of human freedom and that courage to stand up for it, I find rooted in the Book of Job, and I think that's why so many artists and so many thinkers have come back to this book, perhaps more than any other book in the Bible, because it sticks out of the Bible like a sore thumb. It's irreverent, it's blasphemous in a lot of ways and yet, it's not a guide to, good grief, it's not just something to say at a funeral. It's a rebel's book.

On The Book of Job: The Last Word

Job's demands and Job's arrogance and his insistence that he was being unjustly prosecuted forced God to suddenly appear, out of the whirlwind, and God wasn't very happy about being forced to appear, and justify himself before man. And he did—thunderously. And sometimes misleadingly. But you read the Bible and you say, "Here's a man able to irritate God to the point of God coming out and saying 'Let me show you some indication of my grand design. My, my great purpose.'" And that came about, not because mankind was patient or reverent or observant but because Job had guts. And he wouldn't take no for an answer, and he wouldn't accept injustice. I have Joban tendencies, but to be, to be a Job as those criteria set forth, you're talking about Sharansky, you're talking about Sakharov, you're talking about men and women who have really suffered for their conscience. We in America are blessed with such freedom that we don't do that much suffering for conscience. Some, but the dissidents in the world, particularly the ones who broke up the Soviet Union, who broke up the Evil Empire, I think a century from now we will look back and see these were the great heroes of our time. These guys who went to jail, Havel and others, who ultimately achieved a victory against tyranny. And it wasn't America as the super power militarily defeating the other super power. It was the dissidents behind the Iron Curtain and in a Civil Rights Movement here, too, who were able to change the world. —1980

Ken Auletta

Ken Auletta is one of our most perceptive journalists focusing investigative powers on the world of communications. In addition, he is a clear and fluent writer, with books and dozens of articles to his credit. He has been the media correspondent of The New Yorker *magazine for a number of years, and a frequent guest expert on the topic of television. Looking back at our conversations in the nineties, I also find him to be something of a prophet concerning the business of communications. I had asked him what he saw as the upside and the downside of communications futures.*

The upside, simply put, is that viewers, and they may be people who read magazines and newspapers, can view them electronically in the evening. For instance, if you want to watch the *New York Times* instead of running to the news stand as few of us do at quarter to ten at night, you'll be able to view it on your computer screen or your television screen, or maybe your telephone console. So you'll have a democracy of choice. That's the great upside, the upside that will empower me, as a viewer, or a listener, or a participant in this new media technology, to select what I want to watch or listen to when I want to watch or listen to it. Not when some network, or some station, or some channel decides to make it available. So we'll be in a post-channel universe where I can basically plug into my video jukebox and watch any movie, any show, including a repeated show, that I want to, at a time of my choosing. That's, that's a great plus— empowerment, democracy. The great negative is built into the positive. Because within that democracy you will be losing a common frame, a sense of community. We will not have the same shared experience as we had, say, in the earlier decades, when nine out of ten people on a given night were watching one of the three networks, just three networks. And the next day at the watercooler, after 77 percent of Americans watched a miniseries like *Roots* in 1977, the next day at the watercooler they could talk about race relations in America, because they all shared that common experience. You don't have that shared experience now, and you'll have less and less of it in this new technological future, a heavy price to pay in a world that's already Balkanized, or communities that are already fragmented and caught up in special interests and special pleadings.

Heffner: Okay, that answers the question in part. It reminds me that, at the beginning, in the fifties when television was just coming into its own, and there was a wonderful cartoon somewhere, of the man of the future—it was a Cyclops, just one single big eye in the middle of his or her forehead because that's all one needed, focused on the television screen. But what about the content? I mean, for example, did the invention of the telephone in its time give us something new to say?

Well, you can go one of two ways. Either a benefit or a detriment.

Heffner: What's your bet?

I'd say both at the same time. You will have more choices, and you will be able to see documentaries, if you want to see them, and news. You'll be able to see history, call up tutorials—you want to study ancient Greece, you'll be able to do it. Your encyclopedia, whatever—call up books, do it. Your library of choices will be vast. And, if you have special interests—a black network, you have it now, you'll have more. News? CNN, C-SPAN, CNN II, CNN International, you'll have that, too. The, the downside is that good quality programs—I mentioned *Roots*, for example, the miniseries, which galvanized three-quarters of all Americans for an entire week in 1977—an entire week, five nights in a row. Three out of every four Americans watched this single show. I mean that's extraordinary, if you think about it. And it was a good show, but it was an expensive show. And if you no longer have a massive audience, you can't afford the expense of doing that kind of a quality miniseries. That's a major downside, and a major detriment to this new video technology, because empowering people to have many choices means you subtract the ability to have a single wonderful choice.

Heffner: Let's turn to print. You recently moderated a symposium of experts on book publishing. What did you take from that—hope or despair?

I am simultaneously pessimistic and optimistic. Let me tell you what I mean by that. I am pessimistic because I see the business pressures in publishing pushing for more big books, more big first printings, more Hollywood-type celebrity books that they think will achieve the magic mass market they're trying to reach; they will push, and the accountants, who have an increasingly large voice at book-publishing houses, will push to make the decision-making process more rational, and therefore cut out some of those potential backlist books that they shouldn't be cutting out and, in fact, that often make money for the publishing house in the long run but not in the short run. So I'm depressed about that. At the same time, my depression is reduced by the real opportunities offered by technology. Technology might bring about changes in publishing. That is to say: the threatened, midlist book that doesn't sell like a bestseller, and that increasingly is having a hard time finding a publishing house, may well—I'm not saying it will, but may well—find it easier to find a publishing house if one doesn't have to keep an inventory. Online book sales and so-called on-demand printing will become important factors. You take some of the bad economics out of the business, potentially, and you make it possible for people to keep books in stock. Also, a vehicle like the Internet allows us, as authors, to self-publish. And then, if you can figure out some way to charge for what we're self-publishing, you make it possible to keep more books in print, and maybe earn a little money. But I think it's a given that reading will go down. I worry about that. I think it's a given that big publishing houses will get bigger. But I also think simultaneously there's a contradictory given, which is that more people will get in the business, there'll be more competition from smaller houses, and perhaps books that now go out of print will stay in print.

Heffner: Please tell me what you mean by "reading going down."

Well, if you think about your kids (I have a 15-year-old), think about her day. She comes home from school after playing soccer at 6:00, 6:15. She's got to eat. She takes a shower. It's now 7:30. She's had her family dinner with us. She's got a lot of homework to do. She doesn't have any time for leisure reading during the week. She'll say she wants to watch a program like *Mad About You*, as she did last night, and I said, "No, you've got too much homework to do." She wants to go online and check whether she's gotten any mail. "Get your work done." She got her work done. Last night she went online. So instead of reading a book, she checked the correspondence she had from friends from all over the country: the people she went to camp with, people she knows from childhood. So, just looking at her, it's harder for her to read certainly during the week. On the weekend, you can catch up. But do you ever really catch up? And the truth is, surveys show that young people are reading less today than they once did. And part of the reason is that they have many more choices for leisure-time activity, and many more pressures. Not just school pressures, but Internet pressures, channel-choice pressures.

And also, if you think about what television does to the brain, it attenuates the attention span. Reading is a linear experience that takes patience and work. You've got to stay with it. Everything about televison is not about staying with it. It's using that remote control to keep switching.

Heffner: By "television" you mean all modern communications, electronic media.

I do. I do. I think electronic media often subverts reading. And not just because it's an alternative choice, but because the very process is a nonlinear experience. Reading is a linear experience which takes patience and time and work and effort. And television doesn't always take, usually doesn't take, time and work and effort.

Heffner: What does that do, that nonlinear learning that you see, what does that do, to larger questions of public-policy, citizen-participation, or interest in principle?

I think it has the potential to undermine the civic culture, potentially, and I worry a lot about that. For instance, the television culture is one that demands instant gratification: "Give me the answer. Get to the point." You watch television, and you watch kids. They're not only watching television, they're listening to, you know, a CD player in their ear, and maybe they're reading a magazine or reading a book at the same time. They don't focus fully on any one thing. In fact, they feel they can grasp everything, in part because it's not so complicated.

Well, public-policy issues are very complicated, yet this new audience is asking communicators to have sharp points of view, sum them up quickly in a very limited space, or a short period of time.

Being a citizen in a democracy takes time and patience and effort. Most decisions on public-policy issues are very complicated, and they demand more than yes or no answers. And I think we have a "yes-or-no" culture.

Heffner: Then what? What about the next century?

I think there are dangers for our culture, our civic culture. I think you can make an alternative argument and come out a little more hopefully, and I don't dismiss it, which is that technology will allow, for instance, for you to register to vote at home. Then it will allow you to vote at home without having to tax yourself by walking to the polling place. Technology will allow you, and does allow you, to get instant information on anything you want when you want it. Not having to wait for some network programmer to program the evening news at 6:30. And technology allows you many more choices. You have a great number of newspapers in America online today.

So if I want information, I have many more sources of information, as a journalist today, or as a citizen today, than I had five or ten years ago. That's hopeful, but as you go along and report more, and see the consequences of technology and other changes, as you steep yourself in them more and more, you come to new realizations and clearer realizations, and I think I'm learning all the time, and I probably have, it is fair to say that I probably have a more acute sense of some of the pessimistic sides of this potential future today than I did five years ago or two years ago.

But I am, as you also say, by nature optimistic. So I am a guy who finds myself gravitating to that Christopher Morley aphorism, which is, "The truth is a liquid; not a solid." And I think that it is very liquid in my mind. Some days I wake up and I'm pessimistic, and other days I wake up and I'm optimistic. And most days I'm both at the same time. —1993

RACE

MARTIN LUTHER KING, JR. AND JUDGE J. WATIES WARING

It is almost a half century now since I first introduced Martin Luther King to my viewers as a spokesperson for "The New Negro," the title of our program with former Federal Judge J. Waties Waring of South Carolina, whose earlier opinions about segregation helped pave the way for Brown v. Board of Education (the Supreme Court's landmark 1954 decision outlawing segregation in our public schools). In the years after, until his assassination in 1968, Dr. King would play perhaps the leading and most dramatic role in our nation's efforts to right the racial wrongs of its past, dramatically changing the ways in which African Americans view themselves. The very language of our conversation seems almost archaic, certainly in the easy use of the term "Negro." But the thrust of Dr. King's and Judge Waring's argument remains as forceful as ever. I asked Martin Luther King just who and what is "The New Negro."

Dr. King: I think I could best answer that question by saying first that the new Negro is a person with a new sense of dignity and destiny, with a new self-respect; along with that is a lack of the fear which once characterized the Negro, the willingness to stand up courageously for what he feels is just and, what he feels he deserves on the basis of the laws of the land. I think also included would be a self-assertive attitude . . . And all of these factors come together to make what seems to me to be the new Negro.

I think also I would like to mention a growing honesty which characterizes the Negro today. There was a time that the Negro used duplicity, deception too, rather as a survival technique; although he didn't particularly like conditions, he said he liked them because he felt that the boss wanted to hear that. But now from the housetops, from the kitchens, from the classrooms, and from the pulpit, the Negro says in no uncertain terms that he doesn't like the way he's being treated.

So at long last the Negro is telling the truth. And I think this is also one of the basic characteristics of the new Negro.

Judge Waring: My observation of the Negro, and I'm speaking in generalities, of course, has been that up to recently he has been a half-man, or a part-man, and now he at last is waking up to the fact that he's a whole man, that he's an American citizen, and that he is entitled to rights, no more, no less, than just the ordinary run-of-the-mill American citizen. He's never had that before; he hasn't been allowed to have it. He's been under political domination; he's been oppressed; he's had economic deprivation; he's been a servant, formerly a slave; and now suddenly I see the idea has come to him that he's really, truly a man that can stand up on his own hind legs and tell the truth, and say: "I don't want any special privilege; I don't want any special handout; I don't want to be given anything, because the giving idea is all wrong. But I want a chance to become a full man and do my part, be it little or be it big, in the community of our country."

Dr. King: I think it's better to be aggressive at this point. It seems to me that it is both historically and sociologically true that privileged classes do not give up their privileges voluntarily. And they do not give them up without strong resistance. And all of the gains that have been made, that we have received in the area of civil rights, have come about because the Negro stood up courageously for these rights, and he was willing to aggressively press on. So I would think that it would be much better in the long run to stand up and be aggressive with understanding, good will and a sense of discipline, yet things like these should not be substituted for pressing on. And with this aggressive attitude I believe that we will bring the gains of civil rights much sooner than we would just standing idly by, waiting for these things to be given voluntarily.

Heffner: What about the ill will that's generated by aggressiveness? Certainly there is your own experience in Montgomery; you've been the target of strong attacks; you've been the target of verbal and other kinds of violence.

Dr. King: Well, I think that is a necessary phase of the transition. Whenever oppressed people stand up for their rights and rise up against the oppressors, so to speak, the initial response of the oppressor is bitterness. That's true in most cases, I think; and that is what we are now experiencing in the South, this initial response of bitterness, which I hope will be transformed into a more brotherly attitude. We hope that the end will be redemption and reconciliation, rather than division.

But this, it seems to me, [is] a necessary phase of the transition from the old order of segregation and discrimination to the new order of freedom and justice. And this should not last forever; it's just something that's natural right now, and as soon as we pass out of the shock period into the more creative period of adjustment I think that bitterness and ill will will pass away.

Judge Waring: The courts have declared the rights. And I think the Supreme Court decision of May 17, 1954, was the greatest thing that's happened in this country in many, many decades, And I think that it declared in effect that segregation, segregation by law, is illegal and not a part of America. And all the people, the big people and the little people throughout this land have awakened to the fact that they have a right.

Now remember this: it's not a matter of giving rights. Rights aren't given. The right to vote isn't given to you. It's yours and it belongs to you. And the Negro people are beginning to realize that they are ordinary human beings and American citizens and they have these rights. And the courts have told them so.

Now it's up to them to move out. They haven't got to go out with guns and bombs and gas, but they've got to go out with determination and courage and steadfastness like this man Luther King has done and say: Here am I, and I stand here on my rights.

And it's going to prevail; it's got to prevail; and it can't be beaten if we have enough of them who are steadfast enough.

When they begin to compromise and sell out on principles, then they're gone.

Now the matter of strategy is to keep a complete, solid front. There may be tactics as to whether you want to make bus cases first or school cases or railroad cases or things of that kind—those are minor details. But the strategy is: you must never surrender any of the rights you have gained, and you must look forward to the attainment of full equality.

Heffner: Where do you go from here?

Dr. King: That's a pretty difficult question to answer at this point, since in Montgomery we have not worked out any future plans, that is, in any chronological order. We are certainly committed to work and press on until segregation is nonexistent in Montgomery and all over the South.

We are committed to full equality and doing away with injustice wherever we find it. But as to the next move I don't have the answer for that because we have not worked that out at this point.

We have been so involved in the bus situation that we have not had the real time to sit down and think about next moves. But in a general sense, we are committed to achieving first class citizenship in every area of life in Montgomery and throughout the Southern community.

Heffner: Talk about the importance of Brown v. Board of Education.

Dr. King: I think it had a tremendous impact and influence on the Negro and bringing about this new self-respect. I think it certainly is one of the major factors, not the only one. I think several other forces and historical circumstances must be brought into the picture. The fact that social changes made it necessary for the Negro to travel more, so that his rural, plantation background was gradually supplanted by a more urban, industrial life. Illiteracy was gradually passing away, and with the growth of the cultural life of the Negro, that brought about new self-respect. And economic growth, and also the tremendous impact of the world situation, with people all over the world seeking freedom from colonial powers and imperialism, these things all came together, and then with the decision of May 1954, we gained the culminating point.

That, it seems to me, was the final point which seemed to bring all of these things together. And that gave this new Negro a new self-respect which we see all over the South and all over the nation today.

Heffner: Why then do you ask for another act on a national level, an act, let's say, on the part of the President—perhaps an Eisenhower speech in the South? Why is this so important?

Dr. King: Well, I think it's necessary for all of the forces possible to be working to implement and enforce the decisions that are handed down by the courts. And so often in the area of civil rights it seems that the judicial branch of the government is fighting the battle alone.

And we feel that the executive and legislative branches of the government have the basic responsibility. And at points these branches have been all too silent and all too stagnant in their moves to implement and enforce the decisions. With the popularity of the President and his tremendous power and influence, just a word from him could do a great deal to ease the situation, calm emotions, and give Southern white liberals something to stand on, if it is nothing but something to quote.

The Southern white liberal stands in a pretty difficult position because he does not have anywhere to turn for emotional security similar to what hate groups, I mean the things that other groups have to turn to, the hate organizations, so to speak.

But with a word from the president of the United States, with his power and influence, it would give a little more courage and backbone to the white liberals in the South who are willing to be allies in the struggle of the Negro for first-class citizenship.

Heffner: Let me ask you, Judge Waring, to what extent white Southerners are willing to be the allies Reverend King calls for in the battle of the new Negro?

Judge Waring: That's a very hard question to answer. There are very, very few that are willing to come out in the open and say so.

There are a great many in my opinion who would be glad if they were made to do it. I think that there are lots of people—I sometimes use the expression, that the little boy with the dirty face won't go and wash it, but if you grab him by the neck and scrub his face, he then boasts that he has the cleanest face in the land.

And I think there are many of the people in the South, and I saw many of them—my experience was that officially I was quite hated and condemned because I had expressed my views of what I thought the laws of the land were. And I got a lot of telephone messages and anonymous letters saying they agreed with me but they couldn't tell me why or how or who they were.

And those people want to be free, but no politician in the South is going to dare come out and take this position of his own volition. And for example if the President of the United States tells him to, he's going to fall in line.

And if we can get the top Executive people to take action we'll get somewhere.

Remember this, now: the Supreme Court has laid down the law and said what's constitutional. Now that's important, that's most important, it's the biggest thing that's ever happened. But it's got to be activated, it's got to be worked out, and the Executive Department has got to manipulate and work it and enforce it. And the Legislative department should give the Executive Department more power to work and enforce these laws.

Heffner: Let me ask Dr. King again, though, about the feelings of the Southern whites. If you had to give a progress report, how would you evaluate the battle you've fought over the past year? In terms of Southern feelings, in terms of Northern white feelings too?

Dr. King: Well, I think we've been able to see mixed emotions at this point. For instance, from a national point of view, looking all over the nation, we have had tremendous response and real genuine sympathy from many, many white persons; and naturally we've had the sympathy of Negroes.

. . . Many, many white persons of good will all over the nation have given moral support and a great deal of encouragement and that has been very encouraging to us in the struggle.

Now in the South—I guess the lines are more closely drawn. You find on the one hand a group more determined now than ever before because it is a last-ditch struggle, to do anything, even if it means using violence, to block all of the intentions and the desires of the Negroes to achieve first-class citizenship.

But there are also others who have expressed sympathy. There are white Southerners, even in Montgomery, who have been quite sympathetic; as Judge Waring just said, sometimes these people because of fear, refuse to say anything about it. They stand back because of fear of economic, social, and political reprisals. But there is a silent sympathy. And we have seen a great deal of that in Montgomery.

So it's two sides. There's this side where you get the negative response, the other side where you have the positive response. And I have seen both. And I think as time goes on the negative side will get smaller and smaller.

And those who are willing to be open-minded and accept the trend of the ages will grow into a majority group rather than a minority.

Heffner: Gentlemen, do you feel that in the long range there will be violent reactions to the progress that has been made?

Dr. King: No I don't. I think the violence will be temporary. I don't say it will end tomorrow—we will go through some more for the next few months or so, but I think once we are over the shock period, that shock will be absorbed and Southerners will come to the point of seeing that the best thing to do is sit down and work out these problems and do it in a very Christian spirit.

I think the violence that we are undergoing now is indicative the fact that the diehards realize that the system, is at its dying point. And that this is the last way to try to hold on to the old order.

Judge Waring: Mr. Heffner, all these reforms have periods of trouble. Gandhi was murdered, Jesus was crucified, and you find that most great reforms have certain periods of stress and distress.

Now just one last point I want to make. When we speak of the laws it is terribly important that they bring these cases and have a declaration of law, and action by Congress and action by the Executive. Because now, up to the time of the Supreme Court's decision, segregation was legal. And segregation, even people of good will themselves, said that the law says that we have to keep these people segregated.

For instance, it has been illegal for me to ride in a bus with Mr. King here. Now I don't want a law which says I've got to ride with him, or he's got to ride with me. But I don't want a law which says I can't sit in a seat with him.

And we've broken that, and that's an enormous advance. And we've got to do it on every stage right down the line.

The Congress of the United States, I believe—and I've been very cynical and skeptical about it—but I'm beginning to believe, they're going to do a little something this time.

And If they do a little something—they haven't done anything in 75 years—If they do a little something this time they'll do a little more next year, and the President of the United States and the officials in the administration will begin to see that if Congress is moving it's good politics to move, and that'll have a great motivating product on the national picture.

I think we're going forward, we're going forward slowly. We've got to win. And it's a question of whether we're going to win in a short time or a long time. I'm for the short period.

Heffner: How do you project this into the immediate future?

Dr. King: When I think of the question of progress in the area of race relations, I prefer to be realistic and when I say that I try to look at it not from the pessimistic point of view or the optimistic, but rather from the realistic point of view. I think we've come a long, long way, but we have a long, long way to go.

But it seems to me that if we will press on with determination, moral courage, and yet wise restraint and calm reasonableness, in a few years we will reach the goal. I have a great deal of faith in the future and the outcome. I am not despairing. —1957

MALCOLM X, JAMES FARMER, WYATT TEE WALKER, AND ALAN MORRISON

Of the many programs I have done on race relations over the years, clearly both the most dramatic and the most substantive was recorded on June 12, 1963. Malcolm X, very much in his separatist mode, joined me that day; as did James Farmer, National Director of CORE, the Congress of Racial Equality; Wyatt Tee Walker, Executive Assistant to Martin Luther King and Chief of Staff of the Southern Christian Leadership Conference; and Alan Morrison, New York Editor of Ebony *magazine. Roy Wilkins, head of the National Association for the Advancement of Colored People, couldn't join us that fateful morning as scheduled for, hours earlier, Medgar Evers, his NAACP Field Secretary in Jackson, Mississippi, had been assassinated. Evers' life had been repeatedly threatened. Ten days earlier he had said, "If I die, it will be in a good cause. I've been fighting for America as much as the soldiers in Vietnam."*

The day before the program had also been historic. National Guard troops, federalized by John F. Kennedy for the purpose, had forced Governor George C. Wallace and his State Troopers to step aside and, for the first time, permit qualified African Americans to enroll in the University of Alabama. There was no violence. And that night, President Kennedy had appealed for the first time in a dramatic and emotion-laden nationwide television address to what Lincoln had once called "the better angels of our nature" to help set right the relationship of white to black Americans.

"We are confronted primarily with a moral issue", pleaded the young President who would himself be struck down before the year was over. "It is as old as the Scriptures and is as clear as the American Constitution. The heart of the question is . . . whether we are going to treat our fellow Americans as we want to be treated. If an American, because his skin is dark . . . cannot enjoy the full and free life which all of us want, then who

among us would be content to have the color of his skin changed and stand in his place? Who among us would then be content with the counsels of patience and delay?"

The next morning I put my first question to James Farmer, about an Ebony *magazine article that quoted him as saying, "Negroes are fed up . . . are not afraid to go to jail now; they wear jail sentences as badges of honor, not even afraid of being shot. These people aren't going to stop . . ." I asked him how he would conclude that sentence: "aren't going to stop" . . . until what?*

Farmer: We aren't going to stop until a Black skin is no longer considered a badge of deformity by the American people. We are not going to stop until the dogs stop biting little children in Alabama, until the rats in tenement slums in Harlem and the hundred Harlems throughout the country stop biting our people. We're not going to stop until the bigots of the South and the North no longer challenge a man's right to live simply because he is asking for the rights which the Constitution says are his, as happened to NAACP Field Secretary Medgar Evers, who was shot and killed in Jackson, Mississippi. We're not going to stop, in a word, until we have the same rights that all Americans have. We're not going to stop until we have jobs and are not walking the street unemployed in a proportion which is more than two times as great as among whites. We're not going to stop until we have the right to a house, a decent home, an apartment, any place we choose to live. We're not going to stop until we have the right to enter any place which serves the public, all over the country. We're not going to stop, in a word, until America becomes America for all people.

Heffner: What would your assumption be about the time when, as you say, "America becomes America for all people"?

Farmer: Things are moving very rapidly now. . . . This is a climactic stage of the struggle. And I would expect that within two or three years, the most brutal aspects of segregation in the South, that is, formal segregation, will be eliminated; segregation in businesses that serve the public. I would expect, however, that there will be exceptions, that in the hardcore states of the Deep South, such as Mississippi and Alabama, and the hardcore areas of the upper and middle South, it will take a few years longer for us to break down those barriers. I would expect that it will take several years longer in the North for us to wipe out the more subtle forms of discrimination in housing, in employment, in de facto school segregation, and of police brutality. I think, however, that within five or ten years at, the most, I'll be able to take a vacation and go fishing.

Heffner: How do you gentlemen feel about Mr. Farmer's timetable? Mr. Walker?

Walker: Well, I would agree with Jim wholeheartedly that the revolution now has been mounted. What has been seen in the last four or five years has been perhaps the rumbling and thundering of the revolution that had only established beachheads. And I think the critical significance of Birmingham, Alabama, is that here the movement for the Negroes' full emancipation, took a significant turn. And I think the mood of the Negro around the country has been, well—knowing the frame of reference in which Birmingham has existed—if Negroes can stand up like this in Birmingham, Alabama, then—what the hell, we can, we ought to do something here. And I think it has given a new sense of militancy and a new sense of direction to the entire Negro community in America.

Heffner: What do you think was the ingredient here that led to this attitude? And, as Mr. Farmer said a moment ago, this is a particularly crucial period, we're all aware of that. What has changed now? What has changed in this year and the last?

Walker: I think the mounting of the revolution has created the contagion of heroism. I think the human spirit admires heroism and courage. And in an instance like Birmingham they have seen this demonstrated by the young and the old alike, male and female. And it has an infectious quality, and the compounded frustration of 244 years of slavery, and the last 100 years of quasi-freedom with all of the geometric frustrations that the Negro has had. I think this is a part of what Dr. King describes as a zeitgeist. It just had to come. And this is the moment.

Heffner: Malcolm X?

X: Well, as a follower of the Honorable Elijah Mohammed and a Muslim, we believe that Mr. Mohammed has been raised by God to separate the so-called Negroes in this country from our former slave-master, and to lead us to a land of our own where we can stand on our feet and solve our own problems. And because we religiously believe it is intended to be a part of God's plan to separate the former slave, so-called Negro, from the former slave master, the American white man, we also believe that every effort to force integration upon the white man or to force the so-called Negro into the white society is actually in direct and divine opposition to God and will meet with bloodshed and destruction and no progress or benefit either to the so-called Negro or to the white man in this country.

Heffner: Mr. Morrison?

Morrison: I agree with Reverend Wyatt Walker when he says that the revolution which is now going on in America against second-class citizenship and against racial oppression had to come. I don't altogether concur with Reverend King's analysis which I think is well-intentioned, but founded in his mystical philosophy that this is a zeitgeist period. I think the revolution was the result of inevitable historical forces, and we must recognize [that in] our 100 years after the Emancipation Proclamation was issued, that chattel slavery was succeeded by racial segregation, and that as chattel slavery had to be overwhelmed and destroyed by a military conflict, and by force. It may be necessary, as we are seeing today, that racial segregation has to be confronted in a similar manner. And the force and might of the State has to be exerted in uprooting inequality from our society and in destroying racial segregation which is simply the successor to chattel slavery. As for the revolution, I am very glad to note that that word has reached a new significance and a respectability in our culture and language. It embraces all classes of the Negro population, from the young to the old. They are united in the determination which has reached a zenith, a new point. They will not suffer indignities further. Negroes are prepared to die—Negroes are prepared to pay the price of violence in their struggle for equality, as a noted Negro educator stated this week, outside of the United States I may note, but there it is. The confrontation is here, and we must face it, and all of its consequences. And that we must also be prepared to realize that the struggle may take other than nonviolent means. Now this does not mean that the Negro is by nature violent. The Negro wants his rights, and the Negro American will achieve his rights. But it may be necessary to defend his birthright, to defend his heritage and to maintain his status and go forward to goals that he has set for himself, to protect his life, to protect his family, and to protect his status as a citizen. Violence is upon us and we must face it. And I think that there is great alarm in the land in high places as well as low, and I think it is reflected in President Kennedy's great concern about what he calls "moving the Negroes' demand for equality from the streets into the courts." It's been in the courts for a long time, and the Negro became impatient. He became impatient and demonstrated in the streets. Now the power structure of this country wants to contain the struggle. Where it will go from here we now have to consider.

Heffner: What do you mean "the power structure wants to contain the struggle"?

Morrison: I mean that those interests who own, who run, who rule the economy and the political structure of this country are now terribly alarmed that the Negroes' upsurge for equal rights and for the abolition of the badge of color which Mr. Farmer referred to just a minute ago, may result in a grave destruction of the status of the United States and its economy. It could result in serious damage to the image of the United States abroad. A very, very interesting statement was made characterizing this threat. An organization was formed just a week ago by Negro intellectuals and a couple of political people, and the man who formed it said, "It is now easier, and it will become far, far simpler to persuade and prevail upon the legislators in Congress to pass civil rights legislation because the danger, the menace to the system here, to American society, is great and serious." And he put it this way—"The white man is afraid that the Negro is going to tear up the pea-patch of America."

Farmer: I, too, think that the Negroes' revolutionary struggle is a part of a historical process. We see a worldwide struggle for freedom and Negroes could not escape becoming apart of that. Their struggle is going on in Africa and Asia. It's going on all over the world. And certainly the Negro-American was bound to come to the point where he asked, "What about this American fate, and what about these tenets of democracy? Don't they apply to me? And if not now, when?" I think that in historical terms we can date the new militancy of the Negro back to World War II, when Negro boys in uniform were fighting against the master race theory of Hitlerism. Of course, they were bound to ask themselves, what about the master race theory back in Alabama? And Mississippi? Shouldn't I fight against that just as hard? I think another reason for the evolving militancy is the increasing education of Negro youth. As one of the Negro sit-in leaders replied, when he was asked back in 1960, what accounted for the difference between his father and himself. He said, "Well, Pop had only a Bible, I've got the Bible and a college education." How are you going to teach a man about the tenets of American democracy without expecting that, at some point, he will ask, "Don't these things mean me? If not now, when?" A third factor that has created the new revolution is, of course, the emerging nations of Africa. Negroes have gotten a greater sense of identity and identification, and a greater sense of pride as a result of it. You can only push a man around so long. And this has encouraged Negroes to demand that the pushing around stop. Then come the sit-ins, the Freedom Rides—before that Montgomery, the bus boycott under Dr. King's leadership. Now Birmingham. So it's like a fog rolling in now—North and South—Negroes are saying, "Not tomorrow. Not next week. But now."

Heffner: Mr. Farmer, when you talk about the Administration, when you talk about containment, are you talking about containing the acts of violence or near violence, or are you talking about containing the Negroes' effort to secure for himself the equality that is the birthright of all people?

Farmer: We're talking about containing the militant struggle—that is, stop what you are doing and let's go back to the old way of doing it, by sitting around the table, and parceling out a few minor steps here and there. But this is not enough any longer.

Heffner: But do you think that this reflects a basic refusal to accept the development of the Negroes' position?

Farmer: I think in part it's a refusal or failure to recognize the intensity of the demands. Now I think that recognition is coming, I think that the Administration is beginning to recognize it. The speech of the President recently on civil rights indicates that. But this is because the pressure is kept up. And I fear that if the pressure relaxes now that the tendency of the power structure to move will decline. That's why we intend to keep up the pressure as I'm sure the other gentlemen here do.

Heffner: Malcolm X wanted to comment on that.

X: Yes, on this white power structure. When you say, "power struc-ture" I know you mean the white power structure because that's all we have in America. And the white power structure today is just as much interested in perpetuating slavery as the white power structure was 100 years ago. Only now they use modern methods of doing so. And realizing that the black people in this country are waking up and becoming filled with a desire to be looked upon as men, and as human beings, the white power structure uses tricks to slow down that struggle for freedom and human dignity. A hundred years ago they could do it with chains, today they use tricks. And one of the tricks that they've invented is this token integration, to get Negro, so-called Negro leaders to accept a few token crumbs of integration. That don't solve any problems for the masses of black people in this country whatso-ever, but it does make the hand-picked Negroes be satisfied to slow down the cry of the masses. And a good example of that is as soon as the spirit of rebellion, or of revolution, begins to spread among the masses of black people in this country, and they begin to take an active part, and they showed that they weren't confined to this non-violent approach, then the government, or the power structure begin to sit up and take notice and now, as you said earlier, the President is talking about new legislation to take it out of the street and put it back in the courts. Why, as long as it's in the streets, it's in the hands of the masses of black people who will not compromise, or who cannot be brought out.

But when you put it back in the courts, then that puts it back into the hands of the hand-picked Negro leaders who will allow the judges and the other persons that are involved in this white power structure to slow them down. It's only a trick. And as long as the masses of black people are involved in the struggle for freedom, not integration, but freedom . . . a respect as human beings, respect as men, and show that they're willing to die to be respected as men, then the power structure sits up and takes notice. But as long as the mass element is led, and when I say led, I, I use "led" in quotes—actually, contained by Uncle Tom Negro leaders, who hold them back, who tell them "turn the other cheek", and things like that, then the white power structure isn't worried at all. They're only worried when they know that the masses of black people are ready to explode, and in exploding will destroy some of the furniture in their house. And then they react accordingly.

Heffner: Mr. Morrison?

Morrison: Well, I believe that the dominant interests in our society, which are White, of course, are extremely worried that their system will be seriously damaged. It is disrupted now, and they want to halt the, the disruption which is being caused by the rising wave of militancy among Negroes all over the country. President Kennedy in commenting on the efforts and the methods being used by American Negroes to gain their ends and their goals, which simply stated are unrestricted access to citizenship rights—said that it is better to settle these matters [in] the courts than on the streets. But the Negroe started out trying to settle his problems and to correct his disadvantages and destroy the basis for his struggle and eliminate the grievances, very serious grievances he had, in the courts. Our NAACP was set up on the basis of legal struggle and legal tactics alone. And it has had to revise its whole approach to the question.

Heffner: And yet, Mr. Morrison, it seems to me that the President has made certain steps, and he seems to be saying more now. He says, "We face, therefore, a moral crisis as a country and a people that cannot be met by repressive police action. It cannot be left to increased demonstrations in the streets. It cannot be quieted by token moves or talk. It is time to act in the Congress, in your state and local legislative body, and above all, in all of our daily lives." Which is more than saying, "Let's send it back to the courts."

X: Why didn't he say this three years ago? Why didn't he say this when all of these sit-ins and Freedom Rides were very peacefully going on in the South and in other parts of the North? The man didn't say anything until he found out that black people in this country were ready to explode. And as soon as he saw that the explosion, then was a threat to the White society he came up with the mealymouthed speech, which is too late, and it's only a speech. We still don't see any actions that have stemmed from it. It's still only in the stage of words.

Morrison: I think the speech is late, Minister Malcolm X, but not too late. No pronouncement that was that impressive and forthright from a President of the United States—

X: No one made a better pronouncement than Abraham Lincoln made 100 years ago and that still hasn't been put into practice.

Farmer: I applaud words for what words are worth, and those were good and beautiful words. Now we want to see the President follow up these words with deeds. Because we will judge him in the next election. We will judge the entire administration, not by the beauty of the words which they uttered, nor the soundness of those words. We will judge them by what they do. Now what can he do? He will propose legislation—this legislation must be forthright and powerful legislation, covering the whole gamut of discrimination against Negroes in housing, in employment, in schools, in public places. It must strike at the very root of segregation and prejudice. The President must do more than propose the legislation, he must get out and fight for it.

Walker: Yes, I would heartily agree with Jim Farmer, and I can understand the impatience and frustration that Malcolm X evidences—

X: Not frustration, I want to straighten you out. Maybe impatience, but not frustration. You're only frustrated when you don't get what you expect. And a black man is out of his mind, after sitting around here listening to these political speeches by politicians for one hundred years—he's out of his mind if he thinks that he's going to get anything more today than he got 100 years ago.

Walker: Well, I was about to say that Mr. Kennedy probably has another think coming if he proposes legislation, and I personally don't believe that it has a prayer of passing—I hope he doesn't think that this politically will get him off of the hook. Merely to propose it and then it gets killed by a filibuster will not be enough. I don't think it can be solved this summer by proposed legislation which is, it seems to me, destined for failure. I think it's got to come through some strong executive action and it may be that we'll have to see martial law declared in several areas throughout the South—

X: You mean a military dictatorship?

Walker: Well, I don't choose to describe it as such—

X: It'll take a military dictatorship to bring black people and white people together in the same house. If all of the token integration, which you've seen in the South, and it's only "tokenism," and if this has caused the bloodshed that it has, what do you think white people—both North and South—will do on the basis of real integration? If you only ask for crumbs, and you're—and the granting of those crumbs causes bloodshed—what do you think will be caused when you ask for a loaf of bread, or a bakery in which to bake your own bread?

Walker: Let me continue—

Heffner: Go ahead, Mr. Walker.

Walker: —with the business of the power structure, which is the point I ultimately wanted to make about wanting to contain it. I agree with Mr. Morrison in pointing out that they'd like to have the revolution developed on a schedule. But revolutions don't develop like that And I think this is what's apparent to the Administration and to the whole nation. And the reason we're having such a thrust now is because America, as a nation, has never really grappled with the problem of race and color prejudice in America. And it's most grievous error was made shortly after the Emancipation Proclamation, when it made a moral compromise, and we're bearing the fruits of it now. And the revolution is not going to develop in an orderly and scheduled fashion. It's going to develop so fast that the Administration won't be able to cope with it until something is done nationwide—North, South, East, and West. I don't think there's any other course for it to take, and, and in some moments I think it's going to be even more swift than what Jim Farmer conjectured. We may see the resolution of this in another year.

Farmer: Yes, I think what the power structure is really afraid of, more so than guns, because they can get bigger guns. . . . They are more afraid of the dollar. What the businessmen in Greensboro were scared to death of was the fact that people were not buying—not only black people, but white people were staying off the streets—perhaps for different reasons. I'm sure for different reasons—but they were staying off the streets downtown . . . and if they can't make money out of the situation then they want to do a rethink because they love the dollars more than they love discrimination and segregation. Now, we in CORE are going to use the dollar weapon, more than we've ever used it before. We have set a deadline of July 4th and we are calling upon all businesses that are pans of chains, North and South, not only to stop segregating in their facilities, but also to stop discriminating in their employing. That they must employ Negroes and whites in all categories, by July 4th. If they do not, and if they are part of national chains, then they will face our imminent boycotts, economic pressure, and mass demonstrations. We're not saying that they have to complete the process of creating open businesses without discrimination by July 4th. But, at least, there has to be a commitment for the imminent end of segregation and discrimination in their places of accommodation.

Walker: It should be also said to buttress what Jim has just indicated, that this is why the power structure wants to contain it, because granting [civil rights] to the Negro fuels emancipation, means a re-adjustment of the entire economy of the United States. The financial economy and the political economy. Once a Negro is given that, then America has to change its entire posture. I think it's inevitable—an inevitable move toward some kind of socialism.

Heffner: When you refer to the power structure, and you talk about a fear of something akin to socialism—a changing of our economic and political structure; are you saying that this Administration, and all of those political leaders who have stood through the years for the fight that you are waging—that they don't mean what they say?

Walker: I think it's well-intentioned, but when I look at it realistically as a Negro living in the Deep South—I do not see that this is sufficient to bring about what needs to be done immediately. I don't think legislation alone can do it. And I do believe—

X: How can you believe it's well-intentioned, then?

Walker: Well, I'm charitable enough to believe it's well-intentioned. But I don't think it's realistic.

X: That's why we're still in the condition that we're in—our leaders are too charitable toward those politicians who have been using flowery words, but not coming up with deeds that will be equal to those words.

Farmer: I think the real question is not whether they mean it, but what they do about it. Whether they can put it off—because we've heard good words for hundreds of years now, and they haven't come off. Now, maybe they mean it—I don't know. I can't look into a man's mind, but what I know is that those words have not been backed up by deeds. So we will have to judge the Administration, we'll have to judge its good intentions by what it does, not by what it says.

Heffner: But, of course, it all comes back to Mr. Morrison's statement about power structure, and this is why I keep coming back to the question of whether you feel that, basically, the power structure, however one might define that in this country, is opposed to the Negroes' search for equality.

Walker: Yes, and I want to take strong exception to the present suggestion that it's better to move the struggle of the Negro for full emancipation out of the street, back into the courts. And I take the inference as meaning that it is dangerous for the battle to be waged in the streets. But I don't want the public to think that our means of fighting for equality in the streets is an illegitimate method. It's a part of the American tradition. And I do not want it thought that because it is dangerous, that it should be taken from us as a methodology to secure full emancipation now.

Heffner: May I just say as an historian, my reading of what the President said on Tuesday night is not that there is something wrong with what goes on in the streets. He himself, as an historian, knows that this is the way so much has been accomplished in our own history. But rather that he's saying that that has been the prelude to writing into our governmental structure, through our legislatures, through our Executive branch, more fundamental reforms.

Walker: . . . Fortunately, or I guess, unfortunately, John Kennedy has never been a Negro, and I can't wait to go through the courts, because I've seen 100 years of that—and it's city by city, and county by county, and specific instance by specific instance. And that's why the courts alone will not do it, and I can't buy that it's better to move it from the streets into the courts. What this nation must face is that we have a legitimate right under the First Amendment guarantees of the Bill of

Rights, to peacefully demonstrate. And this is what the nonviolent revolution is directed at. And this is why we insist upon it, as a means of, if you will, creating a crisis so severe that the government, the federal Administration has to grapple with it, and do something immediately.

Heffner: But it seems to me that what President Kennedy is urging upon the Congressional branch of government is that the federal government must seize upon this question now that it has been dramatized.

Walker: But let me go a little bit further about legislation. Just Sunday, Anell Ponda, one of our Field Secretaries, and six other ladies and young girls were returning from South Georgia. In Winona, Mississippi, [when] they went into the previously all-white waiting room of the Trailways bus stations—and this is supposed to have been settled by legislation and ICC Regulations two years ago, climaxed in the Freedom Ride . . . they were arrested and beaten and put in jail and held incommunicado and in need of medical treatment that they never did receive. Now this is why the Negro mood is such that we won't buy legislation alone. It's got to be legislation that is enforced by whatever it takes to enforce it.

Farmer: I hope we understand that Negroes don't like being in the streets, I don't like being in the streets myself. But it's something that we have to do. I would much rather stay at home. I would much rather take things easy. I'll only be able to take things easy, you see, when this problem is settled. That's the way that we can get the matter out of the streets, by settling it. And the sooner we do it, the better, for all of us. Until it is settled, we intend to stay in the streets. Not as something we want to do, but as something we have to do.

Heffner: Mr. Morrison?

Morrison: President Kennedy not only stated that his Administration considered it much better—I would also assume, safer—for the struggle of the Negro population to be removed from the area of street demonstrations and protest to the courts. But he also stated, and I quote, "Where legal remedies are not on hand, redress is sought in the streets and demonstrations, parades, and protests which create tensions and threaten violence." Well, I say that responsibility for the tensions and the violence lies not with the Negro people who are proceeding peacefully and legitimately for legitimate rights which the Constitution says they should have. And privileges which have been denied them as citizens. And I also say that in the tradition of the American struggle for freedom, street demonstrations and public protests are completely consistent with American rights and with American history. We must not forget that the Revolution, which created independence for this republic, was started in such a street demonstration on Boston Common. And a Negro played a rather significant role in that demonstration even though the Negro population of that country—of this country, at that time was not a political factor, but was enslaved.

Heffner: Oh, I don't think there was any question that anyone who knows the history of this country would concede, in fact, insist that this kind of street work has perhaps been one of the finest aspects of the American heritage. It was the farmers who said they better raise less corn and more hell. Their actions led to legislative change, which is what the President is now urging, and it just seems to me that the President isn't denying the validity of mass demonstration—of what has taken place on the part of your movement, Mr. Walker, your movement, Mr. Farmer. But rather is saying this must now be institutionalized, which is what I should imagine you gentlemen would want. Malcolm X?

X: You can't compare the revolt of farmers with the revolt of black people in this country because the farmers are revolting over more or less corn, which in no way involves the Constitution or what this country is supposed to stand for; but the black man in this country is supposed to be getting freedom. The country is supposed to be based on that—democracy, freedom, justice, equality, and all that stuff that they teach us in school. And now why should the black man have to go to court to get freedom when a white man in this country is free when he's born. Why should the black man need some legislation to [prove] that he's a human being, when you don't need any legislation to [prove] that whites are human beings. So, I make this point because to come right back to my initial statement at the outset of the discussion, you will never get real freedom and recognition between black and white people in this country without destroying the country, without destroying the present political system, without destroying the present economic system, without re-writing the entire Constitution. It'll be a complete destruction of everything that America supposedly stands for before a white man in this country will recognize a black man as something on the same level with himself. And this is why the Honorable Elijah Mohammed teaches us that the best way to solve the problem is complete separation. Let the Black man, those of our people in this country who want to have a country of our own where we can go and stand on our own feet and solve our own problems, and not have to continue going to court, or waiting for some politician to legislate for another hundred or two hundred years to prove that we're human beings.

Farmer: Mr. Moderator, I've discussed this with Minister Malcolm before, and after seeing Mississippi and Alabama close up, I'd be glad to give him those states if it were within my power to do so. Yet I've said before—

X: Why Mississippi and Alabama?

Farmer: Because, I've said before, Minister Malcolm, the thing that bothers me about your idea of a black nation within a nation, presumably if it can be effected then, is that if the white man hates us as much as you say he does, what a target we'd make if we were all together—

X: —not as much as I say he does—

Farmer: Okay, okay.

X: —his deeds prove that he does.

Farmer: Okay, if he hates us that much, then I would hate to be all gathered in one place. I'd rather be dispersed throughout this nation. He could drop one controlled atom bomb and wipe us out. He could strangle us with a net of—

X: But he's wiping you out—he wiped out the Field Secretary of the NAACP [Medgar Evers—Ed.].

Farmer: May I finish? He certainly did. But he could strangle us with an economic noose around—

X: Strangle—

Heffner: Gentlemen—

Farmer: I would rather be dispersed, Minister Malcolm, and I think then I would make a poorer target. You know, if you're all together, one gun can shoot you.

X: Harlem is all together.

Farmer: But if you're scattered—

X: Washington, DC has already become an all-black city.

Farmer: This is why Harlem is being strangled economically, I think, now. And this is why this summer we plan to have Task Force people, volunteers, working in key sections like Harlem, the Bedford-Stuyvesant [Brooklyn] area, and Newark, New Jersey, to tackle these slums and to organize the tenants for possible rent strikes against the terrible conditions that exist there.

Heffner: What do you think will happen?

Farmer: Well I think there are going to be some that won't come across. I think there'll be some which will offer token compliance with our demands. And tokenism will not be accepted—we've gotten beyond tokenism now. We demand the whole loaf, we want an open city, open states, and an open country. We want, in other words, to get this nonsense of race and racism behind us. So that we can release the tremendous resources that are being tied up. Not only in terms of money, but in terms of talent and intelligence and thought—to work on the problems of unemployment, generally, the problems of disease and health, the other problems that afflict all people in our country.

Walker: . . . We've got to do something about the voting inequities in the South. I was so dismayed at the program *Meet The Press,* when Governor Wallace says to the nation that Negroes are voting all over Alabama. Now I could name almost two dozen counties where a Negro has never voted at all. There are ten counties where no Negro has been on the registration list.

You've got a 21-question form that has to be filled out, and you— the only way you know you're registered is you get a letter from the Registrar—who knows whether it goes in the file 13 or not. Two years ago, we had a drive in Montgomery, Alabama, where 4,000 Negroes applied, and when the registration books were closed, they announced that 210-odd people had passed the test. Well, this is all in the hands of white registrars and white racists. The Negro just cannot get a fair shake at the voting booth. And this is another one of our primary concerns.

Heffner: Mr. Farmer, we have talked about the conditions which would have to exist if there were not to be a march on Washington, if there were not to be the kind of action that you gentlemen have talked about for the summer. It seems to me as you describe what it is you feel must be accomplished to avoid it, that we're not going to avoid that. You seem to be asking for things that are quite legitimate, but it doesn't seem to me that it is too likely that you are going to achieve what it is that you want to achieve. Does this mean that this summer we'll see the kind of action that you're talking about?

Farmer: There will be a march on Washington early in the fall unless these demands are met. And I think that they are legitimate demands. What the federal government has to do, or needs to do in order to prevent such a march is first of all to pass strong civil rights legislation with teeth in it. Second, to see that all places that serve the public are completely desegregated, and third, stop using federal funds to subsidize segregation: For example, in the Area Redevelopment Administration where funds are loaned to businesses that want to build units in the South, factories or what-have-you. Many of these are businesses [that] go South, then employ only white persons. I saw a sign on a highway in South Carolina—just a month ago—stating that such-and-such a firm will build a factory here on this site . . . 500 white women will be hired. Now this was to be with money loaned by the federal government to the concern. Well, that has to stop. We have to put an end to discrimination in employment. I think it can be done. I think it must be done.

Heffner: Do you assume that enough will be done by the fall of the year to avoid the kind of march you've talked about?

Farmer: Well, I'm not assuming anything. These are our demands. And if they are met, we'll be delighted because I don't want to march, I have bad feet. I don't like marching. But if I have to march, I will march because there is something that is more important than my feet.

Heffner: In the criteria you establish, I wonder about the question of federal aid to education, and the importance, in your mind, of preventing such aid from going to Southern states, or other states that practice, officially practice discrimination.

Farmer: Yes. As long as those states practice segregation or discrimination officially, then federal funds should not be used there.

X: Or unofficially.

Farmer: Unofficially, yes. This was a recommendation of the Civil Rights Commission, that all federal funds be withdrawn from Mississippi. I go along with that. I believe in it. CORE is waging a campaign now against school bonds that are issued by school districts, cities, and states in the Deep South where the schools are completely segregated. These bonds are marketed in seven Northern states including New York. Hundreds of millions of dollars are involved. The people who put their money into those school bonds from segregated areas are thereby subsidizing segregation. Now they may be good people in the sense that they don't beat their wives, they don't push ladies down subway steps. They don't realize that the money that they are pouring into those bonds, that they're investing into those bonds, are being used to build and maintain segregated facilities. Well, that should stop.

I'd like to point out that I don't think that the Deep South states can be persuaded or convinced by reasoning or by logic to desegregate. It has to be, as Alan Morrison indicated, by using coercive means. Either economic coercion, or political coercion, or what-have-you, or the type of coercion that we are using in the streets now. And I don't care whether this is done by a Democratic Administration or a Republican Administration. I don't think either one of them would be able to persuade or to convince Mississippi and Alabama to desegregate.

X: Mr. Farmer, why say "the Deep South" when Englewood, New Jersey, is not in the Deep South. New Rochelle not in the Deep

South. Chicago is not in the Deep South. And, by your own admission, there is as much segregation practiced in the North as in the South, but it's done in a more subtle way. And the mistake that is made by many of our people who are in this so-called civil rights struggle—I have to say "so-called civil rights struggle"—is they always make a distinction between North and South. You don't find the Black man in the South catching as much hell as the black man in the North. Only difference is the black man in the South knows where it is, and the black man in the North is being tricked every day by white liberals, who grin in his face and pretend to be his friend, but at the same time is practicing segregation just as much as the white man in the South is practicing it.

Farmer: Well, I don't know . . .

Walker: I don't think I could accept that altogether, Malcolm, because you live in the North predominantly, and I don't think you could speak for the experience I or we as Southerners have. I think the Negro catches hell all over the country, being a Negro. And I think we have said, from our movement—I'm speaking of Jim and the posture that Alan Morrison and I represent—that we say it is a national dilemma, which has to be grappled with. It has different forms. I think, in the South, it's not only emotional and psychological, but it's also physical. And I don't know whether you can put a slide rule on it to measure it; it's just a problem all over the nation and we're on the threshold, I trust, with really grappling with it for the first time.

X: In the South, you're dealing with the wolf who let's you know where you stand. In the North, we're dealing with a fox who grins in our face and makes us think that we're getting some kind of freedom, or that we're in a different place.

Farmer: Let me say, I don't think it's a fruitful discussion as to whether the thing is worse in the South, or worse in the North. It's bad as anything both places all over the country. And it doesn't matter the shape that it takes one place or another. Now, we are in the streets in the North—in Englewood, in California, in New York—just as we're in the streets in the South—

X: And then what has been accomplished?

Farmer: What has been accomplished? . . . Look at Philadelphia, Negroes are now being employed—

X: All Negroes got a job—

Farmer: Now let me tell you, Minister Malcolm, that we have gotten jobs for Negroes in Safeway grocery stores, in Krogers grocery stores, in department stores, in Sealtest Dairies, in concern after concern, and not four—

X: Mr. Farmer—

Farmer: —not forty—

X: —whenever you have—

Farmer: —but they number in the hundreds—

X: Whenever you have thousands of Negroes demonstrating for jobs as was demonstrated beautifully—

Farmer: Yes.

X: —in Philadelphia, and then the leadership settled for four jobs—I can't see where that's progress.

Farmer: Now, let me tell you, in our campaign against a leading dairy in New York, we did not settle for four jobs. We did not settle for forty jobs—

X: The—

Farmer: —now, wait—

X: —the demonstrations in Philadelphia settled for four jobs—

Farmer: I'm not speaking of the Philadelphia demonstration, I'm speaking of the dairy that we had a boycott against. We had more than forty jobs already, and many more coming—now we're after not the token employment. We're after full employment. . . . I think it's no longer adequate for an employer to say that "I don't discriminate, merely because I accept qualified applications and employ the best qualified of the persons who have applied. And it just so happens, accidentally, no Negroes who are qualified, have applied." Now we're insisting that we see some Negroes there, working. We're insisting that there be some dark faces working in those factories, those shops, and those offices. I think that it is impossible for the rear wheels of an automobile to catch up with the front wheels of an automobile while they're going at the same speed. It is necessary for there to be a new push. We say to the employer now that he has a responsibility not only to employ the best qualified person who applies, but to seek qualified Negroes, and if they are not qualified for the specific job, to help train them, and to admit them to all of these apprenticeship training classes. We say the same thing to the trade unions, because we've got to break out of this box where the Negro is at the bottom of the economic totem pole. This is what we're trying to do. It's not confined to Mississippi, Mr. X.

Heffner: Well, of course, this does raise the question as to whether there is not now a search for more than equality. Whether there isn't an effort now to make up, as if one could, for the hundreds of years during which the Negro has suffered outrages within in our country.

Farmer: I think we've got to try. I think that the nation owes us a debt on this. And the nation must pay that debt.

Heffner: You say "the nation owes a debt"—

Farmer: Yes.

Heffner: Is it a debt that can be paid within the context of what it is you basically want . . . the concept of equality?

Farmer: What we're trying to achieve is equality. And we cannot achieve equality while the Negro remains frozen at the bottom of the economic ladder. Now the statistics are rather cruel, and the statistics show that the gap between the average income for Negroes in this country and the average income for whites has not closed. In other words, it is fantastic, as Governor Wallace has done in Alabama, [to] compare the Negroes' standard of living in this country with the standard of living in Africa, or Europe, or Canada. The only fair comparison is with the standard of living in the rest of America. And the gap has not closed. It did close a bit during World War II, but that, as you know, was because of temporary employment in wartime industries. When the war was over, those jobs were lopped off. In the past 15 years, the gap has widened slightly. Which means that if we are to achieve equality, we've got to find some way for the back wheels of the car to catch up to the front wheels of the car without a collision.

X: It means that the only time the black man in this country has made any progress was in wartime, when the white man has his back to the wall, then he lets the black man come forward a little bit. And as soon as the war is over, he tells the black man "get back off me now."

And I think, sir, with all due respect to you and the others who are here, when you sit and analyze the problem as it actually is, and see the hypocrisy that has been practiced by whites when they talk this love talk and equality talk, sooner or later you'll be able to see that since we don't make any progress, only during wartime, it'll take another war for the black man to take any more steps in the right direction.

Farmer: Minister Malcolm—

X: And then—no, I didn't cut you off when you spoke there for 15 minutes—

Farmer: You tried—

X: Moderator wouldn't let me.

Farmer: [Laughter]

X: . . . You see the grip, or the economic rut that our people are in, and as you point out, the union excludes us . . . to keep us out, and if the union doesn't do it, management does it. We are caught in a conspiracy between the union, the management and the government to keep us at the bottom of the economic ladder, the bottom of the housing ladder, the bottom of the educational ladder, and after experiencing that in a country for a hundred years, I don't see how you could have any hope or confidence that this same race that has been doing it is not going to continue to do it, only in a different way, with more twentieth-century, or up to date or shrewd methods today than they had to use in the past.

Farmer: You say, that progress is achieved only in wartime—

X: It has always been achieved by our people in wartime—

Farmer: All right. Now you say that—we're in a war now. We're in a war now, the war is being waged in the streets of Birmingham, the streets of Greensboro, the streets of Danville, Virginia—

X: That's not war . . .

Farmer: Now, wait a minute—

X: No—

Farmer: This is the war—

X: It's not the war—

Farmer: This is the war—

X: It's the result of the war—America is at war—

Farmer: . . . this is the Revolutionary War. The Revolutionary War was not finished at all. The Revolutionary War, 1776, provided independence and freedom in a sense for some Americans, but excluded black Americans. This is Revolutionary War, Part II, so take those beautiful words of the Declaration of Independence, of the Preamble to the Constitution, and make them a reality for black people, as well as white. Now we are waging that war. If you don't like this war, that's all right.

X: Now, wait a minute—

Farmer: But don't deny that it is a war.

Heffner: May I interrupt at this point, and just ask Mr. Walker, who is champing at the bit over here, for his comment.

Walker: Yes, I wanted to buttress what Jim was saying about

employment. I think the Philadelphia instance is one instance. In Atlanta we have what we call "Operation Breadbasket," where we're dealing with one consumer industry, the bread industry, and in less than three and a half months, using the technique that Jim described of buying where we can get jobs on a proportionate basis, we created for the Negro community $400,000 in new jobs. And this means that a man who was a deliveryman and was making $40 a week, now has a job as a bread salesman, and makes $115, $125 a week. He has four children—if he had stayed as a deliveryman, those four kids would not have had an opportunity at college and emancipating themselves educationally. Now they have a chance at college. And when you add $400,000 to the income of the Negro community, in any city, from just one industry then it seems to me, that this is a legitimate and reasonable result for the kind of techniques and methods that we use. And there is a catalog of ills which you recite, which we would agree with. It's a fair commentary. I would like to know what alternative you propose as against what we just—

Heffner: That's a fair enough question. Malcolm X, I'm sure that you'll want to reply.

X: Yes, the Honorable Elijah Mohammed teaches us that after 400 years in this country, a country to which we've contributed our free labor, sweat, blood—we've given our lives to make it, or help make it what it is. And today, because the white man says that it's time now for us to get integration or what he calls freedom, and many of the so-called Negroes who take him seriously and believe that what he says is what he means, they try and take advantage of it, and they end up getting beaten with police clubs, or fire hoses, or having dogs sicced upon them, simply because they believe what the white man says, that he intends for us to have freedom, justice, and equality. So, Mr. Mohammed says in the face of all of this, since we see that we just can't get justice here, and by justice I mean economic security, political security, social security, and so forth, the best solution is for the white man to allow the 20 million black people in this country to go back to our own home—those who want to. Go back to our own home and to our own people. And that the government itself should give us everything we need to go back to our own home and start life anew in our own land, among our own people. And then if the government doesn't want to do that, since we . . . they don't want us to leave and they want us to stay here with them, we don't get along together. Then Mr. Mohammed says that the solution is to separate part of the country here, and give us a place to ourselves, where we can then go and set up our own agricultural system, our own economic system and try and do something to provide food, clothing, and shelter and the things that our people need in order to live. In other words, give us a chance to solve our own problems, among ourselves, on some land of our own instead of continually trying to force us into white society, where the white society knows we're absolutely not wanted, and a white society which knows it will never accept its ex-slave on the same level with itself as something equal with itself.

Heffner: Well, that's clear. You're talking about separatism. Now, Mr. Farmer, what are you asking for?

Farmer: I am asking for compensatory, preferential hiring. I think that it is essential for the salvation of this nation. Now, a study was conducted by the President's Commission of Economic Advisors, which came out with some very interesting, and I think, significant figures. It indicated that the Gross National Product of the whole nation suffers to the tune of 13 billion dollars a year because of discrimination in employment against Negroes. To put it another way, if the training and skills and qualifications of Negro citizens, as they are now, were fully utilized in employment, 13 billion dollars a year would be added to the national economy. Now if, in addition to that the training, the skills and the education of Negroes in this country were brought up to the level of that of whites and then their new skills and training and education utilized in employment to the full, 17 billion dollars a year would be added to the national economy . . . I think that it's in the interest of the nation and its welfare now to adopt a policy of compensatory treatment because of the discrimination of 100 years discrimination in education, in training and in employment. Otherwise we will not break this vicious cycle.

Heffner: Mr. Morrison?

Morrison: Well, this principle of compensatory, preferential treatment for Negro Americans is relatively new and it results from the findings, as Mr. Farmer has outlined, of American social scientists and exhaustive research conducted by Negro leadership organizations, such as the National Urban League. We have discovered that the treatment accorded the Negro in American life has imposed monumental, massive disabilities which cannot be corrected overnight, nor can they be straightened out simply by granting, either by executive order or by legislation, equality of opportunity. Now equality of opportunity used to be the phrase used. But it is not enough. Equality has to be—the word "equality"—has to be broadened, it has to be deepened, and, it has to apply to the tragic circumstances which white America has created for the Negro population. The Negro population is educationally disadvantaged, it's vocationally disadvantaged, and in every other sense it, it has handicaps which cannot be altered or corrected without compensatory treatment. This means that the Negro has to be given more than equal consideration. The American society, federal government, state governments have to inaugurate policies and consistently apply them which take into consideration the historical deprivation of equal rights, the right to education and economic growth of Negro people. Otherwise the Negro will be traveling at a tremendous disadvantage. He's got to catch up, and he has to be assisted to catch up because this is what our society, and let's face it, what white people have done to Negro people in this country. And something has to be done dramatically to make up for the gap. And the gap is widening, incidentally. We used to say that the Negro "condition" was improving and rising. But we now know that the condition of the Negro population ten years ago was actually better than it is now. In other words, the gap in income, the gap in education, is growing and it has to be closed.

Heffner: Mr. Farmer, do you want to add to this?

Farmer: You can call it—the President has called it, incidentally—"positive, affirmative action." The President stepped off of a plane once and this was early in his Administration, and looked, I believe at one of the armed guards that was standing there, and noticed that there were no Negroes. He didn't ask, "Well, now how many qualified Negroes have applied, and were they as highly qualified as the other people who applied?" He called the officer and said, "I don't see any Negroes here in the group." The officer said, "Well, Mr. President, no Negroes have applied." The President, as reported by the press, said to him, "Go out and find some." Now we've been receiving special treatment for 300 to 400 years here. We've been receiving special treatment of a negative nature. Now we're asking for the kind of special treatment that is positive and affirmative.

X: But we've been sitting and waiting for the Man to give us some concessions. Now whenever you ask the white power structure for jobs, that's only a temporary solution. If you ask the white power structure for housing, that's a temporary solution. As Mr. Farmer said where the Negro used to ask for equality, now he's asking for more—he's asking for more than equality. Well, likewise, if they give us more than equality, ten years from now we're going to be asking for more than that because the problem has still not gotten a real solution.

Farmer: Mr. Moderator—

X: —just one moment, let me finish what I'm going to say. As long as we accept a temporary solution, the problem will go unsolved, it will be solved for you and me, right now, but not for our children. If the black nations in Africa, most of which have fewer educated Africans than exist among black people in this country . . . can establish their own independent nations and try and do create a future for their people, then Mr. Mohammed says, here in America, there are enough black people who profess to be educated and with all this talk about equality with the white man, if we're equal with the white man, why can't we separate from him and set up our own government, and grow for ourselves, and solve our own problems?

Heffner: Mr. X, when you talk about black people separating from the White man and setting up their own government, do you anticipate using Gandhi's tactics of nonviolence?

X: Gandhi's fame came from having gotten freedom for the people of India from the English. And he used nonviolent methods, which means you have a great big dark elephant-type creature sitting down on the little white mouse. But here in America you have a little black mouse trying to pull a sit-down, nonviolent tactic—

Farmer: Let me pursue this, Mr. Moderator.

Heffner: Go ahead.

Farmer: Nonviolence is more effective when you have large numbers of people. That is what we've found out in Birmingham, it's what we found out all over North Carolina—

X: What did you gain in Birmingham—

Farmer: Now, wait a minute—let me tell you what we've gained in North Carolina—

X: What'd you gain in Birmingham?

Farmer: Let me tell you what we've gained there. Mr. Walker can answer that. This was his campaign, in Birmingham. Ask me about our campaign—

X: What'd you gain in North Carolina?

Farmer: Let me tell you what we've gained. We've gained jobs, we've gained open employment. In Greensboro, North Carolina, one of the officials of the city who was in charge of employment has announced that, hereinafter, all city employment will be on a merit basis, and there'll be no discrimination. A committee has been set up whereby grievances of individuals who feel that they've been discriminated against because of race will be dealt with. We are represented on that committee. In six cities in North Carolina, the theaters have desegregated. Places that serve the public in five cities have de-segregated, and the whole state is becoming an open state—now, wait a minute—

X: Is it a gain to go to a theater for a man who hasn't got a job?

Farmer: It's a gain to get a job . . . and it's jobs that we're providing. Now it's a gain, also, to go to the theater, it's a gain because it's not the theater so much—it's not the cup of coffee at the lunch counter. It's the dignity that a person achieves. Is it a gain to have a business over on the other side of the tracks to which you can go, but when you walk down town you're discriminated against and cannot go there?

X: It's a gain—

Farmer: What I say, Mr. X, is that all places that serve the public, black and white, must serve all members of the public. We are members of the public. Whether you want to admit it or not. If we are not members of the public, then what are we?

X: Why do you have the race problem in this country, if we're members of the public?

Heffner: Now, next—may I—

Farmer: We're members of the public and that's why we're trying to wipe out racial discrimination.

X: You'll never wipe it out with a desegregated theater—

Heffner: Gentlemen, this is the last of our discussion, and it seems to me, and you all will grant that quickly, that we could go on forever with it. I would just like to say, as the moderator who shouldn't involve himself overly much that, still as a white man, I'm concerned with the notion that there is just one type of white man in this country, and that he feels a certain way. I think that you probably recognize, as there are differences among you concerning certain tactics and approaches that you would take, there are many, many differences among whites. And I think that would be a mistake not to think in terms, for a few moments, of interracial activities. Mr. Morrison, I wonder whether this theme has any meaning, validity for you?

Morrison: Yes, it does. America's destiny in my opinion is to be one nation, united, undifferentiated according to degrees of citizenship, in which racial chauvinism is outlawed and prevented from being expressed. I feel that this dramatic drive which we are witnessing and in which some of us are participating, toward real equality, which means desegregation and integration, can only be accomplished by an increasing cooperation, collaboration between the Negro people and enlightened white people. And there are many enlightened white people. Unfortunately, too many of them are not disposed to express themselves or to join with Negroes hand-in-hand in the struggle. We have here, tonight, two men—Mr. Farmer and Reverend Walker, who represent organizations that are founded on that principle, that white and Negro Americans can join together in this great crusade. It has to be done because the question of the Negro status and the abolition of the injustices which the Negro suffers is the dominant question in American life today. To me, it takes precedence over any other issue you can name. It should have priority. The priority is so important that I think it demands that President Kennedy perhaps suspend his European trip and stay in this country and fight for the legislation which he will introduce next week. America has got to achieve this destiny of equal rights for all its citizens, or else it will not survive.

Heffner: Mr. Farmer, do you find that interracial efforts continue to have the validity that you've hoped for many years that they would have. Or do you feel that perhaps Malcolm X's emphasis upon real separatism is beginning to seem more and more correct.

Farmer: No. Needless to say I'm opposed to separatism. Now, I do not say that Harlem and a hundred Harlems throughout the country should be destroyed or Negroes cannot live together. It's not that Negroes don't like to associate with Negroes and want to associate with white people. What Negroes want is a choice. They want to be able to live in "Gorgeous Gardens" if they choose, or "Lovely Lane." [Or] they may not choose. They may choose to live in Harlem, as many of them will. So we have to clean up the problems there. Now this is the approach that CORE takes, and CORE is an interracial organization, always has been. We feel that this problem is not just the black man's problem. It's a problem for all Americans, whether white or black. All of them suffer. I look at the white man, even in the South. I pity the segregationists. I think that he is as much a victim of the historical forces about which we've been talking as the Negro is. Now, we are trying to free him as we gain freedom for ourselves. One white student down in Lebanon, Tennessee, said to me, when I was talking about freedom, after the speech he said, "Well, Mr. Farmer, I'm not free either. I have a Negro friend and I can't go downtown and have a Coke with my Negro friend." So we're trying to provide freedom for the white people as well as the Negroes in this country. Now I think that there should be an increasing pride among Negroes, or black people. I think that there should be pride among all Americans because we ought to be proud of what we are, our heritage and our traditions. America is not a melting pot in the sense that people disappear. America is a melting pot in the sense that people come together out of proud traditions, out of cultures, feeling that they have something to contribute to the total, overall culture. Negroes increasingly are finding something in their background, their heritage, their culture to contribute. This, I think, is the future of America.

Heffner: Malcolm X, I wonder whether you can accept the notion that a White man is no more responsible for his skin than is a man who is black?

X: If he's not responsible for his skin, he is responsible for his deeds. And that collectively the white people in this country are guilty today, and must accept the blame for the collective criminal act that was committed against black people by bringing our people to this country. And if it is not the whiteness of his skin for which the Honorable Elijah Mohammed teaches us that he's entering into condemnation today, it is his deeds. And he can't separate his deeds from his skin. The country that has been established here has been established by white people for the benefit of white people. The economic system, the political system, the educational system of America has been set up primarily for the benefit of white people. Our people were brought here in chains, forcibly, not on the *Mayflower*, but in slave ships to add to the American economy, and we've been exploited politically, economically, and otherwise ever since.

Heffner: I think that there is no one at this table and there are very few people I know, Malcolm X, who would deny the validity of much that you say. But I turn to Mr. Walker, and ask him whether in his own activities in the South now, which have achieved certain things—whether they haven't been achieved with the assistance, North and South, of certain white men?

Walker: Oh, absolutely. Perhaps I could hinge it on the question raised by Malcolm a little earlier. About what has Birmingham achieved? Maybe there is no one, two, three to add up, and what was resolved in the agreement or truce that was made is minimal when you consider how completely emasculated the Negro community was in Birmingham. But as over against the mayhem and the murder and the police brutality and the economic deprivation that the Negro suffered in Birmingham particularly, and Alabama generally—the Negro has proved in this new militancy that has been evidenced by Birmingham that, when we rise up in mass numbers, we can completely immobilize not only a city, but the police force of an entire state, and further dramatize to the nation the urgency of the problem which is exactly what Birmingham has done. It represents a watershed in the revolution of the Negro community in America.

Heffner: And the impact of Birmingham upon white support for your movement in the North as well as the South?

Walker: I think I can describe it this way. There are two kinds of white people in America. One is committed *to* the movement, which is a small number, and then there are those who are committed *by* the movement—that we have so dramatized; this is a nonviolent technique, and I speak of all the organizations—

X: Was Birmingham nonviolent?

Walker: Not altogether, but 95 percent so, it was. We have dramatized that the urgency of the problem has got to be dealt with now. There are some people who expect the resolution of today's problems to come in on the wheels of inevitability, and it doesn't happen like that. Somebody's got to prod it, somebody's got to push it, somebody's got to put severe pressure on it to create the kind of crisis that Birmingham represented so that it becomes a national issue—which is what we're facing now.

Heffner: Of course, I'd like to ask Mr. Farmer, too, what he feels the impact has been, of the actions of the past two years upon support, and understanding on the part of the White community.

Farmer: I think there's been much more support. There is growing evidence that many people in the white community are now waking up to the fact that this thing has got to go. Segregation has got to be ended. And I think they're determined to do something about it. Now, we will keep up the pressure, we'll stay in the streets. And I would welcome white persons to join us there. I would welcome allies in the struggle. We need all the allies we can have, all that we can get, because this is a tremendous struggle. —1963

JOHN HOPE FRANKLIN

History is not just a subject taught, but is also a great teacher. And John Hope Franklin, the distinguished chronicler and interpreter of the American past, refines that rather simplistic statement in assuring us that "The historian is not in the business of protecting the morals of the people, but as the servant of the past is in the best position to provide a rational basis for present actions." Franklin's collection of scholarly essays, Race and History, *provided the basis for a conversation about history and the making of public policy. I asked him first about the uses of the past.*

If people do not heed the lessons of history, if they indeed look at the historical past and ignore it, if they create instead a set of myths that they call the past, and then act upon the basis of those myths, they will undoubtedly be led into policies and actions which are unrealistic, which are themselves misleading, and which of course will cause them to end up on the wrong side of a particular problem. I think that we have too much of that in our present as well as in our past. And I think that's why we have such difficulty in being realists in this country, looking hard and long and carefully at the facts of history. I think, if we were to do that, the facts would tell us a great deal about what we are, where we've been, and they might even suggest—I say this very tentatively—where we might be going.

Heffner: Why do you say "tentatively"? Don't you think that history should be a guide for the future?

Yes. I say "tentatively" because I don't want anyone to get the impression that I would imply that history repeats itself.

Heffner: Only historians repeat themselves.

Only historians repeat themselves. But with respect to history being a guide and its being instructive, I have no reservations. I don't speak tentatively. . . .

Heffner: Don't we think, though, that we're quite a historical-minded people? We're constantly concerned with what Jefferson would have said, or what Washington would have said. And yet, as I read your essays, I find there a thrust in the direction of saying that we have been at least as frequently misled by those who would use history as propaganda.

I think that's quite true. We do have a fascination with what we call history. But it's a fascination with a kind of superficial history. We like to think of the Founding Fathers in the most romantic way, the most uncritical way. We like to place them on a pedestal, so to speak, and regard them as demigods without looking at them critically, without subjecting them to the kind of scrutiny and examination that all persons deserve who are human beings like you and me. And this is what I think we do so often with our history. On the one hand, we regard it as a very romantic and wonderful and inspiring kind of story. On the other hand, we look at it superficially, in quite another way, mainly as a set of almost disconnected, disembodied facts. So that when some of our institutions get us disturbed about the performance of young people on historical tests, let's say, and so forth, we in turn get very disturbed that students can't remember the decade in which the Civil War was fought, or the year in which the Declaration of Independence was signed and issued, or they don't remember the opening and closing years of Reconstruction, let's say. But I would be much more distressed if they did not know what the Civil War was about, even if they couldn't remember that it was in the 1860s. I would be much more distressed if they did not know the inconsistencies that the stands that the Founding Fathers took in the Declaration of Independence, inconsistencies represented by their, on the one hand, fighting for their own independence, and on the other hand, holding a firm grip on the slaves to be certain that they did not have human freedom or independence. And in much the same way, I would be very disturbed if Americans paid more attention to these factual data generally than to the causes and the consequences of our great historical events and developments.

Heffner: But I must press you then, because it is my impression that as a people we know neither.

No. . . . And so I'm distressed on two counts. But if I had my preferences, I would prefer they know a good deal about the causes of the Civil War, even if they can't quite figure out that it started in 1861.

Heffner: You know, the early essay that you wrote on [*The*] *Birth of a Nation* seemed to me to focus so importantly upon the myths that have been perpetuated in our own history, in our own larger culture. Do you think that has been remedied since the early years of this century?

Remedied to a very limited degree. I would argue still that after all these years and after all the remarkable scholarship in the field, say, of Reconstruction (because that's what *Birth of a Nation* deals with), but even with the efforts of Kenneth Stampp in his book, *Era of Reconstruction*, or my book on Reconstruction after the Civil War, or to the vast number of books that have come along, like Eric Foner's book on Reconstruction and many monographs on Reconstruction in the various states, and Leo Litwack's remarkable book, which won the Pulitzer Prize, *We've Been in the Storm So Long*—in spite of all that, I am fearful that there is the impression still conveyed that the Reconstruction period was similar to that depicted in *Birth of a Nation*, or in the volume that became an early choice of the Literary Guild, *The Tragic Era*, by Claude Bowers, or in a much more recent work that came out in 1948, *The South During Reconstruction*, by E. Merton Coutler, I'm afraid that they still dominate much of the thinking about Reconstruction that most Americans subscribe to and worse still, I'm so afraid that much of the public policy that is being worked out in the 1990s is based on a conception of African Americans in politics that draws heavily on the so-called experience of African Americans in the Reconstruction years.

Heffner: When I try to make that point to my students, I'm afraid it just passes over their heads. Those horrendously brutish caricatures of the newly emancipated slaves and of everything about so-called Black Reconstruction that fill *Birth of a Nation*, D. W. Griffith's classic pro-Southern 1915 film—along with its deeply sympathetic portrayals of defeated Southern whites, even of the creation of the Ku Klux Klan—created images and stereotypes of black Americans that are still very much with us and that surely account in important part for this nation's languorous approach to civil rights.

It happens because we've had a persistence of practices that fed on these stereotypical notions, that, say, kept blacks out of politics for the most part for several generations after Reconstruction, and that in turn was renewed by *Birth of a Nation*, by Claude Bowers' *Tragic Era*, by Coutler's *The South During the Reconstruction*. So that it's what you want to see that you see. And there develops, as I tried to say in my presidential address before the American Historical Association, which was called "Reconstruction: Mirror for Americans," it recalls very clearly in the minds of so many people that Reconstruction is synonymous with black rule. It is synonymous, in turn, with malfeasance, and misfeasance in office. And that even in 1990, when there is reference to, say, a black candidate for public office in this years, sometimes you will see in the media a reference to the fact that this will be the first time, if this person is successful, if this black person is successful, it will be the first time since Reconstruction. That conjures up, you see, a whole set of notions about what went on during Reconstruction. It's not merely that blacks have not had any power since Reconstruction. It is also that, when they had power, they misused it. This is what you might call a subliminal effect. I'm not suggesting by any means that everyone who uses the term even knows what it means, Indeed, there's a lot of inaccuracy. For example, when Harvey Gant announced his candidacy for the United States Senate in North Carolina in 1989, and then made good in running in 1990, many of the writers referred to this as the first time that a black from North Carolina would go, if he's elected, to the Congress since Reconstruction. Well, the last black from North Carolina in Congress . . . left the Congress in 1901, which was long after the Reconstruction. Or they will say that he will be the second senator elected from the South since Reconstruction. That also is wrong. There were two elected from Mississippi during Reconstruction. Not only, then, do we have our facts all mixed up, muddled up, and inaccurate with respect to this problem, but much more important, it seems to me, is there is this undercurrent of fraud and implication that if they are elected they will somehow return us to that awful period which is called "The Tragic Era."

Heffner: I often paraphrase Beard's notion that all written history, all recorded history is an act of faith. And what you and I would consider misinterpretations of the past, are indeed acts of faith that stem from a very present-minded attitude toward blacks and whites.

Yes. By all means. Right. Well, I couldn't agree with Beard more when he said that history is an act of faith, and said it in his presidential address. But I think that Beard would be the first to criticize the use of history in this fashion, that is, as though this is what history is rather than merely an act of faith.

Heffner: But isn't that the danger we run whenever the historian becomes involved in—and now I go back to the beginning of our discussion— becomes involved in controversial issues? Doesn't he almost necessarily lend his perspective and perhaps even shape his perspective relating to the past to his contemporary-minded, his present-minded wishes?

I think that's always the danger. And I think that's something about which one must ever be conscious. I don't see anything wrong or objectionable about being present-minded, about the historian being present-minded, as long as he understands what he's doing, and as long as he doesn't take the historical fact for the purpose of somehow distorting it to fit into a present context, into a context that will somehow lead down a certain road that does not necessarily follow. Let me, if I may, just illustrate that very briefly by suggesting that if you feel deeply about say, the way in which the Reconstruction has been misinterpreted, if I'm going to use that as an example of how one must guard against repeating that during the present, then I have to be aware of the dangers of this misrepresentation. I have to be aware and be very sensitive to the possibility that even I, in using that material, might misrepresent it to make my point, you see.

Heffner: Are you satisfied that generally the disciples of Clio today are that aware of the dangers and that aware of what they must and must not do?

Oh, no. I'm not at all satisfied. Certainly not about all of the disciples of Clio. I see still too much use of Clio's work for purposes which it seems to me would not be for the common good or for the best interests of historical facts and historical knowledge itself. You know, there is always, as I suggested in one of the essays in this book, there's always the dilemma that the historian faces of being on the one hand a true, diligent, committed disciple, the muse of history, and doing precisely as one should do in order to carry out her wishes and the accurate portrayal of history. On the other hand, every historian is a human being, with deeply held beliefs, passions, desires, aspirations, criticisms about the present and the future, and wants to do whatever he can to improve the chances of a better world in which we live. If that is so, then he walks a kind of tightrope between, on the one hand, being certain that he is true to his principles of writing fair, objective, unadulterated history, and of advocating to the extent that he possible can the improvement of our social order on the other. The extent to which he uses the materials of history to do that is limited, I think, because he must be certain that in using these materials he does not fall prey, does not become tempted to twist them or distort them just to make his point. —1990

KENNETH CLARK

Writing now, one might hope that Kenneth Clark's comments in the late 1980s about racism in America could be relegated to past history. Dr. Clark was the psychologist whose studies of the impact of segregation on African-American children gave Thurgood Marshall his most powerful ammunition in successfully arguing Brown v. Board of Education before the Supreme Court in 1954. But despite the increasing political power of African Americans, despite the rise of a black middle class, and the rising importance of black intellectuals as well as black creative artists and entertainers, Clark's pessimism now seems to me to remain appropriate. I asked him whether the hopes and expectations raised by Brown, and later by the Civil Rights Movement of the 1960s, were generally justified.

They were justified in the sense of hope.

Heffner: And accomplishment?

Well, accomplishment in some areas of American life. Oddly enough, in the Southern parts of the United States, there have been accomplishments that one just cannot ignore. One cannot pretend that the problems of racial injustices and segregation and cruelty are as flagrant today as they were before Brown. Where I find the keenest disappointment is in the Northern areas of the United States, in places like New York, Boston, Philadelphia. I did not, and I make the confession very bluntly and clearly—that I did not believe that racism was as deep and as pernicious in Northern states, in Northern cities, as it turned out to be since Brown.

Heffner: Do you find that any inroads at all have been made in the North? In the non-Southern, non-original slave state areas?

No. In fact, let's take a very specific example of racism, namely segregated schools. In the 1950s, there were segregated schools in New York City. In the 1980s, a much greater number of children attend segregated schools. There is a much higher percentage of children in New York City, white and black, attending racially segregated schools than was true in the 1950s. I do not see that education has avoided racism in Northern cities.

Heffner: Because of educators? Or because of other factors?

Well, certainly the educators have not communicated to the public that being afflicted with racial prejudice interferes with their ability to communicate to American children what education is about. I just don't understand that. Educators seem to be timid. Either they themselves have been so afflicted by the racism of their own education that they don't want really to turn the system around, or they're afraid—they don't want to alienate the black or white public officials, or the public.

Heffner: Can they do anything about this within the context of not only our political system, but within the context of the way you now believe Americans think?

Well, they can't do anything about it as long as they don't believe they can, as long as they don't take any risk or chances. In the area of race, American educators are less willing to take chances in terms of helping the American people to grow up, to become mature about this issue than they are about anything else. Now they're talking about—and maybe rightly so—AIDS and sex education and things of that sort, but they are not talking about how to improve the moral, ethical, and human qualities of the children in our schools. They consider this more risky than to talk about sex, which I think is fascinating.

Heffner: Please explain that. It's not that you've shocked me into speechlessness, but I would like you to explain that psychologically.

I guess it's a totality. Racism perpetuates itself. I did not realize the depth of American racism until I observed what was happening in the United States since Brown. . . . Howard Beach [a race riot in an area of Queens] and other examples of white adolescents venting their racial hostilities through violence . . . South Boston, where white children took the American flag and used it as a basis for striking out against blacks. I didn't realize until I saw these examples and the extent to which racism in our educational system impaired the ability of our children, white children and black children, to be human, once color becomes a factor. This is a terrible thing that we are doing to our children. I felt terribly sorry for the white children in South Boston when I saw their faces on television, corroded with hate. Ironically, I feel sorry for those white children in Howard Beach because we defaulted in not helping them to understand that you cannot vent hostility on other human beings because of color. But our educational system has defaulted.

Heffner: But Dr. Clark, I'm really asking where we begin, given the equipment we start with? Where do we begin? Having to be taught to love? Or having to be taught not to hate?

I'm not talking about loving. I'm talking about—

Heffner: Accepting.

Yes. I believe that the most important goal of education is that of teaching human beings to understand and see the commonality among their fellow human beings. Our American educational institutions do not see this as a major priority or as a priority at all. As long as you have racism, as long as you have segregated schools, you are not going to get this kind of approach to the meaning of education.

Heffner: It's been thirty-four years since Brown v. Board of Education. Where do you think we'll be thirty years from now?

I'm afraid to answer you because, you know, I made all these positive predictions—

Heffner: Well, go ahead, be my guest.

I don't know. I really believe that color is an infection—a psychological infection which is extremely difficult for human beings to deal with and to remedy. I really feel today that the chances of Americans having their educational and their religious institutions turn around and begin to see the need . . . to respect their fellow human beings, are pretty slim. Now, they'll do it rhetorically, I mean, they'll do it with words, but I'm talking about even the Church. The religious institutions are, to me, as much in default as our educational institutions. It just so happens that I'm more identified with educational institutions than I've been with religious institutions, but you associate color and status, color and economic levels, and continue that, and it is not likely to change very much except verbally.

Heffner: You still feel then, in the debate that has raged, that this is a matter of race, not economics.

I think it's race, I think it's color. I think white ethnic groups have a much greater chance of upward mobility and acceptance, even with class distinctions, than do black human beings or brown human beings. And I think that color and race are the barriers to understanding and decency.

Heffner: What do you advise the black population to do? If you posit, as you do, this future? What is the advice that you give—

I don't know that the black population is particularly interested in my advice because there was a time, not so long ago, that I kept arguing for integration and fighting for integration while the popular group, not necessarily the majority by the way, of the black population was asking for racism and asking for separateness and black separatism. And my particular position was not popular at that time.

Heffner: Has your position changed?

No! I don't believe that blacks have any more justification for racism than do whites. What I thought the black separatists were doing was just imitating white separatists. And I thought it was kind of stupid. However, they didn't lose anything nor did they gain anything by this, it was just going around in circles, color being a stupid basis for making judgments about human beings.

Heffner: A few years ago you were very, very angry. What you said in print seemed to me to indicate that you were at the height of anger about the question of race. Do you feel that now, or have you just given up?

I'm not angry as I used to be because I have taken it for granted. I've accepted the fact that America will continue racism and what we'll have to do is to try to prevent the more violent and cruel manifestations of it. —1987

DERRICK BELL

Law School Professor Derrick Bell was called "one of our movement's giants, one of our true heroes," by Jesse Jackson. Less visible as a public intellectual than writer-scholar Henry Louis Gates, Jr., he was also called "energizing and infuriating" by Gates himself. Certainly our conversation in mid-1992, following publication of his book, Faces at the Bottom of the Well: The Permanence of Racism, *deserved both of these adjectives. I was struck most by his statement early on in our conversation that he meant "to tell what I view as the truth about racism without causing disabling despair." What did he mean, I asked.*

It seems to me that history, my experience, [and] current events as we read them, all point to one conclusion about racism in this society, and that is that it is permanent. That it is an essential, it is not an aberration, it is not what most of us believed it was—30 or 40 years ago—a pimple on the otherwise beautiful complexion of America as a place of freedom and equality for all. We all believed that, at one time. That was the conclusion of the Gunnar Myrdal report—the huge study of racial discrimination in the '40s, and we all accepted that. As a litigator, I acted on that belief. And I think though that even if it means tearing down, in a way, much of what I've done, much of what others have done, that on the tatters of what we thought would be a wonderful edifice—on even the ruins—we have to see what there is to be seen. And that leads me to my conclusion.

Heffner: You seem to have adopted a determinism here that cuts out room for anything other than despair.

Well, it's—and I certainly have to acknowledge it—the temptation to depair that this leads to because it's so different from that we have followed and believed. The fact is though that to continue on with those beliefs leads to a more definite despair. Moreover, it does not provide any insight to where we should go from here. I think that there is something that is the stuff of revival in speaking the truth. The truth of individuals who learn that they have terminal cancer, let us say—if we put it on an individual basis. For some, they jump out the window. For many others, though, after they get themselves together, they live more purposeful lives with whatever time they have. Why? Because they have gotten beyond that which afflicts us all at one point or another, the belief that though death is something that happens to somebody else, it's not going to happen to me. And we live our lives often enough like we're going to be here permanently, and that wastes an awful lot of our lives. I think there's a similar situation in regard to our commitment to racial equality. If we face up to the reality of racism and the role it plays in our society, then it's not simply an aberration; it's a necessary stabilizing influence in a society like ours. That doesn't mean we give up. It means that we are able to face the real problems, the real enemy, if you will, and to fashion tactics and strategies that are likely to be more effective. Not guaranteed, not likely even to bring about the kind of era we thought about when we sang "We shall overcome," but likely to lead to more meaningful endeavor than we're now engaged in.

Heffner: In reading *Faces at the Bottom of the Well*, at times you seem to be saying, "We have seen the enemy and it is "us."

To the extent that we continue in our own direction, often enough it is us.

Heffner: What would change that direction?

I think we must change our attitude with regard to where we're going, what we're doing. In the last few months, for example, there's been a lot of controversy about the worth of all-male, necessarily black schools in the inner city as a means of dealing with the genocidal situation that is facing so many of our young black males. Many of those who held the original dream of both racial and gender integration, have been very troubled by that. Have opposed it. Some organizations have gone into court to actually halt such programs. Well, I think that that is at least mischievous, and perhaps more dangerous than that, because it is not allowing a potentially effective procedure to even be tried. And we can repeat that example in many other areas of the civil rights struggle. To continue in the same way, I think, is a mistake. if you ask me "Well, what should we be doing differently?" I can't give you a blueprint. If I could I would have written a better book than *Faces at the Bottom of the Well*, but I can say that once we adopt a different outlook with regard to the causes of racism, how we deal with it, I think that individuals particularly in their own areas of education or employment or whatever it is, will be able to fashion ideas that make more sense in our present world.

Heffner: What is basic to your thinking, your fix on human nature, that leads you to write about the permanence of racism?

There is something about humans because, as many of my critics often point out . . . the United States is not unique in its willingness to subordinate an identifiable minority, either minority identifiable by race, or religion, or ethnic grouping. It's a worldwide phenomenon. What would seem to make it different here is our commitment to our earliest documents, the Constitution and others, that seem at one level to be pointing in a different direction. When read carefully, of course, they already inculcate some of the essence of the problem that we face today.

Heffner: Well the compromises in the Constitution certainly put their stamp on racist attitudes.

. . . The essence of slavery was a belief by whites that blacks could be reduced to slavery and that that would be somehow beneficial to them, it certainly was going to be necessary to move the society along. When slavery was replaced by segregation, no whites had ever been segregated in the way that blacks have been. And again that policy came about as a compromise needed to move whites of differing views, different politics, ahead. So that if you look at almost any of the positives or negatives in terms of the racial policy in this country, you will find that at the bottom, whatever it's been said, it was intended to further the ends of the whites, often differing whites on a partic-ular issue. Slavery itself was a manifestation of this deep sense of white superiority and that blacks, while we would like them to be treated better, if we have to make a decision between treating better and not treating better, then we're going to follow Lincoln's example. When he wrote back to Horace Greeley in regard to slavery that "I will do," he said, "anything I have to do to save the Union. If I can save the Union by freeing all the slaves, I'll do that. Keep them all in slavery, I'll do that. Freeing some, leaving some in slavery, I'll do.

Whatever it takes." I love that quote because it reflects his candid nature, but it also reflects American policy-making both before and after Lincoln.

Heffner: Let me come back to the question that I asked you before about the nature of human nature. Is what we're talking about, the need to oppress or the need that you may sense of whites to prevail over blacks? If that's the case, mustn't blacks feel the same way about whites?

If we're just talking about Africans, I don't see any lessening of some of these unhappy urges by people of African background when they get power. Even over their own people, so I can't say that there's something in the genes that makes one group good and one bad. In this society, though, there are several levels, you see. The fact is that race has always served as a diversion. The piece that I wrote at the beginning of *Faces at the Bottom of the Well* talks about "black people are the faces at the bottom of the societal well. whites, many of whom occupy a level only slightly above the blacks, reach down and are mesmerized. Some reach out and try to pull us up, they know that unless they help us up they won't be able to move to a different level. But rather than look up at the top to see who it is that's keeping us both down, they remain fixated on us and determine that they will stay where they are if it means we can stay down further below." Well there's something of that, and it is encouraged by varying groups at the top because it takes the heat off them. That's George Bush, isn't it? We're coming up to another election, but the last time Bush—who came into power on Reagan's policies, where there had been a greater growth in the disparity between the upper class and the rest of us, almost in the history of our country—didn't talk about that at all. He talked about waving the flag and talked about the Willie Horton case. He moved the focus away from where the problems really are and focused them in one way or another, somewhat more subtly maybe than Reagan (some would say not so much more subtly), on race. And it works every time.

Heffner: You seem to be saying that it works every time not in terms necessarily of Reagan or Bush or of X or Y or Z, but in terms of whites and blacks in America.

The individuals change over time. But the willingness to use race as a detour, as a change of focus away from where the real issues are has been the same. That's how slavery got started. Those able to afford slaves were able to convince those whites who could not afford slaves that somehow, even though the presence of slaves meant that the rest of those whites were going to be in a disadvantaged economic position, that they needed to stay together to fight off the slave revolts and all the rest. And we have the same thing today with affirmative action, don't we?

Heffner: What, if you forgive me, bugs me so about your book, *Faces at the Bottom of the Well: The Permanence of Racism,* is that I find so little hope in it. Now tell me again, what is that mystical connection between recognition of what you want the black community to recognize and a kind of transcending of the despair that there must be. How do we get from here to there?

A couple of things. One is that we are here basically to recognize and fight evil, whatever that is. I mean, we certainly want to be successes and support our families, but life, the miracle of our lives must be more than a house in the suburbs and a fancy car in the driveway. So that if, by some miracle, racism ended tomorrow, those of us who feel that our lives are to serve others, to look, find evil and try to deal with it, we would look around for and deal with poverty. We would deal with some horrible disease. So that in some ways the fact of racism being permanent is not automatically, "Oh my God, there's, there's no hope," because our efforts are always to recognize bad stuff. The more important thing though I think is the fact of slavery, because slavery was a horrible time, but it was also a time of magnificent overcoming by any number of the slaves to a situation that must have been worse that anything we can imagine today. That these people have no rights, that they were chattel, that they could be bought and sold and beaten and killed and raped, and there was no relief. That must have been very despairing to many. But we know, from the history and legacy of the spirituals, that for some there was a recognition that as bad as their lives were there was something beyond that. And not simply a hope of a place in heaven. That they had a faith that transcended even their situation. And I think they were able to gain that faith out of an honest recognition of just how bad their situation was.

Heffner: I started off our conversation quoting you, that your objective was to get people to understand the realities of racism and without despair. How sanguine are you about the future?

I think that I am not sanguine. But I do not despair. The slaves had no reason to be sanguine about what was going to happen, they hoped for freedom. We hope, too, things are going to get better. But all of the indicators point in another direction. That is a reason, though, for recommitment in keeping with the miracle of our existence, our responsibilities. What makes us feel good about life. And that is fighting through. Let me end with a quick story about an old woman down in rural Mississippi who I asked a question like this, because she was pushing back at the whites.

Heffner: I loved her answer.

They were shooting at her house at night, they were trying to take her farm, and I said, "You know, Mrs. McDonald, why do you do it?" And she said, "Oh—." She said, "Derrick, I'm an old lady. I lives to harass white folks." Now this Mrs. McDonald, as a matter of fact, lived in a basically white community, and her neighbors were very supportive of her. So she wasn't condemning all white people, but those who were "on" her, who were pressing her. Her talent was not to beat them—because they had the money, the power, the guns. Her determination was, in her words, "to harass them." And to get from that harassment, whether she recognized it or not, a kind of existential triumph.—1995

HUGH B. PRICE

A "younger" African-American leader emerged in the mid-1990s: Hugh B. Price, then the newly selected president of the National Urban League. Though not in the virtually daily limelight of those in the preceding generation—Roy Wilkins, James Farmer, Martin Luther King, and others—Price nonethless exerted real influence both as a spokesperson and executive in the "Movement." He had noted that "this ruthlessly competitive world waits for no nation, no ethnic group, no individual." I asked if this meant he would focus his energies on African Americans' economic improvement.

There are a number of issues that we have to focus on. I think that if you consider the fact that, in the social compact, there are individual responsibilities and societal responsibilities, it's my belief that the compact has broken down on both sides. The breakdown has fed the problems on both sides. On the individual side, we have seen a retreat from individual responsibility, the obligation that parents have to bring children into this Earth and to be in a position to nurture and support their children economically, the increase in violence and loss of respect for human life, all of those kinds of issues on one side of the equation are quite, quite serious.

On the other side of the equation, we've seen the major economic changes in our society that have made it much more difficult for people to support their families, and that have fostered, in my judgment, much of the tension between races as people are scrambling for position in the economy. What's happening in the economy is not unlike a basketball game, where you've got people jostling under the backboards for the only rebound that's coming off. And I think that if we're going to pull our way out of this we've got to repair and redefine the social compact on both sides, which means that we've got to go to work. We, of the Urban League, for example, have to work in our own community and with our own folk to take individual responsibility much more seriously, and I think that's a broader societal issue, by the way, not just an African-American issue. And secondly, I think on the side of the social obligations, we've got to look at where is the work going to come from and where are the livelihoods going to come from that enable people to live with dignity. And if we don't address both sides of the compact and concentrate only on the personal responsibility side and not on the opportunity side of the equation, we're going to have an imbalance and a continuation of the problems that we have.

Heffner: Obviously, what we live in now is a society in which there are those who may give lip service to the notion of compact between two groups, but who generally come back down and emphasize one. "It's your responsibility to do this," rather than, "It's a responsibility for both of us." How do we get out of that situation?

I think it must be an understanding in the society. These are the key ingredients of social cohesion. It is entirely appropriate to say, "Thou shalt do this, thou shalt do that. You have certain responsibilities." But there also is the Preamble to the Constitution which posits the notion that government and society have to look out for the social welfare, provide for the common good, and, in effect, manage an economy that makes it possible for people to prosper. After all, we left feudalism centuries ago, the days of a handful of well-endowed overlords and the rest of the vassals on the farm struggling away as best they can. The whole greatness of this country was the opening, the broad opening of economic opportunity to those who wanted to participate, and the prospect of upward mobility, the prospect that, no matter how humble your beginnings and how modest your skills, there was a blue-collar economy all the way up to a white-collar economy that provided a place for you and an opportunity to share in America's bounty. That part of the social compact, the expectation that the economy will deliver for you if you play by the rules, has broken down for millions of Americans. It hit African Americans earlier because of the urban base, but it is hitting everyone now as well.

Heffner: But you seem not willing to make any concession to the notion that, just as the frontier lent itself to that fluidity, that flexibility, that upward mobility, in fact the frontier is gone, and so are many of those good things that historically always went with the American experience.

Well . . . well, we're in a period where upward mobility seems to be in a holding pattern for millions of Americans. If you talk to macro-economists, they would suggest that, as in the past, with the Industrial Revolution, we will work our way out of this; there will be opportunity for decent incomes at the back end of the transformation that we're going through.

Another view, if you talk to many business CEOs, is that we've only just begun to see the impact of technology and the globalization of labor on the American worker, and that the picture is not that pretty at the back end. And it's fascinating that many economists say that the CEOs have a short time horizon, and the CEOs say that the economists have their heads in the sand. It's hard to reach any consensus about this.

What I think is also fascinating is that, in this grand, global realignment of work and wealth, wealth is moving toward the Third World. And there are many who are saying that, in the grand scheme of things, that is appropriate. That if we're going to have prosperity and comfort in parts of the world where there's devastating poverty, if we're going to staunch the flow of immigrants from very poor countries into First World countries then we've got to grow the economies of those societies. But in the process there's a wrenching price that we're paying in this country.

Heffner: Where do you find the optimism to make the assumption that, in this grand transformation, to balance things out between the First and the Third Worlds, within the foreseeable future, we're going to return to America, the land of opportunity?

Well, I don't think you have a choice but to be optimistic. And certainly when you work with real people in real communities, you have to do whatever you can to help them navigate the real world as they see it and as they encounter it. So, in our work, we know that children in inner-city schools are capable of higher levels of achievement and of performing more challenging material. We know that they're capable of getting better jobs in the communities where they are. There is growth in some communities. There's a great deal of economic churn and job churn in communities. There are opportunities to participate in those parts of the economy where there's growth and where there's wealth to be made. And we need to do a better job of positioning African Americans to participate.

What I'm suggesting is that the macro-picture is the harder one to get one's hands around, and, in fact, where there's less of a knowledge base. There is a lot of knowledge about how to do a better lob of educating inner-city children who don't seem to be doing well in school. I've seen those instances. You've probably talked to people who can talk to you for hours about the wondrous things that are done. So we know at a micro-level how to do a much better job of preparing people. What we don't know at a macro-level yet, and aren't even willing to discuss in this country, is: Where are we headed as an economy? What are the characteristics of the kind of market economy we have now that might not address all the problems that we have? Will the kind of economy, with its emphasis on highly competitive capitalism, deal with the pockets of high unemployment in this country, and are there compensating mechanisms that we need in public policy, such as public-sector job creation, in order to make sure that people have a chance to work where the private market doesn't work?

Heffner: But where does race come into the picture?

Where does race come in? It was once said to me by somebody that when the tidal wave of major change hits the beach, African Americans are invariably engulfed first because they're closest to the water but, if the change is big enough, it works its way up the beach. And I think that's what's going on now: it's working its way up the beach. Race is clearly a factor in the exaggerated impact on us. Race is clearly still a barrier in getting certain kinds of jobs, getting access to housing, getting access to lending, and the like. The Urban Institute has sent out applicants in the last several years, to white and blacks, equally qualified, applying for jobs. The pattern, not surprisingly, is that white candidates get more favorable consideration. So we've got to continue to fight racism wherever it's encountered; but, in addition, we've got to focus on preparing all of our young people to participate in this economy that's before them in their communities and in this country.

So, on the ground, we have to do our level best to prepare our folks to navigate the real world as they see it. And in our policy and advocacy work, we've go to partner with others who are beginning to ask hard questions about how the economy is working, whether it's creating enough opportunity, and what kinds of compensating mechanisms there must be in order to enable everyone to participate again. Because I think if we don't get at that question, and if we have larger and larger pockets of African Americans who really don't have a place in the economy, don't have a place with dignity in the economy, and you engraft upon that other people of color and angry white males who don't have a place in the economy, there's the potential for the creation of a very large, disaffected class which, if it ever stopped warring against itself, and instead, coalesced, might provide a basis for some more compassionate policies. Which isn't to say one's looking at alternative economic systems, but just looking at compensatory mechanisms to take the hard edge off capitalism.

I think there's a growing realization that there's a lot of discontent in the land and a lot of alienation that is spreading beyond people of color to the majority culture. Will that crystallize in compassionate public policies that take the edge off of things? I don't know. A couple of years ago there was an increase in the wage supplements provided under the tax system through what is called the "earned income tax credit," which was an effort to do that. But I don't see a lot of evidence otherwise. And, of course, there's a lot of talk in Washington now about retreating from the public policies that help. And I just wonder, you know, do we want to toss mothers and children off welfare and run the risk that, as is the case in some Third World countries and even on the Riviera, that we will encounter mothers and children out begging on the streets. Do we want that in this country? Do we want to run any risk of that? Are we prepared to toss people into a labor market that is very soft and has a lot of unemployed folks and for whom there may not be adequate jobs? What are we going to do if there's no room in the local labor market, if, let's say, the unemployment is seven or eight percent, if people are tossed off welfare?

If we were to create public-sector jobs or have publicly stimulated work to provide a compensating mechanism, it would be fine to have a hard-edged welfare with a time limit which forces people to become self-reliant. But if there is slack in the labor market and there aren't enough jobs, what are we going to do? If every time the unemployment rate dips below six percent, the Federal Reserve Board hyperventilates, raises the interest rates, puts more people out of work, and at the same time we're saying to poor people, "You've got to be self-reliant and work," there's a disconnect there between our policies and our realities. And we want to work with others to try to establish a connection between the two phenomena.

Heffner: Yet, with an unemployment rate that isn't all that high, one could hardly say that we see signs of the compassionate society that you urge upon us.

I see the precursors of it, which is the beginnings of an openness in communities about what's really going on. And I think the last elections were, in part, about that: "This isn't working. I'm in pain. The people who are in office aren't responding to my pain. So let's get a new cast of characters." But I don't see the constructive impulse coming out of that yet. I think that's got to grow from the ground. I think that's an op-ed debate that's got to happen. I think that the impulse for compassion and inclusion has got to come back up from the ground. The American people have got to say, "We want to live in this society; not that kind of society." And that means that groups like ours and others have got to work the turf out there on the ground so that people speak to their public officials about the kind of world they want to live in.

Heffner: How well are you going to be able to do the job of leading that kind of society—and that's the only way to put it—when there still are extremists in the area of race, both black and white? How well can you maintain this thoughtful, moderate approach, the concept that there is a social compact with two sides to it?

I think we'll be able to do our work. And I'm not going to war with the extremists. We've got hard work to do. And I understand some of what the extremism is about. It's about extreme exasperation with the way things work. I mean, there are other factors as well sometimes, and a lot of it sometimes is deeply rooted in racism. But a lot of it's rooted in sheer exasperation and a sense that America is not willing to live up to the Constitution and not willing to live up to the obligation to provide for an inclusive society and for the well-being of all.

I often say that there are people who operate solidly inside the mainstream—that's the Urban League—and we help build bridges and help people across. There are some groups that have a hard advocacy edge to them that believe that folks need to function inside the mainstream, and they're forever pushing on the outside to get people into the mainstream and to make the institutions that set the rules to be more compassionate. And then there are people all the way on the outside who say, "I don't believe it's going to work. I don't think they're ever going to open up. And besides, there's a whole history of racism and discrimination in this country to undergird our belief," and also believe that, "If you get up on that bridge, somebody's got a depth charge, you know, connected to them, they're going to blow it up when you're up there and vulnerable as you try to cross over. So, we're skeptical. We're profoundly skeptical, bordering on cynical, that America's ever going to be serious about this, so we're going to do our own thing."

That is the extremism rooted in exasperation with the American system. I understand what that's about. But I think the game is inside the mainstream. That's the only way you can go. —1995

OTHER VOICES

Stephen L. Carter on Affirmative Action and Racial Discourse

Professor of Law at Yale, author of Reflections of an Affirmative Action Baby

Affirmative action has done a lot of different things and it's important to talk about what kind of affirmative action one has in mind. In my book, I talk mostly about the kind of affirmative action one encounters in moving upward in the professional world . . . college and professional school admission . . . entrance to a profession, and so on. Most of those benefits have, indeed, gone to the black people who are best situated, if you look at whatever socio-economic measures you'd like to look at. On the other hand, there are forms of affirmative action such as the use of affirmative action programs to break up lily-white trade unions and things like that, that have clearly benefitted working-class black people as well. So it depends a lot on what you're talking about. But there's one reality we do know: that since the enactment of the Civil Rights Act in 1964 and the increasing move toward affirmative action programs in the late 1960s, the income gap between the top and bottom fifth of black wage earners has increased faster than the income gap between the top and bottom fifth of white wage earners. I don't want to insist that affirmative action has caused this phenomenon, but what these data do tell us is that affirmative action is not solving the problems of those who are nearer the bottom.

Heffner: Why do you have this reputation for being so negative about affirmative action?

You know, I don't think of myself as negative about affirmative action. I think of myself as realistic about affirmative action. My view about affirmative action is that it can be a useful tool in some circumstances, but it has to be used sensitively and what's vital is that we dethrone it from its centrality of being the main tool most often debated and most often talked about in the move to racial justice. It can be very useful and has its place, but too often, a rhetoric on both sides of the issue is structured as though it's the only important tool, or the most important tool, and those propositions I deny.... if one criticizes affirmative action, especially if one is black, there's a vision one must be against it, one is either against it and wanting to tear it down in every respect, or one is playing into the hands of those who are against it. This notion that affirmative action should be above criticism, that we shouldn't have realistic conversations about it's weaknesses, as well as about its strengths, that notion is part of what I talk about in the book, when I talk about putting people into little boxes. That one can't hold what one might think of as the intellectual middle ground, one can't stand off from affirmative action and say, "Let me be critical without necessarily being in opposition." Instead one is forced into one camp or the other, and if one says some critical things about it, people say, "Oh, that's that anti-affirmative action fellow ... Professor Carter."...The problems of race are too important. I'm not willing to accept the idea that in dealing with people's views about race . . . all we need to do is slip people into categories and not deal with what they're saying. My view is that what matters is the argument, not the person who's putting the argument forth. —1991

Thurgood Marshall on Lawyers and Unpopular Cases
Counsel for National Association for the Advancement of Colored People in Brown v. Board of Education (1954), and future Associate Justice of the United States Supreme Court

I think that theory is as old as the practice of law, that when a lawyer is in court defending a client there is no connection at all between his philosophy and that of the client. Of course, speaking for myself as an attorney for an organization more or less my ideals and philosophies are much the same as the organization. If even in that capacity once I am in court with the client the rights of the client come above any philosophy that the organization might have. And so is it possible, and indeed it has occurred that I have found it necessary to do what the client wanted and in many instances it would be against my own personal philosophy, but if the client wanted it done that is what a lawyer is to do. He is the legal technician, and there is no connection at all between the philosophy of the client, and I have never understood why a lawyer should he blamed for it.

. . . Once you agree between the lawyer and the client to take the case over, then the one agreement is that the man is going to get a fair shake in court. And once you get to that point the ideological background passes out; you want to see that the client gets a fair trial.

Heffner: Knowing about this program and my guests, some people just couldn't understand Edward Bennett Williams' willingness to represent the late Senator McCarthy, Jimmy Hoffa, and gambler Frank Costello. This is the difficulty.

I think that it is this simple, that if Senator McCarthy had come to me instead of Mr. Williams and asked me I would have taken the exact same position Mr. Williams took, and if he still wanted me, I would have defended him.

Heffner: But what about the others? Your cause, that of your organization [the NAACP] and of your individual clients, is unpopular in the American South. As a consequence, is it hard there to find lawyers to face down public opinion?

We are having increasing trouble in the Deep South, and we are having considerable trouble in other areas. But fortunately we have never yet had a case that we really wanted to take up that we didn't find the lawyer, and in the deep South, I hate to bring race in, but it's not restricted to Negro lawyers in the South. We've had outstanding white lawyers, who have in the past stopped forward.

There are men who will come forth, but Morris Ernst's point is that any lawyer who does not come forth, has not performed his duty as a lawyer to do it within his means. I don't mean that he should starve to death as a result of it, but there are plenty of lawyers in the country who could bring the necessary legal extras to these cases that would mean something.

Heffner: And I gather they are not doing that,

They are not doing it. —1958

WOMEN'S
ISSUES

GLORIA STEINEM

Gloria Steinem has been a leading planner, inspiration, theoretician, and spokesperson for the women's movement for decades. Through her activities, as the founding editor of Ms. Magazine, *writer, and lecturer, she has taught us that feminism and humanism can be synonymous. One of our several conversations took place early in 1987, soon after publication of* Marilyn, *the book for which Ms. Steinem wrote the text and George Barris provided the photographs. The talk initially focussed on Monroe, but soon branched out to more general aspects of the Feminist Movement, at moments even with a note of belligerence—at least on Ms. Steinem's part. And if the conversation had taken place in 2003 instead of 1987, it's likely that she would have even more right to be belligerent. Not that much has changed in 16 years.*

Heffner: Why Steinem on Monroe?

It's a hard question for me to answer because it seems so evident that it becomes difficult to explain. I think she was an exaggerated version of what women are very often encouraged in general to be. All the more so in the forties and the fifties, when she was alive, but even now. Remember that she was encouraged to be childlike, to be ornamental; she was valued for her looks rather than for what was in her head or in her heart. She played a role of the role, that is the classic dumb blonde role. And in addition to that she was encouraged to conceal the real Norma Jean who was inside her in somewhat the way women—men, too—but I think even women more so, are encouraged to hide behind the stereotype. Yet that internal woman had experienced a lot of the things that we now know have happened to large numbers of women. Being, for instance, sexually assaulted as a little girl. I mean when she was alive, she may have felt quite alone in this experience, but since her death many more women have come forward and talked about this. And we know more now about its consequences. And fearing aging, much more than men do. And wanting desperately to be taken seriously and not being able to. So her existence in the culture is this massive mythical figure who exaggerates what women are supposed to be, and thus conceals her real self; a kind of larger projection of the individual woman for a lot of us. So I got hooked on Monroe. I got hooked on trying to find out who she really was inside that mythic projection.

Heffner: When I saw the review of your book and asked you to be here with me, I went back to your earlier book of essays and read one you'd written years ago on Marilyn Monroe. And I guess the further question I want to put to you is whether there really was that much more that would have surfaced and would have developed if we were then where we are now in the feminist revolution?

Well, it's hard to know what would have surfaced, but I think there's a good chance that she might be alive. And that's very important. I mean, if a movement can save lives, what more important is there to do?

Heffner: She died, then, because—

She . . . Well, she was, she felt very alone, very isolated. She was a child-woman trying to grow up, but was rewarded for being a child; she was trying to play serious roles, but wasn't allowed to. She was trying to get her identity through a man as we were then taught to do, to marry whomever it is we wanted to become. An American hero in her case, Joe DiMaggio. A serious person, Arthur Miller. And so on. She was trying to come to terms with that person inside herself, as we all are, I think. And had the movement been around to let her know, movement just means people moving, I don't mean in any formal sense, but women telling the truth, perhaps she might not have felt so alone.

Heffner: And how do we behave differently now? How would it have affected her? You said she would have talked. She could have given expression to—

She did talk, but I mean she would have known when she spoke that she was not entirely alone in those experiences. She would have known, for instance, that about one in six little girls is sexually assaulted by somebody in their households. And would have had other people to confirm what the consequences are—that you feel as if you have no value but a sexual value. And that it's somehow your fault. She might also have had other actresses who were saying as she was saying, "I want to be taken seriously. I don't want to play dumb blonde roles, I want to be a whole person on screen." And she might have had a few more roles that were serious roles. She might have had her own identity instead of having to marry it. I mean we can't know, we can only speculate. But there seems very good reason to believe that if she had been born later or the movement had been born earlier, she might be with us today.

Heffner: A person of real talent then?

I think so. I think she's now recognized as a wonderful comedienne and also quite a serious actress in some of her earlier movies especially, though she never was given the scope to really do a wide variety of work. Nonetheless, she's spoken of by Strasburg and others, as you know, as one of his most talented pupils. He places her up there with Marlon Brando.

Heffner: You've just said that she would be alive, perhaps, had the Feminist Movement, the "moving of people" taken place earlier. I want to ask you what the downside would have been in the life of Marilyn Monroe, whether there would have been any downside in the context of what has happened with this movement?

I don't think so, because it isn't as if she enjoyed or loved being thought a dumb blonde, in which case the movement might have had a downside for her. To the contrary, she wanted very badly to be taken seriously. And the end of her last interview was just that. She pleaded with her interviewer, "Say what I really believe." She said. "I believe, you know, in world peace and, you know, serious subjects. Please don't make me a joke." Of course the interviewer didn't use that at all.

Heffner: I was very much taken by that, "Please don't make me a joke." Obviously you felt that that was a motif in her life.

Yes, I think that she feared very much being humiliated, being laughed at, and yet she was in a bind, in which to become successful and to become visible, she had to take those roles.

Heffner: Well, let me move the question away from Monroe. What has been the downside, because there has to be?

I know what you mean and yet I question your approach. For example, would we say there has been a downside to combating anti-Semitism?

Heffner: Fair enough. But you say you know what I mean. So can you take it from here?

Well, I think the trendline, as they say, is clearly up. I mean women are living longer, we're healthier, we have much less incidence of depression and mental illness, we're less addicted to tranquilizers and other things than we used to be. We report ourselves to be happier. So the trendline is up. But, of course, until you really have equal power in society, then anything you do, to some extent, will be used against you.

Heffner: But I thought there were a number of people who have said that indeed for many women, or for women generally, there were many areas in which they were taking on the problems, as well as the power of men. Is this not true?

No, actually it's not true. Women are living longer and are healthier. And, part of the reason that women are having more heart attacks is because we're living longer after menopause, when hormones cease to protect women from heart attacks. Thus more heart attacks. But it's precisely because we're living longer that we're having more heart attacks. And in fact the group that always had the highest incidence of stress-produced illness is and was poor black women. In other words, there's not much to the idea that only rich white male executives had stress and health problems. I mean I have a lot of empathy for their stress and health. But they're not the group that has it the most. What produces stress, it seems, is a feeling of being out of control. That's a primary component of stress. And that is much more likely to happen among poor people than well-to-do people.

Heffner: You mean it is not power that tends to corrupt, but powerlessness.

Yes, I think powerlessness corrupts absolutely.

Heffner: And do you think that at this point we're moving into a period where there is more of a feeling of power on the part of women?

More, but there are other problems, transitional problems that are very tough. Middle-class women have the problem that previously poor and disproportionately black or minority women had, which is having to maintain two jobs. So often a woman is both working in the labor force, the paid labor force, and then having to come home to take care of children and the house and so on.

Heffner: Why do you call that a transitional problem?

Well, it's a transitional problem because we're on the way to men being equal parents, for which we need to change the job patterns, which we're only beginning to do. So that men get parental leave and can stay home when new babies arrive. So that there's a shorter work day or a shorter work week for both the parents of little children. So that there's equal sharing of parenthood and work outside the home. Instead of giving two jobs to one person. And, of course, you know we're the only industrialized democracy in the whole world that does not have some national system of childcare.

Heffner: You see any potential for that soon?

The last time we really had full-fledged national legislation that was possible, however fragmented, was in the Nixon Administration. It was passed, but Nixon vetoed it. And since then there hasn't been any real opportunity for national legislation. But we have made a number of advances in terms of tax deductions for child care expenses, and tax rewards for corporations that provide child care, either on-site or through a chit system, you know. So there have been little advances, but not the kind of broad national policy, pro-child policy, that we need.

Heffner: You say, pro-child. You think it has been a matter of Americans not really having been concerned with children, as always touted?

Yes, I'm afraid so. If we just look at the way the society treats children and how little we welcome them into the work place or public buildings or—you know, we segregate kids terribly. When I give a lecture, very often there will be a parent, usually a woman, but sometimes a man, with a baby, at least one if not more, and the baby will start to cry. And that parent frequently feels bad and like he or she has to leave. And I always stop the lecture and I say, "Please do not leave." I mean a child crying is much more human and pleasant sound than a jet overhead—which we put up with. Why can't we include children in our lives? I mean at *MS Magazine* we have children in the office.

Heffner: There have been those who have been saying in the last few years that there is a reversal. That there is a movement away from embracing the very kinds of ideas and ideals that you talk about.

There's certainly a backlash, yes. Absolutely.

Heffner: Backlash implies a truly reactionary movement. You think that's true?

Well, I think that's true. Yet it's very easy to think that it's bigger than it actually is because, for one thing, it's represented in the White House. I mean Ronald Reagan is a representative of the backlash in this regard, in terms of equality. On race and sex both, for example, he stands against the major concerns and legislation and gains. But if you consider that a backlash is in itself a proof of success, you know what I mean. That is you don't get serious organized opposition until you are, in fact, taken seriously. Also that the public opinion polls have been getting steadily better. *Newsweek* did a cover story on women in the labor force not long ago. And the cover story was full of quibbles and pessimism and so on, but the public opinion poll that they had sponsored was fabulous. I mean it said that more than 60 percent of women feel that the Women's Movement has affected their lives positively, more than half consider themselves feminists. The poll was almost the opposite of the article.

Heffner: I really didn't mean the political movement, which as you say is a sign of success in itself. You don't move against something that hasn't achieved a considerable amount of success. I meant what one hears about the attitudes of women themselves.

Do you know anybody who wants to go backward?

Heffner: Go back? That's not a fair response. But I rather felt that attitudes towards motherhood perhaps, toward what one could do, toward an appropriate relationship to children, that there has been some feeling that the, well, the almost anti-motherhood attitude—

Did I just sound anti-motherhood?

Heffner: No, no, not you.

Okay, but who sounded anti-mother? Frankly, it's only the women's movement that has been trying to make pro-child attitudes and legislation, trying to honor motherhood and to honor work that's done in the home, and so on. Here's the problem, I think. It's a problem in perception that I don't know how to deal with. I think it's almost inevitable, when women rebel it's assumed that they want to be like men. Because, because what could be better, you know? And we never said that, actually, we never said we wanted to be like men. We wanted to be like people, we wanted men to be more like people, too. We wanted to share all of the human qualities. So there was a feeling that women who wanted equality didn't want to be mothers because men were not mothers. And didn't want to be housewives because men were not housewives. That's never been the case. We want everybody to be able to be everything.

Heffner: Some years ago, in another conversation with you, Betty Friedan, and others, I said that we men needed the compassion that you've just demonstrated. I had the feeling at that time that you didn't think that all of your sisters were quite so involved in that kind of compassionate and humanist approach to this movement.

Well, I think the women who actually were homemakers were the most bitter.

Heffner: That's interesting.

Yes. And they were very involved in the movement. They were active before I was, in fact.

Heffner: What are you saying when you say that the homemakers were women who were the most bitter?

Well I think that they had felt marginalized and isolated, off in the suburbs, in their houses and without adult companionship and so on. I mean they had personally experienced real hardship. You know, being a homemaker is psychologically, physically, healthwise, economically the worst job in the United States. So their experience of that caused them to tell the truth in a way that may have made people feel that the very job of homemaker should be eliminated. But in fact, what those women really wanted and what has become certainly clear since then is the need for respect and support and pay for this job. Whether it's done by men or by women.

Heffner: Do you think it's still considered the worst job in the United States?

It's not that it's considered so. Objectively, it *is* the worst job in the U.S. I mean there is no guarantee of salary at all, it's just room and board, legally speaking. That's all your husband has to provide. "Ahh, and, by the way, what did you do with the fifty dollars I gave you yesterday?" And women who are homemakers work longer hours than any other class of worker, longer weeks; have more incidence of drug addiction, of violence. I mean the most dangerous place for an American woman is not in the street, statistically speaking—it's in her own home. She's most likely to be beaten up by a man in her own household. She has the most likelihood of being replaced by a younger worker—

Heffner: That's an interesting point.

I think, just objectively, it isn't the intrinsic work; I mean the intrinsic work is really interesting. Raising baby humans is a lot more interesting than a lot of what goes on in this building and in factories and with a lot of the rest of the paid work force. Which is why men should do it, too. I think men would enjoy it. But when it's privatized and pushed off in the corner and not rewarded and isolated, it gets to be very tough.

Heffner: Do you think anything very significant has happened about changing that privatization, pushing it off in the corner, making it very tough.

Well, I think that two things have happened. One is that the huge influx of women into the paid labor force has reduced the amount of time they have to spend in the home and also encouraged some men, I wouldn't want to oversell the number of men who are doing a lot of work in the home, but there are some who are now helping with the child-rearing. Helping, I say advisedly, not sharing. But at least helping. And that has made a difference, I think. And also precisely because women now are in the paid labor force and still expected to raise children, there is a kind of baby strike going on, as you may have noticed.

Heffner: I thought that had ended.

No, it's still going on. It's not just that fewer women are having fewer children, but because women are also having them older, a new group of women is now having children, if that makes sense. But the per capita birthrate is still very far down. The Right Wing sort of so-called pro-family groups are now trying to restrict birth control, restrict abortion, you know, all the things that we know—in large part because they're alarmed by the plummeting birth rate. And if they want the birthrate to go back up again, what we need to do is not to force people to have children, but to make it more possible for people to have children. And to provide child care and to allow a work pattern that means that fathers can be real parents.

Heffner: I hope that what you're doing is predicting that that will happen.

Well, I don't know—the answer is blowing in the wind. It depends on what you and I do every day and what everybody does every day. Which is why I say, literally, a movement is what we do every day. I'm always really worried about thinking that a movement is organizations or top-down activity. Because revolutions, like houses, just don't get built from the top down. —1987

NAOMI WOLF

Of all the aftershocks caused by the social and political earthquakes we know as the Feminist Revolution of the 1960s and 70s, perhaps none was more unsettling than that caused by Naomi Wolf and her book titled The Beauty Myth. *Ms. Wolf later gained (short-lived) attention as a result of her own questionable "image" consulting to the Gore Presidential campaign in 2000. A decade before, however, our conversation explored ideas and convictions about beauty and society with unsettling predictions, as I asked my guest just what the "beauty myth" is and how it becomes the beauty trap.*

We've lived under a patriarchal system for as long as there's been recorded history and, ever since there have been records, women have been controlled in various ways. And you could say that the cult of beauty is ancient. What I'm pointing out, though, is that just as those historical moments when other material constraints on women loosen, the beauty myth, especially here in the West, tightens to take on the work of social control that other myths about femininity, like "the feminine mystique" for example, which we so recently freed ourself of, can no longer manage.

Heffner: But are you so certain that those holds, those restraints have tightened recently?

Yes, by all means. There are two points I want to make about that. One of them is that we're supposed now to be free. The Women's Movement of the '70s was a tremendous revolution. I believe it was the greatest revolution in the history of the species. We should not be victims—actually I would argue with that word—we should not be survivors of a system that's still trying to manipulate and control us in this particular way. The second point I want to make is that you ask, "Has it gotten worse?" . . . you look at the numbers that I cite, and my book is full of quite shocking and horrific statistics—eating disorders, just to take one example, have grown so exponentially in Western industrial nations that now, according to *Time* magazine, 50 percent of all American women between the ages of ten and thirty suffer from either anorexia or bulimia. That's mind-blowing. Cosmetic surgery is the fastest growing medical specialty. The profession of "image-consulting" grew by eight-fold over the course of the '80s. Clearly something's happening here. It seems to me inarguable that if now half, roughly half, the women on American campuses can't eat properly something profound and terrifying is happening.

Heffner: But why say that women are "victims" and why say that they can't eat properly? Who is doing this to whom?

Who is doing this to whom? Western women since the beginning of the Industrial Revolution have been uniquely controlled by ideals. In the nineteenth century, the perfect beauty was an ideal of sickness. And I argue repeatedly whenever there are classes of Western middle class women who are literate and idle there's going to be a ferment of feminism in the air, as there was in the nineteenth century. Some ideal is going to be needed to control them and make sure that things do not get out of hand. And sure enough, this cult of individualism in the nineteenth century grew and flourished, publicists all around told women, middle-class women—that they should be sick—a booming industry of sexual surgeons attending to "female" complaints grew up, telling them that normal, healthy processes were, in fact, diseased, that menstruation and sexual desire were manifestations of disease. And middle-class women got sick. Again in the 1950s, when the economy needed women to leave their war work, when men were returning from the front, this society desperately needed an ideology that would drive women back into the home and convince them that the ideal woman was the full-time, happy homemaker, absolutely obsessed with the shining, perfect floor. Well, Betty Friedan and *The Feminine Mystique,* her book and the Women's Movement of the early '70s took apart that domestic fiction and I argue that we're seeing exactly the same process again, that this society controls women through notions of perfection. And that this is just the latest example of this means of societal control. And that it's working. When I say "victims," I want to point out that women do very creative things with the circumstances handed to them, but that since the Women's Movement took off in the early '70s and just simultaneous to that, the weight of fashion models plummeted by 23 percent below the weight of the average woman. And the average woman wants to lose 23 percent of her body fat to fit the ideal, and at a body weight loss of 23 percent all kinds of psychological disruption sets in, as my research shows that it does, and this leads to the levels of eating disorders that I cite in my book. So that it seems to me that we have to stop looking at the ideal of "thinness" for example, as an aesthetic ideal and start looking at it as a political ideal. In other words, beauty is always the idea, is always prescribing behavior, not appearance.

Heffner: Do you think men are equally the victims of this ideal?

Certainly in the past five years or so, advertisers have figured out that it works, that you can target a vast market by making people feel sexually inadequate and sexually insecure, and increasingly there's a new beauty myth being developed in mainstream media, aimed at men, to undermine their feelings of aesthetic self-worth. And psychiatrists are predicting eating disorders among young men. However, I don't believe in my lifetime, as long as men hold the balance of economic power, that they will feel that their appearance determines not only their attractiveness to women, if that's who they're interested in, but their entire self-worth as a human being. In other words, men have role models in the world all around them. Women's role models that they see are largely confined to fashion models. And so until the balance of power in society changes tremendously I doubt that men will see fashion models, male fashion models, and view them as role models.

Heffner: Then you are essentially talking about power.

. . . That's precisely what I'm talking about. But I left out an interim link there when I was explaining who's at fault, who's to blame.

Heffner: Go right ahead.

I described a social mood in which a new ideology was desperately necessary. One of the new themes, one of the important new points that I make in my book is that I am not blaming men as individual

lovers, husbands, fathers. I don't believe that the pressure this intensified, what I call "beauty-backlash" comes from individual men. I
believe it comes from institutions, male-dominated institutions that
are safe-guarding political power.

Heffner: Can you give me an example?

I'll give you a very good example. In the early '70s, feminism, thank
heavens, made it illegal to discriminate against women in the work
place on the basis of our gender. Case law then evolved . . . in Britain
and America, that makes it legal to discriminate against women in the
workplace on the basis of appearance. So now there's this Byzantine
legal situation where you can be fired or demoted, if you're a woman, if
you look too feminine, and fired or demoted if you don't look feminine
enough. And as women entered the professions, television is a wonderful example, qualifications from what I call the "display professions"
like fashion modeling and prostitution, increasingly were applied to
them by employers as a way to have risk-free employment discrimination. In other words, it puts discrimination back in again through the
back door. And what this safeguards is a situation where, according to
my research, 25 percent to 40 percent of the gross national product of
Western countries is work that women do for free, or for less pay. It is
unpaid female labor, and the economy depends on it. You have a situation where women have come to feel that they're worth half as much
and work twice as hard because they're being told, quite legitimately,
that their appearance is part of what makes them valuable as a worker.

Heffner: As I read your book, I had the feeling that what you were
talking about was exploitation for profit on a much narrower basis.

Yes. The link I left out was in the midst of this demand for social control of women and for a new way to put discrimination back into the
work place, four major industries exploded over the last twenty years.
One of them is the 20 billion-dollar cosmetics industry, which censors

mainstream women's media. Increasingly, mainstream media sells use-
less anti-aging creams, but the fact that the manufacturers are some of
the major advertisers in mainstream and women's media means there's
very little room to negotiate with the beauty myth within those pages.
Another industry is the 33 billion-dollar dieting industry. This industry
would vanish overnight if low feelings of self-worth were not instilled
in women. And again there are major advertisers in women's magazines. They have the same censoring effect and promotion of the beauty
myth that advertisers of domestic products and household appliances
used to have in propagating the feminine mystique in the fifties. So
there really is a limited debate and the range of role models that women
can see out there in the world. The third industry is the 300 million-
dollar cosmetic surgery industry, the fastest growing medical specialty,
and totally unregulated—87 percent of the patients are women. Finally,
the 7 billion dollar pornography industry, which is, incredibly enough,
larger than conventional films and records combined, with more out-
lets than McDonald's. All of these industries desire to manipulate what
women can see and take in in terms of the media environment. And
they do so in a rising economic spiral.

Heffner: Do you feel yourself to be capable of being manipulated
that way.

Absolutely.

Heffner: You do?

Absolutely. I'm a woman in this culture.

Heffner: Yet you're also a scholar, and you have developed a protest
against what you've been talking about.

Finally. But my protest came out of the experience of having the beauty
myth used as a political weapon against my advancement. Let me give

you an example. I pointed out in the book that, according to my theory, the closer women get to power, the more intense the pressure the beauty myth places on them, as a way to undermine that power. It's not surprising that the ground zero of anorexia and bulimia is at the most prestigious men's and women's colleges, in other words the most prestigious Ivy League colleges. Usually the most brilliant students, women students on these campuses are the closest to full starvation. This is not an overstatement. I was anorexic, so was almost every one of the other women Rhodes Scholars that I knew at Oxford University. I think that we've got to recognize that you do not become free of the beauty myth by living from your neck up. In fact the way the beauty myth undermines women's power is to say, "You can either be serious or sexual, but not both." Of course, to make false choices, to make the false dichotomy absolutely weakens women. Men are not expected to choose between being sexual or serious. In fact, their seriousness is taken to enhance their sexuality. So I would say that, just because I was well educated and fortunate enough to be educationally privileged, doesn't exempt me in any way from these things. It simply makes me angrier.

Heffner: Today there is the "mommy trap," there is the "beauty trap," there was the feminine mystique, which was the "feminine mystique trap."

Yes

Heffner: And you put it all on a political basis, and an economic basis—

Absolutely.

Heffner: But why haven't you been willing to limit yourself and your critique to the economics of salesmanship or saleswomanship?

Because that's not adequate. You have a choice, when you're being bombarded with advertising. Ultimately you have a choice whether to buy or not buy a particular product if your livelihood doesn't depend on it.

What's happened over and above the ways the four industries I talked about are manipulating mass media, is that increasingly the beauty myth is being used to make women not only feel, but believe, to make it be true; that their careers, their income, their livelihood depends on conformation to these stereotypes. That their sexuality depends upon confirmation to these stereotypes. That their sense of self-worth as human beings depends upon it. Now those are very different things to negotiate with. Impossible, I would say. And I think it's therefore inadequate to stop short—also it's certainly been done before and it's not an adequate explanation to me to blame either men's sexual desire which I think is not, as I said, the source of this pressure or, you know, the capitalist economy. I mean certainly the capitalist economy stimulates and exacerbates this, but it would not have the breakneck power that it increasingly has—look at your own profession. It's no news that you will not vanish from the airwaves because you're mature and have the appearance of authority.

Heffner: You mean an old man.

But a woman in your position is likely to vanish from the airwaves because she's no longer what the industry calls an "anchor clone." And that that paradigm on television of the older man, who looks like an individual, and the younger, nubile, interchangeable heavily made-up anchor clone, who disappears as soon as the first wrinkles show up on her face, has become the paradigm for the relationship between women and men in the workplace everywhere. And I'm just suggesting that with this development, the backlash has used much more powerful weapons than it's ever had before.

Heffner: You know what took me so about your book is that I agree with so much of it. But there is one part that concerns me greatly and that is the—and you as a scholar will recognize this phrase—the "Devil Theory" of history. . . . you're looking for a devil and you don't find it inside yourselves, you find it in a manipulation, in a creation and a manipulation of that creation by forces outside. And you're not even satisfied with an economic approach.

Yes.

Heffner: You want to make it something larger. There are forces at work in our society that purposefully manipulate women to keep them in the house.

Yes. Or to keep them feeling imprisoned in their bodies. Yes, I have no apology for that. The way I put it in the book is not a conspiracy theory, it doesn't have to be. I've become convinced, and I'm very influenced by the work of Barbara Ehrenreich, who I think proved this absolutely in her book, *For Her Own Good: 150 Years of the Experts' Advice to Women,* that if you look at the history of how middle-class women do—and are made to do—what the economy and what society need them to do at any given moment, you're looking at manipulation which is so necessary and so, almost reflexive, that it doesn't even have to be conscious.

Heffner: How different is that though, from the way men are manipulated when you're talking about advertising, when you're talking about what appears for commercial purposes in the press.

Two big examples. One, I talked about employment. As long as men are not judged on what I call the PBQ, or Professional Beauty Qualification, in the work place, men will have freedom to negotiate their version of the beauty myth far beyond what women have. And that leads directly to whether they can feed their families or not. Another example is—and this is a sensitive subject—in terms of their sexuality. In the last 20 years, I think there's been a real generation gap. In about 1960, I think women born after 1960, like myself, were developed somewhat differently than women born before 1960. And I call us the anorexic, pornographic generations. What I mean by that is that there was, in the '60s and '70s, a spillover of imagery from soft-core pornography increasingly into

mainstream culture and women's culture and movies and television—
MTV—and what this means is that women my age and younger learned
about what sexuality was supposed to look like, if you were a woman, and
what sexual perfection looked like, before we learned about sexuality from
other human beings. And this, I think, means that the beauty myth in
our generation goes deeper than skin deep. And it's much more difficult
to negotiate with something that's telling you it's held your sexuality for
ransom, and again that's a distinction that I think most heterosexual men
just don't feel. I don't believe that they feel as sexually vulnerable in relation to images of male physical perfection as women feel. And those are
two enormous changes. I think we underestimated just how much threat
a truly successful women's revolution would have been to this culture.
Particularly an economic threat. I think it's not surprising that institutions would collude right now in very overt ways to protect power,
because there's a lot at stake. If women really moved freely, in free bodies,
through a free society, and were judged according to their merits, 50 percent, at least 50 percent of the top jobs would go to women.—1991

GAIL SHEEHY

*Gail Sheehy had been a highly successful magazine journalist for many
years before she published her first major book. This was* Passages: The
Predictable Crisis of Adult Life, *a work of popular psychology that
swept away both reviewers and best-seller lists. She then, and very successfully, met the challenge of a follow-up study with* Pathfinders, *a work
based on the author's personal research efforts designed to explain and*

define the qualities of the human spirit that enabled some to make new paths and to create and cultivate the capacity to make life work rather than to succumb to its difficulties. When we spoke early in the 1980s, I noted that Pathfinders *is about amazing people—and it is about amazing people—people Ms. Sheehy searched out for their achievements so that she could follow their lives for some years and identify the qualities that make them pathfinders. And I asked, what relevance, then, do their lives have for the rest of us who are basically just followers?*

Well, I don't think of these as superhuman people. Anyone can be a pathfinder, because the qualities that they have are learned, are not innate. There are only three genetically determined qualities that seem to give people a head start, at least only three that have been identified in all the twin research. One is high energy; that is, as you and I know, the more involved you become, the more energy increases and multiplies. And it's cumulative. The next is social style. Someone who is outgoing is going to get more commitments and engagements with other people than someone who is very retiring and withdrawn. And the third is a tilt toward the optimistic. It's my feeling, and I have no hard proof of this, for people like Jonas Salk, who I interviewed on this subject, seem to agree that it's possible that there's something like an optimism-negativism dial that we're born with and we sort of tilt toward the negative charge or a little bit to the positive charge. And certainly if you have a more positive outlook you will probably take more chances and be less upset or set back if you fail. But apart from those three slight advantages, no other advantages of background, class level, even education, really marked a difference between a pathfinder and anybody else. The qualities that they had developed were qualities that one learns and increases by living.

Heffner: You mean your message is: Anyone can be a pathfinder.

Yes, I mean there are people in the course of my research whose great achievements have been inner achievements. For example, there was a young welfare mother who at 18 had as impossible a hand dealt to her as one could imagine. She had a child, she had to get out of a terrible marriage to an alcoholic. When she did that she violated the code of her socioeconomic background, her ethnic background. She was almost ostracized in her neighborhood. She found another love, a childhood sweetheart. She invested all her hopes in him. He encouraged her to go back to school. Things looked very rosy. And suddenly he died. Accidentally, but he was gone. And she was left with a tiny baby, ostracized from her neighborhood, no support system, no job, having to go on welfare. Now that's not somebody who is way ahead of the game. What did she do? She picked up a bottle of pills. She thought about killing herself. And one day she put her fist through the window and she realized that she was going to start hurting her baby, and that scared her. So she went to the community mental health center and she got help. That helped her to take the next step, which was, one day when she was bathing the child, she said "He's so beautiful! I want to see him grow up, I want to see him as a teenager, I want to see him as a grown man. I'm going to have to find some way to independence and self-respect so that I can be here to see his growth." And she went back to school, became a practical nurse, went on, and is now at 23 planning to take her master's degree next year. And she knows that she can't get married for at least five years. She can't even consider it, because it's going to take her that long to grow into a full person. That tells me she's developed one of the cardinal qualities of a pathfinder: She's learned how to look ahead and anticipate what she's going to need in the next stage. And she's extended her anticipation by probably five years because one of the truest measurements of social class is one's ability to anticipate. Previously she probably thought ahead only week to week. Sometimes, when times were really bad, from day to day. You often hear people say, "I'm just living day to day."

Heffner: Gail, do you think you would have been as involved in this research, would have continued it, indeed, if your first returns had indicated that genes had played a larger role, that luck rather than pluck was more important?

I'm enough of a journalist so that I'm quite sure that I would have gone ahead. And it would have been a different book. It would have said, you know, you're dealt a hand of cards before you're born and that's the way it is, you know, you play it as it lays. But I'm happy to report I was rather surprised and quite delighted that that did not appear to be the case; that the strengths like developing the capacity for loving, for not being afraid of loving, for not being afraid of mutually loving, respecting someone's differentness, are things you can work on. Learning how to cultivate friendships and how important they are. Very difficult particularly for men because they never know when they're going to be competing with each other or hiring each other or firing each other, so it's very difficult for them to form close relationships with other men. And that's why one of the unhappiest creatures is the recently divorced man, because he's lost the one person he usually was able to confide in—his wife. But men do learn, and male pathfinders do have twice as many friends as the average man.

Heffner: But it seems to me somewhere there you've picked people who were by nature endowed with the capacity to do the things that you now identify that they did. Not so long ago the *New York Times* ran a column by Jane Brody about beauty and stature and the advantage that one has if one is good looking and tall. And I wondered whether these pathfinders aren't people who do start out with all that which enables them to develop these qualities that you said we could all—

Well, let's knock them down one by one.

Heffner: Go right ahead.

That's a straw man, beauty. One of the pathfinders in the book was a very much overweight, genetically overweight woman who was huge in stature, very tall, and very strong. She lived in the South, and of course did not measure up to the female idea of beauty and womanhood in that part of the U.S. Her husband was a dentist. She reached the age of 30, having had four children, and felt, "Am I going to be nothing but pregnant for the rest of my life?" She noticed that a lot of her friends, women friends, didn't do anything substantially, seemed to be in the business of criticizing what other people did, almost acting as professional critics of other people's creative efforts. Her life was narrowing. Many, many people would have stayed in what were very comfortable circumstances with a nice living in a nice part of the country and just said, "Well, see, I just can't make it because I wasn't born beautiful; I was born fat and big." Instead what she did was go to Alaska. She found her way to Alaska, her husband joined her. He refitted his practice to a little Cessna, and began flying around having the time of his life going to native villages and practicing medicine with people who really, really needed it and appreciated it. She became the great earth mother of the community in western Alaska where they settled, and where her ample frame was nurturing, was wonderful. In fact, she ended up at one point when her husband was away on a dentistry trip and the town ran out of oil and she had to unload an oil drum from a barge when she was seven months pregnant. She rolled it up the beach to keep the town from freezing to death that night. Now, she had learned how to turn obstacle into opportunity, and to make herself value herself and to make others value her. And they are the most loved couple in western Alaska, I'm sure.

Heffner: Isn't this just an anecdotal approach, a reporter's story-by-story approach? I thought this was a work of science.

Well, I hope it's both. But I don't think that science by itself really touches us, really makes us understand in our pores what it would be like to live the life of a pathfinder. And I don't think we have the courage to try it until we see them, see other people walk us through it, walk us through that obstacle course. You know there are many languages of living. You know there are many ways of handling situations that otherwise might have seemed dead ends. I really don't think there are many dead ends now, categorically. There are certainly many people who would find what they thought was a dead end. But individually, is paralysis a dead end? There's a woman in the book who defeats paralysis, who makes something of it. Is losing a job a dead end? Is being passed over when you're 55 and you've given your loyalty to a company a dead end? Maybe not. Maybe it's an open door to start your own business and begin doing something you really believe in that then is reflected in a revitalization of your marriage, and perhaps in your spiritual life, and a sense of purpose instead of just a sense of being a hypocritical wage slave. I learned that the chief characteristic of a pathfinder, man or woman, that of having a purpose behind him or herself. This is not what the average American would answer on a questionnaire at this time in our history. I think we're in an aberrant period. But the answer to the question, "Do you have a purpose or cause beyond yourself or larger than yourself?" brought in as the average response, "No." Reason: "My cause is me." Pathfinders never answered that. They may not have had an absolute cause or purpose developed yet, but they were working towards it or they were trying to find time to do it. but most of them had, it was a very important part of their lives, that they either, whether it was Bingo Dillon and his community in Charleston trying to save his neighborhood during the busing crisis, or whether it was the nuclear engineers who resigned from their industry to alert the public to the debate about safety, although they had lived the most conformist lives up till then till their forty-second year. So did their wives. Why did they jeopardize that? Why didn't they say, like most people would, "Look, I've got children to put through college. I need financial security. I can't jeopardize my family."

Heffner: OK. Why?

Because this couple, after five years in passage, began thinking they needed to revitalize their marriage. Then they realized that really life is about what one does every day. That they were supporting an industry that they couldn't change from the inside, although they attempted to, by their daily work. They would not compromise their beliefs. As the wife put it, "I don't want to go around, walking around in a body that's dead. I want to believe in myself." And the fact that they left the industry, made a public resignation, were ostracized, opened up all kinds of new avenues for them. They made common cause with two other engineers and their wives who did the same thing, they started an energy consulting business on alternative sources of energy, so that now they have flexibility in their lives, they could spend more time with their families and children, they were doing something they believed in, they did it better than they had ever done their jobs before. It did not hurt them to shrink their incomes by about $10,000 at first because they didn't need all those status things once they were no longer fighting for attention in the corporate circle. And ultimately the wife found herself having to take over for her husband on a speaking engagement in Australia. There were 5,000 people there. She walked up to the platform like a zombie and then opened her mouth and it all came out, because she said, "I found something. When you believe in what you're saying, you don't have any trouble finding the words." Another lesson I learned in my research was that people who came out at the top of the well-being scale in whatever group they were among were the most likely to have made some major change in their values and attitudes or life structure at some point in their adult lives; not people who had lived consistent lives. The same finding was made at the University of California, in the human development program at San Francisco, where they expected the consistency of values and psychological behavior would be the key to a healthy mental life. It was quite the opposite. The healthiest, mentally healthiest people had made a major change. And I think if you think about this country, that's what it's always been about. We are always ready, when we find ourselves in a corner, to try—even when we have no idea how it's going to come out—to try a change. And think of the luck, think of what makes this system possible. We have the freedom to change, more than any country in the world. People have the chance to seek well-being in their individual definition in this country. —1981

HELEN GURLEY BROWN

The most superbly empathetic listener, and the cleverest interviewer I've encountered in all my years of listening and interviewing is, hands down, Helen Gurley Brown, the former longtime and hugely successful Editor-in-Chief of Cosmopolitan *magazine. Her Cosmo Girl has now reigned as an American icon for many decades, albeit a most controversial one among both Feminists and their detractors. Author of the just-reissued 1960s best-selling groundbreaker* Sex and the Single Girl, *over the years Ms. Brown has had as many insights, or more, into men and women as anyone in America. She still does. Once, in the late 1980s, when we discussed her recent* Having It All, *I decided to needle my good friend by asking, since in real life men don't have it all, where does Helen Gurley Brown get the idea that women should?*

I'm going to parry with a question and say—where do you get the idea that men don't have it all? You have a wife or a loved one, usually a wife, you have the children, and you have fantastic careers. And nobody ever questions that you'll continue to have those three commodities in your life. It's never suggested that you might go home and work three days a week, or that you might take a lesser position. For women, having it all is very challenging these days and some women figure they just can't support all that carrying on so they have to give something up. Frequently it's the man. They have the children and the job, but he had to go. Now, what was your original question?

Heffner: The original question was why in the world you think we have it all, and perhaps so easy?

It's easier for you because you don't do most of the nurturing. The reasons why women don't get as far ahead in the business world, the commercial world, and politics, any formal profession, is that we have the children and we do most of the nurturing. Men adore children and they're very good fathers. You're a wonderful father, now a grandfather, but you still don't do the day-to-day work, the orthodontist, the pediatrician, and getting them to the tennis lessons, buying the clothes, getting them off to school. Women do that. So having almost total charge of the children, during the daytime anyway, it has to come out of someplace else, which is a woman's professional life.

Heffner: Well, then, you seem to be describing a situation out of which they'll find no exit. Is that true?

No, that's not true. There has to be an exit. For one thing, American business has learned the efficacy of not only employing women, but moving them up the ladder into better and better jobs. It's because women are so good at what they do. There has to be an answer, and soon men are going to have to learn how to be better helpmates at home, better nurturers, and better, in some ways, fathers, because your crowd loves the double income. You got very used to that, but you want it both ways. You want the double income, but Mummy should do what Mummy has always done, including baby you. So, men have to make a few concessions, I think, so women can have it all. There is a way out, but the government and U.S. corporations have to come to the rescue with some help.

Heffner: You seem to make the assumption that we're going to continue to insist upon having those double incomes. You obviously mean just that, and that's not going to give. What's going to give are the traditional, cultural, social patterns that you've been describing, the psychological patterns.

It would seem so because of college education alone, we're going to need the double income, let alone the mythical Jaguar and country house. Just paying the mortgage on your present living arrangements means that the money has to come from both places very likely. It was thought originally women would just do it so you could take a good vacation, or she could have a little pin money to buy a fur jacket. Well, that went bye-bye a long time ago. Yes, women are going to be in the workplace permanently: I believe the statistic is about 68 percent of all women with children under the age of 18 are working. And I'm not a great predictor, or prognosticator, but I would say that's not going to get any less so.

Heffner: Is that a good thing? No downside to that, Helen?

You know, not being a mother, I shouldn't be allowed to comment. How do I know whether it's good for the kids or not?

Heffner: What's your guess, though?

My opinion, my guess, is that having a working mother is neither good nor bad for the children. It's bad for her to be at home if she's miserable and she'd like to be out in the workplace. It's bad for her to be in the workplace if she'd like to be at home. So far as the kids are concerned, then it's up for grabs. But for her own sake—this I do feel passionately about as you know— women are happier [when] we achieve something aside from just being the honor student's mother, or the football player's sister, or the account executive's wife.

Heffner: But that opens up the first question. When I asked you what makes you think that men have it all, you then listed the whole litany, but having it all, is it worthwhile? You're making it sound as though the men in America, men generally, are leading the lives of not quiet desperation, but of enormous happiness, that it all pays off, and that women want to cut into this too.

I'm not a fool. I'm certainly not silly enough to think that men have a wonderful, halcyon time of it every day that they get up and go to the office, or the library, or the schoolroom, or wherever it is they go. But it is better to achieve, and it is better to be recognized for what you do, and although it takes a tremendous effort to be successful in a career, it's very rewarding. And my research tells me the reason that women don't always get to the top is not only that we're the nurturers, and take care of the children and the men at home, it is that some women have looked at what men go through to be CEOs and chairmen and they say, "Gee, I don't want any part of that, that's horrible. Phil comes home and he's half dead. It's like they've run tractor over him. Poor thing is working 30 hours a day." Some women have eschewed that, they don't want it. Not to be able to do what you're capable of doing, or want to do is really heinous. We've kind of gotten beyond that now.

Heffner: Were women to gain the power you want for them, the power you say men have, would they become like men?

That's an interesting new subject: violence, and how violent are men intrinsically, and how violent are women. I don't know that we are as gung ho as you are. If we had the guns would we shoot them? I'm not sure. But, I do think that she will be more like a man when she gets power. I believe when women get into positions of power, just as a head of a company, or having 100 employees, or 30 employees, you pretty soon get off the passive kick and you start being quite strong and steely, and if that's masculine so be it. I don't think so, I think it's just a human condition. When you get a lot of power in your hands, you get tough.

Heffner: Then having brought women into this situation, and you applaud it, as a matter of fact you look for more and more of it, where do we turn for the softer, gentler, kinder influences in our lives?

Men are going to have to get to be more like women, and that's a thought from both you and my friend Gloria Steinem. Women have become more like men, at least we've gotten positions of power in the workplace, and positions of economic parity. Now, for us to continue to do that, and rise and climb, then men are probably going to have to do things we did, like sewing on buttons and scrubbing the floor, and being nurturing to their boy children. It's going to have to be known that men care about these things. A man can be a good daddy, a good nurturing daddy, even as a mother has always done those things. So to some extent, I don't mean to be facetious, I think the gentler, softer, kinder side is not going to revert totally to men, but you're going to have to do some of it, and be some of it.

Heffner: Tell us about the changing workplace.

When I was getting started, 18 years old, my first secretarial job, no woman in the world had a secretary of her own. I mean, you were a secretary, or a clerk, or maybe a librarian, or teacher or worked in a department store. The changes that I have seen wrought in my working life have been thrilling, and exciting, and horrendous. Horrendous because for so many years, any of us who got to be in a position to have our own secretary were so thrilled just to have that prerogative that we would never have worked less hard than we did.

Heffner: You talk about all the changes that have taken place in your working lifetime. Do you see a continuation of those changes? Do you think that we're moving further along those lines as we get into the twenty-first century?

I think we're definitely on our way, and I don't see any backsliding. We've got legal identity now, we're no longer chattel, like chairs, and possessions of men. Now we have to get legal equality, another thought from Gloria Steinem. But in addition to that, we have been proved so efficient, and successful, and wantable, and terrific in the workplace that I don't think it's going to slide back. Some women may stay home more than they did, or maybe not go into the work-place at all, if that's what they're after. It's just options, you should do what you want to do, what works for you, and I predict, if I may, that we'll have more women in politics. It's been a very slow area, in big political jobs, House of Representatives, the Senate. I think that's going to be a big push.

Heffner: And I notice that you say in speeches that you make, you trust, you hope, that when they play "Hail to the Chief" someday in will walk a very fashionable lady. Now, do you think that's going to happen soon?

It's going to be a long time before a woman is the Chief Executive of the United States but, yes, it is going to happen.

Heffner: I'm not baiting you, but when you talk about the positive changes that have taken place, do you also see them at all connected to the problems that we have in this country now, the family prob-lems, the social problems, the cultural problems that we have? Do you see any connection between the change in the status of women, and the sorry state we find ourselves in, in so many areas?

That is a baiting question, and the answer is no, I don't see very much connection because you can still be a hard-working woman outside the home and raise good kids. Remember that among minorities, women themselves, poor women, always worked in factories or were other women's maids. We've been working outside the home forever, since the twenties, so it isn't a new phenomenon. So I don't think you can stick women with the drug problem, or those other problems. That's got a great deal more to do with family life than anything else.

Heffner: I didn't mean to be confrontational. I just wondered, as a viewer of the American scene, whether you thought there had been some connection.

Let me repeat that it never was realistic to think that all women stayed home, and didn't work outside the home. It's just that they didn't have terrific jobs. They had scruffy jobs, and children were raised very successfully. My mother was a teacher, many women worked in department stores and as clerks, and stenographers, and they raised good kids. They just have bigger jobs now. —1988

BETTY FRIEDAN

As a writer, lecturer and political activist, Betty Friedan contributed mightily to the birth of feminism in America in the 1960s. Her ground-breaking book, The Feminine Mystique, *offered an intellectual challenge to the status quo, and the title itself became part of the language. Thirty years later, in 1993, Ms. Friedan's* The Fountain of Age *set out, as* Time *noted, "to do for the image of older people what she did to dispel the feminine mystique." Our conversation that year began when I asked this icon of feminism why she wrote that "The mystique of aging is much more deadly than the feminine mystique."*

We absolutely have no image of age in America, except deterioration and decline from youth. Age is a problem, a terrible problem and burden for society. Age is to be denied, you know, denied as long as possible, surrounded by a miasma of dread. Age only as nursing home, only as Alzheimer's, senility. So people want to deny it. And there is no image at all that fits the reality of the new years of human life that people now have beyond 50, beyond 60, beyond 70, even beyond 80, that the increasing lifespan in America in the course of this century has given us . . . The average life expectancy of Americans is now over 75. For women it's nearly 80. And if you are already 60 or 65, your life expectancy is even longer. And these, for the great majority of people, will be healthy years. And they will be years that we can live vitally in the community, love, be productive. But there's no image of that. You have just senility. So we deny age. We try to give the illusion of youth as long as possible, have our face lifted five times, look like a mummy—not young, but like a mummy—and not even, if we really buy that obsession with youth, that denial of age, that dreary dread mystique of age, then we don't even let ourselves know the new possibilities that are evolving in us as we grow older, We don't let ourselves live our age as fully as we might, freed, liberated from the strictures of our youth.

Heffner: But isn't there something self-defeating, as self-defeating as the search for the fountain of youth, in the search for the fountain of age? Isn't it a quest for something that can never really be?

I don't agree with you. I mean, *The Fountain of Age* is a very deliberate title because the fountain of youth denies the possibility of age. You cannot be young again. And why should you want to be? Does life peak at 25? You know, is there nothing good that develops in people as they go along with experience in life? I mean, I wouldn't want to feel the way I felt at 25 again. If I could be 25 and know what I know now, and feel what I know now, that would be a different matter. But I can't be . . . it's futile. But the fountain of age is not futile. In other words, you'd have to break through, just as women had to break through the feminine mystique to see the new possibilities of life for women and for themselves and to define themselves as a people that they are. Take off that girdle, you see. So the blinders of this dreary dread age mystique, if we get rid of that, then we march into uncharted territory. There are no road maps, there are no rules, there are no role models. And that means, as no other time in our life, it's up to us. But you have to be able to avoid getting stuck by the sort of false syllogism and no-win proposition, [that] you have to love the way you loved when you were 30 or you don't love at all, [that] you have to work the way you worked when you were 30 or you don't work at all, [that] you have to have the power you thought you needed when you were 30 or 40 or you're utterly powerless and passive. You have to break out of all that, and then see where you really are. What I'm trying to do, and it's not unrealistic, is to say—let us look at this period of life, these new 25 years that people have that they didn't have before, as a unique period of human life. The things that are important to human life continue to be important, but you don't have to love the way you loved when you were 30. There may be new possibilities of intimacy and love that don't fit those youthful models. Your sexuality doesn't have to fit the measures that Kinsey [the famous sex researcher] took that peaked for your sex . . . before you were 30. You can be freed of that, you know, the macho mandate. Your memory even—I mean, the research that I cited in *The Fountain of Age* shows that if you give 17-year-olds and 70-year-olds memory tests, that if it's unrelated words, numbers, you know, lists, school stuff, 17-year-olds do better. But when you give meaningful material, the 70-year-olds do better. Because they get it whole and they slough off the irrelevant materials. In other words, your intelligence, your emotions continue to evolve. I don't use the world "old," I say "growing older." And yet there's no denial in it. And there's an openness and a readiness to experience this new period of life for what it is, full of surprises, not free of pain, but one in which you can continue to be vitally living your life as the person that you more and more are. All the research in my own interviews shows the one thing that happens to people is that they that continue to evolve and develop in their later years. One becomes more and more authentically oneself.

Heffner: What do you mean? I know you say that in the book, but what do you mean, "authentically oneself"? Weren't you authentically yourself when you wrote *The Feminine Mystique?*

I certainly was ... a process that really began then of throwing off the false mask. And that continues. It's such a liberation, just as it was a liberation for women, to say, "All I am I will not deny." You know, that began for us. But for men and women not to have to live up to the false or no-longer even true mandates and masks that we carried with us from youth, free of the games, free of the pretenses, free of the illusions, free of these strictures and restrictions, to be ourselves fully ... There's also a crossover that takes place, the research shows. Men develop the side of themselves that's been suppressed because it's supposedly feminine. Women develop some side of themselves that's been suppressed because it was supposedly masculine. And so you become more a whole person ...

I mean, we do, we are, we know who we are in our sixties, seventies, and more. We are the pioneers of a new kind of age. And right behind us are the baby boomers who survived the traumatic period when they thought you can't trust anyone over 30. Being 40 was even more traumatic, but now they're facing 50. And they're this huge, bulging market. And, you know, the women have broken through the feminine mystique, and the men have helped take care of their children in ways that they never did before. And they're poised behind us with enormous power ... I mean, one of the newsmagazines a year ago showed a cover with a youngish looking man with a gray hair saying, "Oh my God, I can't believe it. I'm going to be 50." It's amazing how young men and women come up to me and they say, "Oh . . . I'm going to send your book to my mother or my father." And they then say, they start talking to me about what's in the book. And I say, "Well, you're so young yet. You really read it?" And they say, "Oh, yes. It's gotten me over my own dread of age." You know. Well, I would have thought this person was so young she or he wouldn't have had the dread, a dread of age yet. But it's interesting to have these baby boomers behind us who are not babies anymore. I mean, I think they're going to be moving into this new territory that will be the social revolution of the turn of the century. Just as the youth movement in the '60s, [was] the songs, The Beatles, you know, the new music. Then, you know, everybody was so obsessed with the 18-to-39 market because they were the big group. Now, the turn of the century, our generation and those coming into age behind us, we will be the cutting edge. And the music and the songs and the values in society. But it's not, it's not going to be, it seems to me, a movement of older people against young. It's not a polarizing thing, you see, the battle against ageism like the battle against sexism. It's larger than that.

Heffner: But now let me ask you about the resources that are needed to support the kind of generation you're talking about. Will these resources be available?

You are buying the dreary, dread mystique of age in a way that tries to make older people the scapegoat for the crisis of health care in our whole society, or the economic crisis of our society. And that is wrong. Older people tend to be healthier than younger people. They need hospitalization less. And the idea that this is an enormous, costly burden on society, comes solely from the doctors prescribing high-tech procedures, giving people a day or an hour or a month more of painful life when they are in a terminal state. The thrust of health care should not be just the diagnosis of esoteric symptoms and the attempt to cure what can't be cured. The effort should be made to keep the ill functioning in a human way, in the community for as long as possible, not these costly nursing homes they are sentenced to.

Worse than death, you know . . . Medicare and our health insurance doesn't even cover the non-medical and preventive measures that can keep people going in their community so they don't need nursing homes. I don't want to define people or define ourselves in age only as objects of health care, as objects of medical care and the effort to cure the various conditions typical of older people. This is what the age mystique does. But society has to face the realities, that health care is needed. But a health care that is based on a youthful model of medicine isn't working for people now either. If doctors are locked into the age mystique, and a woman or man comes in with a real problem, the doctors can say, "Well, that's just age," and they don't do anything about it. Or, they prescribe all these drugs to sedate you, and then the drugs themselves create the problem. But instead of looking at the whole person you are and see what's happening to you, the health care professionals won't accept the fact that even some of the supposed symptoms of senility, even physiological complaints that some older people do have, come from depression. And there's every reason, given the way society treats older people now, for people to be depressed in age. It takes a real strong person who is able to get angry and is a truth-teller to make it to the vital age, to really partake of the fountain of age the way our society is structured now. But don't make older people the scapegoat, the scapegoat for the health crisis caused by the profiteering on drugs and the high-tech procedures. There's got to be a revolution in medicine. There's got to be a way of caring for older people in terms of the people they are, keeping them functioning in the community. But that does not mean that anybody over 65 should not have certain necessary operations. Health care shouldn't be rationed that way. It should be rationed in terms of possibility for human function in life.

Heffner: Do you anticipate that the search for the fountain of age is going to experience the same incredible surge that feminism did?

It looks as if it is putting into words what people needed—to be able to name their new place. That it may lead to some kind of movement, I could no more say now than I could, 30 years ago, have predicted the scope of the Women's Movement. But I don't think it will be like the women's movement. I don't think it will be older people against young. And I don't think the Women's Movement was that way either.—1993

OTHER VOICES

Elizabeth Holtzman on the Birth of the Equal Rights Amendment
Former Congresswoman and Brooklyn District Attorney

Heffner: It wasn't so long ago that Thurgood Marshall indicated that all of this talk about the Bicentennial left him a little bit cold because the Constitution itself had been so thoughtless and careless about minorities, about women. I wonder how you feel about that.

Well, I've been saying some of the same things as Thurgood Marshall for some time. I mean obviously having been in the House of Representatives and having sat on the [Nixon] Impeachment Hearings and having studied the Constitution in law school as well as in Congress, I became increasingly respectful of what a wonderful scheme it sets forth for democratic self-government. On the other hand, being a woman and living as long as I have by now, I'm increasingly familiar with the extent and depth and pervasiveness of discrimination. And as a lawyer, as a woman, as an American citizen, I find it personally offensive, indeed, horrifying that we come to this birthday of the Constitution 200 years later and the Constitution, itself, does not say that women are equal under law. More than half of our population at the time of the celebration of the Bicentennial will still not be equal under the law. And that's really something that's a very sobering fact. And while we have a lot to be proud of in terms of the celebration of the Constitution and 200 years of self-government, we still realize and must realize that there's a long way to go.

Heffner: Do you think that the changes that are needed are so fundamental that you would go beyond amendment to restructuring the Constitution?

No, I'm going to be very conservative about this. I think that the Constitutional framework has worked for 200 years to preserve self-government. But it needed to be changed to abolish slavery, that was one of the very sad factors that it enshrined, the notion of human property. It's still sad, today, to find that it does not treat women as equals under the law, that has to be changed. But I think these changes can be accommodated. Actually, if the Justices of the Court would interpret the Fourteenth Amendment appropriately, there would be no need for the Equal Rights Amendment, but they haven't done that yet. —1987

Diane Feinstein on Being a Woman in Politics
Former Mayor of San Francisco, current U.S. Senator

Heffner: I want to ask whether we as a people have won anything substantial with the rise to power of a woman in politics and statecraft.

. . . I don't know whether the nation overall is better off or worse off in terms of policy, because that's dependent on brain cells and wisdom and common sense and judgment. And that's not necessarily a sexual attribute, that's based on one's conditioning, training, education. I think the nation is very much better off with the sharing of power. And everything that this democracy purports to be and is is an open system, that people can share power. Women have to do their apprenticeship just as everyone else. They have to be effective, because effectiveness is the ultimate test of leadership. They've got to have drive and staying power and motivation over a long period of time. I believe they can be effective, and I believe they carry with them certain attributes which have their upsides and their downsides, depending upon how those attributes are utilized.

Heffner: What are the downsides?

The downsides are, I believe, when you become the first of anything, the first black, the first Hispanic, the first woman, the first Jew, the first Catholic, to cross a line and occupy a new position, there's a great deal of curiosity. With the curiosity comes testing. Some of that testing may be fair, some of it may be unfair. But it's testing. The press are going to press the question to see how much does he or she really know. The electorate are going to question as well. The public policies of the individual are going to be looked at and debunked and tested, if you will. And I think the testing is a little bit beyond that which someone that isn't the first [is subjected to]. After that period I think it evens out. And after that period I think that it's performance, it's effectiveness, it's delivering the bacon that makes the difference. —1985

MEDICINE

LEWIS THOMAS

At the height of his powers, Lewis Thomas was better known to the general public as a writer than as a distinguished scientist/educator of international renown. The critical and commercial success of such books as The Lives of a Cell *and* The Medusa and the Snail *ultimately earned him the sobriquet of "Poet Laureate of Twentieth-Century Natural Science." And in our dialogues about some of the more provocative issues facing the practice of medicine as well as the construct of modern science, Thomas displayed the same level of perception and insight that a reader would find in his stylish and graceful essays. In one of his essays, he had quoted the phrase, "The long habit of living does not dispose us to dying." I asked if he would elaborate on that.*

I suppose one universal attitude that we've always had about dying is an apprehension that it might turn out to be something awful. And, of course, none of us really knows what it's like. Odds are, I think, that it's really not a bad event in the sense of being either painful or agonizing or dreadful.

Heffner: Why do you say odds are?

Well, William Osler, who observed a great many patients living and dying, in his career, wrote some trenchant things about dying. He became indignant about the notion that there was such a thing as a death agony. He'd never seen it. He'd never seen anyone experiencing anything that could be interpreted as agony. And I must say that I agree with this. I have not seen this myself. Montaigne was the first person I know of to write about what dying might be like on the basis of an experience that he had or nearly had with dying. He was run over by some horsemen in a narrow ravine, and became for all intents and purposes dead. He was carted off home by friends, and remembers and writes about how curious it seemed to him that the people around this makeshift litter were distressed at his death. He could hear what they were saying, and he had never felt so tranquil. He felt absolutely at peace with himself. And there are similar observations described by others. David Livingstone, the explorer, was caught and mauled and very nearly killed by a lion that bit him across the right chest. He came within a few seconds of dying. Livingstone wrote about this later on in a puzzled essay in his memoirs. He said that he knew perfectly well where he was. He was in a lion's mouth, and he was being crushed. And it didn't seem bad at all. He postulated in an essay that during the process of dying something must be turned on that produces an absence of pain, but in addition, a very real sense of tranquility. He was quite eloquent about this and quite sure of his ground. Some of the accounts that we're now getting from people who have gone through all the motions of dying, cardiac standstill, say, and then have been resuscitated, carry a similar note of astonishment that the process seemed in retrospect something almost enjoyable.

Heffner: You say something must be turned on as death approaches. What do you mean?

Well, I'll try. There is, as you know, a totally new field now in neuro-biology which came into being a few years ago with the discovery that there are some very small peptide hormones secreted within the brain that have the properties of morphine. They are called the opiate-like peptides. There are certain cells, chiefly in the brainstem, that are specifically designed to receive hormones of this kind. Oddly enough, it turns out that the same cells and the same receptors receive and bind morphine. It is as though morphine is itself a kind of biological accident, with the real opiate being secreted by the brain for its own purposes. And I suppose one of those purposes could be to provide something like anesthesia or analgesia at times, which would otherwise carry unbearable pain. Perhaps, that's the mechanism that's involved.

Heffner: Yet, despite this, in your writings you seen to indicate that today there is such an incredible, and I gather you feel much larger, apprehension on the public's part. Do you think that the causes for this "fixed anxiety about health" as you have called it, might help or hinder the "turning on" or the "turning off" of this mechanism—if it exists— that enables us to die in peace?

I doubt that it could really effect the mechanism I'm suggesting. That's probably built into all of us; and I don't think it's a mechanism to be fiddled with. The whole aspect—the increasing apprehension about dying and about disease in our time—puzzles me. I really don't understand it. We are by all the numbers the healthiest society in the history of mankind. Our life expectancy for everybody, all comers, men, women, all economic levels, all races in the Western world is something like 72 years, and evidently going up every year. And a lot of the diseases that used to terrify us, for example tuberculosis, most notably, and tertiary syphilis, are now behind us. We've got them under control along with most of the serious, formerly lethal, bacterial infections, even and some of the virus infections. We're left still with some very serious and disturbing, alarming, chronic illnesses, but we've got much less to worry about than we did when I was a medical student 40 years ago. And yet we seem to worry more about our health, and we worry an awful lot more about dying than used to be the case. Some of the ceremony associated with dying has been lost in our kind of civilization. It used to be a great occasion. It used to be something that happened in the home with the family around, with a lot of meaning attached to it by everyone concerned, including whoever it was that was dying. And that seems to have been lost in our time. Maybe this is also one of the reasons why there is so much more fear of it than used to be the case.

Heffner: What do you think are the contributing factors to this strange fixed anxiety about health?

It may be that we've done so well. That is, having got rid of the very diseases that used to kill most of us, particularly the infections diseases like TB that were responsible for death early in life, in childhood so often, our expectations went up. And having done part of it, the public at large asks why can't we go the whole distance and get rid of the present major diseases—cancer, heart disease, stroke, and all the rest.

Heffner: Well, why can't we?

I think we can. I think it's been demonstrated clearly that once you get to understand the underlying mechanism of the disease, as happened with tuberculosis and pneumonia, and the infections in general, you can then begin doing the kind of basic research needed to do something about it. The trouble we're in today is that we still don't understand enough about underlying mechanisms in cancer or heart disease or stroke or schizophrenia or arthritis or any of a long list of other major troubling or chronic illness. If we keep at it, perhaps over the next decades, maybe 50 years, maybe 100 years, we will have learned enough to be relatively free of disease.

Heffner: And then?

Everyone wants to know what then. I mean, how can you die if you don't have a disease? Oliver Wendell Holmes wrote a dandy poem about this. This, I think, is what the famous poem, "The Deacon's Masterpiece or The One-Horse Shay" was really all about. "The One-Horse Shay" kind of sounded like a metaphor for the human form. Absolutely perfectly made. A marvel. And when it finally had aged to the time, however many years it was, when the clock stopped for the one-horse shay, it fell apart all at once. There was nothing but dust. And I have the feeling that's what natural death, a term we don't use so much anymore, really amounts to. And I think it's inevitable. I don't think much would change if we did gain control over the most miserable diseases, as I'm hoping we will, in the years ahead. I think that we'd just age. We would ultimately come to an end as happens today with many old people, and simply stop living.

Heffner: What is meant, what do you mean by the overutilization of medicine?

I don't believe in the notion one sometimes reads about in newspaper columns, particularly health columns, that we are fundamentally fragile creatures, that we've always got something just about to go wrong, and unless we're propped up all the time by a health care system, running in and out of the doctor's office, being checked up, we might fall apart. The average human being in our affluent and well-nourished part of the world is extraordinarily healthy for most of his life, and doesn't need to become involved in what it is fashionable to call the health care system. I'm not a real believer in the annual complete physical examination, for example. And I'm not a believer at all in the use of complicated screening techniques to do a whole lot of laboratory procedures in order to find abnormalities. I think it's probably better for patients to consult the physician and to become involved in clinics and hospitals when there's some real sense that something's gone wrong.

Heffner: Yet it is in your own field of expertise, cancer, in the great institution that you administer [Memorial Sloan Kettering Cancer Center], that I think that we find the greatest concern. I think most people probably take themselves to a physician for a checkup most often in terms of concerns about cancer and heart problems. And we are urged on every side to have that checkup, because the condition may be cured more readily if it's caught in time. How do we respond to that?

Well, there are some things that really should be done, but they don't require laying on the whole technology of medicine all at once. Obviously, or it seems to me obvious, the earlier a breast cancer can be detected in a woman the better are her chances of recovering and surviving for a normal lifetime. But early detection is best done by the woman herself. And what we need really is more information disseminated about how to go about self-examination of the breast. The Pap technique for the detection of cervical cancer is highly effective, but that is itself a relatively simple procedure, and does not involve a lot of expense or a lot of cost or a lot of time. Those are the two main types of cancer that one can detect early and where the detection makes a lot of difference. There's a technology of search now being worked out for the detection of blood in the lower intestinal tract, which will turn out to be of great importance in the early detection of cancer of the bowel. And if that one can be detected earlier, the survival rate will be vastly improved. These are all relatively simple things. This is not what I would call the usual annual checkup with all the laboratory tests that can be done and the full array of the facilities of a clinic.

Heffner: I'm interested that you put your emphasis on self-examination because it's clear, from what you've written and what you've said, that you have a major concern that we as individuals know so little about our bodies and about our bodily functions that perhaps one of our problems in seeking too much medical assistance, inappropriately, comes from our ignorance.

Yes, I think this is true. I'm always surprised by how little my most intelligent, best-educated friends, not doctors, know about their own body. And what extraordinary misapprehensions they have about what and where, for instance, the liver is, and what the pancreas does for a living, and how many kidneys are there, this kind of thing. And I've thought it would be a very good thing if we could get embedded somewhere in our primary and secondary school education much better courses than are now provided in physiology and pathology.

Heffner: In the essay you call "Anatomy," I gather you refer to biofeedback and its techniques exercising control over ourselves and our bodily functions. You write, "On balance, however, I think it best to stay out of this business. Once you began, there would be no end to the responsibilities. I'd rather leave all my automatic functions to work as they please and hope for the best." And I have the feeling that you were to a certain extent putting down some of the newer—you might call them self-help—medical approaches.

Not all of them by a long shot. But I do have some doubts and misgivings about the devices and the techniques that are now popularly talked about as though they were a way of controlling your own internal functions. I think I said in an essay that if someone told me that it was now time for me to take charge of my liver and give it instructions, I wouldn't know what on earth to say to him. The cells of my liver are very substantially more intelligent than I am, and they know what they're up to. And I think that if I were in charge I might be inclined to meddle and get myself into trouble. The same thing is true for the cells of my central nervous system. They are entirely on their own, and neither I nor anybody else should really be allowed to meddle with them.

Heffner: Where might you meddle with relative impunity?

There's some evidence, tentative, that one can gain control of blood pressure. And perhaps it will turn out that some people may be able to maintain lower blood pressures using techniques of this sort. The work is still highly experimental, and I've got some doubts about its future. But there aren't very many other occasions that I can imagine where making efforts to get control over your own autonomic nervous system holds much in the way of what I would regard as promise for the future.

Heffner: Is this part of the whole effort, basically in the psychological area, to control ourselves, to exercise what you call autonomy?

I suppose so, and one of the reasons that I object to it, and I'm kind of intemperate about this, is that it seems to me to carry a certain disrespect for the human body. The body is really very well made, and left to its own devices and supported by good nutrition and reasonably sensible living, it does very well. And I'm not attracted at all by the notion that we can just make up our minds ourselves to fix things differently and meddle. My own view is that the tissues and organs of the human form were designed to function, and do function optimally, and I don't think any of us know enough yet about how these functions are mediated at their fundamental level to warrant stepping in and meddling.

Heffner: What is your response to those who insist on seeing medicine as all art or all science?

I would like to have the practice of medicine continue to be, as it's always been, a kind of combination of art and magic, and at the same time have it be the science that it's now showing signs of becoming. I'd hate to give up what I remember from watching my father practicing general medicine 60 years ago, when I was a small child. And indeed I'm reassured from time to time that colleagues much younger than I am do indeed use what I call the art of medicine.

There's a difficulty in having turned medicine into a science with a high degree of precision and with instruments that are capable of making diagnoses, and therapeutic agents that are capable of changing disease in ways that we couldn't have dreamt of just 30 or 40 years ago. A doctor's life is transformed. He's much busier. He has to rely much more heavily on technology than ever before. The busy ones have less time to talk to their patients, to listen to them. It's a very difficult profession to practice. But the real good ones, the ones I know who do general medicine even in towns as busy as Manhattan, still do a good job of the art. They are reassuring, they care about their patients, and they know the families. They may not necessarily know the name of the family dog as my father did when I was growing up, but they're good doctors. It's harder now, though.

My father began practicing in 1905 or 1906, and continued almost until the time of his death in the late 1940s. And throughout most of that time, although he made a lot of housecalls, got up at night and went off to see patients carrying a black medical bag that had a few odds and ends in it, he was never convinced that what he did at the bedside or in the home really made a difference—technologically anyway. There weren't any medicines that anybody was sure of except liver extract for pernicious anemia, insulin for diabetes, and a few others—digitalis, for example. But mostly what doctors did in all those years was to use what they had in the way of common sense and a certain amount of science that had been inherited from the nineteenth century in the study of the natural history of disease, in order to make a good diagnosis. My father felt that his job was to make an accurate diagnosis and then be able to tell the patient and the patient's family how it was going to turn out, and then to stand by and give whatever support he could give. And when I went to Harvard Medical School in the 1930s, I was taught exactly that kind of medicine. We had a little book we carried around with us when we made rounds. It would fit into one's jacket pocket; it was called *Useful Drugs*. It was about 80 pages long, as I recall. It had some things in it about cathartics and opium and aspirin and other odds and ends. It was very rarely opened. Our instructors at the medical school told us quite plainly that our job was to make a diagnosis, make a prognosis, give support and care, see to it that the patient got good nursing care, and not to meddle.

Getting away from meddling was the great accomplishment of early twentieth-century medicine. If you got sick in the early nineteenth century and fell into the hands of a doctor, you had a pretty good chance of dying from therapy. That was abandoned around the time of Sir William Osler, and medicine became very conservative. It was even called nihilistic for the first third of the twentieth century. And then to everybody's astonishment came the sulfonamides, then penicillin, and then all the rest of the antibiotics. Medicine was off and running and hasn't stopped since. In the end, a lot depends not on the educational experience of a young doctor in medical school or during his house officership, but on what kind of a man he is or what kind of a woman she is. There are some people who are very, very good at the management of illness because they like other people. They have a kind of inbuilt affection. Some of these people are in the middle of their class as far as grades go. I'm afraid some of them—maybe a lot of them—are not being admitted to medical schools these days because of the competition for admission based so heavily as it is on grade achievement. But still there are some. They are very good doctors, and they learn during medical school and during their residency period how to handle the technology of medicine. And they already know, because they were brought up to have character, how to deal with patients with care and affection.

Heffner: You feel strongly, don't you, about the importance of nursing?

The people who really hold the hospital together and really make patients feel secure and really know what's going on from minute to minute, day and night, are the nurses. I have a vast respect for the nursing profession. The nurses and the doctors quarrel sometimes about the autonomy of the nursing profession. But I'm all for them. If I had a lot of power I'd say double all nurses' salaries overnight and look up to them. They're a good bunch.

Heffner: But is this perhaps because they're removed from the necessity of making the same kinds of scientific judgments that doctors, residents, and interns must make?

No, in a sense they have an even harder time than the doctors do. Most nurses come into the profession because they like people, they like being useful and they want to help. And what have they been discovering and confronting for the last 25 years or so is more and more in the way of administrative chores, a lot of desk work, a lot of management work, and a lot of technology. I think they have an even harder time than doctors because of these two sets of quite unrelated duties that they're obliged to carry. —1978

OLIVER SACKS

Like Lewis Thomas, Dr. Oliver Sacks has made his public presence known more as a writer than as a physician. His essays have been collected in numerous volumes, most notably The Man Who Mistook His Wife for a Hat; *his patient profiles or "neuro-histories" have gained him fame as one of the great clinical writers of the past 50 years. In a conversation in the late 1980s, we talked about some of the "knowables" as well as "unknowables" of medical science and practice. I asked him what vision is it of human purposefulness that informs his medical work and his continuing efforts to reach and to teach his ever larger and more enthralled readership.*

I feel in some ways that we are insufficiently grateful for what we have, that we take everything for granted. And in health, everything is given to us. We think, for example, visually, that the world is given to us in all its richness of color and depth and movement and form and meaning, but then you have someone like Dr. P. [a character in a Sacks essay] who sees, but sees without sense. To understand that, is not so simple. A patient I'm seeing at the moment, who sees, but suddenly lost all sense of color, allows us to realize what a miracle is performed by the brain in putting things together. Although I seem to write about disorder, I think some sort of lyrical feeling for the organism, and for being alive, and for the brain, is involved. And I suppose the other thing is this sense of the immense resilience and resourcefulness of patients, and people who've lost faculties of one sort or another. For them, coping is much too mild a word; transcending is a little too ethereal; but my interest is in survival, and survival in the face of the strangest sort of neurological disorders.

I think there's a fundamental difference between the sort of things nature does to us and the sort of things other people may do to us. And I see again and again that patients can take the hurts of nature with a sort of equanimity. People can get used to blindness or paralysis; they can't get used to being ill-treated. On the whole, I tend to work in chronic hospitals with some of the sickest patients, and the first vision may be a very dismal one and even one of horror. But then I think one has a very strong sense of these people as survivors. I can't bear to see a place where there is any negligence and cruelty; I think that's entirely different—then there's moral agency at work. But somehow the indifference of nature, I think does make it bearable.

Heffner: You just used the word "coping" and I can't help but ask, "Why do we cope and how do we cope?" What inner mechanism is there that enables us to cope?

One somehow wants to use a common phrase like "the will to live."

Heffner: What does that phrase mean?

I know that mechanism can take a beating. For example, after a massive stroke or massive heart attack, something about the will to live may not be there for a while, and the person may need to be, how shall I say, carried tenderly. But then the personality reasserts itself. It certainly does when there is caring.

Heffner: You mean other people's caring for us?

Other people's caring for us. And also our caring for ourselves. There were some famous studies some years ago of an orphanage in Mexico where the children had every sort of hygienic and mechanical care, but no human care. All of them died by the age of three. The will to live didn't seem to be established there. I think that caring and being cared for is quite essential.

Heffner: Now in a society in which medical care is provided for larger and larger numbers of people, and perhaps better medical care, scientifically speaking, but is provided without that human touch you're talking about, what does the future hold for us?

Well, I think the present position is one of paradox because the accomplishments of technology, neuroscience, have risen meteorically. Things are possible now that couldn't have been imagined ten years ago. But human care, I think, has taken something of a beating. People come in with a headache now and they're sent for a CAT scan straight away. When the first thing one should do is listen. Listening and paying attention is the beginning of medicine. Physicians themselves also are beginning to suffer from this lack of human contact. There's talk about "burnout," boredom, which there never used to be a few years ago. I think there has to be some sort of revolution, or bringing back the human touch, to go with the high tech.

Heffner: Well, where and how does that take place?

I think it largely has to happen with individuals. Say with individual doctors who will listen intensely to their patients. Who will try and imagine what it's like to be the patient and at the same time can call on all the technology and all the new concepts. It doesn't seem to me an impossible thing; frankly it seems to be a crucial thing. I don't think that time and busyness are sort of adequate excuses for not paying attention. I remember a former chief of mine who would see 50 patients in his outpatient clinic on Friday afternoons. Now, true, these were all people he'd seen before, but somehow in 30 seconds or in 60 seconds, he would concentrate so much they'd feel themselves the only person in the world. And, I think that a great intensity of care and concentration is possible in a short time. But I agree it's very difficult and I suppose there's the same problem in education, where there's a question of a sort of mass versus individual tutoring.

Heffner: I wonder whether there is a force at work now, in the medical schools for instance, that would tend to institutionalize the concerns that you've expressed and the solutions that you offer?

I think there are some changes that are coming in now. It's realized that students have to spend time with patients and that this can't be hurried, that things can't be passively learned by lectures. I think it's also realized that something like an apprenticeship, which sounds so medieval in a way, is still necessary. I think also that there is growing interest in the medical literature in individual case histories; by 20 years ago it had become almost impossible to publish an individual case history. And everyone said we've got to have a series, tell us what happened with 50 patients, you have to have double-blind series, or whatever. I think the feeling is now coming along that a single patient, studied with enormous detail can illuminate a great deal and, I think some sort of respect for the individual, whether it's the patient or the student, is on the way back. But there are also forces going in the other direction.

Heffner: You say that apprenticeship, "which sounds so medieval," is still necessary. Why?

I think there are many things that can't be taught, but that can only be learned. And they can only be learned by working with someone who is experienced or who is a master.

Heffner: You know, going back to your word "coping," which certainly surfaces again and again in your books, I wondered, as I read *The Man Who Mistook His Wife for a Hat* and the others, whether this case-by-case example of coping leads you to feel differently than other physicians might, about our capacity now not only to manipulate genetic content, but perhaps our responsibility to take life at the end, which is, in a sense, the antithesis of an involvement with the human coping mechanism. How do you find yourself responding to those physicians who look for—not that they welcome—but look for, of necessity, the right, the authority, to be involved in euthanasia.

Well, I think first that there's a tendency to medicalize birth and death, which occur in a hospital and without much human content. The situation now is changing in an unprecedented way because we have the power to maintain a sort of life in people who are brain-dead and really have no possibility of consciousness. It's a terribly difficult question because where is one to stop? I think that certainly patients themselves, especially elderly and chronically ill patients, should be able to express, and strongly, their feeling that after a particular point they don't want any more endeavors made or any further resuscitations.

Heffner: Would you accept their conclusion?

Personally, I would, but I'll say that this may in a sense be theoretical because I don't, myself, carry this sort of life and death responsibility.

Heffner: But you are a medical person, observing what is going on in this field of concern, and you must have some very visceral responses to it, too. As a citizen as well as a physician.

Well, yes, I certainly have visceral responses, but that response starts in one's own family. There's a very favorite aunt of mine, I describe her a little bit in *A Leg to Stand On*, who had a wonderful life until the age of 86. And she was full of good activity until that age. She then had to have some surgery, and everything went wrong. And she said very plainly that so far as she was concerned it was not worth continuing life on these terms, it would be a misery to her and a burden for everyone else. She therefore declined to eat. A psychiatric opinion was sought. But the psychiatrist said, "This is the sanest person I know. And she's an adult. Let her do it, you know, if this is what she wants to do." Clearly that was a responsible decision on her part. But equally clearly one's got to protect people against self-destructive sorts of things.

Heffner: And the mechanism must be what? For protecting, for permitting? Autonomy for the individual and yet for protecting us against whatever it is you want to protect us against.

I'm hopeful that we could bring all this up to the level of rational discussion and openness.

Heffner: What must the mechanism be then in the medical field, in the medical profession, in order to reach the level you hope for. A board, a group of physicians? How are we going to make this incredible decision as we go into the future? And it's going to come up more and more. More of us are living longer and longer. And clearly we're going to be affected by that. What would you do?

Well, I confess I haven't thought a good deal on this, but first and foremost I think there needs to be a renewed respect for the patient's experience. The patient has to be listened to. He has to be allowed to express as fully as he can, his own situation. Both his medical situation and his human situation. And, that door of listening and attending has been partly closed. That's got to be opened. I think if that door is opened a great deal else will follow.

Heffner: But haven't physicians generally said, not that, "We need not listen" but rather, "We need to present an authority figure. We need to be those who know to start with what is best in order best to serve the patient."

Well, there are different sorts of knowledge. The patient has his experience, we have our expertise. But I think there needs to be more of a sort of collaboration. I describe this in a story, which is, metaphorically as well as literally, called "On the Level." I describe in the story an old man, in his nineties, very bright, with severe Parkinson's disease, who tends to lean to one side. He doesn't know it, but other people comment on this. And I ask if I can take a videotape of him. He hadn't believed it to be true. And he thought people were pulling his leg, joking. And he was amazed when he saw the video but said, "Sure, they're right, they're right." And then he thought. He said, "Is there a sort of sensor in the brain that will normally tell you if you're on the level or tilted?" And he said, "And could this be affected in me?—Is it affected in Parkinson's disease?" I said yes, yes. And then he thought—and I call this the therapeutic moment, and it was very, very moving. In that moment he thought about things and he made a suggestion. He said, "If this level in the brain isn't working, or if I can't make use of it, would it be possible to make an external level (he used to be a carpenter), so that something like a bubble-level, or a spirit level, would be attached to the spectacles, which I could use to monitor my walking?" And I said I thought it sounded bizarre, but it was also, I thought, a brilliant idea. Anyhow, it was made and first of all he was rather cross-eyed, gazing at this thing, but then it became automatic, like looking at the instruments of his car, and it worked very well. Now this really is a lovely example of a sort of collaboration between patient and physician. Obviously, there are many situations in which that's not possible, but there are other situations in which it is. . . . —1987

ISADORE ROSENFELD

Dr. Isadore Rosenfeld, a New York City internist and cardiologist, has been, over the past few decades, an effective spokesman for a commonsense approach to medical information for the general public. His many books, including the best-selling Second Opinion, *along with popular magazine articles and radio and television appearances, have reached millions of Americans. Dr. Rosenfeld has offered advice, comfort, and clarification on medical issues that cloud our lives and commented as well on their broader social implications. It's amazing how many of his opinions a generation ago ring true today. In one of our programs in the early 1980s, I asked him about the many steps medicine had taken toward longer life.*

. . . I'm not a geneticist, but I think that our cells are programmed to live for a certain length of time. Now it may be that in the future, with genetic manipulation, we're going to be able to change that. A more realistic objective, though, should be the attainment of old age with satisfaction. I mean for people to enjoy old age. One of the very greatest problems that we have now is that we can keep people alive, you know, their hearts may be good, their limbs may be good, but they are senile. They have no memory, they can't take care of themselves, they're a burden to society, to their children, to themselves. The question of the aging of the brain is one very much in focus now, and an area that, I think, will be productive in the next few years. The reason I'm optimistic about this is precisely because we now call it "aging." I don't think the chemical changes that occur in old people's brains are due to hardening of the arteries. That is a common misconception. The research that's being directed now is toward the belief that what happens in senility—in confusion, memory loss, paranoia—all the things we recognize among our very old citizens— are caused by chemical changes that may be reversible. There is already research under way at the National Institute of Aging in Washington, testing new compounds which will act on enzymes in the brain. These enzymes affect the metabolism of the brain, causing problems that are really independent of hardening of the arteries . . . .

Heffner: And in the field that everyone either skirts or plunges into, cancer, do you have the same kind of optimism?

We have made a lot of progress in the cancer field. It's a dread word and a dread disease. It seems that the more types of cancer we're able to control or to cure, the more there appear to develop. The numbers of cancer cases are on the increase, although there are certain kinds of cancers that we can control. More and more doctors every day are seeing patients with different kinds of cancer who, 15, 20, 30 years ago, would have died quickly. These people are now able to live longer in greater comfort. Some of them are being cured. We're able to cure more cancers by means of early detection, by surgery, some by radiation, and the addition of chemotherapy, immunotherapy, and other various treatment forms. But despite this there is a very discouraging increase in the total number of cancer cases.

Heffner: How do you account for that?

I'm not sure. I think it's probably the environment. I think there's pollution. I think it may be in our food, in the air we breathe, in the clothes we wear. I can easily account for cancer of the lung in women. You know, even when I started the practice of medicine 30 years ago, to see a lung cancer in a woman was very unusual. Today there's virtually an epidemic of lung cancer in women. And it's caused by tobacco smoke.

Heffner: Is there any validity to the notion that the more specialists in other areas are able to control those diseases and extend life, by definition we'll see more cancers?

No. Cancer is not a degenerative disease, although cancer does occur for the most part in older people. There are many important cancers affecting children. So I don't think one has to view cancer as an inevitable accompaniment of aging. Cancer is a disease.

Here's where we stand with cancer. We have made tremendous progress in early detection. For most cancers, because we don't understand the basic underlying mechanism, it's very important to pick them up early. Hand in hand with early detection, we have very sophisticated surgery, very sophisticated radiation by which very high-energy beams can be pinpointed so that the cancer the surgeon is burning out is hit hard by a narrow beam, and the rest of the body is much less affected than it used to be with the older methods. The new CAT scanners, or the sonograms that go deep inside the body without invading the patient, can identify tiny cancers at their earliest stage. One of the exciting things is a blood test that will indicate the presence of a cancer in an apparently healthy individual.

The basic question with cancer, unfortunately, is one that is not yet understood: Why a cell in an organ follows a rational, orderly existence, as do its cellmates, and then something suddenly triggers that cell to go crazy? It invades the bloodstream, goes to different parts of the body, and literally chokes the life out of a patient as it metastasizes. We don't yet understand that mechanism. For example, we know that tobacco is responsible for most cases of lung cancer. But there are many people who smoke and who smoke heavily who don't have lung cancer. Now why? What is the difference? What is it in one person that makes him or her vulnerable and another not? Those are the questions that have not been answered. We have made very great progress in all kinds of drugs to kill these bad cells. We've made progress with radiation and surgery. Now we're trying to stimulate immune responses, to have the body's antibodies move in to kill them. That's the therapeutic thrust. The true answer will come when we begin to understand the mechanism of cancer.

Heffner: What about preventive medicine?

You see, when we started this conversation, I talked about the immediate short-range effects, and the long-term effects. In heart disease for example, the long term effort is to understand what causes hardening of the arteries. We now know that there are certain things that make an individual more vulnerable to developing a stroke or to developing heart attacks. Those things include cigarette smoking (the old evil back again), high cholesterol or other abnormal blood fats, high blood pressure, lifestyle, weight, exercise, personality factors, all these things. And they are all, as you know, called "risk factors." But these risk factors are not the cause of the disease; they are things that accelerate the development of the disease. The underlying cause is something we don't understand. We try to prevent the disease by controlling these risk factors, and we are only modestly successful, I must say. So that over the long term we will exercise prevention when we understand the fundamental underlying causes. Today we can only effect cosmetic prevention, in my judgment.

Heffner: Dr. Rosenfeld, are you saying, when you talk about "only modestly successful," does that mean the profession has not been successful in getting people to abide by preventive measures, or that the measures themselves have not really worked out?

Well, both. As people become educated they realize the importance of keeping physically fit and of watching what they eat and controlling their blood pressure and not smoking, and there has been an impact on public opinion in those areas. But quite frankly, given all that, the predictability of preventing a heart attack is not 100 percent. I think one can reduce the likelihood of a heart attack, for example. That's the area we're talking about. We can reduce the incidence of heart attack, perhaps, and have a 25 percent chance of doing it in the vast majority of cases. If I see a patient whose mother died of a heart attack, whose father died of a heart attack, whose brothers and sisters have heart problems, who comes to me and says, "Now, look, I want to prevent this fate," all I can do is give advice and watch him very carefully. But in the majority of cases we will not be able to prevent the heart attack. It will require careful watching so we can intervene with drugs and surgery and so on. But the control of risk factors is far from 100 percent effective. No cardiologist can guarantee any patient that if he does this, that, and the other thing, he will surely be protected against a heart attack. We will reduce the risk in some people. But we cannot now interfere with the genetic expression of this disease until we understand the basic underlying cause of hardening of the arteries, which we at this moment do not understand.

Heffner: Moving quite far from such medical mystery, is it perhaps an act of arrogance to put an artificial organ into a creature of God?

I don't think of this as an act of arrogance. I think that the whole question about an artificial heart is viewed from an emotional point of view because it's the heart. There are thousands, hundreds of thousands of people the world over who live by virtue of an artificial organ other than the heart, and who would be dead without it. I refer to kidney transplants and to kidney dialysis. There are people who go three or four hours a day three or four times a week to have the impurities washed out of their blood through the artificial kidney. For me as a doctor there is very little difference technically to choose between the artificial heart, the artificial kidney, or the artificial liver that you've begun to read about. I mean any organ without whose normal function life is not possible is to a scientist and a technologist and to a physician equally important and drastic. So the fact that this is a heart and not a liver and not a kidney doesn't change things.

I've heard doctors say, "Well now, we ought to spend the money on prevention and not fiddle around with an artificial heart." The fact is you can't stop such a process. You can't stop people going to the moon. You can't stop these interplanetary expenditures. You can't stop the challenge. And the challenge is a surmountable one. You can be sure that, within our lifetime, people will be getting artificial hearts routinely. Almost as routinely as kidney transplants.

Heffner: Where then do we draw the line? When do we say, "This is a bionic man or a bionic woman, and that's not for us"? Can we replace the lungs? Can we replace the liver? Can we replace the kidneys? Where do we stop?

Well, at this moment we're limited in the organs that we can replace. But I don't think that there should be any proscription or limit to our biological attempts to improve the quality of life. Now, I want you to understand, I'm not talking about living forever. But I see nothing wrong if somebody has been plagued with a congenital or terrible disease of the lungs or of any other critical organ, if medical science can devise a way to replace that particular affected organ—and you know we're replacing kidneys by the thousands with kidney transplants, either from relatives or cadaver kidneys, and we're keeping thousands of people alive with dialysis. And you ask any of these people who is living a normal life now by virtue of the fact that they have somebody else's kidney in them, whether they think they are bionic. They're not bionic; they're just healthier.

Heffner: You're begging the question, if you'll forgive me. Let's take someone with a kidney transplant. That person then, getting along very well, does he or she become a candidate for an artificial heart, too, at some point? What would you say? Fine, why not?

Absolutely. If that person is now living normally, but with a transplanted kidney that's been successfully grafted, and that person is still young and develops a disease which precludes his or her continuing to live because of some problem in the heart, and if science has developed either a heart transplant, which we're now able to do much more easily because of new drugs that prevent rejection and so on, or by virtue of some technical achievement, I find absolutely no moral, ethical, or philosophical objection to that at all, provided that this is not a method of prolonging suffering. The point I want to make is that we must not be frightened by progress. I think that if the motivation, is not simply to prolong old, infirm, feeble, suffering lives, I'm all for it. If in fact the objective is to help an otherwise healthy person lead a normal life by virtue of some operation, we should do so.

Heffner: Let's go back to the crucial matter of preventive medicine.

Mention the word prevention, and most people say, "Oh well, it's the same old stuff about smoking and weight and watch your diet." As a matter of fact, there are thousands of useful, new facts that have become available. I think such information can make a difference not only in the prevention of major killers like cancer and heart disease, but with problems such as kidney stones, gallstones, seasickness, mountain sickness, snoring, all kinds of things that interfere not only with the duration of life but with its quality.

I think there is a problem in communicating medical facts to the lay public. This is not because doctors don't want to communicate or don't know how to communicate, or that patients are not interested. There's a tremendous interest in medicine. The problem is that in the real world you go to a doctor only when you're sick. And the doctor will address himself to your sickness. Doctors are really too busy to sit down and tell people what they have to do to avoid or prevent illness.

And as a result there's an information vacuum and people go to all kinds of gurus and to all kinds of magazines and all kinds of resources, some of which or many of which are of questionable validity.

As things are shaping up in the delivery of health care, with less and less of the traditional doctor-patient relationship active in the future, what we're going to be seeing is the delivery of health care by corporations which will then make this kind of communication even more difficult. And less common.

People don't apply the new developments in preventive medicine because it's boring, and the idea that, "It can't happen to me." Especially with young people. People also look for a quick fix. You know, I think that 35 percent of the cancers could be eliminated by diet. And I have spelled out the kinds of diets for particular types of cancer. I mean, cancer of the stomach would have a different diet than, let's say, cancer of the bowel. There's a different one for cancer of the breast. And there are specific diets that we think may reduce the likelihood of specific cancers. You don't find people paying attention to that information. We could reduce the number of heart attacks. We already have substantially. We could reduce them even more by control of certain risk factors. And not only control of risk factors but also the administration of certain medications that people won't take.

The economics of medicine is a factor in this matter of prevention. You know most people are covered by insurance for their visits and for hospitalization and so on. But in many cases, insurance will not pay for a checkup. Insurance will not pay for an educational lecture . . . .

Most doctors I know, including me, work 18-hour days and our phones ring day and night dealing with emergency situations, people who are actively sick. The way medicine is now structured, the doctor's role is to take care of sick people. It is not currently structured so that the doctor has the luxury and the time to sit down with a well person. It should be. In the ideal world, it should be. It isn't. And we're going to have to realize that. The reality of life now—and again I keep talking about reality—is that in the current priorities, the health establishment is in fact being cut back. There are fewer dollars for research. I think the emphasis on group medicine, the HMOs where the one-to-one relationship is disappearing is all for cost effectiveness. Immediate cost effectiveness. I don't believe that there is a concern among the authorities to maintain and deliver the kind of quality health care that we are all interested in. And I think that the next five or ten years will see a dramatic decrease in the quality of care in this country. So it would be illusory to talk about a system in which not only the level of care of the sick is maintained, but educating well people is also an objective.

Heffner: Is the good doctor an artist or a scientist?

The good doctor is both. Now, I know that sound platitudinous. I think part of the problem that we're facing today is that we have such a preoccupation with technology, which has its place, and for which I thank God, and which saves lives, and without which we would be where we were in the eighteenth century vis-à-vis disease. Despite all that, I think today's problem is the preoccupation with technology at the expense of some humanity. I think there has been and there still is a dehumanizing element to the practice of medicine. You see, we're given marvelous statistics. How many people die of infection anymore, how many people are in iron lungs? Look at all the cancer patients we cure. Look at the life expectancy today. Things have never been better on paper. Yet it's a curious paradox that if you ask people about their perception of medicine as it is practiced vis-à-vis their interpersonal relationship with their doctor, you will hear that some of them find it difficult to establish a relationship based on the doctor's function as a healer, a counselor, and confidante. Many people, unfortunately, view their doctor as a technician. Today's doctor comes off poorly when you compare him with the doctor in the good old days of horse-and-buggy medicine. In the old days, everybody loved the doctor. Yet curiously enough, the doctor could do very little for you at the time. He was an observer of disease. The textbooks of those days showed the graphs of how fevers develop in the course of an illness. Nobody could cure pneumonia. There were no antibiotics. There was very little surgery except amputation. Yet, despite the fact that the doctor was limited in what he could do, he was universally loved and respected. And that was because he comforted, he communicated, and he consoled. Whether or not he treated [disease] was beside the point, because patients in those days were very fatalistic and nihilistic. If you lived or died was the will of God. Today, the doctor knows that he's more than a hand-holder, he's a doer. And he is so preoccupied with working you up and getting you cured that he doesn't feel he has time for the other niceties that patients traditionally still expect. Now, the great pity as far as I'm concerned is that the doctor, or some doctors, don't feel they can do both. I think they can, and they should. There's room for both. At the same time, if given the choice, of course, I would rather be cured impersonally and technically than go to my death very comforted.

Heffner: With your hand being held.

With my hand being held. But the point is one shouldn't have this kind of extreme choice. The options should not be so polarized. I don't think that the fault lies with the medical machine, so to speak. I think the fault lies with the man. I don't think that factors like a busy schedule, or knowing when and how to used sophisticated tests to arrive at a diagnosis or implement treatment, make a warm and compassionate and caring approach impossible or difficult. Some of the busiest and most harried doctors I know always leave you with the impression that the time you spend with them, however brief, is yours, and that nothing else matters to them but you. I also know other doctors who, if they had all day to spend with one patient, could never convey that. Now that is not, in my judgment, a matter of education or a matter of machines or technology; it's a matter of character and temperament.

Heffner: How can you reconcile what I think is the obvious need of every patient for seeing in his physician a source of strength and of real help with the need for a second opinion, for second-guessing that doctor? We all accept the notion, forgive me, that doctors aren't gods. But I've got to believe in you, and I've got to believe in what you say because part of your relationship with me and mine with you has to do with my faith and trust in you. How does that correspond with this notion of looking for a second opinion?

I don't mean to suggest that every medical situation warrants a second opinion. I think there are certain well-defined circumstances, however, under which one is well advised to get it regardless of whatever threat to the doctor-patient relationship it might constitute. First of all, I think that where a good relationship exists in the first place, the doctor should initiate that procedure of the second opinion. I know in my own practice when I make a decision for a major recommendation in which I have complete confidence in my own judgment, I nevertheless offer the patient a second opinion. Because I think in the back of everyone's mind, if you give them a dire prognosis or a diagnosis, you tell somebody they have, or you imply to somebody that they have a cancer or tell somebody they have a bad heart or need cardiac surgery, and so on, I think it's only human that in the back of every patient's mind is the hope that perhaps you're wrong. So I think that, in the first place, in such major situations, doctors should take the initiative. Where the doctor doesn't take the initiative, however, I think that it is important for us to change the kind of mindset that you describe because nobody has a monopoly on wisdom, judgment, or information. And there isn't a doctor practicing today who has not at some time or other, and more than once, made an error in a major recommendation to a patient. So I think that the situations in which a second opinion becomes warranted really, in the circumstances, become quite clear. In the interpersonal relationship, that is how the news is broken, how it's received, I think it's almost a self-determining situation. The sensitive doctor will know when the patient is worried or insecure, and should initiate it. And if he doesn't, the patient who is worried and insecure should be able to say to his doctor, "Look, I have great love and confidence in you. We've had a great relationship. But this is a very terrible thing you're telling me. Let's get another opinion."

Heffner: It's interesting to me that, with the people I've discussed the question of second opinions, usually the focus is almost immediately on surgery. The patient thinks one is talking about surgery. But I gather from your book, *Second Opinion,* you're talking about a much wider field of medical alternatives than surgery.

Yes, yes. If you stop to think of it, surgical operations happen very rarely in the course of one's lifetime, if at all. I can name many people, including myself, who have never had an operation, but who have serious illnesses. You know . . . there is diverticulitis, there is peptic ulcer, there is heart trouble, there is stroke. There is a whole variety of serious, disabling or life-threatening diseases in which the treatment can vary, and in which differing degrees of expertise by a practitioner can make a great deal of difference. I think one of the saddest things to observe in the practice of medicine is to see people suffer unnecessarily. To suffer because they are following the recommended advice, the recommended regimen of their doctor, following it to a T and not getting any better. And they are so wrapped up with this attitude that they don't want to hurt the doctor, after all it's the doctor and he must know what's right, so that the patient suffers unnecessarily. Whereas it may be that some other physician is working at a new approach, or has had a new approach. You know, we often get set in our ways of doing things—doctors, that is. Doctors get into the habit of treatment by rote, and do things in a certain way. It may be that in some cases that aren't responding, a different approach would be preferable and more effective.

Heffner: That brings us again to the whole matter of the doctor-patient relationship.

I try in my one-to-one relationship with patients never to allow anybody to leave my office until I've asked them two questions: "Do you understand everything that I've told you?" and, "Is there anything else you want to ask me?" Because so often patients leave or feel rushed, they walk out in the waiting room, the door is shut and the next patient is in. There may have been some things that they needed to have clarified, "Now, what did the doctor mean? What did he mean when he said this?" And then they go home and stew over it. So I never let anybody out until I make sure that they understand what I've told them.

Heffner: What about informed consent? I've often heard from my medical friends that in the final analysis in this day of high technology, the patient really doesn't have much of an opportunity to be informed, much less consent.

Absolutely. For example, with respect to breast surgery, I don't think that any woman who is found to have a lump and who is having a biopsy should give carte blanche to the surgeon to do whatever he deems necessary while she is under anesthesia. There's plenty of time to wake, discuss it with your family, with your family doctor, and then get a second opinion as to the extent and nature of the surgery. I think the key to it is the relationship between the patient and the primary physician. People don't go to surgeons de novo. I mean, you don't phone a surgeon and make an appointment with a surgeon, as a rule, unless you've, you know, broken your hand or something. If it's a matter of an operation, whether a coronary bypass, or a gallbladder, or hysterectomy or what have you, you call your doctor. Your doctor makes the assessment. Your doctor recommends a surgeon. You go to the surgeon. The surgeon talks to the doctor. The doctor talks to you. There is a dialogue, or at least there should be. So it's not as if the patient finds himself on a medical moving sidewalk that he can't get off. Hopefully, he has the kind of relationship with his doctor that permits him to say, "Look, you've sent me to Dr. Smith about my gallbladder. He says that I should have it out. Now, I want to tell you, my father had a gallbladder operation when he was just my age. And you know, he died. And I am convinced that if I have surgery, I'm going to die too. I don't want to have the operation. What are the alternatives?" Now, if you and your doctor are a team, he will give you those alternatives. I mention some of the alternatives to that particular disorder. That's why knowing your medical alternatives is very important, and discussing them with your doctor is very important. So there isn't anything inexorable. There shouldn't be anything inexorable as long as the patient can communicate with his primary physician.

Heffner: But it is said that when you get into a giant hospital, a teaching hospital, you do get on a moving sidewalk, and the relationship between the primary physician and the patient becomes minimal. Is that a fair statement?

Yes. There is a tendency, which I personally deplore, that once a patient is admitted to a hospital, members of the staff do things and cause things to be done which are not always approved by or ordered by the patient's primary physician. That happens, but it should not happen. The machinery is there to prevent it from happening. It requires a greater sophistication on the part of the patient to say, "Hey, wait a minute. Where are you taking me? You're taking me down for a cardiac catherization? You're taking me for an intravenous pyelogram? My doctor didn't say anything to me about that." And then, "Hold off a minute. I'm going to call my doctor and see if he ordered it."

The fact is that people are more sophisticated now. Patients know more today about their own individual illnesses. A patient with myasthenia gravis will come in and say to me, "Now, I've heard about removal of the . . . whatever." People read about it because medicine is no longer a secret. It's no longer the private playground of the doctor. Medical information is widely available. And if you had some major illness, you would have to read about it. You would find out who the best people are to treat it. You would look for any breakthroughs. You would do anything to save yourself. And so you should. They used to say that a little knowledge is a dangerous thing. But I don't go along with that. I think a little knowledge is better than none. And I think this whole trend to educate people so that they can communicate intelligently with their doctor can only elevate the quality of medical care that people get, and keep the doctor on his toes. You know, the old days of the doctor saying, "Listen, you take this pill and go home and don't ask me any questions, and call me in a week," that's finished. First of all, the bottle in which the pharmacist had put the pill, by federal law, now must state all the things that the pill does and doesn't do, and all the harm that it can cause. Remember, in every medicine there's a little poison. And it's a good thing to have all that information in the package insert. So that people no longer will accept—and I don't think they should accept—dogma from on high by the high priest of medicine. The doctor is a dedicated practitioner who has at his command certain facts. He doesn't have all the facts. And he does the best he can. And if the patient can help him with some news, that's fine. I don't get insulted if a patient tells me that they've read something that I don't know about. Mind you, it happens very infrequently. [Laughter]

Heffner: What about malpractice? What has been the impact of malpractice suits on the conduct of your practice and the practice of most of the doctors you know?

It's not been good. And I'm not talking about the premiums that doctors have to pay. I believe that anybody who has been harmed by a physician or a surgeon by virtue of negligence should be compensated. I think, however, that the current malpractice situation is a farce. I think that innocent doctors who do their best and who perform procedures which don't work out because of, you might say, the will of God, are made to pay enormous, inflated sums. The most important impact this has had is that doctors now practice defensive medicine. People complain about all the tests that they're doing. The doctors have a tendency now to do every conceivable test for a given symptom so that they will not be dragged into court to be asked, "Hey, why didn't you do an X ray here? Why didn't you do a blood test? Why didn't you do a stress test? Why didn't you do an angio?" So doctors do everything that could possibly be related to a symptom so that if anything adverse happens they can't be accused of having shortchanged the patient. The result is, I think, less time spent with the patient, less of a detailed history, less of a detailed physical exam, more impersonal medicine, more costly medicine, and shotgun medicine.

Heffner: What do you mean by "shotgun medicine"?

Well, you know, somebody comes in and says he's got a little ache here or there. The great majority of complaints aren't serious. Instead of sitting down and taking the time to find out, maybe it's digestive, maybe it's nothing, give him a couple of aspirin and see if it goes away and call back in the morning, what doctors now will do for this thing, they'll get a cardiogram, they'll get blood tests, they'll get X rays, they'll get stress tests, they will think of radionuclear scans. The list is endless. You could walk out with a $3,000 bill for a hiccup.

Heffner: Okay, except for my pocketbook, am I better off as a patient, or worse off?

You are better off, but only if you are subjected to the tests that you need that are reasonable and that are pertinent to your specific complaint, and which are ordered on the basis of judgment. You know, you can't ask that question, "Am I better off because of all these tests that are done?" because cost of health care delivery is a very real thing. I don't know the percentages, but thousands of dollars are spent by an average family each year either to pay health premiums or to pay for what health insurance doesn't cover. And you are not better off if you are broke or if you are financially threatened or if the health system is going bankrupt because of a lot of unnecessary testing.

Heffner: Okay. But the answer you gave me first of all—and you were very quick to put it in when I started to ask, "Am I better off?"—is "Yes."

Yes, health care is better than it ever was before. But that doesn't mean that we must lose our vigilance and that patients and doctors shouldn't continue to toe that line. —1981

KATHLEEN FOLEY

Pain and death are not my favorite subjects, even for cocktail-party conversation, much less television. But in 1995, when the opportunity arose to have a dialogue about both, with Dr. Kathleen Foley, then head of the Pain Service at Memorial Sloan-Kettering Cancer Center, who also directs the Project on Death in America of George Soros' Open Society Institute, I found it irresistible. Perhaps I was drawn to the issues just because, as I found confirmed, discussion of pain, death, and dying, are so often avoided, swept under the rug, as it were, in our culture. Thus, Dr. Foley's comments were as thought-provoking as they were wise. I asked her about the Project on Death's statement that "The possibilities for a gentle closure of life are often overwhelmed by uncontrolled physical pain . . ."

I think we really have an opportunity now to treat patients with pain and to provide them with, in fact, a comfortable death. And yet one of the major barriers to patients obtaining effective pain relief as they die, is the patient's own fear of the drugs that may provide them with pain relief, as well as physicians and health care professionals' lack of knowledge. There have now been a series of studies in the United States showing that cancer patients, for example—with cancer being the second leading cause of death—are sorely undermedicated for their pain, are not effectively treated. Physicians who care for this population have themselves been evaluated and agree that they really don't have the tools and knowledge to treat pain effectively. So that the evidence is that nothing would make a greater impact on controlling pain for these patients than to institute educational programs for the public, specifically to deal with treating pain.

It's critical that we educate both patients and physicians. And it's critical that we educate the public. Because the public thinks that cancer is painful, and really doesn't recognize and doesn't know that cancer pain can be treated. It can be treated apart from treatments for cancer, and it can also be treated by a variety of approaches. Recently, the Agency for Health Care Policy and Research has defined guidelines for the treatment of cancer pain, and has argued that probably upwards of 90–95 percent of patients' pain can be controlled. But the average person doesn't really know that, and so patients generally aren't good advocates for themselves in requesting pain relief from doctors. They want to be sort of macho; they don't want to complain about pain, they don't want to place that in the forefront of the discussions of their disease. And because of that, they are often undertreated for their pain.

Heffner: What about physicians?

... What's happened in the last ten years has been the advance in our understanding of how to use drugs with patients. Our scientific underpinnings have advanced so rapidly that this whole area of pain management has not been integrated into the medical school curriculum. It hasn't been integrated into residency programs. Clearly the American Medical Association, the American Cancer Society, other major organizations are advocating the incorporation of teaching about pain management in medical school curriculums. But it hasn't happened sufficiently as yet.

Heffner: Is their resistance because of the general American attitude towards drugs?

I think, clearly, for the public as well as for physicians, the use of drugs is markedly affected by the fear of drugs. I mean "Just say No" [was] a very powerful and important campaign. But the problem exists because these drugs for the cancer patient or the patient in pain are the same drugs that are being abused. However, that's only part of the problem. The much greater problem is that of government restrictions. And those government restrictions have to do with very strong policies about regulating drugs. So, for example, physicians are under strict rules in using these drugs. Pharmacists are under strict rules in dispensing them, and patients then get all of this as a third message that they feel like they must be taking something that's wrong or illegal. And crossing the fear-of-addiction barrier and the ignorance about these drugs and how they should be used effectively is, I think, one of the major thrusts in informing the public.

Heffner: How real is this fear of addiction?

In the cancer patient, it is really a minor issue. By that I mean that the data we have now suggests that only .04 percent of cancer patients who are treated with drugs on a chronic basis have the potential for becoming addicts. And what's evolved—and I think the public is beginning to hear this and understand this—is that the cause of addiction is not the drugs, but the person and the setting in which the individual takes drugs. Cancer patients are taking these pain medications for relief of their pain. They're taking these pain medications on a regular basis. Patients don't escalate or take more than they should take. They typically take less. They are not getting high on them. There is a perception that these drugs are bad for you. Yet for cancer patients with significant pain, it often is the main way that they are able to function on a daily basis, take care of their children, take care of their families, go to work. And we've had the incredible opportunity now with the cancer patient population to look at patients over a period of about 20 years and to follow them repeatedly during this period of time. They've taken chronic narcotics; they've taken chronic morphine, for example. Yet they've been able to function. They are not selling them on the streets of New York. They are not dispensing them to their family. They are not using them recreationally. They are using drugs in order to function. And so it's in that framework, with this natural experiment, which is the first time we've ever had an opportunity to study a group like this. We've seen that control is the important thing.

Heffner: Could it be that some physicians would disagree with what you've said?

I think there's been a period of time during which we've had clinical experience, and there also has been a period of time during which we've had to define how we use these drugs appropriately. And within that framework, we've been able to demonstrate that the development of an addiction was a myth, not reality. So it has, I think enhanced the physicians' comfort with using these drugs. Also, even more importantly, it's enhanced their knowledge.

Heffner: Do you think there's any danger that the medical acceptance of these drugs will allow their spread into society in general?

There are always dangers when you make drugs more available and when they're put in a more open context. But I think we have very strongly made clear distinctions about taking analgesic drugs. You take them for pain. You don't take them just to feel good. And the most interesting thing about cancer patients is that, when their pain is treated they say, "Well, I don't need to take that drug anymore." So they are not getting some secondary gain from taking the drug. We've begun to see very different effects of the drug. The main reason for their development was to treat pain. We have almost comparable compounds within our own bodies. We have peptides that mimic morphine completely. So we already have these as our own endogenous substances. But patients are taking them in this setting, for pain relief, because their own endogenous system doesn't work as well as it should in acute, stressful circumstances. The education that's gone into making pain medications available for cancer patients, making narcotics available, making drugs like morphine available, has been to indicate that there's a right place to use these drugs. That's why they were developed. Other areas, primarily the recreational, are the wrong places to use these drugs. And when you make that black and white, and you make the distinctions clear, then it is, I think, a very compelling reason for the right group to obtain these drugs and not, in fact, be hurt by the wrong group. The saddest thing that happens daily is that cancer patients are undermedicated, they have difficulty finding and getting their drugs in drugstores, and their families are concerned that they may become addicts.

Heffner: Of course I can better understand the reluctance of the patient than I can the reluctance of the physician.

You're right. It is astounding. So what is it about pain that makes it hard for doctors to see it, to hear it, and to treat it? And not just doctors, but, in fact, our society.

Heffner: I share your concern. What is there about pain?

Well, if we understood that, we would solve this problem, I think. But we're beginning to understand the following: When a patient reports pain, and is seen by a physician or a nurse in a certain context—and there now have been three major institutions that have studied this and demonstrated this—the physician will always underrate the pain of the patient. The house officer, nurse, or physician will underrate the pain. And yet the patient will rate their pain at an eight or a nine. The higher the patient rates the pain, the more discordance there is between what the patient reports and what the physician or nurse reports. The fact is this subjective symptom isn't a priority. As physicians or as other health care professions, and, in fact, as the public, we tend to de-emphasize it. We keep saying, "Well, it can't be that bad." So, one of the problems is: How are we ever going to treat it if we don't agree on what it is?

I don't think it's a failure of compassion. I think it's a failure, in part, of empathy. I think it's an inability to recognize the patient as an individual, or the setting that he or she is in. And I think it's a failure of time.

Heffner: Time. What do you mean?

It takes a lot of time to take a pain history from a patient and to tease apart the medical aspects of the pain from the psychological aspects. And to make distinctions between a patient's reports of pain and to decide whether it's a physical, psychological or a mixed phenomenon. And that kind of time is no longer available in a ten-minute interview with a patient or even in a 20-minute interview in which a physician might attempt to sort out these issues by taking a very detailed psychiatric history as well as a medical history. But we don't have that kind of time. So in an attempt to get around that kind of time issue, the American Pain Society has come out with guidelines that they suggest every inpatient health care delivery system should have posted at the bedside of a patient which is monitored at the same time blood pressure and pulse rate are measured. And, in fact, we've instituted this in our hospital. The nurses can rate the pain. Because the evidence we have is, if you rate it, if you measure it, then you'll talk about it; if you talk about it, then you'll probably try to treat it. And it's also for the nurses as well as the patient to articulate a language of pain.

Heffner: Do I guess wrong that nurses are much more—I guess the word is not "sympathetic," though that may be—empathetic? They deal with the patient more directly over a longer period of time, and you say time is of the essense here. Are they better attuned to pain felt by patients?

Yes and no. I think the time isuse is the critical issue. They spend more time with the patient, and they have the opportunity to see the patient in many different dimensions that the physician doesn't often have. So that I think that physicians often see glimpses of patients; whereas nurses see them chronically, and see them and understand them better as persons. In the same vein you can misjudge people. This is commonly a problem with patients with chronic pain, who have significant pain all the time, so they're not screaming in pain, they're not moaning and groaning, but they are in terrible pain. And the nurse might say, "Well, they jumped out of bed this morning, so how could they be in pain?" Or, "They were able to walk down the hospital walk. How could they be in pain?" And use these kinds of physical observations as a way to negate a patient's pain,. So what I'm really, in a way, describing, is how complex assessing this subjective symptom is. Yet all of the studies we have suggest that you should believe the patient. That should be the principle. You start with believing the patient. And over time you'll sort out the contributions of physical pain and psychological issues related to the pain.

Heffner: Do you think it's true that physicians generally pay less attention to a patient's evaluation of pain than to other aspects of their illness?

Well, not to chest pain. Because chest pain might mean a heart problem—which might mean a death problem. So chest pain clearly is a very important symptom.

Heffner: One that scares the doctor.

It scares the doctor. Scares the patient so they'll come to see a doctor. And scares the doctor because it might mean misdiagnosis and death. So there's one pain that clearly has enormous, significant implications. The others don't have that same implication. And there really is a belief that, well, you don't die of pain. So it tends to be trivialized.

Heffner: You don't believe that, though, do you?

I don't believe that, because patients almost die of pain. What pain does to individuals . . . has been demonstrated in animal models . . . in which Scottie dogs . . . were continually provided with a painful stimulus to the point that they really couldn't escape easily, and what the dogs did was that they went off into the corner of the cage and just stopped eating, and they stopped interacting and socializing with the other animals, and they just curled up in a ball and lay on the floor.

Heffner: So it was fatal in another way.

And that is clearly what happens to patients. They become withdrawn. They can't function. They can't go to work. They can't interact with their families. And they become profoundly depressed in the setting of a persistent, chronic pain.

Heffner: Dr. Foley, you're head of the pain clinic at Sloan Kettering. Is there a field of medicine that perhaps can make up for the general ignorance, unwillingness, lack of sophistication about the role of pain? Can persons trained as you are trained substitute for the understanding that you wish were there with internists and other doctors generally?

Yes and no.

Heffner: Can you intervene with such a specialty?

Yes, we can. There are pain services now in many hospitals throughout the country, and there are outpatient pain clinics. But I don't think any of us want to intervene in that way. I think we really want to help educate physicians to be able to do this in their own practices. And I think we're moving in that direction. It's slow, but I'm much more optimistic now than I was 20 years ago. There are [pain] specialists, and they are needed. But the majority of people—more than the majority—99 percent of people will be seen by their own physicians. And so we need [patients] to advocate for their own pain relief. We need them to say to their physician, "Well, how are you going to treat my pain if I have pain?" Or, "Would you send me to someone special if I have pain?" We need to teach family members to advocate.

In fact, we need to encourage our patients to use patient representatives to advocate for them if they feel they are not getting effective pain relief. Instituting this broadly in many hospitals are "continuous quality improvement programs," where the whole institution tries to respond to improving pain in its patients. And that means making pain visible, using it on the blood pressure and temperature sheets, and also improving pathways for nurses to treat patients. And then, if th patients' pain is not adequately controlled, to speak to the physician. And if the physician does not respond, to sort of go up the scale of hierarchy to make sure that the patient obtains pain relief. So it's empowering not only to the patients, but empowering the staff, to do a better job.

Heffner: What have you and your colleagues done on the subject of dealing with death in America? And what do you think you can do? What are your objectives?

Well, we think that there's a need to transform the culture, and to realize that there are many facets playing into the culture that we need to understand better. So, in part, we want to understand better what the issues are. Why do we avoid talking about death? What is the level of death anxiety? Death is all around us. It's all around us in the newspapers, in the various illnesses that patients are dying from now, and it's constantly being put before us in television programs. So what is this disconnect between the fear of our own deaths and talking about it, versus the public discussion of death? And in attempting to look at the subject, one of the major issues is that, at this point in time, 80 percent of Americans die in hospitals. They are dying in institutions. Dying in institutions has led to, in part, an over-medicalization of death. What we really want to advocate for is the improvement of the care of the dying. Yet there's clearly a debate about the way patients can have control over their own deaths. Which is to have legalized physician-assisted suicide or euthanasia. That is polarizing the issue at the present time. I think the discussion should start with consideration of our dying, about preparing for our death, about talking about death and, most importantly, about creating health care systems and societal systems that respect and care for the dying. Because in our society the dying are the most vulnerable. We need to respect them, and we need to have systems in place to care appropriately for them. To do that is problematic when we have so many other pressures in our society that have little to do with caring for the dying.

Heffner: What do you mean? What other pressures?

The pressures that relate to the economics of health care, the pressures that relate to the caring for patients with curable diseases, public health issues. And we have tended to trivialize the care of the dying in the same way that we have not fairly and appropriately addressed long-term care for our aged population.

Heffner: I'm interested that you use the word "trivialize." Please explain.

Trivialized in the sense that we have not given it the credit that it is due, and we have not focused on death as an incredible life event. In that context we have finally begun to look at the multiple factors that have led to or influenced a lack of appropriate care for the dying. I think I would argue that we need end-of-life care to be appropriate. Obviously the specifics would vary from patient to patient. But this care can only be appropriate if patients, the public, and the health care professional will talk about dying—will acknowledge to patients that there is no other therapy available; but will also assure them that the system will not abandon them, will be there for them and take care of them and say, "I wish you to live until you die and to have a dignified death, and that requires medical care."

Heffner: That means that you're opposed to physician-assisted death, I gather.

I personally am against physician-assisted suicide because I think that's not what the issue is. I mean, I take care of large numbers of cancer patients who go on to die, and that is not their issue. Their issue is living well until they die, getting adequate pain control, dealing with their psychological issues, and trying to come to terms with their life and with their families, the impact of their death on their families. That is really where the public is. The public is concerned about how to care for family members, to have home-care programs or hospice programs that provide effective, compassionate, medically supervised care for individuals at home, that the government helps underwrite the costs of care in that setting, that families are not devastated financially, socially, or psychologically by this care. It's very difficult to care for someone at home, so we need systems in place to do this. The hospice program currently supported by Medicare is a very good example of the provision of this type of care for patients at home. And it's been demonstrated to be cost-effective. It's allowed patients to leave the hospital, to be cared for in their home settings. So we have these kinds of approaches available in part;

but we need a much broader discussion of ways and means to respect the needs of this group of patients.

Heffner: Do you think our concerns are more attitudinal toward death and dying than they are economic?

Yes, I think they are more attitudinal. Patients often say, "I've never died before. So how do you die?" And asking what it will be like. How will I feel? Will I have pain? Will I suffer? Who will be there to take care of me? Who will be there to treat me? Those are the questions that the public, the patients, are asking. Moreover, we, in hospitals, cannot admit patients to the hospital to die. When a patient who is, in fact, dying is brought to a hospital, there must be a convoluted diagnosis—such as pneumonia. He has to have some treatment or the hospital will not be reimbursed. So we have a system, a health care delivery system in place that is, in fact, making it more costly because we're not acknowledging that people are dying. If a patient could be admitted to the hospital with the diagnosis, "Process of Dying," then that would facilitate a system of care that could be less costly and equally or potentially more caring. It could attend to issues that dying patients need to attend to, which are often more existential and psychological and spiritual and personal, and not necessarily medical.

Heffner: How do you bring about the cultural change with respect to concepts of death and dying, that you feel is so necessary?

. . . The hard part is that the dead can't vote. The dead can't tell us what they would have liked to begin to have influence in the next election. But their caregivers can. Caregivers, I think, are the powerful voices that can begin to help us move and change this culture. I think there are several groups now, in the AIDS population, particularly, a group of individuals who probably will demonstrate for us more than any group has ever done, the sense of community for individuals taking care of one another, and for a community responding to people with chronic illness for a long period of time. And their articulate ability to live in the shadow of death and to talk about it is educating all of us around them. So I think that a cultural change is happening in the AIDS epidemic that will affect all of us.

A second area that I think is important is the large number of individuals with cancer who are in remission, but have been given a fatal diagnosis. That's a second group of individuals who themselves are now living in the shadow of death, who are able to begin to articulate this and to make choices and to help move this cultural discussion.

Heffner: Do you think that the rest of us don't realize that we are living in the shadow of death?

Come now, do you realize you're living in the shadow of death?

Heffner: I think I do, because I'm so darn long in the tooth now. And as I become aware of that more and more, my thinking has been modified a great deal. Which leads me to ask again, don't we understand that we all have a death sentence? Is it that we try to look beyond the end? Do we try to shut our eyes to it? What part do our religious institutions play?

I don't know the answer. I think this is the kind of issue that we keep arguing over and trying to understand—how deep, how personal is this death anxiety? And it's different for different individuals. For some it's an incredibly powerful force; and for others it's not. And yet it has created a sense, at least in one population, the caregiver population, the medical world, a death anxiety and a death-denying frame of mind so profound that it may even be in opposition to a public much more able to understand and to deal with the issue of death. —1995

ROBERT MICHELS

Dr. Robert Michels is the single most brilliant and articulate physician I have ever met, which clearly is the reason we have been talking together on the air for nearly 30 years. He was Chair of the Psychiatry Department at the Cornell University Medical College and Psychiatrist in Chief at New York Hospital when we began our marathon discussion, later serving as Dean of Cornell's Medical College before returning to his distinguished psychoanalytic practice. Some time ago, I asked him about the future of our major medical research and teaching institutions.

There are major issues of concern to academic medicine, but also to the health care system and to the nation. In many ways, the accomplishments of academic medicine have been the pride of our society. Most people in the health field provide health care to citizens; they care for the sick. But, in addition to that, the academic institutions do two other things. One is they train, they educate professionals who will be future health care providers. They run 125 medical schools. They train nurses and social workers and psychologists, pharmacists and other health professionals. The other thing they do is develop new methods of treatment, new drugs, new diagnostic procedures, new strategies of health care that will be more effective and more efficient. And if there's any area that our nation has excelled in, in the last few decades, it's in the study and development of new methods of health care, pharmacologically, in terms of systems of imaging the body, in terms of methods of delivering treatment. From the economic point of view, one would see that academic medicine is a very small part of the total health care bill. The health care industry spends a much smaller percentage of money on research and development than the automobile industry does. But it's a vital part of what we do because that's what makes our children's health care better than ours, just as ours is better than our parents' was.

Historically, over the last few decades, academic medicine has largely been funded by subtle, often invisible, cross-subsidization from the resources that were developed in the health-delivery system. To put it briefly, health care in the private sphere, outside of academia, made a profit. In the academic sphere, that same health care made a surplus that was used to support the expensive cost of research and education. But the changes we've been talking about, the shift to managed care, the rationalization of the system, the concern with cost control, have reduced the profit in the private sector, but they [also] reduced the surplus that was used to subsidize research and education in our academic institutions. And those institutions don't have a substitute source of support. So as we're rationalizing our health care system, an unintended but extremely important consequence is the starving of the academic institutions that have provided the research and education.

Heffner: When the late, great Lewis Thomas, was here, he said very much what you're saying, but also said that in the whole scientific endeavor we were still living off the fat of a decade, two decades, three decades ago, when more resources were devoted to basic research.

I think that there was a period in which we weren't even aware of resource constraints as the country enthusiastically supported such research, and good science didn't have to worry about adequate support. We have a problem today in that the number of good scientists seeking support, and the ratio of their numbers to the support available, makes being a scientist a dangerous game of chance. Only a small percentage of all the applications for funded research get approved and funded, and scientists see excellent applications for research funding get turned down. Some of them get discouraged and leave the field. Even more tragically, others are discouraged from entering the field in the first place. And we're worried that we're, in effect, destroying our seed for the future in this area. And what this means in many areas is consolidation. It means recognizing that hospitals with small or borderline programs should close those programs, that the great teaching institutions with the finest faculties should concentrate more effort on teaching, and that we need a reimbursement system that recognizes the cost of that and provides the money to do it.

Heffner: Now, how do you see all of this as developing in the opening decade of the twenty-first century? How do you see all these chairs being placed around the large table of medical care?

The American way is not to find a solution to a problem, mandate it from above, and enforce it in all 50 states at the same time and thereby solve the problem.

Heffner: Maybe it needs to be.

If we were absolutely confident in the total wisdom of our national leaders, perhaps. But I don't think most of us are. And I think what you're going to see is some experiments. I think you're going to see experiments in various components of the system. Perhaps in the states or regions. Perhaps in a network of medical institutions. I think you're going to see some of the for-profit health care systems that are developing decide that they want to have their own medical schools training physicians for their specific needs. I think you'll see some of our great research universities recognizing that the training of investigative or academic physicians is sufficiently different from the training of primary-care clinicians, that new curricula will be devised. I think you'll see communities trying different experiments going in many different directions.

Heffner: Let's move on to the question of HMOs. Do you feel comfortable with the notion of making medicine a profit center? I know your answer is going to be, "It always has been." But institutionalizing it this way, is this a source of comfort for you?

Medicine's a profession. And that's good. It means that a physician isn't only trying to maximize his personal gain, but he or she has a very important mission of doing what's best for the patient. That's not the classic market situation. And if you're buying an automobile or buying a new suit, it makes perfect sense to go into a market situation where the seller is trying to maximize gain, the purchaser is trying to maximize benefit. But if you're in pain, or scared that you might die, or need to tell somebody all of your secrets to make sure you can get the best possible help, you don't want to be in a quasi-adversarial relationship. How we can maintain the profession of medicine and the nature of the relationship between the physician and patient and all that implies, with the economics of a for-profit system, is a major problem. I guess I'm old-fashioned in the sense that I think it's an unfortunate way to organize health care, despite the advantage of forcing efficiencies on the system. But I wouldn't be surprised if, once those are forced on the system, if its disadvantages loomed so large that it withered away and was replaced by something more supportive of the professional ideology of health care in medicine.

Heffner: How would you describe that something?

I think that if we get an organized, efficient, less cottage-industry health care system going, we may find that the competition squeezes the profits out of it. So either a kind of regulated-industry approach or a public-industry approach becomes more politically palatable, and, at the same time, more ethically acceptable both to the public and to the health care professionals in it.

Heffner: Is it possible that a major change is in prospect? A great many private physicians who had almost automatically opposed the notion of the Canadian system, a single payer, are now, having been caught up in HMOs, looking in that direction again, saying that the single payer is desirable. What do you think?

I think the surveys that have been done suggest that Canadian physicians are happier with the setting and ambiance and the structure of their health care system, and that their patients seem happy, too, compared to American patients and American professionals in some of our HMO structures and our managed-care structures. When the first health care changes were proposed, physicians reacted very negatively to the notion that the government would be telling them what to do. What they discovered is the government may be a more benevolent manager than a for-profit health care organization trying to squeeze the last dollar out of the bottom line. Some of them now long for the government to look over their shoulder rather than an accountant. I think you're going to again see a lot of experimentation in that area. I wouldn't be surprised if some states go all the way toward a publicly organized system while others encourage competition in managed care, and we have a kind of period of competition among models of care. I think that would be interesting, and we might even be able to do some good studies on the way in which different models influence the quality of care.

Heffner: Meanwhile, you said you were old-fashioned, and the concept of the marketplace, the concept of medicine as a profit center, disturbs you. It doesn't fit with your traditional approach. What about the younger doctors?

I would say the people entering the field are better than ever before. They're brighter, they're more well-trained, and their personal goals couldn't be more desirable. I think that, in the old system, there was a profit element in the individual practitioner's practice. And I think, as that's getting shaken out, it's probably good for medicine and for health care. What I'm concerned about is, if medicine becomes a job rather than a profession, another way to make a living, and if the work is defined as an occupation without a special moral, almost a religious quality, is it going to attract a different kind of person.

Heffner: Now, just take that point. That has been the criticism of a fairly recent generation of doctors, leaving out the question of HMOs and huge companies in this business. Did they bring this on themselves?

I think in part. I think that, if you look at the history of medicine or you do a cross-cultural look at medicine, physicians in the United States in the last 50 years have been more affluent than at any other point in time or in any other culture or nation. And I think that's probably an accidental blip because of changes in federal reimbursement systems of Medicare, and because of the economy after World War II. I think that that's going to get corrected. What I'm hoping for is that, in correcting it, we don't throw out the baby with the bath water; we don't end the profession of medicine and replace it with the occupation of applying biologic knowledge to disease care by somebody who sees himself or herself as working from nine to five, Monday through Friday.

Heffner: Do the young people you've been dealing with view medicine as a calling? Why do you say they're trained better than ever before? That I don't understand. Trained better at the university level? At the college level?

We're going through a revolution in medical education, and it's a wonderful revolution. And there are several components to it. One is that our basic science training, which had often been boring, rote memory of many, many facts, has been so enriched by new knowledge that its content has become intellectually more exciting, and, at the same time, it's expanded so much that there's no possibility of learning all the facts. And the leading medical schools have shifted their curricula so that learning the basic sciences of medicine is now intellectually challenging. Learning how to use methods of problem-solving rather than memorizing lists of facts, is a great advance. Secondly, our clinical training, which had, over the decades in most medical schools, become more and more a series of sequential rotations in the various medical specialties— four weeks of this specialty, four weeks of that specialty—has become a more integrated and organized health care system with an emphasis on primary care and ambulatory care, and a much more cohesive sense of knowing what it's like to be a doctor with patients rather than learning a series of technical sub-specialties of medicine. Finally, a third theme of medicine, ignored in the past to a great extent: the sociology of medicine, the economics of medicine, the politics of medicine, the ethical aspects of medicine. The significance of medicine and its role as the physician and the patient are together in a social structure, has become an educational theme; attention is being paid to it in our teaching and our curricula. Medical school curricula are much better than they were a few decades ago, and the students like them more.

Heffner: You're very optimistic then, about the nature of medical students of the future.

I think the medical students we're getting are great. We're getting many more women, we're getting many more minorities, and we're getting the brightest and best. I'm very optimistic about the students. I hope we live up to what they deserve. —1996

STUART M. BERGER

American society was, in the 1980s, more than mildly obsessed with food, with dieting to lose or even gain weight, with achieving good health through food. It had been thus many years before, and still is to this day. One of the medical stars of that earlier period who had only a brief ascendance, was Dr. Stuart M. Berger, author of the huge best seller,

The Immune Power Diet, *and a ubiquitous commentator whose bold views about food, medicine, and society went far beyond calories and vitamins. I asked Dr. Berger to comment on obsession with food as well as dieting.*

American society in general perceives the word "diet" as a "weight loss regimen." It's grown to have that meaning as a result of all the diet books trying to teach us how to lose weight. That is not what the idea of diet consists of. One can concern oneself with dieting that has nothing to do with weight loss. For example, if you are a cardiac patient, you can be a thin cardiac patient and still be on a diet very low in fat and high in complex carbohydrates. There are many other examples. If you were prone to gout, you would be on a diet low in urates. The point is that proper diet is an essential part of good health.

Now, as to our obsession with food, I don't know that we have a monopoly on it. When I was in France last month, it seemed to me that the French were pretty obsessed with food, and so are the English. I think that what we have done is export a brand of bad food around the world. For example, in Japan, up until we kindly gave them McDonalds, they did not have cardiac disease to any extent. And now we've donated to the Japanese society the opportunity to have cardiac arrests on a regular basis. That's the American impact on the world. I mean, it's poor nutrition, and it's quick food, and it's the kinds of high-fat, poorly developed foods that have become so popular here over the past 30 or 40 years.

Heffner: I like those words, "poor nutrition." Do you think that's really where we are now?

I think that the major national problem that we have, the number-one health hazard in America today, is poor nutrition. I think it's responsible for more illness than anything else. For example, I think poor nutrition is even worse than the epidemic of smoking; it kills more people, clearly. There's no doubt about it. Poor nutrition probably contributes to the development of cancer. That's been clearly documented by the American Cancer Society in connection with colon cancer, the number-two cancer in men, breast cancer, uterine cancer, and probably all others. It affects the immune system rather dramatically. We're talking about all immune-mediated problems, from arthritis and headaches to MS and others. It clearly undermines one's heart and affects diabetes. I mean, we've known that for many years.

Despite all this, the ignorance in the area of nutrition and prevention is absolutely staggering. There was a study released from Washington . . . citing the fact that doctors know nothing about nutrition, literally nothing. When I graduated from medical school in 1977, I'd had two hours of nutrition during my four-year course. That is not an adequate amount of training. And remember that's a doctor, someone who treats the human body. The nutritionists in the nutritional centers are still working with nutrition standards and information going back to 1940, 1950. The recommended vitamin levels we see coming out of government studies have not changed significantly in ten years. Our environment has changed enormously. It's much more toxic. If there is a role for vitamins, it's a function of our lifestyles. Why doesn't that happen? Why aren't people considering it? I think that at every level the degree of nutritional ignorance is extraordinary.

Heffner: And do you think this poses a real danger to Americans?

I think that the medical epidemic of the twenty-first century will be in immune-mediated disorders. And there are already all too many examples. I see today women and men in their 50s and 60s coming into my office for the first time with allergy-related asthma, who had no history of allergies in their childhood. That was unheard-of ten years ago for a physician. I see patients who have viruses, CMV virus or Epstein-Barr virus, that last two and three years. And they suffer with chronic fatigue and low-grade temperatures for all that time. When I was going to medical school, people didn't have viruses for that long. A good case of mono was four months, five months. Now it can be three or four years. Then there's the epidemic of cancer. And believe me, it is an epidemic. There's a reason for this. It's not just serendipitous that, as a nation, our immune system is falling apart. And the reason is, in my opinion, that our environment is increasingly more toxic, that we breathe more chemicals, that we're surrounded by pollutants, that our foods are full of all kinds of [chemicals] with side effects we know nothing about. In addition to this there is also stress, and obviously stress plays an important role in undermining one's immune system. Clearly there's a problem.

Heffner: But are you saying that, through diet, we can compensate for poisons in our environment?

Exactly. That's what I'm saying. And perhaps more succinctly, that what we have to focus on is preventive immunology. We didn't do preventive cardiovascular treatment in this country for years. And as a result, we had an extraordinary amount of unnecessary disease. When we thought of preventive cardiovascular treatment, we saved a lot more lives than we have with transplanted hearts. Now we have to think in terms of preventive immunology. How do you make your white blood cells live longer? How do you augment the integrity of your body before you become ill? How do you protect yourself against certain illnesses?

We know that if you have a high-fiber, low-fat diet, there's less likelihood of developing colon cancer. That's preventive immunology. We know that vitamin A and vitamin E are antioxidants, and that free radicals are critical in the development of all cancers. That's preventive immunology. There are very real things based on well-established facts—from medical schools, the finest institutions around the world—that one can engage in in terms of preventing catastrophic illness. That doesn't mean we're never going to get sick, and it doesn't mean that it's a cure-all. But what it does say, simply, is that the likelihood of illness is reduced. If you have a family predisposition towards colon cancer, you should be watched no matter what kind of nutritional program you're on, because there's a genetic predisposition towards colon cancer. But clearly, you should also be having a high-fiber, reduced-fat diet.

Heffner: All right, I understand what you're saying, but where do we go from here, what are we going to do about all this? The medical profession, society in general, you and I.

We're in trouble, big trouble. I think that it's a very difficult problem. I'll tell you why we're in trouble, or why I believe we're in trouble. This is a nation whose medical system is illness oriented. And we focus on disease states. We don't think like the Chinese, that a physician should be paid as long as the patient remains healthy, and that when the patient becomes ill, then the physician hasn't done a proper job. As a result of that, you have a kind of abdication of responsibility on the part of the medical community. Despite the desire on the part of the nation to be more aware of nutrition and prevention and health, you have a group of quacks—totally uneducated, irresponsible people who dominate the airways and who give bad diet information and bad advice. That's insane. I'm certain that we could extend our average lives by about 15 years if we integrated healthy nutrition, removed cigarettes, and concerned ourselves with basic stress control and good exercise. —1995

JONAS SALK

When Dr. Jonas Salk and I talked in the mid-1980s, he had long since achieved world renown as a medical scientist, the discoverer of a vaccine with the capability to eradicate polio, one of the world's most deadly diseases. I had expected to hear a pragmatic voice, that of the ultimate laboratory investigator. Instead, Dr. Salk expressed great eloquence and perceptiveness as a humanist and social philosopher, a spokesman for the future of the race. I began our conversation by asking him to explain his intriguing statement that we must be wise and good ancestors.

Well, I'm sure that just as we look back into the past to those who preceded us we recognize that some of those who have gone before have been wiser than others. And the question that I have been asking in recent years, amongst others, is whether or not we are being good ancestors. And I pose that question because I believe that future generations will look back and judge us as to whether we have been wise or not, or whether we have been profligate and wasteful and destructive of the opportunities for their future as well as the further future of generations to come.

Heffner: And your answer?

I think we are being both wise and unwise. As I said in one of my writings, in which I spoke about the survival of the wisest as distinct from the survival of the fittest, I thought that wisdom had become the new basis for fitness. At the present time, the future is very much in our own hands. We can control whether we will destroy ourselves and the planet or use science and technology and the knowledge that we possess for better, rather than for worse, so to speak. I have the impression that the new generation of young people are coming upon the scene with a sense of ancestorhood and with more wisdom at an earlier age than was evident before. I think this comes about as a matter of necessity, almost as if there is something innate, something inherent in us that is destined for a longer term rather than a shorter term future. And I think that many of the things happening in the public domain cause us to say, intuitively, that there's something wrong and that something has to be done by way of correction. We wish our leaders would listen.

Heffner: Yet it seems to me that in years past there has been a rejection of that concept of ancestry or ancesterhood.

It seems that way. And it's for that very reason that I think it's emerging now with greater strength and greater force. So that it is as if evil in a sense evokes good. So that it is as if when things get bad enough then something happens to correct the course. It's for that reason that I speak about evolution as an error-making and an error-correcting process. And if we can be even so much better, ever so much slightly better, at error correcting than in error making, then we'll come through.

I speak about evolution as both a biologist and a philosopher. If you like, as a bio-philosopher, someone who draws upon the scriptures of nature recognizing that we are the product of the process of evolution. And in a sense, we have become the process itself. Through the emergence and evolution of our consciousness, our awareness, our capacity to imagine and to anticipate the future. And to choose from amongst alternatives.

Heffner: But you used the phrase "our consciousness" as a generalization, and as I read your book, *Anatomy of Reality,* I was particularly interested that you write, "There are some among us who feel or see more clearly than the rest. They are the ones who illuminate and reveal reality for others." There is a sense of elitism there. How do you identify those who do have this sensitivity?

Not really elitism. In nature we see different kinds of structures, different functional elements. For example, we know about DNA and about proteins in living systems. We know about the genetic code. And we know about those structures which express the genetic code. I imagine humankind is an organism and that some parts in this complex organism perform special functions for the species as a whole.

Heffner: But where does the rest of the species come in this process?

It's all a part of it. Think of each of us as a cell performing a different function, a different role. And if you would see it that way then you'd say there is a place for everyone. And that one is not better than the other. It is that they play a different role and perform a different function, one that is consistent with their genetic endowment.

Heffner: But what happens to the rest of society when we begin to identify those who can see more clearly, those who can think more clearly, about the future challenges that you identify? And you identify so many of them. Are you being—shall I say—autobiographical?

Well, I suppose so. I always felt that I did for the rest of the world what the rest of the world could not do for itself at that time; when I was doing the kind of work I was doing earlier on in immunology, vaccinology. But yet I depended upon the public at large to provide the funds and the support so that work could be done. I look upon ourselves as partners in all of this. And that each of us contributes and does what he can do best. And so I don't see a top rung and a bottom rung. I see all this horizontally. I see this as part of a matrix. And I see every human being as having a purpose, a destiny. And my hope is that we can find some way to fulfill the biological potential, if you like, the destiny that exists in each of us. And find ways and means to provide such opportunities for everyone. Now at the moment the world is suffering from large numbers of people who have no purpose in life, for whom there is no opportunity. And that's sad. It is in this way that I think about the problems that we have today. I don't worry about those who have great potential other than when it's wasted, when it's not being utilized, not being fulfilled. And I'm as interested in those who are ill, shall we say, and need help, as in those who have a great deal to contribute. . . .

Heffner: In terms of the engineering of biological bits of inheritance, the manipulation of DNA, what impact will that have on the potential, the destiny of which you speak? Those are very powerful words, very important ones. What will they do to what nature hath wrought?

As you use it, the word manipulation sounds pejorative. I'd rather say it will provide us with ways and means of extending our survival time on the planet by developing more efficient and effective ways for providing food supply for so many more billions of people that are still to be sustained at any one time. You see we've become completely dependent upon science and technology for the number of people that exist. At the moment, there are about 4.7 to 4.8 billion people on the face of the earth. Each one is out there hunting and gathering. In view of that, it becomes necessary in order to maintain a population of this size, to push the frontiers of science and technology as far as possible. Advantages will then accrue to humans for maintaining a life of high quality, especially for the many more individuals than those existing today and who will be alive for longer periods of time. What is important is that we, number one, learn to live with each other, and number two, try to bring out the best in each other, the best from the best and the best from those who perhaps may not have the same endowment. And so this bespeaks an entirely different philosophy. A different way of life, a different kind of relationship where the object is not to put down but to raise up the other.

Heffner: Dr. Salk, you are concerned with raising not the combative stance but the helpful stance. But do your studies of the past indicate that this is a notion shared sufficiently for us to assume that it will happen?

It's altogether possible. As I indicated earlier, I see signs of this in some segments of the younger generation. I can also see other signs. The clinical judgment, if you like, the qualitative impression that I have from those I know and those with whom I'm working convinces me that there's more than a grain of hope. And that it is worthwhile to presume that this can be done, that we can increase the population, if you like, of the few to which you refer.

Heffner: But I thought you were suggesting that there is room for that increase but that there is nothing much that we can do to increase that population, at least through genetic manipulation.

I wouldn't think of genetic manipulation as the way to do it.

Heffner: Why not?

Because it can't be done.

Heffner: I'm surprised to hear you, of all people, say it can't be done.

Well, it can't be done for the following reason. You can engage in genetic manipulation if you're talking about a cell, but not about a human being. A human being is far more complex than a cell. A human mind is quite different from a cell that can be manipulated from within its universe.

Heffner: And yet from your own writings and elsewhere I have the sense of man making man. This is tremendous optimism on your part if you say we can create ourselves and our future.

By shaping ourselves, not our cells. That's the important distinction.

Heffner: But why do you stay away from the issue of shaping cells?

We are shaping the cells, to be sure, but we will not change ourselves in the course of shaping our cells. Because we're dealing with something that is far more complex. We're dealing with the mind, which is different from the cell. We're dealing with the human consciousness, which is different from human life in the strict biological sense.

Heffner: Yes, but you, yourself, write about the importance of shaping consciousness in such a way that we can survive the incredible challenges that we face now. Is this shaping, this molding, a threat?

No. It will happen through experience.

Heffner: Do we have enough time for experience?

Well, if we don't then there's nothing to worry about. We do have enough time if we don't waste it. And it's for this reason that I write as I do, that I speak as I do. Because I'm convinced that we do have enough time. And we will not have enough time only after the fact.

Heffner: Well, this amazing sense of man creating man that you convey in all that you write, I wondered whether you saw the potential for using that sense in addressing contemporary political or social issues. How do you see those formulations having an impact on these contemporary problems?

I see them as very relevant to contemporary problems, and I see my thoughts arising from observations and experiences in the contemporary world, from my own life's experiences. So that my present view, in a way, emerges from my own life's experiences. I have for some reason the instinct, if you like, the intuition of a healer. That's probably why I went into medicine. That's why I chose science as a way in medicine. Now I seem to have the desire to fix things when they're broken, when there's something wrong. And at the moment the planet is sick, humankind is sick. We seem to be suffering from all kinds of addictions. We see drug addictions, addictions to tobacco, addictions to alcohol. We even see addictions to the making of nuclear weapons, which seem to be super-fluous and unnecessary. Why can't we stop? Well, there's something about human nature that has to be understood. And so, if you like, I've shifted my attention from an interest in immunity to an interest in creativity and recognizing the importance of creative approaches to the solution of these problems. Meaning unusual approaches, uncommon approaches, approaches that may, perhaps, not even as yet been recognized. And it's for this reason that I focus attention on others like myself, those who are interested in these questions and who perhaps have visions and percep-tions and imagination that allow us to look into the future.

Heffner: And your sense of that future now?

My sense is optimistic, positive, hopeful because I find enough others like myself who have the same sense, who have the same commitment. And I think that we're driven by an evolutionary instinct. Not a sur-vival instinct mind you. An instinct to survive through evolution, through overcoming the kinds of obstacles and difficulties with which we're confronted. And I see also the perception of the importance of the human being, the importance of the human mind and of human creativity in all of this.

Heffner: Dr. Salk, if we were to turn the clock back, would you have imag-ined as you watched the announcement about the success, the achieve-ment of the Salk vaccine, would you have imagined that your own life would have taken this kind of course, have followed in this path?

Well, not in detail. But I will tell you one thing that did happen at that time. I realized then that I saw the way in which people reacted, people of all kinds, many of them I thought reacted inappropriately, to the availability or the prospect of the solution of a problem that clearly plagued us at that time.

Heffner: Why inappropriately?

Inappropriately? I will give you a very good example of that. There still continue to occur in the world about 500,000 cases of paralytic polio a year. Now the fact that the disease has not been eradicated from the face of the earth is testimony to me that all of the problems of man, all of human problems if you like, will not be solved in the laboratory alone. And that was what I said at that time. And it was that which set the future course of my life. Even though I've continued to function as a biomedical scientist, I have continued also to develop these ideas, in trying to understand these paradoxes. And in the course of this, I recognize that there is an instinct I recognize in myself and others, which is to reach into the future. And this instinct for what I call ancestorhood—a concern that we begin to be conscious of after we've been through a period of parenthood, the period of adulthood . . . There is a phase in our lives in which we seem to have an instinct and a desire to leave something meaningful behind, to have done something meaningful. And I see this in many people who have become very wealthy, very successful. There's something gnawing in them that says that there's something more to do. And I find this encouraging and refreshing. I see this as a sign in such people and in younger people that there is developing a force that will express itself in a very positive way . . . .

Heffner: Does this mean transcending the nature of human nature?

It means expressing human nature. It means expressing the potential that exists in human nature to save itself from itself.

Heffner: And has it always been there?

Yes, it has always been there.

Heffner: But where do you get the notion that if we haven't in all man's history tapped those resources of optimism, that they really exist?

We have been optimistic. That's how we got here. That's why we're here today.

Heffner: A fair enough answer, I guess. But you're fearful that we may not stay.

Well, I believe that we do have to participate actively in the process to avoid the equal probability that we can undo it all.

Heffner: Dr. Salk, as a physician, if you didn't believe that was the answer to my questions, would you take a more pessimistic note or would you as a physician still feel the need as a healer to be optimistic?

Well, it's too late in my life to ask me that question because I already see enough evidence for optimism. And in recent years I find that perhaps what I'm seeking is a scientific basis for hope and I think I've found it.

Heffner: Why does there need to be that scientific basis when you have become so involved in the idea of creativity. This stands apart from the scientific pursuit to a certain extent, doesn't it?

Not at all. It's the essence of a scientific pursuit.

Heffner: Dr. Salk, can you tell me briefly what you mean by what some might call a paradox?

Well, I believe that I have been expressing this both in this conversation and in my life, that my work does represent and reflect the process of creativity in the human realm. And it is creativity itself that's going to save us.

Heffner: In the world of science or in the world of the humanities?

In the world as a whole. —1985

OTHER VOICES

Norman Cousins on Treating and Preventing Illness

Professor at University of California at Los Angeles School of Medicine and Editor, The Saturday Review

. . . I think that we've been so educated about certain aspects of health, that we tend to overlook some simple truths. In fact, I think we have not been served well by public education on health. I think that the general trend of thought makes us very timid about ourselves. The things that we read, the things that we're told to do, all these things give us great insecurity about our bodies, and I think we're becoming a nation of hypochondriacs and pill-poppers. . . . There's so much emphasis on annual checkups, for example, that physicians' offices are clogged with people who have no business being there. Then too, you turn on your TV set and it's impossible to look at it for a few minutes without seeing this or that analgesic for this or that pain. And we're almost made to feel subversive or un-American unless we begin to pop pills to take care of these pains. The curious thing is that we're not taught to pay attention to the cause of the pain. Everything is geared to giving us labels. If you have symptoms, then you want a label. What is the name of the particular illness? But it's not just what is wrong that's important. The question that has to be asked, the primary question, is, "What is it that we are doing that we ought to stop doing?" Because we don't stop doing it. Then it'll only be a matter of time before we have to take more pills.

Heffner: There is an assumption on your part then that, to a large extent, when we're ill it's a function of the way we have been living. Is that a fair statement?

Yes . . . You see, for a long time we had the germ theory of disease. The notion that we were in a crowded thoroughfare or crowded room, and one of our apertures happened to be open, and a bug spied the aperture, dove in and dove down and took up residence, and kicked up a fuss, and we became ill. But a lot of people may have had their apertures open under those circumstances, but it didn't happen to them. Why not? It didn't happen to them because their bodies were equipped to take care of the problem. When you become ill it simply means that your immune system is not working as it was intended to work. Well, what is it that makes it difficult for that immune system to do its job? Here you have to look not just to disease germs, but you've got to look to the way we live, to our emotions, despair, depression, prolonged grief, frustration, exasperation. All have an effect on the body's immune system and open us up to attack. So psychological factors play a very important part in bringing on disease. It's not just the bug. Our bodies can handle the bugs. It's the deterioration of the defense mechanisms in our body that we have to be concerned with. —1993

Peter D. Kramer on Medication and the Self

Associate Clinical Professor of Psychiatry at Brown University, author of Listening to Prozac.

About three or four years ago, I started writing articles for psychiatrists saying, "Patients aren't just getting over their depressions, they are changing in ways that go beyond recovery from depression." I think . . . if there was one sentence that made me think about writing this book, it was a patient who came in and said, "I'm not myself." And I said, "What do you mean, you're not 'yourself.' " And she said, "I'm the way I was in the past, but that isn't myself." And I said, "You were one way for 35 years and then on this medicine for five months you were some other way . . . would you never have been yourself if the medicine hadn't been discovered . . . might have gone your whole life and never been yourself." And I think, I think she said essentially "yes" . . . that there was some marker for selfhood, that she recognized what was self and what was not self, and that the person on the medicine was herself. And I thought that was remarkable and maybe even correct.

Heffner: You say "maybe even correct."

I think it's very uncomfortable to think that there are . . . were people throughout history who never felt themselves, or never were themselves . . . you know, in the absence of these drugs, which have only been around a few years. I think that on the one hand it seems a bizarre hubristic kind of statement that we can produce true selves through medication. On the other hand I think there are people we see who just never are comfortable, it's as if you had a migraine all your life, and it went away, you would know that that was a change toward your more comfortable self, or your more true self. That the migraine, even if it had been with you for many years wasn't really a part of you that was meant to be there. And I think that some people find that the degree of . . . social inhibition, or inhibition to new experiences, or pessimism, stickiness, sentimentality, that goes away on these medicines really feels like "not self" when it disappears. —1993

B. F. Skinner on the Psychology of Freedom
Professor of Psychology at Harvard University

Heffner: Do we dare think the unthinkable . . . whether there are limits to human freedom?

It's so hard to define freedom that to measure it, see how far it extends, where one could cut it off and say it goes no further would be a particularly difficult thing. I like to distinguish between our feelings of freedom, which I think are extraordinarily important—and life without a feeling of freedom would be unlivable—and the scientific case, whether or not human behavior is indeed free in any literal sense, or whether it is caused, as de Tocqueville says, by genetic endowment, the product of a long history of the evolution of the species, and by the life of the individual member of that species from birth to the present moment, and by the present situation. I, myself, I should make quite clear, believe that our search for some reason to hold to that kind of freedom is to a considerable extent simply a measure of our ignorance. And the time which has elapsed between de Tocqueville and the present has, I believe, narrowed the circle very considerably by revealing kinds of control of which he was not aware. I would say that Freud made a very great contribution here. I don't like the Freudian mental apparatus, but Freud did reveal kinds of orderliness and behavior that have been dismissed as accidental caprice. I think we've gone beyond that by studying the relation between behavior and the environment of the individual which, although it cannot of course ever be said to prove that there are not elements of freedom in the system, make it reasonable to me to proceed on the assumption that man is not in that sense free, and to ask what are the sources of the feelings of freedom which are so important to us. —1974

POPULAR
CULTURE &
THE AMERICAN
SCENE

ROBERT REDFORD

I'm one of those who feel strongly that Hollywood has had an enormous impact on our lives. But because of my twenty years as Chair of the motion picture industry's voluntary rating system, out of respect for possible conflict of interest concerns, I only rarely invited people identified with the industry to The Open Mind. *At times I did, however, and among the most interesting has been Robert Redford, in his various creative roles a "star" of the first rank. In fact, of all my guests over the years, Redford was perhaps the most disarmingly forthcoming when it came to evaluating both the power and the responsibilities of media masters.*

We spoke together in May 1994, not long after his evocative direction of Quiz Show. *He had recently been quoted as saying, "Something changed irrevocably with this event, the quiz scandals. It really marked the end of a period of innocence in our social history." So I began, "Well, historian Redford, explain yourself."*

As a historian?

Heffner: Well, you are a historian now.

I think probably that's true. I mean, it sounds a little heavy-handed, but I think it's true. I think my interest, as long I've had the authority to be the author my own work in film, it always goes in the direction of history, socio-history, sociology, anthropology, if you will. In other words, what we're about as a culture, what we're about as a society, is endlessly fascinating to me. Because I'm in it. It's part of me, who I am. It's part of my heritage, and it's now part of my children's heritage. So it's a matter of great interest. This specific event interested me because, if I look at it from the historical point of view, which I now can (because it's 35, 40 years later), I can see certain things I couldn't see then. At the time, I could only feel them. I could only feel things like the energy of the period. I don't think one can feel one's innocence. Only when one gets past it, when one gets to the point where it doesn't exist anymore, and one says, "Oh, I see. That's what I had. Innocence."

But that's what it was. It was the energy available at the time in this city in particular, New York, where it was the energy of innocence, and it was also the energy of hope. And that innocence was directly related to television in the sense that, I think, that was the time—and I can speak firsthand on this—that that was a time when we still believed that what we got on television was the truth, or the way things were. And I think that incredible shock of the exposure of TV was the first real shock to hit a nation uniformly, that began a series of other shocks. Kennedy's assassination. Bobby's assassination. Martin Luther King's. One shock after the other. And along with these shocks, I think, came a series of crushed hopes. Because these were figures that brought with them a certain degree of hope. As television did. And I remember that, in those early days of television, I bought into the miracle it was advertised to be. I bought it totally.

So when that show [*The $64,000 Question*] was on, I remember that, as a young person having just arrived from California [to] New York, I was 19, and I watched those shows. And I couldn't help but watch them, because they were hypnotic. They were meant to be hypnotic. They were purposely made mesmerizing by the producers. And so that part worked. Where I was critical was in the performance of the contestants. I didn't buy it. I didn't buy it because I was an actor myself.

Heffner: You mean they weren't good enough actors?

They were not good enough actors. Of course, I was critical of every-thing then, because I was a young actor, and most young actors are critical of most other performances, no matter what.

So, I remember looking at these characters on television and thinking, "I don't buy this. Something's just too weird here. I don't buy it." On the other hand, the characters themselves were doubting the context that it was in. They were doubting the show. Even though the show seemed to have all this integrity. It was hyped-up, but not nearly as over-the-top and cartoonish as the shows are today. It had more integrity to it. So did television in general. And so one bought it. One bought the idea that the show was okay, in spite of the weird-ness inside it. So that was my impression. So I had that history, and I had my own reasons. I was actually on a quiz show once.

Heffner: Did you get the answers ahead of time?

Well, no, I got the whole show ahead of time. I was told what to say, and what to do. So I had that kind of firsthand experience. It was on a show, a Merv Griffin show. I think it was called *Play Your Hunch.* And I was not one of the contestants. I was one of the subjects. I was silhouetted behind a screen, to be or not be somebody's twin brother. There were two other screens with two other guys. Is it . . . X, Y, or Z? And the contestants would argue back and forth and they'd say, "Well, I think it's . . ." And there was this, kind of nerdy-looking guy standing in front of the screen. And they said, "Now, which guy," in that booming voice, "which man behind the screen is this man's twin brother?" Pretty heavy material. So I stood back there being this guy that wasn't his twin brother. . . . And they said, "Well, he's too tall, he's too short, he's too fat, his shoulders are too wide, they're too narrow. I mean, it looks like he has a big head." And everybody would laugh, on cue, of course. And I felt like a complete idiot standing behind there, because I didn't know what I was getting into. I went down there for the money, because I was in dramatic school and I was married, and my wife was pregnant at the time, and we had no money, and I was desperate to get some money from somewhere. We were living off her salary to get me through school. So I went down there because I was told it was going to be $75 to $100. So I go down and they put me through the interview. And they said, "What do you do?" And I said, "I'm an actor." He said, "No, you're not." I said, "Yes, I am." He said, "No, no, no. Please. You don't understand. You can't be an actor. We can't have an actor on the show. Are you kidding?" I said, "Okay." So then he said, "What else have you done in your life?" And so I told him. Construction, you know, I'd worked as a laborer, and that I had been an artist. He said, "Art. I like that. That's good. Artist." So he [wrote] down: Artist. He said, "So, Merv will come out and ask you a few questions after it's over, you know, about yourself and where you're from and about your profession. But remember: Artist, not an actor." I said, "Okay." And I said, "So when do I get the 75 bucks? At the end of the show?" He said, "Okay."

So then I go behind, I do this thing . . . and I'm feeling pretty stupid. And the things come up. And they say, "Okay, now we're going to find out who it is. Is it X?" And I was X, right? The screen comes up, the audience sees me, and they boo. So my first experience in front of an audience is that I was booed, because I wasn't the twin.

Heffner: [Laughter] I trust that was the last booing.

So then Merv comes out . . . And then the other guy, the final guy was [the] twin. Everybody applauds like it's a big deal. And then Merv comes out and talks to me, and he says, "So, you know, what are you?" I just felt so stupid. So that was my experience actually on a quiz show. That was 1959. And that was actually the year that the quiz show scandal broke. So I was aware of the scandal and I had seen the show itself, *The $64,000 Question.* There was something wrong with it, but you didn't want it to be wrong, so you bought it . . . You know, 55 million people at once were buying the show. So when, years later, when I came across the *Quiz Show* script, that had been laying around for about a year or a year-and-a-half, it hit a nerve not only from my own personal experience of remembering the country and New York City at a time that is now pretty well gone, but also it raised issues that I thought were important to look at—ethics, primarily.

Heffner: But you know, in your film, *Quiz Show*, when Goodwin says, "We thought we were gonna get television, but it's gonna get us," I was thinking of something that Walter Goodman wrote in the *New York Times*. He said, in reviewing a television program about the quiz scandals, "Although the quiz scandals had never been repeated, whether television remains a money-driven, ratings-driven operation with the same pressures and incentives prevailing, and the reach for ratings as relentless as ever, is an easy multi-million–dollar question. Not $64,000, but multi-million–dollar question. Is much of television a long-running scandal?" And I had the feeling, when I saw your film, that you have a personal stake in saying that much of television is a long-running scandal . . .

Well, perhaps, but I must tell you, first of all, that my place in television is really a transitional one. Because I grew up with radio. Radio was with me at birth. And television came along when I was about 13 or 14, I guess. My family couldn't afford television in the beginning. It was like this wonderful thing out there somewhere that other people had. And I remember the first time we ever experienced it, it was advertised, I think rightly, as a miracle. The idea that somebody could be on the other side of town talking, and you could see them, was just a miracle . . . And of course with it came all this incredible hope of what it would bring to you. It would bring incredible education, it would bring phenomenal entertainment, exposure to world events, you know, all of which is true. But how much is done in terms of what it could do, and what is its abuse? Certainly the scandals were a flagrant abuse of the integrity of a new institution.

So, I did not grow up with what young people today do. It's all part of the fabric of their lives. It was not mine. So I never quite got on board with television, except as an actor. And I think I got quickly disappointed by what television failed to do in the context of my own expectations, what it could do. And the only way you knew what it could do was when you saw something of real quality. It made you aware of what wasn't there. And the continued amount of money that was thrown at a lower-grade experience was just depressing.

Heffner: And when you go to the movies, you feel differently?

I don't go to the movies. So it's hard for me to comment on that.

Heffner: But I'm serious about this. Because you've picked one medium. One of the two major mass media of our times: television. And when you have Goodwin, in the film, say, "I thought we were gonna get television, but television is gonna get us," *you're* saying something.

Well, that had a lot to do, of course, with the subtheme of the movie, which is ambition. I mean, Goodwin's an extremely ambitious man, young man, and the other two characters are as well. They have that in common. They have ambition in common, and to a degree, greed in common. And so when he says, "I thought we were gonna get television," he was speaking about his ambition. Here was this guy who was first in his class at Harvard, right. But he was a 29-year-old guy who was extremely ambitious to think that he could go, under the guise of the governmental subcommittee, that he could go after television. He was extremely ambitious. And he failed at that ambition. And he also had his eyes opened to the fact of how really powerful this instrument was, and that the collusion between government and business, which he just experienced, was a real eye-opener. And that realization, which is a realization that I share, having to do with power and how power works in our country, was what prompted him to say that "Television is gonna get us." Because television, I think, at that time, was about to replace religion as the new opiate of the masses, which I believe it has already done. And I think he got a real lesson, first-hand. And that's the drama of the piece for the audience, the lesson that Goodwin gets about the collusion between those two powers, the power of law and the power of business. It's what made him realize that TV was going to survive, and he may not.

Heffner: Well, I don't want to push you in a direction you don't want to go, but you seem unwilling to contrast television with that other great medium with which you have been much more familiar. Is it any different in film? And I don't mean as an aesthetic experience.

Well, how do you mean, then?

Heffner: I mean in terms of the impact the medium has upon us, its influence upon us, and the nature of that influence.

I'm not sure I know. I think the question would probably be best answered by a sociologist looking at television in a very close way. I can only speak from my own experience, which is that television has become pervasive, and film is not as pervasive. Film can afford a different kind of treatment. Television has a real meter ticking behind it all the time. Television has become an instrument by which we get our information on a rapid, daily, regular basis, whereas film is not. We get information from film, but we don't necessarily trust it, because it's usually fiction. And non-fiction pieces usually go into the documentary category or are supposed to be reserved for television. So I think it's different in that regard.

Where it's similar is that we are given images that we digest, images that affect us one way or another.

Heffner: But as to *Quiz Show*, for example, don't you think your picture of that time and of those events will be implanted much more deeply in my students' minds than anything I have to say as a historian?

Well, that'll be interesting to see. I'm not so sure about that. Maybe I'm a little on the cynical side. One would have thought that films like *All the President's Men* and others I've made would have had an impact. I'm not sure they did.

Heffner: You don't think that *All the President's Men* did?

No, not really. I think that, starting with *The Candidate,* for example, where I honestly felt that in showing our political system and its emphasis on cosmetics—and that was 1971; it was released in '72 to show that how we get people elected in this country has little to nothing to do with substance; that it has to do with the cosmetics of how we present an image to the people. I thought that really going after that in a slightly black-humorous way, but being very accurate, might have some effect, because that was the year of the 18-year-old vote. And I was, along with a huge sea of people, very, very hopeful. I saw that as a tremendously encouraging time. And thank God the 18-year-olds were going to be able to vote, because maybe we might return to something that I had lost with the death of Jack Kennedy, someone of my own time. I mean, Kennedy was replaced by people not of my time. Johnson wasn't, Nixon wasn't. And we've had a succession, with the exception of Carter, of people who were not of my time. And that was a great loss. So here was an opportunity to get it back with the 18-year-old vote. The 18-year-olds would have a voice. And they might elect someone of their time. It didn't happen. And I was quite taken back by that.

Heffner: You know, I'm astonished. Most frequently when I'm with people who come from the printed word, and talk about their power, they say, "No one's in here but us chickens. We don't have power. Television does. And film does." And yet you honestly don't believe that what you have done in film has had any kind of mind-changing impact.

I don't. I really don't. And I'm not being falsely humble, I'm not being overly cynical; I just have learned the hard way, again based on this sort of odd hope. I thought, well, this film can belong to the generation about to vote. They can take that. But it didn't happen. The 18-year-old vote never produced. It just didn't. They didn't show up at the polls. Now, the cynicism had already set in pretty hard. The film became a kind of underground favorite, I'm told. A chic film, if you will. And then *All the President's Men* was, I mean, you know what a struggle that was. I mean, that took three years to get to the screen, and I had to wade through all kinds of obstacles, including the *Washington Post*, and including the fear and anxiety and suspicion of the press itself about how it was going to be portrayed. But finally we got there. And it was a film that I had a lot of pride in—in its accuracy and that it was not taking an overt, cheap shot politically, which I would have probably personally loved to do, considering it was [about] Nixon. And I did carry a tremendous amount of heavy negative baggage about Nixon based on my own experiences as a child growing up in California with him as a senator. But I resisted that because I felt it was more important to show that this was a film about investigative journalism and how it worked. Using that incident in that time as a backdrop. And I was hopeful that the lesson to be learned would keep us from ever repeating it again. And ten years hadn't even gone by before not only were we repeating it, but worse. So look at those events, and you say, "You know, I wonder, maybe all that gets really affected by films is fashion." You know, somebody wears a hat in a successful film, everybody wants to wear the hat. Somebody wears a moustache—I remember when I wore a moustache in *Butch Cassidy*. Everybody at the studio didn't want me to do it. My agent said "I'll resign because of this." And I said, "It's what I want to do. Look at the pictures. That's what the Sundance Kid looked like. And that's what I want to do. I want to play that character, and this is how I want to look." So I did it, and then, ironically, the film caught on, and what came with its success was an interest in the fashion of what we were wearing in the movie. Who would have known it, you know?

Heffner: But you know, if you have ambitions, if that's the word, to function as a historian, how are you going to maintain the sense of responsibility in your historical interpretations if you don't recognize the power of what it is you do as a historian with your films?

It's just that I don't recognize the power you talk about. One wants to assume that, and you would like to think it. But I don't. If I recognize the power of it, it's not so much in the hope of what, how it can affect people, as the responsibility it carries to be accurate. That's a big thing with me. Because you're in a business that fictionalizes very easily. You're in a business where the public at large is just buying these images. There are so many images coming at them so rapidly, that there's very little digestion time, there's very little analysis time. I mean, there's not a whole lot of analysis going on about the information age we're now in, questioning whether it's good or bad. It's just accepted as a new technology, therefore it's got to be good because it's progress. Okay, as long as that's going on, then the public is going to be less inclined to say, "Wait a minute. Is this true or not? Or is this real or not? Or is this . . . " The blurred line between fiction and reality gets worse and worse. So what do I do with that? All that I do is accept a certain amount of responsibility to be accurate. —1994

SISSELA BOK

Sissela Bok is a philosopher for our time, one whose teaching résumé includes Harvard and Brandeis, and whose books, including Lying *and* Secrets, *address moral issues and the way our society deals with them. It*

was actually the subtitle of another of her single-word-titled volumes—
Mayhem—*that drew my attention:* Violence as Public Entertainment.
*My years in Hollywood, and my enormous concern with violence in film,
as well as on television and the other mass media, drew me to Dr. Bok's
argument that every child in our society should have, as a birthright, "basic
nurturing and protection" from the impact of unfettered media violence. I
asked her, however, whether, aside from the people we would expect, the
psychological and psychiatric associations, the PTAs and the other groups
concerned with children directly, she thought that, as a people, we've really
begun to have a sense of what this mayhem may well be doing to our
youngsters.*

. . . I think that we may, to some extent, have a skewed sense. Many in
the public believe that the main problem with entertainment violence
has to do with children, adolescents, adults, becoming more violent
themselves. And I think research shows that that does happen to some,
definitely. But it's not the major danger. To me, the major danger really
has to do with something else, which is that people can become desensitized to violence. They see so much of it on the screen; children grow
up with it from the very beginning. So how do we shield ourselves
against that? Well, we shield ourselves by developing a kind of callus
almost, to be able to take violence. Interestingly, a lot of adolescents go
to violent films to try to learn to take it more. This is one proof, perhaps, of their manhood or something like that. That's the great danger,
one of the great dangers, to me, that we become less able to respond to
violence when we see it, either on the screen or in real life. And that
may be something that Americans should be very worried about.

And there I come back to this word "mayhem." "Mayhem" comes
from a French medieval word for "maiming." Now, the question is
whether there's a part of our spirit that can become maimed if we expose
ourselves a lot to violence, if there's something that is stifled or maimed,
and that might just be our capacity for empathy for other human beings.

Now, that's one thing for all of us as adults. We have to make our
choices, and we have to learn to deal with that. But it seems to me to

be very unfair to make the choices for children before they are old enough at all to decide what they want to do about it. And, as a philosopher, I would also say that that capacity for empathy underlies everything else about our moral development. If we can't even feel as much as we should for other human beings, then we can't really understand the Golden Rule, "Do unto others as you would have them do unto you." We can't really understand that because we're not thinking enough about other people. And then we can't even make choices that are sufficiently rigorous with respect to, for instance, doing violence to them or hurting them in some way.

Heffner: Do you feel that there is any indication that we are coming to understand that this desensitization is precisely what's happening?

Yes. From all the social science studies that have been conducted, and there have been a great many studies now, and a lot of meta-studies, so-called—that means studies of the studies—does seem to be the case that entertainment violence and media violence generally can have four effects, really. One, perhaps the most common, is to make people more frightened, more fearful. They see so much violence on the screen, they wrongly conclude that is all around them sometimes. People are afraid of doing things in their communities. Children are more afraid of being kidnapped than of anything else. You know, the greatest fear of children is of being kidnapped, amazingly enough. So that's one fear.

Second is the desensitization we had been talking about.

The third is a kind of growing appetite that can come. The more desensitized you become, the more your appetite can develop for more and more violence on the screen.

And the fourth is greater aggression.

Now, all of those have been studied. And, of course, they hit different people differently. Some people may only, for instance, experience the fear, not the other things. Some may say, they may experience the fear and say, "I have nothing more to do with this kind of programming." Others experience the fear and then want to stick with it and are drawn to staying with it because of all the advertising, and become more desensitized. Some develop the appetite, and some are more aggressive as a result. But it's pretty clear from the research that's been done that these effects are in play.

Now, then, you might say, "Well, it's not necessarily going to bother my children." And that could be true. And I think, actually, that in the supportive, loving family, those children are more likely to be all right, however much TV they see. It's the children who are most left to themselves, whose parents care least about them, whose parents have least time for them, sometimes because of tremendous demands at the workplace, those are the children most at risk.

Heffner: But the number of these latchkey children is legion. Doesn't that mean, then, that organized society must do something for them in particular, though for all other young victims of media violence as well?

It certainly seems to me that society must take much more of an interest. And here I would argue that this is not only a matter having to do with television or the media at all. Our society, America's society, does less with respect to the general support of children and the general attention to how they should be nurtured than any other industrialized democracy. And this is very peculiar since we talk all the time about how much we love children. We do less. And there are more children in poverty, more children exposed to violence in the home and on the street, than in any other society.

Heffner: Mustn't you, then, argue forcefully that we should remedy this situation, beginning with the very "mayhem" you identify so graphically?

The First Amendment, I think, has become a kind of cannon for some people that is wheeled out to shoot down anybody, in fact, who wants to raise any questions at all. And so they're using the First Amendment to shut down debate, not to allow it to go on. I think that's one thing I very much wanted to argue against in the book. I do think it's important to beware of censorship. Having written, on the one hand, a book called *Lying*, and on another a book called *Secrets*, I couldn't remain more opposed to censorship. In this book [*Mayhem*] I looked at countries like China and Vietnam and others that do exercise tremendous amounts of censorship over what comes over the screen and over the Internet. And that's clearly not the way to go. And I do believe it's true that once we begin to censor media violence, the next thing could very well be something else. It could be political, it could be religious. . . . But that said, there are so many other things that people can do. Caveat emptor, what people can do as consumers, that's only the first step. Then I do think, because of what you say, so many other children being exposed to all of this, that we have to do much more in our communities and in our society. And there I was looking first at Canada, where there has been a much more coherent debate involving teachers, producers, and the entertainment industry, people in the churches, children, young people. They've had a longer debate, I think, than we have. And then I looked at Norway also. They, of course, suffered from censorship during the Nazi period and so are very wary of that also. And they have a campaign against violence in society more generally, including entertainment violence.

Heffner: Let's just be so honest and forthright as to abandon the word "censorship," which is the dirtiest word an intellectual can use, for obvious reasons. Let's try to talk . . . about regulation instead. Actually, ours was a nation that, until two, three Presidencies ago was essentially a regulatory nation. We began, at the turn of the twentieth century, to think in terms of "caveat vendor" with our Pure Food and Drug Acts, so that shoddy products could not be pushed upon an unknowing public. What's happened to that notion? Have we succumbed so thoroughly to the deregulatory mantra of the past 15, 20 years that we can't think in terms of regulating media any longer?

Well, you know, regulating speech is a little different from regulating food and everything else, as we know. We have to be especially careful with respect to speech. I would say that the way to go, to me, seems to be, for instance, what was done in Canada. As a result of this debate, pressure was put on the industry to self-regulate. And that is being done elsewhere, I think, to some extent. There are always questions of how long it's going to last. Self-regulation on the part of the industry with a lot of pressure indeed from the public, I think would be a very good way to go.

Heffner: I suppose that I shouldn't comment that in the entertainment-for-profit world, voluntarism, or what you refer to as "self-regulation," has been proven very much to be the scoundrel's last refuge. Instead, let me just ask what evidence there is that parents are going to participate in the kind of consciousness-raising that you talk about?

Well, you know, if you take child rearing in general—and, by the way, I think this problem has to do also very much with us as adults—but if you take childrearing in general, there are all kinds of shifts over the course of history. Right now, for instance, breastfeeding is something that is regarded as better for children, and that many, many more mothers do than did 10, 20, 30 years ago. I think parents are often willing to do more for their children if they have a sense that it matters. So again we come back to this question then of how to raise the consciousness, that it does matter.

Heffner: And you think this can be effective?

I think that, to begin with, certainly parents can do a lot more now than they could even five or ten years ago, partly because of technology, new ways of protecting themselves. But I also think that it's possible for communities to do much more and for societies to do much more. And that's why it's important to think about how other societies have responded, not always just feel stymied and powerless because of our own sense that it isn't going to work in our country.

Heffner: And you see international communications, the crossing of borders, as the most difficult thing we have to face today?

Both the most helpful and the most difficult. The fact is that we can look for solutions crossing borders, even though, yes, the problematic aspects of entertainment violence also cross borders. The internationalization, I think, works in both ways, and the sense of hopelessness that so many people have. I've talked to people who are all in favor of censorship, but they don't think it's going to work, so they have a pretty great sense of hopelessness. On the other hand, the people who don't want censorship also feel despair because they don't think there's anything to do. And I guess I just want to alter that discourse a little to say there's a lot more that we can do.

One thing that was so interesting to me just in the last year or so, was to find that an international clearinghouse has been set up on the Internet to deal with the issue of children and media violence. What that means is that, for the first time, all kinds of different groups and individuals in so many countries can actually tap in and see what other people are doing. So there's a whole world now of information that we didn't have even five years ago, I think, available to parents and individuals looking at their own lives. —1998

FLOYD ABRAMS

I have had a great many heated, though gratifying, conversations with Floyd Abrams over the years on The Open Mind. *Abrams is a good friend by now, and an enormously gifted and unusually highly regarded constitutional attorney, best known to the general public for his defense of freedom of speech and First Amendment rights. This subject was at the top of our agenda when we spoke together in early 1994, shortly after Congress, and even Attorney General Janet Reno, had voiced concerns about the level of violence in the media. Further, U.S. Senator Ernest Hollings had weighed in with a* New York Times *op-ed piece entitled "Save the Children," and Abrams had countered with his own, "Save Free Speech." The* Times *had called theirs "A Dialogue on TV Violence: Survival Versus Censorship." And I said to my friend, "I feel constrained to ask if you ever think that there is reasonable ground in contemporary America to find media violence a serious evil, wreaking serious injury. That's not an unfair question, is it?"*

It's a very fair question. I think on one level, the answer is "yes." But only one. I don't think that media violence causes crime. I don't think it causes violence. I'm very unpersuaded by the so-called studies that are so often cited in support of that proposition. But I do think that speech matters, and that if speech glorifies violence, people will tend to become persuaded that violence is an acceptable form of conduct. I think if someone writes comic books, or even higher-quality books, saying something or urging something or advocating something, people are sometimes persuaded. I don't think media violence is irrelevant. But I don't think it's anything Congress can or should try to do anything about. I do think that the impact is, like all communications, long-, not short-range. What it affects is values, the way people think about things. That's, on the one hand, just the sort of thing the

First Amendment protects and, on the other, it matters. And so if we can jawbone some people to persuade them to avoid gratuitous violence or the glorification of violence, I think that's fine. But in my view, nothing more than that is constitutionally appropriate or ought even to be tried.

Heffner: If we were to take the word "constitutionally" out for a moment—you say nothing more is "constitutionally appropriate"—then would citizen Abrams, father Abrams—because you're concerned about your children and their well-being, would you then have some feeling about the importance of, and perhaps the necessity for doing something further?

With or without the word "constitutional" in, there is a level of desirability in having higher-class, rather than lower-class, literature, movies, television, and the like. Certain types of television degrade the people that watch it. They have a right to watch it, but if it were up to me—and at one point it was, when my children were younger—I kept them from watching, and my wife, even more strongly than I, kept them from watching all sorts of programs that we thought weren't good for them, or might not be good for them. Or might be scary. I remember being terrified as a kid listening to the radio to some of the programs that were then on and that existed for the purpose of scaring people then my age. I wouldn't have thought of taking it off the air. As a parent I might have thought of restricting a little bit of access to it.

But in general, look, I think a lot of this talk is overdone, overblown. We are deliberately not facing up to real-life causes of violence, but trying to put the onus on Hollywood, on television, on media. If it has an impact in the sense that I'm talking about, if it has an impact of harming or encouraging certain values to be something other than what I wish they would be, yes, I wish somebody would move a little bit away from that. But that's really not a central or even a serious problem in America today. And people don't like to talk about real problems. I mean, people don't want to talk about poverty, because we've pretty well given up. They don't want to talk about guns because it's too controversial . . . So what do we do? We talk about violence on television as if we're talking about something which really has direct impact on the violence in our society, and I just don't buy it.

Heffner: You know, Floyd, I'd like to challenge this notion, that we do the one rather than the others. If I may, I challenge that, because we do talk about crack, we do talk about guns, we do talk about all of these social evils. But the communications industries seem to get very much involved in this notion that we should not also talk about the violence that you refer to. You say, there are values perhaps pushed here, attitudes that are perhaps exacerbated here. But you don't seem terribly excited about it.

No, I don't think it's much of a problem. But it's real. That's the only reason that I'm even prepared to say, look, for those people that really believe that the depiction of violence on television has an impact of a more direct nature than I think, yes, we want to put some pressure on Hollywood. You want to call in the television executives and have Senator Hollings yell at them now and then. That's okay. It's not important, but that's okay. What's important to me is that Congress might pass laws which Congress shouldn't pass, and that we still have a free system of communications in the country, understanding that the nature of freedom is that there'll be some publications, some broadcasts, some films that you or I or others will find unattractive or which we will be very uncomfortable to have certain people watch.

Heffner: "Unattractive." That's an interesting word. That's perhaps as far as you'd go. It's "unattractive"?

It's that sort of word. Yes, yes. When I read about kids, young people applauding a murder in a movie theater, that's disturbing. It's a disturbing commentary on our society. It is much less a commentary on the movie than on what we have become as a society. But if you ask me, "Do I think that movie is good for them?" No, I don't think it's good for them. I think people have a right to put it out, and the audience has a right to watch it. But the fact that, even if I'm right in what I say, there may be a right to do it, doesn't mean that I think it's a wonderful thing . . . It's simply one of a lot of things in our society which are available to people.

Heffner: Well, suppose we go at it in the other way. You say, hey, pressures are fine. I think you would say that. Jawboning—

Yes, jawboning is okay. I mean, I'm not going to raise my First Amendment flags and fire my First Amendment cannons every time some government official, either because he believes it or because he thinks he gets good publicity from it, starts yelling at or mocking officials from Hollywood or television, many of whom aren't all that attractive anyway, and put on their material for motivations not always terribly attractive. They can have at each other. Where I get off the boat and where I get very disturbed is when we even start talking about this in terms of law, where we even start saying, "Look, I've got a wonderful idea. We have too much television violence. Let's pass a law about it."

Heffner: Well, how do you account then for Attorney General Reno's seeming feeling that, yes, there is something that can be done, should be done, and within the framework of the Constitution of the United States?

I can't, except to say I believe she's wrong, that she's poorly advised, that her position is insupportable legally, and more, that it is insupportable as a matter of social policy. I would be much more comfortable with Attorney General Reno if she had played the role that I and some other people who happen to be on the same side of this play, if she had been the one saying, "You know, we really would like to get less violence on television, but there really are limits, serious limits, institutionally imposed,

Constitutionally rooted limits on what Congress can do. And one of them is that Congress can't pronounce that there may or not be violence on television, and when or when not violence may be had on television." That seems to me contrary to the heart of a lot of First Amendment law and even more First Amendment policy. So I would have hoped that she would have played the role of the defender of the law against this year's efforts to do something on the cheap about violence by focusing on media violence instead of the wide range of other real causes of violence.

Heffner: But Floyd, the fact is that she didn't. The fact is that she seems to be joined by an increasing number of public officials and by an increasing public opinion.

Absolutely. That's why we need the First Amendment. We don't need the First Amendment to protect speech which is popular. We don't need the First Amendment to protect speech when Congress likes the speech. The only time we need the First Amendment is when the Attorney General and the Congress and the public together join up and say, "You know, this is terrible. We just shouldn't allow this sort of thing." And the answer, then, is, you know, isn't it wonderful that we have this bar embodied in our law and in our history to say, "Yeah, we understand that you're really upset, and you still can't do it."

Heffner: Of course it's wonderful, until one takes exception to the title of your recent Elliot Lecture at Yale Law School, "Serious Injury, Serious Evil, and the First Amendment." You seem to be saying, as you follow Holmes and Brandeis, that if there is indeed demonstration of, proof of serious injury, serious evil, then the First Amendment may have to be reconsidered, not as an entity, but in terms of its immediate appropriateness to be brought into play. And you quote Brandeis here: "It is the function of speech to free men from the bondage of irrational fears. To justify suppression of free speech, there must be reasonable ground to fear that serious evil will result if free speech is practiced. There must be reasonable ground to believe that the danger apprehended is imminent." Well, there are more and more and more people, Floyd, who believe that there is "reasonable" ground. At some point, must not respect be paid to those conclusions that "reasonable" people feel that there is "reasonable" ground?

First, Dick, you have with your unerring eye picked out the one weakness in Justice Brandeis's opinion. That's the use of the word "reasonable." We've come a lot farther along the road of First Amendment protection since then. But the basic thrust of that is, in my view, quite correct. And what Justice Brandeis was saying was, "Look, be careful here. It's not enough that you are afraid of speech. It's not enough that you have some sense that serious harm will result. You really have to be quite sure that it will and that it will be imminent." And in the most famous line from that, one of the most famous of Supreme Court opinions, Justice Brandeis said, "Men feared witches and burned women." That's the sort of thing that I'm afraid of as Congress, with the support that you rightly point out of an increasing amount of the public, says, "Well, this is something we can do." And then the Attorney General comes in and weighs in, so far at least, along the side of saying, "Yes, I think you really can do that as a constitutional matter." And we're on the lip, as we meet right now, of some sort of legislation in which Congress is going to presume to tell broadcasters when they can broadcast what sort of material on television. And I find it very, very disturbing. That doesn't mean that there are no situations in which Congress can act about certain types of speech, you know, certain types of national security harm, certain types of truly imminent danger to the country. But we have nothing like that. Nothing.

Heffner: Well, of course we have nothing like that in your estimation. Imminent danger does not exist, as far as you are concerned.

Because of television? It is a joke, Dick, really. It is a joke to say that our country stands in imminent danger because of violence on television.

Heffner: You know, Floyd, you're so wonderful at smiling and saying that, that who could not believe . . .

Do you disagree with that? Do you really think that we are in imminent danger as a people?

Heffner: I disbelieve the notion that one can shrug all this off quite as easily as you do—and I accuse you of shrugging it off, okay? So what?

No, it's not so what.

Heffner: No, no, no. Wait a minute. Let me finish.

All right. All right.

Heffner: I'm not talking about television alone. I believe that there is a quality to our society that has been exacerbated by the violence in media. Maybe it's because I sit here every week, but I do believe that we may not be, as the kids used to say, "what we eat," but that we sure as hell are becoming very rapidly what we see and hear. And yes, I do believe in the power of the media. I do believe that you can have a society whose values are to some important extent not created, no, but to some considerable extent exacerbated by the media, yes.

And that's the classic argument against free speech. I mean, that's what it is. It's the, "If we let this thing go on, people will learn from it. Learn wrong things, learn dangerous things from it. So let's crack down." That was the argument against having public libraries in the first instance. That if we expose the masses to all of this stuff, they would do terrible things.

Heffner: I wish I could do what you do, to drag in public libraries and—

But I'm right.

Heffner: —make the comparison. No, you're wrong.

[Laughter]

Heffner: You're wrong, and you're so eloquent in doing it. You're more eloquent than those tobacco people who kept insisting there is no way of identifying the connection between cancer and tobacco, or heart disease and tobacco. Therefore, let's not take these enormous steps. Well, Floyd, I go along 1,000 percent with you that there'll never be a way of clearly identifying a connection between violence and the media and what happens in the streets.

And if there'll never be a way of doing that, my argument is that we ought to be awfully careful about starting down a road where the government tells the speakers out there, the broadcasters, the filmmakers, other people who write or compose or the like, that because even though we're not really sure that what you do does this terrible harm, we think it really might, so, you know what, we're going to err on the side of safety. That, more than anything, was the lesson that Justice Brandeis was opposing . . . in saying, in substance, that our devotion to freedom of expression involves risk taking. It involves all the risks of speech. And I would add to that, that what Congress is considering doing, what the Attorney General has so far said is constitutional, involves all the risks of suppression of speech.

Heffner: That's why I wish you were on the other side. I wish you were taking that great intelligence and putting it to bear on how we deal constitutionally with a risk. And I concede that it is just a risk, a potential, somthing that I feel and many others feel, but is not going to be proven. I wish that you were using your deep and profound concern, which I share, for free speech and for the First Amendment, not in that traditional absolutist Abrams way, but in a way that might help us out of this situation, because it seems to me maintaining the posture you're maintaining is going to lead only to slapping the wrists of media miscreants . . . and nothing will happen.

Well, I want to be really candid. I don't think we're in a situation in which, you know, we need fear that if we don't act today or tomorrow or soon or sometime, that the country will be the victim of some terrible harm because of what it is we're talking about. We have a violence epidemic in America. And in my view, to focus on television as the cause of, even as a major, as a serious cause of that, is simply a cop-out, to avoid dealing with problems we don't want to deal with, that we can't deal with, that are too expensive to deal with, that we've given up thinking we know how to deal with. And, you know, there'll be members of Congress who will vote a bill that might even pass in the courts. I'm not saying for sure that my views are going to be vindicated in the courts. I think they will be on this one. But they might not be. People get frightened enough, who knows what will happen?

Heffner: You make the point, eloquently as always, that there's probably no way of writing laws that could be effective in this region without doing damage to First Amendment provisions.

Yes. My point is that you either have to write a law where the language allows predictability, which is, for example, in some of the proposed laws, citing any act of overt hostility of one sort or another involving physical conduct between one person or one image and another, then I understand the problem is that it sweeps in most of the best of literature. Or you can have a law which says "no" to gratuitous violence. You can use adjectives to try to define what it is you don't want on television. Not violence, but violence that we think goes too far. And that, I would say, is by its nature vague in the sense that we don't want and don't allow our laws to be.

Heffner: What is going to happen, Floyd?

Right now I don't think that we're likely to have legislation immediately. There are negotiations which go on sometimes between broadcasters and the Congress. It may be that broadcasters will say some things and do some things which will satisfy Congress. It's sort of ironic, I think, that . . . Congress talks about violence at a time when there's probably less violence on broadcast television than any time in the last ten or twenty years. If you just check out primetime television on the networks, you have a significant diminution of the amount of violence that's on. That is not true of some cable channels, and it's not true as much of the independent stations. But I guess I don't think anything is going to happen short term . . . But I wouldn't be surprised if at some point we have legislation. And that's why we need a Supreme Court and the First Amendment. —1994

NORMAN PODHORETZ

Norman Podhoretz is one of several elder statesmen of Conservatism in America, others being men like William F. Buckley, Jr., and the Reagan White House favorite, Irving Kristol. Though the Podhoretz Conservative credentials are impeccable, it should be noted that he was more than a bit to the left early in his career as an author and editor. He was also a charter member of the New York intellectual elite, post–World War II generation, as a Columbia College graduate and long-term editor of Commentary *magazine. His memoir,* My Love Affair with America: The Cautionary Tale of a Cheerful Conservative, *had recently been published when we talked early in this new century. I asked about his use of the phrase "cautionary tale" in the book's subtitle.*

A cautionary tale is directed at some of my fellow Conservatives, friends, who in recent years began talking about this country in terms that were uncomfortably reminiscent of the terms that the Left-Wing radicals of the '60s did, and in fact, it was that kind of talk, the anti-American talk of the '60s that drove me out of the Left and into the Conservative position I've been rather happily occupying for the last 30 or more years. And then suddenly I discovered that my present group of friends, not all of them, but some significant ones, were beginning to talk about the illegitimacy of the American regime, about the possibility that civil disobedience might be called for. Some even said a revolution might be called for. Now the issues that were driving them were totally different from the issues that drove the radicals on the Left in the '60s, which were Vietnam and civil rights and so on. The issues driving the Conservatives of the late '90s were the use of power by the Supreme Court and some of the decisions that the court had made. And also, more immediately, the quite puzzling fact, that every time Bill Clinton told another lie, his approval ratings rose. It was just the opposite of Pinocchio's nose. So the phenomenon of Clinton's great popularity called into doubt one of the fundamental beliefs of contemporary American Conservatives, which is that while the elites, summarized by the national media, Hollywood, New York, the universities, might be against them, most of the American people were on their side. The locus classicus of this belief is a wonderful crack made by William F. Buckley, Jr., that he would rather be ruled by the first 2,000 names in the Boston phone book than by the combined faculties of Harvard and MIT. Well, suddenly it seemed as though the first 2,000 names in the Boston phone book were not fit to govern us—so it seemed to some of my friends. And I violently disagreed. Not necessarily with some of the particular judgments they were making, but with the attitude toward America that was arising out of these judgments. And so—seventy though I was and weary of battle, I donned, as I put it, my rusty old armor, reluctantly, and the aged eagle spread its wings—to steal a phrase from T. S. Eliot—and went into battle again in defense of America.

Only this time it was to be not a defensive defense, but an aggressive one. A wholehearted, full-throated assertion of the greatness of this country and of the institutions on which it is founded. And the cautionary note was aimed at my fellow Conservatives.

The "cheerful" Conservative, the adjective "cheerful" in the subtitle, refers to the fact that so many of my Conservative friends are glum. As Judge Robert Bork put it in a book of his, "we are slouching towards Gomorrah." That's a phrase he took and adapted from a poem "The Second Coming," in which W. B. Yeats referred to "what rough beast, its hour come round at last, slouches toward Bethlehem to be born." He was talking about the Second Coming of Christ. Bork was in effect hinting that we had already arrived at the place of evil, we had already gone to hell. I don't agree with this view at all. On the contrary.

There are other examples of what I'm talking about. I'm cheerful about the condition of America. And I'm cheerful about the future of America to the extent that I can foresee what is likely to happen out there. Though it's hard to predict next week, let alone next year.

Heffner: Back to Buckley's comment about those 2,000 people in the Boston phone book. What do you think has brought that about? Have they changed? Have the American people changed?

I think that the American people are rather more complicated than some of my friends believe or have imagined in the recent past. I ought to say, in all fairness, by the way, that most of them have backed down from the positions they were taking that provoked me into writing this book. I'm glad to say that because as you know my last book was called *Ex-Friends*, and I didn't want to make another set of ex-friends. I have nowhere to go from here. But I think that a lot of my current friends—I'm glad to say that they have not become ex-friends as a result of this book, had, well, you might call it a morally romanticized view of the American people.

Heffner: You said that about yourself as a younger man.

I did indeed, and I talked about my Utopianism as a younger man. They're not Utopians, the Conservatives I'm talking about. It's a slightly different mind-set. No, what I actually think is that they fail to take into account the complexity of sentiment. This is a very big country and there are a lot of things going on all the time, swirling around, many in contradiction with one another. Say one thing—others seem to say the opposite and people seem to be able to live comfortably with these contradictions. Walt Whitman, you know, once said, "Do I contradict myself? Very well then I contradict myself, (I am large, I contain multitudes)." Well the American multitudes contain contradictions. And I think that some of these complexities which are reflected very much in the culture around us and the polity, were ignored by many of my friends who put too much emphasis on one side of the whole bag of elements rather than looking at the entirety.

Heffner: What are we going to do with your broadness of scope, with your ability to accept and embrace?

Well, I'm glad that you think I'm broad. I wish more of my critics shared your view.

Heffner: Well, you've accepted many positions.

In a way, I always did. I mean, I'm idiosyncratic in that sense. Even when I was a radical of the Left, as I explain in *My Love Affair with America,* I loved this country. And as I discovered, many of my fellow radicals not only did not love this country, they hated it. And made no bones about that. Many of them now deny that they ever felt that way. But it was not for nothing that so many of them spelled America with a K to suggest an association with Nazi Germany. And it was not for nothing that so many of them said that the country was so rotten that nothing but a revolution could save it. You know no reforms could do any good. I was always uneasy and finally revolted by this attitude toward America. And, so again in one sense there's a consistent thread in my own point of view, certainly with respect to the nature of this country. And it's odd that the nature of this country should be an issue . . . it's America as a sort of ideological issue. Is it a good thing or a bad thing that there is such a place? You know, does it set a good example or a bad example? Is it a force for good or a force for evil? Both within, to its own people and to people outside the world?

This is an argument that's been raging practically since the birth of the republic. And the other curious feature of this argument is that [it's] unlike every other country of the world [where] Conservatives tend to be very patriotic and even aggressively nationalistic. Patria— pro patria is the essence of conservatism all over Europe, everywhere. Whereas in this country, at least since the Civil War, not so much before it, you've had a tradition of conservatism that was and I make no bones about using the term—anti-American. I don't say "un-American," I say anti-American. That is the figure I always single out as the sort of quintessential embodiment of this tradition—[was] Henry Adams, who was the the grandson and great-grandson of two American Presidents, and [he was] a great historian in his own right, who came to loathe this country with a ferocity that is almost hard to take, to believe, unless you actually see the words he uses, especially in his private correspondence, about this place in which he was born and to which he had such a deep and strong attachment.

Heffner: But now you're saying that his counterparts today have begun to have similar feelings about this nation.

Well, very few of them are as virulent as Henry Adams was. But I think that it is true that a number of Conservatives had a kind of fever a few years ago of, almost an infection of anti-American feeling, and though that has subsided I worried about it very much at that time. I'm a little less worried about it now because unlike so many of the Leftists, my Conservative friends have actually responded to criticism. I mean some of them have bethought themselves in fact, when it was pointed out to them, "Do you hear what you're saying?" And they didn't like some of what they were saying themselves. But the tradition is alive.

Heffner: Of anti-Americanism? Do you see these people as becoming radical and trying to bring you with them? . . . Is that why you wrote, "I did not become a Conservative in order to become a radical, let alone to support the preaching of revolution against this country . . ."

That quote came from a letter I wrote to Father Richard John Neuhaus, who was a friend of mine and the editor of *First Things*, a journal of religion and public life. He had run a symposium in the magazine called "The End of Democracy?" in which some of the ideas that I described earlier were expressed quite forcefully by people like Judge Bork, Charles Colson, who is a born-again Christian, and Richard Neuhaus, himself, as well as couple of other Catholic contributors. And it was about that symposium that I wrote Neuhaus a letter. And his response was that I had misinterpreted the symposium. Well, I don't think I did misinterpret it. But I found that his own interpretation of what he himself, and the others had said was a lot milder than what I found on paper. That's why I say they back down a bit.

Heffner: You mean the matter of looking back at what they've said, and saying "this isn't what we meant."

"That's not what I meant, that's not what I meant at all." Well, they may not have meant it, but they said it. And, and I thought it was dangerous for them to be saying things of this kind. And I felt that it was my duty even at the risk of making a new set of ex-friends, to tell them so in no uncertain terms. And I did. And then I wrote this book, *My Love Affair with America*, in which I tried to combine, as I have in other books, elements of memoir or autobiography with social criticism and cultural history. It's a kind of peculiar mélange in which I feel comfortable. And the point was to say that the American, and this country, represents one of the highest points of human civilization known to history. That's a very strong statement. And I tried to, I used my own story as a way of making the abstract proposition more vivid and concrete, but I also write a good deal about the history of some of the ideas and attitudes that I'm trying to analyze and criticize. And finally I try to make the case for this very, very positive judgment of the United States. That is, I put it up there with fifth-century Athens and Elizabethan England and Renaissance Italy as a great, as a high point of human achievement.

Heffner: You and Victor Navasky, another old friend, participated recently in an exchange in the *New York Times,* titled "Debating How Best to Love Your Country." And I wanted to ask you about this exchange in which Navasky, the publisher now of *The Nation* magazine said, "My definition of patriotism would involve fighting to make sure your country lives up to its highest ideals." And you had the opportunity, a moment later to say, "I would like to take issue with the definition that Victor is offering. To define American patriotism as struggling to make the country live up to its best ideals has in practice generally meant denigrating the country for not doing so. The ideal is very often the enemy of the real." Why would you say the ideal is very often the enemy of the real?

I say it because it's true. Just as it's often said, "the best is the enemy of the good." People who are intoxicated with the ideal, we sometimes call Utopians. The word "utopia" is a Greek word, it means nowhere. And there is a very ancient tradition of fantasies about some place that doesn't actually exist, but that is perfect, depending upon the author's or the imaginer's idea of what perfection consists of. And the real world, which of course is imperfect, and always is imperfect and always will be imperfect, is invidiously contrasted with this Utopia that is conjured up by some author or other, or some fantasist or other. Now, many of us are subject to the Utopian temptation. I have been subject to it. I was seized by Utopian fevers around 1960. This led me into a period of what I describe as "infidelity" in my love affair with America or, if you like, my marriage to America. But as sometimes happens in love affairs or marriages, this period of infidelity ended with the relations strengthened rather than weakened. My view is that it is one thing to try to make life better. And we have an obligation to do that. You might even say we have a religious obligation to do that, if you happen to be religious. But at the same time I think it is incumbent upon us to be cognizant of what blessings are available or accessible in the real. And it is incumbent upon us to be grateful for those blessings. Incumbent in the sense that it is spiritually necessary to a healthy soul. And not to mention intellectually honest when such blessings exist. In actuality, the so-called idealism of certain movements has gone hand in hand with a virulent attack on what is sometimes called the "status quo" or "the system," which tends then to get generalized into the nature of the country as a whole and leads to outbursts of anti-Americanism. As happened most recently in the 1960s on the Left.

Heffner: But must this be the case when there is a wrong, when you see what is an evil within your country?

No.

Heffner: Do you not want to correct it?

Yes, I do. I said I thought it was an obligation to do so and to try to do so. But there's the question of the spirit in which such an effort is undertaken. If it's undertaken—as corny as this may sound—with love, that is with a genuine desire to improve what is, or to rectify a wrong, if that's the spirit in which it's undertaken, you have one kind of phenomenon. If the spirit in which it's undertaken is destructive and full of hostility, you have something else again. Let me give you a homely example that I may have even used in my argument with Victor Navasky at the *Times.* You know there are people who say, "Well, I love my wife, or I would love my wife if only she were perfect. If she were perfect, I would love her. But so long as she's not perfect, I'm going to hector her, badger her, bring her to court, maybe even beat her up, and until she sees the light, I will continue harassing her in this way. And then someday perhaps she will become perfect, and then I will be able to love her." And, you know, I don't think that's such a bad analogy. I also said to Victor Navasky, and what I believe. I do not see how you can say it is more patriotic to burn the flag than to wrap yourself in it, which is what some people claimed. What he claimed, actually. So, you're talking here partly about the spirit in which reform is undertaken. You're talking here about the—to put it bluntly, the honesty of the case that's being made. In other words, some people pretend to be for reform when they are, in fact, for revolution or for undermining the entire system.

Heffner: So where would you put the Civil Rights Movement of the sixties?

Well, I think the Civil Rights Movement has to be divided into various phases. The early Civil Rights Movement, starting not in the sixties, but in fifties. I would put that movement very high on the list of noble political endeavors in the history of this country. And that very much included the spirit with which it was infused, which was a spirit of love and nonviolence. And the objective was for people who had been illegally, as well as unjustly, excluded from American life, from the centers of American life, it was an effort that they made on their own behalf to be included. Later, in the mid-sixties, you had a new movement arising, which rebelled against this entire phase of the Civil Rights Movement. It came out of the tradition of black nationalism. It called itself Black Power. It was not integrationist, that is it wasn't seeking to be included, but was separating itself from the country. It was defaming the country, it was saying the country was so infested with racism that there was no hope for any justice within the so-called system. That it had to be smashed or replaced. That violence would be necessary. "Pick up the gun" was one of the slogans. And you had the irony of an organization which was called the Student Non-Violent Coordinating Committee, becoming an advocate of violence some ten years later.

Heffner: But do you think if there had not been those episodes of violence, if the cities hadn't been burning, that the right kinds of steps would have been taken anyway to correct the evils that the Civil Rights Movement was designed to correct?

Well, I not only think so, but I think that the wrong steps were taken in response to the violence—wrong steps meaning the adoption of a system of reverse discrimination, or preferential treatment that people euphemistically called "affirmative action." This was profoundly, profoundly antithetical to the American tradition, this idea of treating people as members of a group, rather than as individuals. And it was out of the panic that seized what the black radicals themselves called the white power structure that this whole approach was born, adopted. I think it's caused a lot of damage to this country, I do not agree with people who think that it has been beneficial to its intended beneficiaries. I think it's injected a new kind of poison into the relations between the races, and that it has undermined the feelings of pride and achievement that might otherwise have been felt by some of its intended beneficiaries. I think it's undermined a system that I deeply believe in, that is the merit system. I think it's helped to dilute and lower standards of achievement in various areas.

Heffner: Do you think, though, that there was anything to the question that Martin Luther King asked in his letter from prison, his letter to the ministers. "How can I tell my child—'wait.' How can I tell my child to wait for justice, wait to be treated as you need to be treated"—for another generation.

It was a good question, and I don't have the answer to that question. But I don't think Martin Luther King can be cited as someone who supported these changes in the Civil Rights Movement that I deplore. I mean, you don't know what somebody would have done had he lived. But we do know that Bayard Rustin, who was one of his chief disciples and the architect of the 1965 March on Washington was strongly opposed to the turn that was taken by the Civil Rights Movement after 1965. It no longer was a Civil Rights Movement. It was something else. And it had lost the nobility that we associated with it under King's leadership and the leadership of some other people like King. So, you know, this is the kind of argument that's impossible to resolve in a brief discussion

Heffner: It's not an argument, it's a question, a question about your feelings about these things.

Well, my feelings—as I say, my feeling is that more harm than good was done by the turn that was taken in the mid-sixties in this area. That's my feeling, yes.

Heffner: And you . . . would you apply this thinking to other great social problems, the assumption that one waits and hopes and uses love?

No. It depends, it depends on the context and it depends on the problem. Look, let me try to put it in another way. This country, which has been highly heterogeneous, ethnically, racially, religiously for at least—well, from the beginning, but even more so since the Civil War and since the millions of immigrants came pouring in from Southern and Eastern Europe—Italians, Jews, Germans, you know, all kinds of people. It developed a way of dealing with this problem, a problem incidentally that has led to the shedding of a great deal of blood in other countries. Well, most recently we saw it in Yugoslavia and ex-Yugoslavia. The English have terrible trouble with this problem, because they're not used to it, they were a homogeneous society for most of their history. Well, we had developed various methods by which to, as we used to say, "Americanize the immigrants."

Today, you'd say, "bring them into the middle class, create upward mobility"—however you wish to put it. Nobody sat down and devised it as a plan. You know, a ten-point plan. But, it emerged and it had various instrumentalities. The public schools, as I wrote in detail in my *My Love Affair with America,* were a major instrument. But the basic idea was the Constitutional principle of treating individuals as individuals without regard to race, creed, color, country of national origin. That used to be the Liberal catechism. Now, of course, it was violated in practice very often. But in principle, as Gunnar Myrdahl pointed out a long time ago, it had, because the principle was announced, it had and was bound to have enormous influence and practice, as indeed it did.

Well, it was working, it had worked for millions of other people, it was not working as well for blacks, for a variety of reasons about which a thousand, ten thousand books have been written by now. But it was in fact beginning to take hold among blacks, as it had among other groups. And what we did, as a nation, in the late sixties was to simply turn our backs on, "discard" that system which had worked wonders.
—2000

NICHOLAS LEMANN

Nicholas Lemann is not only the new Dean of Columbia University's distinguished Graduate School of Journalism, he is one of the famed American breed of "new journalists." His progenitors were the likes of Gay Talese, Hunter Thompson, and Tom Wolfe. While perhaps more sedate as a stylist than those earlier reporter/writers, his concern with various aspects of American culture are no less intense, ranging from Washington politics to the seemingly mundane issues involved with the world of educational testing. In our conversation in late 1999, on the heels of his book, The Big Test, *Lemann described the various tests—SATs, Regents, etc., the bane of all secondary school students' lives—as a very consciously developed form of social engineering, with enormous implications for American society and culture. I asked him about those implications.*

There's a kind of SAT and university-generated elite sitting at the top of society running everything. Several books share the idea that there's a new elite; it has all the economic, political, cultural, social power and everybody else is being left behind. I've thought about that a lot. My own book is really a history of how that elite was created. But I think of the country as being more complicated. The people I've been talking about, this elite, I call the Mandarins. And as a kind of pretty serious parlor game—in my book and elsewhere—I have divided the country into three success groups. And those would be Mandarins, these are the test-takers, university-educated professionals. Talents—people who just kind of go out and do whatever they do. They don't need any particular credential. You know, small-business people, big-business people if they started the business, entertainers—people like that. And, finally, Lifers who are people who go to work for big organizations and spend a long time and kind of rise up to the top. So, my theory is that there are three groups—Mandarins, Talents and Lifers. They're distinct from one another. They compete with each other to run the country. Each controls some territory. I don't think that the Mandarins run everything. All of America is potential Mandarin territory, which is a good thing. I don't think it would make this a better country if it were all Mandarin territory, which is what the founders of the system, you know, wanted and hoped for. I would like to keep the Mandarin track small and focused and keep a more unstructured form of opportunity the "norm" in this country. I don't know exactly how much turf the Mandarins control, but to the extent that it seems to be increasing, I'd like to ratchet it back. . . .

Heffner: But you say "increasing." Are you so sure about that?

It's actually a big debate right now. It's pretty complicated. Let me divide it into political and economic spheres. Politically, the Mandarins were created almost in a test-tube laboratory so that they could assume political power. The people who built this system assumed that its products would be, you know, Plato-style philosopher/king/statesman types. They, the Mandarins never really gained political power and, if anything, I think their political power is decreasing now. It looked, at the beginning of this decade [the 1990s], as if the moment had arrived because the Clintons had taken power. They were the first Mandarins to come to the Presidency. And then there were all these other sort of SAT and Admissions characters around them, like [Robert] Reich and Ira Magaziner and others. There was a feeling in this class that, you know, their moment had arrived. But my position is that they didn't successfully establish themselves as the political power in the country. And, indeed, they're more important politically as an object of populist resentment then as the rulers. So that's on the political side.

However, on the economic side, I think the Mandarin space is increasing. In other words, one of the ironies of all this is a system set up to generate political leaders is viewed by the American people, as a system for handing out economic rewards. So, even as the system has failed in a sense, if its job is to produce a political leadership group, its succeeded enormously in being perceived as the gateway to getting through to the goodies in America. So that's why you have 25,000 people applying for 1,500 places at Harvard and all these other elite schools. That's why every time you get in the New York subway, there's a prep course ad saying essentially, "If you take our course, we will guarantee that you will be rich and successful." So the system is seen as a route to economic success, and I think it turned out to be a route to economic success. Not all types of economic success, but it tracks into a type of economic success, and, in that sense, it's expanding, I think. So political contraction, economic expansion.

Heffner: But let me go back and ask you for your evaluation of those at the beginning who wanted *The Big Test* to do the right thing, presumably—Henry Chauncey, James Conant and others.

Well . . . All these people were idealists. I don't agree with all of their ideals, but they were all idealists and it should be said that when this system was started, it was not started in a kind of open way, with public debate. It was started privately. These were all establishmentarians.

Heffner: And that bothers you, doesn't it?

That bothers me, yes.

Heffner: Why?

It's too important to do something this big without public discussion. It affects too many people.

Heffner: How would it have been discussed? How could it have been discussed? Seriously. I mean it's one thing to say, "They did this themselves. They did it behind their own closed doors." But how could it have been otherwise?

Well, you know, we're playing historical "what if" here.

Heffner: Right.

And it's very easy to play. You could say the Educational Testing Service, rather than being a private, non-profit organization, should be a government agency, as the national testing operations are in most advanced countries. It performs a public function, it allocates opportunity. It slots people into institutions that are either government-owned, like public universities, or heavily government-financed, like private universities. And therefore, it should be a government agency. So let's have a piece of legislation, let's set up this agency, and then have a debate on it, just as when the Civil Rights Act was passed. That's my model for how to have a national conversation. A bill is written, the country goes insane talking about it, but by the end something passes. Compromises have been made, but there's a kind of consensus reached on what the organization and its goals should be.

Heffner: Do you think at any point this country would have been prepared to deal with the question of an elite? That we would have admitted to ourselves what the elite was in this country? That we had a Mandarin group?

I'm not sure. But I don't think that would necessarily be a bad thing either. I'm not a great believer in the whole prospect of having kind of an engineered elite selection ... During the 1930s and 1940s, there was a fight between two ideas about education and opportunity in America. One idea, which was the idea of the people who started ETS, like Conant, was this very elite top-down idea based on intelligence testing. It was that colleges should be small, should serve four or five percent of the population, people carefully picked, probably on the basis of their mental test scores, and slotted for leadership, or picked for elite status. So that's one camp. The other camp—the camp that lost in the fight over starting ETS at least, is the expansion camp. These people's vision was (you know Truman appointed a commission on higher education in the late forties, and this is what its report said, even as they were losing in real life), "Let's just expand higher education. Let's make it big, with relatively open admissions, let's not have any selection tests or very minimal selection tests. Instead, let's have placement tests and let's not use the education system to pick an elite. Instead, let's use it to just try to equip as many Americans as possible with both a Liberal Arts education and specific work skills, then let the chips fall where they may." And I find that idea much more attractive. So had the whole system been decided legislatively, where it would have come out, I suspect, would have been more along the lines of the Presidential report that came out in 1948. Less along the lines of the Educational Testing Service regime that was established at the same time.

Heffner: And what do you think the result would have been?

There would have been a lot of results. You would have had less of a big fight over affirmative action than you have now. That's one thing. And you would have had a less distinct kind of Mandarin class of the kind that I talk about, for good and for ill. They would have been less of a sort of fortunate group in the society, but they would have been less controversial and less of a target also. I suspect that the elite universities would have retained more of their sort of "old preppie" tone, which probably is a bad thing. So that the good side of this whole revolution is the change in the elite universities from preppie domination, or what I call . . . "the episcopacies domination," to domination by a kind of academically chosen group. If you had to choose between those two, I'd choose the side that won.

Heffner: Well you're clear on that point . . . But do you think we can ever move away from that? Do you think there's any possibility that at this stage of this nation's life we can move away from judging by the numbers?

Well, I'm going to give you a sort of qualified answer. I do think, you know, Pandora's box is open. . . . It would be very hard to go from the situation we're in now to life without tests. And I'm not for that. I hope if we can get to a more sophisticated understanding of tests, to where the debate goes beyond tests, pro or con, to what kind of tests, what they measure and how they're used. . . . And once you go to that place, you see that, within the word test many, many, many things can be done. In other words, just to give you a couple of examples, the SAT is an aptitude test that is meant for selection. In other words, what it originally is supposed to do and to some extent does do is say, "We're looking for 1,000 kids or

10,000 kids every year who score very high on this test, not because of what they learned in school, but because of something that's already in their brains. We're going to whisk them out of the school system and send them to elite universities on scholarship." So that's what the SAT does. At the other end of spectrum you have a test like NAEP . . . the National Assessment of Educational Progress, also an ETS test. It's given in public schools in America, it's given to a sample of students, there are no consequences for the students of the test score—it's a random sample. The only purpose of that test score is to tell whether the schools in the state are doing a good job of teaching their students. So it's a test for a completely different purpose which is to improve the quality of public education. The SAT is specifically not designed to address the quality of public education. So one is a test I feel much more warmly toward than the other. Another point that's just sort of a general point about tests is, there's a cart and horse issue. Very often, and certainly in the case of the SAT and many other tests, what you have is some outside force requiring a test of all students. And the test lands like a flying saucer and everybody says, "Oh my gosh, here's this test and it has huge consequences and now let's all adjust what we do in our lives and in our schools in order to try to produce higher scores on this test." That's putting the cart before the horse. What we should be doing instead is saying, "First, let's decide what we want our schools to do, what we want our society to look like." And then once we've decided that, and what we want to teach kids, then let's design the test. Let's design the test after making those decisions. Instead of reverse-engineering life to meet tests that are handed down from outside.

Heffner: And as the father of two sons, how do you conduct yourself in relation to the phenomenon of tests?

Well, I divide the issue into three categories. They take ETS tests that we've talked about, and they take state-mandated tests. All sorts of things. And here's what I do, since there are tests and then there are tests. The test I like the best for my kids is the New York State Regents. And the reason I like the New York State Regents is that the message to the kid is that you start in the Regents course, and at the end of the year you will be given a Regents exam. There are no secrets about what's on this exam. It's a curriculum-based test on whether you learned the stuff in the course. So, for example, I say to my son, "You know you've got a Regents exam at the end of year. You know what you should do, knowing you have that? Study your biology and learn the stuff." And he does. It's a really good system. It motivates the kid to study and learn and it's also a way of measuring whether the school is performing on a state standard. So I like that test. As to the SAT, I tell my kids, "Don't study or prepare in any way, and let's just take the test and see what happens." And if you get a high score we'll never worry about it again. And if you get a low score, then we'll plan our next move. But I don't want to start with the obsession. I only want to obsess if there is a reason to obsess. And the final kinds of tests are state reading tests and the state skills test. There, my objection is that the state picks a test. They buy off the shelf from the test publisher, then they announce to the local schools, "This is going to be the test." And then everything is distorted because the school starts teaching to the test. And what the kids do in elementary school becomes "test prep" for whatever tests the state decided to pick.

Heffner: But isn't that very much like your approach to the Regents?

No. Because the Regents is the cart and horse point. This is the key point. With the Regents and what I'd like to see happen with the reading test is, first you decide what your curriculum is, then you design the test to be a test of the curriculum. With the state reading tests, both the old one and the new one, it's the opposite. First, they buy a test from a commercial test publisher. Then, what happens under the school roof changes to produce a higher score on the test.

Heffner: So the commercial test publisher becomes the Board of Regents.

Right. Exactly. . . . I think there should be a state reading test in the third grade or the fourth grade . . . I'm all for that because you're really "out of town" in America if you don't know how to read. And we need to make sure schools are teaching kids to read. But I say, "First develop a state reading curriculum, then develop the test." And that way you will not have literally a separate course in many schools, a test prep for the reading test. Now that's bad.

Heffner: Still, the trouble is that you live by the numbers.

Yes, you live by the numbers, but we don't end up after many years, with just saying "Well let's just not have tests." Instead I want to have a more fine-grained debate and say, "Let's have the right kinds of tests, instead of the wrong kinds of tests." —1999

DAVID BROWN

David Brown has been a major Hollywood presence for decades, first as a studio executive, later as a producer. On his own or with partners, he has been responsible for films such as Cocoon, The Sting, The Verdict, Patton, Driving Miss Daisy, Chocolat, *and, most notably and profitably,* Jaws. *Earlier in his career, he was a successful magazine editor and writer, so that the writing of books came naturally when, during the 1980s, he decided to enjoy a hiatus from filmmaking with an autobiographical account,* Let Me Entertain You, *followed by the equally engaging* Brown's Guide to Growing Gray. *About the latter, I recalled that its number one point is "Don't retire." I asked him why not?*

Well, because when you retire, you accentuate the dying process. And when you work, at whatever you like, whatever you like to do most, if you're fortunate enough to do that, you perpetuate living. You go on living. The ideal thing is to work until you die, it's the best way to live.

Heffner: What happens to the people who don't continue to work?

They die before their death. I've seen them all. I've seen their vacant look. I know there are a lot of people out there who say, "I've been working all my life, now I want to take off and retire for a while," but I don't think they're telling the truth. I think all of them would like to be involved. All of them would like to be reeled back into the real world.

Heffner: But, David, you know, a decade ago, a quarter century ago, the emphasis was upon getting people to phase down, to phase out, to get ready for retirement, to plan the ways they were going to vacation, the places they hadn't been to, etc. What's happened?

Well, what's happened is that it's a great growth industry. I mean photographs of babies now, with their retirement age being calculated by some of our insurance companies. And I think it's wrong. I think it's a cheerful con game that America's played on people saying, "You work so that you can have a happy retirement." I'm not for a happy retirement. I've never known a happy retirement. And I'm not a workaholic.

Heffner: So what are some of the themes of growing old that you took on? What's important to consider, rethink?

Well, in all cases, the work theme is the pervasive theme. And in order to work successfully, you have to have some kind of a life. I don't believe in people who just live for work . . .

Heffner: But you talk here about "the end" and you quote Dylan Thomas: "Do not go gentle into that good night. Old age should burn and rave at close of day. Rage, rage against the dying of the light." But you're not a raging kind of person.

No, not at all.

Heffner: How do you interpret that? What do you make of it? What do you do with it?

I make of that having a fighting spirit. Really wanting to live, wanting to live in the full sense, in every sense. That—it isn't rage so much, but a determination, a zest for life.

Heffner: Can you find that thing in your life, if you don't already have it? Teachers, for instance, presumably, are born, rather than made; so how do you find what to fight for?

If one person's absolute experience in life is of any use to another person, it can work. You're looking at an almost pathetically shy individual. Somebody whose knees knocked when he had to make a speech in college on a stage; someone who would flee rather than be surrounded by a lot of people. To this day I'm extremely shy, except when that red light of the TV camera is on. And I say, "Yes, I am an example of a kind of a misanthrope, kind of a—what they now call a "nerd." I was a nerd and I got out of it by looking at role models, by studying other people. I didn't have a strong parental background or any of that stuff. The answer is, resoundingly, you can improve your life, your mental posture, and everything else. Yes, you can go raging if you wish, but by following my rules, following what I perceive to be a universal truth, you can change yourself.

Heffner: I was very interested in what you wrote about the role of depression. You said that your wonderful wife Helen Gurley Brown had told you, when you said you were going to write about getting over depression, that she thought you were probably very well qualified in certain ways to do just that. You had met the problem. Why do you write about depression?

Because depression is endemic in our lives and particularly in the lives of older people. From my early fifties, the first intimations of mortality came into my life. I began to lie awake nights and said, "Hey, I'm past the half-century mark. My life is more than half over, probably two-thirds over by all actuarial statistics." And I got depressed. And I get depressed at so many things. The only cure for depression is maniacal activity and—for me—work. Work is the greatest therapy.

Heffner: What other roles does work play as you see it in this aging process?

. . . The other roles of work have to do with interpersonal relationships, the workplace is the place you meet people, it's your extended family. You spend often as much time or more time in the workplace than you do at home. Heaven help you if those hours and days aren't good. You're in your family, if you're in a happy workplace. And if you're not, get out. Find something else.

Heffner: Aside from "Dont retire, continue to work," what are the most important practical matters that you would put to those of us who are getting on in years?

I have a chapter, somewhat combustible, called "Let a Woman In Your Life, Preferably More Than One." Now, lest you leap to the conclusion that this doesn't have a high moral tone, let me suggest that hypocrisy is the lowest moral tone and some of my suggestions there have to do with making friends of women. We're living in an increasingly nonsexist society, I hope, and women are out there. Some romances may take place. Someone once said, "Life happens when we're making plans." No one knows what those relationships will do.

Heffner: You really feel strongly about that, the importance of the exchange between the sexes.

I feel very strongly that the feelings should exist. I don't believe in a cutoff of feelings. I believe that men and women should be attracted to each other ad infinitum, but I don't believe that one should go around shucking off responsibilities and leaving a lot of people around whom you've abandoned . . . I believe that the sexual urge is a very strong, life-sustaining one. And it goes on for all of your life, unless you permit yourself to be cut off from it. And society has this cutoff. They're trying to tell us we're old and we're not supposed to feel that way. Well, check a few retirement homes, you'll be surprised.

Heffner: You won't accept the notion that we're not supposed to be that way, right?

I would accept the notion that we are what we are. And I believe that many of our attitudes have been the result of society's own brain-washing. We are pretty solid physically for a long, long time. I quote some medical people on that. Until ultimate senescence, the body moves. We do live on reduced brain cells, but those that are left do a wonderful job of keeping us going. —1987

OLIVER STONE

Film director Oliver Stone's JFK *had been in release only a few weeks before our conversation. But already—indeed, even months before his brilliant film was completed—his critics had us see Mr. Stone only as a subversive distorter and devaluer of our history as record. A modern-day Socrates comes to mind, too, if you will, subverting the Establishment with incredible skill and power, always urging our young to question, to doubt, to distrust accepted wisdom about our national past—this time, with the murder of our young President as a particularly bitter case in point.*

Indeed, the extreme and seemingly endless press attacks upon Mr. Stone lacked only the hemlock to signal his critics' determination to mute his message, to counter the doubts Stone's film raises about the Warren Commission's single-assassin theory with doubts about the filmmaker himself. Writ so compellingly large on film, his speculations were clearly anathema to those who themselves created, or at least embraced or repeated in the press, the official version of Dallas, November 1963.

I wondered about whether the Lords of Print feared and deplored the very skills of this celluloid Pied Piper because, finally, they would otherwise also have to recognize and concede the power that they themselves have so long wielded: the power to create the past in their own imagery—as Oliver Stone did in his. Demanding responsible use of his medium might, perhaps, command more responsible use of theirs. What did he think?

I think that the journalists' community failed in 1963 to examine in detail all the discrepancies that became apparent in the following year when the Warren Commission Report was released. I think that they accepted the cover story that Oswald did it alone a little too readily. And I would think that if we had been a little less naive, I guess, the press, at that point in time—these are men, after all, who had been in who had lived through the 1930s, and the 1920s, when there were coup d'états, when there were world revolutions—these people I think really missed the boat. They didn't look inside their own country because they didn't think it could happen here in America, that a President could be killed by his own government, or by a coup d'état.

Heffner: But it can happen here and these are men now still writing, and writing about your film in a . . . in a very negative fashion. They weren't "true believers." Why were they taken in by the cover story?

You're asking me a very, very difficult question. It was certainly a good cover story, because Oswald had [a] biography that was immediately available. They had the Russia business, this man had been there—I think he had a profile as a Communist in Russia, he had one in New Orleans, and he had one in Dallas, as a Communist. Subsequent investigation has revealed that in New Orleans, on the contrary, he seemed to have been used by an anti-Communist group. He was given a profile as an anti-Communist but, at that point in time, what was quickly available to us was a picture of a solitary, lone-nut Marxist. And as we now know, he wasn't even a very good marksman. No one at that point questioned: "how could he have done the shooting job that he did?." As you know, the FBI tried, with Olympic caliber marksmen, to match his shooting feat and failed.

Heffner: Well, you suggest that the press people missed the boat, to use your expression. How do we explain it? Was it that Camelot had dazzled them and they didn't want to besmirch it? Was it that they didn't want to dig into the Kennedy past? What was it that led them to be so much less critical than journalists are today?

There are so many questions and answers in connection with that. We didn't question the CIA in the 1960s. The CIA was looked upon as a heroic organization. For somebody like Jim Garrison in New Orleans to come out and say that the government killed its own leader was shocking and horrifying. And the press turned on Garrison with all its power and destroyed his credibility. Dan Rather was under a spell, it seems, when he saw the Zapruder film two days or a day after the assassination; he described President Kennedy as being propelled violently forward when he was hit. How blind could he be? Is such the power of the sort of the event that Oswald was presented to us hours after that killing as a fait accompli, and we bought into it because we had to believe that one person was responsible for this tragedy, like a car accident. And then, of course, [Oswald's] being killed two days later was an extremely convenient historical exercise. The *New York Times* headline on that day said, "The Assassin of the President Was Killed." They didn't even say the "alleged" assassin of the President was killed by Jack Ruby, they said, "the assassin." So, right away, because of the fact that Oswald was killed immediately, it was perfect. It fell into place.

Heffner: Now how do you feel about the fact that there are so many who make of you the historian of this period? Do you want to be that?

Hardly. I'm not a historian in the sense of having all the facts. I don't. I admit to that, and I have constantly said that from the beginning. I've been attacked for it. I only have certain facts and the rest is speculation. I called the film a 'counter-myth.' It's essentially a hypothesis made of fact and speculation. I've been faulted again and again for not having more facts, and my response to that is, "Then let's unlock all the files we can get our hands on, including the House files on the assassination, the CIA files, the FBI files, the Office of Naval Intelligence files, and the Army Intelligence files." Let's get them out and then maybe I can have more facts, and we all can have more facts with which we can intelligently deal. No one will not deal with that issue. Nor will they deal with the discrepancies that my film raises. All they do is attack me for speculating. At the same time, they don't deal with the discrepancies that we show in the Warren Commission Report. Such as: How did Oswald get the job at the Book Depository? Who was Ruth Payne? Why is Margaret Oswald, two days after her son's arrest, saying that her son is working for American intelligence? How does he get into Russia and out of Russia, and does not get debriefed, although 25,000 American tourists are debriefed coming back from the Soviet Union? There are at least two dozen of these questions, questions that no one in the press has dealt with.

Heffner: But now how do you deal with the criticism that you are such a master of celluloid that you have become, literally, a Pied Piper, that your skills as a filmmaker take what you call speculation and make it, for millions and millions and millions of people, particularly younger people, a fact. If not a fact, something much, much stronger than a speculation. How do you deal with that?

As a criticism, that I'm not selling the movie as a fact.

Heffner: No, no, no. I understand that. How do you deal though with the criticism that says, "Look, this fellow Stone has made this superb film that he is now wielding as a weapon, using a medium that doesn't deal only with facts, but deals with speculation in a dangerous way."

Oh, I think that's nonsense. I think the average moviegoer, who sees a few movies a year, knows that it's a movie and, and realizes where I'm speculating. Where I am speculating is very clear. The dialogue says, "What if? Maybe possibly?" Jim Garrison in the courtroom says, "Let's speculate on what happened that day in Dealey Plaza." The viewer is not unintelligent, and can see the difference between what is fact and what is speculation—in my opinion.

Heffner: Look, I love your film. I think it's magnificent, but I wonder if you really mean that the average moviegoer can distinguish between what they see in your films, and what they then come to believe is reality. They've had no other exposure to this material.

Listen, my critics have had 28 years to sell the American public on the "Oswald-did-it-alone" mantra. Which they've done. The newspapers, the Warren Commission, TV, have told us for 28 years that Oswald did it alone. And the American people were not brainwashed by that. That's interesting—that they resisted it. They didn't believe it in 1964, the polls show they didn't buy it. And as the years have progressed, there have been fewer and fewer people—11 percent was the last quote I got that believed that Oswald did it alone. In a *Times*/CNN poll, 75 percent believed there was a conspiracy, 50 percent believed the CIA did it, and 18 percent believed the military did it. If you realize that the CIA and the military are not necessarily disassociative that they could work together, you have 68 percent of the American people saying that the American government killed its own leader. That's a pretty signifi-cant belief that, or let's say "undermining" of the priesthood's, the media priesthood's belief that Oswald did it alone. It also goes very far towards really saying that our government is far less trusted by the American public than heretofore.

Heffner: You and I know that. You and I know that with the assassi-nation and then Watergate and then the other assassinations, and so many other things that you can tick off, our government is not believed. Do you believe that our government—you say "put together the mili-tary and the FBI and the CIA"—that they killed the President?

I'm saying, well, what the movie says, is that there are elements in the government that did it. And, you know, we're not that precise. The one area where we deal with it a little more specifically is where the Donald Sutherland character talks about it, and he does say, "It is a conspiracy with no face." There is nothing on paper, everyone has a plausible deniability, and he points to a possibility where one phone call, he says, "Only at the most secret point, only at the most secret point is there a connection made." And that is the phone call from a higher up, let's say an Allen Dulles type who goes to a mid-range technician—we show that on film that technician puts into operation a plot—let's call it a cellular plot—like a terrorist cell in Beirut, or a guerrilla warfare cell in Vietnam. You're a mechanic, you go, you're given orders, you don't even know who you're working for, you don't know who your boss's name is, you have nothing on paper. So my critics say, "How can there be such a conspiracy of so many people?" It doesn't work that way, it's not like 4,000 people have a convention in Miami Beach and agree to kill Kennedy. It is really secret and probably could involve as little as five to six people, or maybe ten people.

Heffner: But there are two basic levels on which your critics operate. One is, "What are the facts of the matter in terms of the Kennedy assassination, who did it, and why?" But the other one is, and this comes up again and again, the sense of "dis-ease" that a film-maker has at his disposal, the skills and the resources to put together pictures that don't even claim to be totally factual in a way, and here they and I would contradict your point about "the American people are wise enough, we know enough and we're clever enough to know that's not reality." I mean, for instance, if you read *Gone with the Wind,* or if you see *Birth of a Nation,* don't you think that those amazingly powerful media presentations are capable of leading people to believe "that's the way it was"?

I guess you're right. I'd say so.

Heffner: Then doesn't Oliver Stone's *JFK* lead us, of necessity, to believe that's the way it was?

I suppose you could argue that, but I guess 9 million Americans have seen the film in the last four weeks and many of them have told me, "Well, I believe part of what you say," or "I believe all of it," or "I believe none of it." So, I mean each person is quite capable of going to a movie and making up his or her own mind. As a parallel argument, one could point to the very strange Zapruder film, which we show in the movie five or six times. That is an extremely powerful piece of film. It is a clock for the assassination. It shows you in detail what happened. And that piece of film is somewhat parallel to my own story with my film that has been for the last 28 years denied completely by the government and by the newspapers. Denied in the sense of, first of all, being locked away for 12 years by Time/Life, and barely shown. It was subpoenaed by Garrison. But what you see is, they constantly keep reminding you, is not what you actually see. In other words, Kennedy may be leaning forward here, but there's 1.6 seconds that has to occur before Connolly gets hit, and you can see it on film, and it's ridiculous. On paper, you can justify that it takes 1.6 seconds for this bullet to exit Kennedy's throat and then make this crazy turn and tumble around and then go through Connolly. But on film it doesn't work. And then, the final headshot, frame 313, you see Kennedy shoot backward like that, hit by a shot coming, I think, obviously from here. And on paper they will convince you that this shot came from back here, but Kennedy went backward when he got hit. So they have taken the power of film and they're saying that this is not what you see, but is the exact opposite of what you see. And that's interesting as a strange sort of contradiction. I guess that they just have a thing about film. I guess they don't like film because the film goes right to the point. You can't lie on film.

Heffner: But what about *Birth of a Nation*, which you would say "lied on film," right?

I'm not that familiar with that film, but I assume you're talking about the Ku Klux Klan scenes.

Heffner: Yes, I'm talking about the feelings generated by that film. Or the anti-black feelings generated by the book *Gone with the Wind*, which created or helped foster a sense of our black community that certainly stood in the way of any meaningful civil rights actions, until the Kennedy, June 1963 civil rights speech. That's what I'm getting at.

First, concerning the accuracy of the point that you're trying to put across, or the speculation that you generate. Secondly, the power of the film. You know, when I have press people here, on *The Open Mind,* mostly they're saying, "Nobody's in here but us chickens—don't talk about our power—after all the American people know better—they know what they read is just what one reporter or one editorial writer believes, or says." And now here are the two media really pitted against each other.

Yes. There's no question that the media has been an enemy to this movie.

Heffner: Only print media?

Well, no, CBS News has attacked the film twice, editorialized about it. Dan Rather has, in the middle of programs, attacked the film without even having seen it. He called it "hokum." Mr. Rather has a stake in the assassination, I think, because he made his career out of it. But we've been attacked on *Nightline.* I had an argument with Ted Koppel recently about that. He accused me of mixing my re-staged footage with my documentary footage, and I said, "Well, you do the same thing," and he said, "How's that?" and I said, "Well, you have a *Nightline* on the KGB, and you put Oswald's fake diary on the screen as if it were real. Oswald never wrote that diary, even the Warren Commission said so. You bring out two witnesses, Priscilla Johnson and Richard Snyder, both of whom are questionable, both of whom have CIA and State Department ties, and they tell you what you want to hear so, you know, don't tell me about your objectivity."

Heffner: Is there any uneasiness on your part about the power of the medium that you wield?

Actually, no. Not enough . . . I think that films should go further. I mean I think they will. I think with the new techniques we're going to

get—we're going to use everything, sound, picture, states of consciousness. What's interesting about the movie, which nobody points
out because it's all about the politics, is that as a piece of movie, it's one
of the fastest movies that goes right to the mind. It's like splinters to
the brain. We have 2,500 cuts in there, I would imagine. We had 2,000
camera set-ups. We're, we're assaulting the senses with a new-wave
technique. We admire MTV editing techniques and we make no
bones about using them. We want to get to the subconscious, get to
the dreamlife and, and certainly seduce the viewer into a new perception of the reality of what occurred in Texas that day. Do you
remember the old *You Are There* television series?

Heffner: Yes.

Which we all—I think we all loved in the fifties—where they put you
into the spot. Well, this is what we are trying to do now, but with
superior techniques.

Heffner: That's the point. Suppose—

Suppose I'm wrong, you're saying—

Heffner: No, no, no. Not "suppose you're wrong." Suppose another
Oliver Stone comes along and uses those even more advanced techniques that you're talking about, aren't we then going to be caught
between the technicians, the film and print technicians, who are
simply massaging our minds to make their own faulted points?

Well, in any given year with 300 movies, you know, probably 280 of
them are bad. I think the audience has to make its own mind up. It's
a democracy and they're quite capable of doing that. And kids are,
too. Don't think kids are as ignorant or naive as we think they are.

Heffner: You say "ignorant" or "naive" and I would simply make the point—and I think you've just made it a hell of a lot better than I could—that we are susceptible to manipulation. Maybe not manipulation, but we are susceptible to being worked over, to having our brains massaged.

I think it's our way of life. We get up in the morning and your wife or your lover makes the point and tries to massage your brain to buy her or buy him something, or you go to your office and you're immediately assaulted by 14 phone calls and 14 different people who want 14 different things out of you. We are always being pulled and tugged. This is life. I don't know that movies are supposed to be some kind of sauna-bath escape from reality.

Heffner: Is there no sense of responsibility then, that the press, or the print media generally or the film media should have in terms of going beyond certain boundaries in manipulating, using their capacity to convince us . . . the viewer, the reader?

Hopefully, there is a responsibility to the facts. For example, we had an excellent research staff, which went over with a fine-tooth comb all the facts as we know them. And as I said before, there are so many un-agreed-upon facts in this case. But we went over it all with a fine-tooth comb and we tried to be responsible to the facts as we know them. The speculation, that's obviously my own, but it also is supported by people like Fletcher Prouty and Jim Garrison and Peter Dale Scott, that the motive, the possible motive for the murder was that it was Kennedy's winding down of the Cold War. But that is obviously theorizing. Arthur Schlesinger, Jr. also agrees with the premise. So it's not that crazy and "out there." But as to the rest of it, the facts—we did the best we could, we exercised a self-appointed responsibility.

Heffner: You will concede that there are many people who would say, that wasn't enough. Differences remain.

Differences in the evaluation, but when we show David Ferrie dead, that was the crime scene at that point and the coroner did say that it looked like a natural death. Which we showed in the movie. We have Jim Garrison walking through the apartment and in his mind, we go to black-and-white I think four times, four cuts, with him imagining, speculating about David Ferrie having pills forced down his throat. Now I just want to point out that that is a speculation, but we also know from the autopsy that there were contusions on the inside of David Ferrie's mouth.

Heffner: You talk about four cuts, but now I've gotten a final cut, and we must end our conversation.

It goes too fast. —1992

OTHER VOICES

Max Lerner on American Civilization

Journalist and author of America as a Civilization

Heffner: Is there a peculiarly American civilization?

For me, a separate civilization is a culture, a society which has moved beyond its own limited, national boundaries and has been creative enough so that it has cut a wide swath in history. In that sense, China was a civilization, Russia was, Greece was, Rome was, France was. And I think America started as a civilization probably, somewhere in the mid-nineteenth century. When Emerson declared that there was, in fact, an American scholar.

Heffner: And today?

I think we are very much a civilization. For many around the world, we seem to be Rome, perhaps a perverted version of Rome. But at any rate, very much a civilization, the center of a Western imperium.

Heffner: But Rome fell.

Yes. And some day America will fall, of course. Civilizations are organisms. The difference between a civilizational organism and a human organism is that our lifespan is limited rather strictly, the lifespan of a civilization is not. And, sometimes when we think a civilization is in decline, it goes on for centuries and centuries.

Heffner: ... Many years ago, you said you were a "possibilist" and you seemed to believe that the possibility, the likelihood is that this nation shall survive now. That we're not in the death throes, this isn't Rome yet. Is that fair to . . .

Yes, I think so. I would say that those who talk about the decline of America don't have a very long perspective. And they don't really think in civilizational terms of the organism. I would say that America is not senile, but probably it's juvenile.

Heffner: Still, Max, still?

It is . . . yes, I think so. It is not senescent, probably adolescent. And our energies, if we die, we will not die as Rome did from a running-down of energies, but perhaps from an explosion of energies. —1988

Harold Evans on American Freedom
Journalist, author of The American Century

I think Americans don't fully appreciate what they've achieved. And I think they certainly don't, as a general mass, realize quite how free they are by comparison with the rest of the world. And I think it's very, very important that they know how it was achieved. The individuals who helped to make it. The ideals. And the failures, too. Because unless a country knows its past, it cannot even begin to think about its future.

Heffner: When you talk about freedom . . . is that the singular quality, if not the only quality that you would put first?

Well, I think freedom is the overarching [quality] . . . obviously Americans I think are, individually and communally, generous, expansive, and enterprising. And it's not a chicken-and-egg situation. I think all

526

of those things flourish in an atmosphere of freedom. And when you don't have freedom . . . freedom of speech, freedom of religion, and freedom of travel, freedom from arbitrary arrest, all these other things, the human personality withers. And we've seen this. Look what happens to art in the totalitarian societies, whether they be Left Wing or Right Wing totalitarian societies, it withers. Creativity does not flourish in an atmosphere of repression.

Heffner: The question for the next century is whether capitalism can triumph over its own contradictions. What are those contradictions?

Well . . . The major contradiction, of course, is that the American economy . . . allowing individual liberty to create wealth . . . also tolerates the largest gap between the rich and the poor in the industrialized world. And the interventionists, who began with Teddy Roosevelt and then Franklin Roosevelt, want to redress that balance. Certainly Franklin Roosevelt did. And always [there is] the dilemma that if you redress it by restricting economic enterprise and freedom, you might actually throw out the baby with the bath water. And this tension is a permanent feature of the American landscape and it's still unresolved because it's quite clear that the economic freedom isn't completely pure and perfect. The kind of unregulated capitalism that we've just seen collapse in the Soviet Union was what America had in 1889. We've gone beyond that, we've regulated capitalism . . . "welfare capitalism" it's called now. But at the end of the day we still have this large gap between the rich and the poor, we still have the blacks in the ghettos getting a lousy education, we still have the corruption of politics by money. So how do we resolve these final things without limiting freedom too much? And I think that is such a fascinating exercise. — 1998

Robert McGuire on American Susceptibility to Terrorism
Former New York City Police Commissioner

Heffner: To what extent to you think we are going to make terrorism succeed by enabling it to disrupt our own sense of well-being—and what do we do as citizens?

I think what we have to understand as Americans what terrorism is. It's a violent act, a very, very fortuitous, serendipitous, accidental violent act. It doesn't matter who it's directed at. And it's designed in effect to achieve a political objective by frightening people, by terrorizing them, by forcing them or their government to do something or inducing them to act on their government to do something in the political context. Americans . . . we're very brave people, but we also have a very short collective fuse. We're impatient. We like solutions to problems. We want this war [the first Gulf War] to be over within ten days. And as anything gets played out in America that's unpleasant, we don't like it. I think we're going to see some of that frustration and impatience if there is an escalating series of terrorist acts. We just have to keep talking about it. We have to educate each other about what is the effort behind these terrorist acts and how will we basically insulate ourselves from what they're trying to achieve . . . They tend to frighten people in the collective sense, and that works its will on the government that's involved. And that's what you really have to guard against because you don't want your government making national security judgments based upon what comes out of various terrorist activity.

Heffner: Are you suggesting that we Americans are more susceptible to terrorism than perhaps other people?

I think in a sense we probably are. We haven't seen it so we don't know. But I think our concern for the individual human life, of even one person being maimed or killed, the fact that we enjoy such unbelievable freedom and liberty in our country I think makes us a little bit more susceptible. The fact that we also, as I said before, are used to quick solutions, quick fixes, we don't like unpleasant things playing out over a long period of time. I think all those things suggest that we might not be the best group of people to confront and resist escalating terrorism. —1991

Dr. Benjamin Spock on Childhood and Social Obligation
Pediatrician, author of books on child-rearing

Heffner: When raising children, where does old-fashioned morality come in?

I think that all children should be brought up in the United States with a feeling that they have strong obligations to society. That the society has enormous problems that could be solved and aren't being solved. And so I would say they ought to be brought up with this kind of moralism. And, in a sense, that would be a kind of patriotism. I think when the young say they don't have much belief in patriotism, they're thinking of the kind of patriotism that made a great majority of the citizens follow Lyndon Johnson blindly into a war. That's the kind of patriotism they're disillusioned with. I want to steal patriotism back. I think it's a perfectly good word, and that all Americans should be brought up with that kind of patriotism. —1974

Dr. Ruth Westheimer on Sex in America
Sex therapist, author

Heffner: Why do you want to add to what you have called the American craziness—talking only about sex?

I realize that there is a tremendous need in our society for this kind of information. And while I still am saying let's not talk about sex all the time, at the same time I'm saying if we can use the power of the mass media in order to educate, in order to tell a woman if she has difficulties having an orgasm, don't just sit there and suffer. Don't fake it. Don't be unhappy and frustrated. But do something about it. Take that aspect of your life, sexual feelings and activity, into your hands by doing something about it if it is not satisfying and pleasurable. For people who will say, "I don't want to have an orgasm," I say wonderful. I hope you have a good meal tonight. But people who do have problems with premature ejaculation, or, for example, older men who might have some difficulties obtaining or maintaining an erection and very often are unhappy out of ignorance, because they don't know that they need to be physically stimulated in order to obtain an erection. So very often what happened is a lot of unhappiness out of ignorance.

Heffner: Doesn't so much talk and so much sexual activity in our media add to the frustrations, to the concerns of the troubled women and men you talk about?

What adds [tension] is unreal expectations. If the soap operas tell us that a healthy couple is having sexual activity every night, then I have to smile and say, look, I'm a very mature older woman. I see a lot of people coming in to my office and talking to me. It's not so. But when you do engage in that activity, that is after all given to us, that is free, that is there to be enjoyed, do it so that it is pleasurable for both of you.

Heffner: How would you evaluate the changes in our sexual mores and behavior over the decades in which you have played a major role in increasing our sexual awareness?

When I started in 1981, the radio people would not use specific, explicit sexual terminology. They would still say that someone is pregnant . . . "she's with child." So what has changed is the vocabulary.

The problems have not changed. The issues between men and women, the issues in terms of sexual literacy, of knowledge. The only thing that has changed is in this country we have the best scientifically validated data about human sexual functioning that has ever been available, and we are talking more about it. We do have less unintended pregnancies in this country, but we still have too many. We have less women who have difficulties having sexual satisfaction. So there is that change.

Heffner: Is there a conviction on your part that with all the emphasis on sex there is still something new to learn?

Yes, we do have some new data. We can send a man to a sleep laboratory and the next morning he walks out with a computer printout of his erectile activity. We now have data that women can be aroused by visual stimuli. So in terms of knowledge, even that pill Viagra is a fantastic pharmaceutical invention. That is if properly used, with a medical doctor saying "okay," with education making sure that that man doesn't think he pops that pill, he goes home, he hasn't brought her home any flowers, he hasn't taken the garbage out the night before, but he's going to say, "I now took the pill, hop into bed." I can foretell lots of problems, and then I would say, " I told you so." [But] we do have a tremendous amount of good scientific knowledge, which we have to use but properly. In sex education, it has to be a combination of parents, schools, churches, and synagogues, everybody together, And I do believe that we need that information and still be able to say, "There have to be boundaries." There have to be boundaries of good taste.

Heffner: What do you see as the major developments that lie before us in your area of expertise?

I think that more and more because of television, because our children are more sophisticated, because of the Internet, I think that more and more people are going to do sex education. Everybody has to be an ask-able parent. I believe there will be more and more education. There will be kindergarten teachers who will sit with parents and say, "Okay, let's do this together. We have to talk about how babies are born." There are going to be more grade-school teachers and parents who are going to say, "How are we going to control what our children see on computers and on the Internet?" I'm an optimist that all of this is going to bring about more education and less problems. —1985 and 1998

Norman Mailer on Writers and Writing
Novelist, journalist

I think most writers, most serious and talented writers, are generally opposed to the government of the state they live in. I think this is natural. Untalented writers are often highly developed functionaries; they are functionaries of the word and the paragraph and they can write manipulative prose. There's a great difference in my mind between people who write manipulative prose, that is prose to try to get people to do certain things in certain ways (inspirational books would come under the head of manipulative prose). And there are people who are really trying to communicate a vision of life such as it is. It can be a warped vision of life. An angry vision. A satiric vision. Or whatever, but it's their vision. And when they're trying to do that, they're trying to write as well as they possibly can. And they tend almost always to be critical of the country that they live in. And thereby serve an immensely valuable purpose. That's the critical factor you might say. Where would we all be if we didn't have a critical side to our brain that was always monitoring our actions and saying well, you've made a damn fool of yourself again?

Heffner: You know, Neil Postman, the social and cultural critic, seems to believe that, given the electronic media of our times, we may become less and less involved with the written word. Does that seem to you to be the case?

Oh, it's a great concern of mine. I think it quite possibly can happen. I wouldn't know how to put it, but I just feel that television leaches out interest in the written word. And I think we're all becoming reduced, serious novelists are becoming almost as rare, almost as much a luxury to culture as poets were just twenty years ago. In other words, 20 years ago people would read novels and wouldn't think that much about reading poetry. They didn't feel any longer that they really had to read poetry. Reading a good novel was enough. Or even reading any novel was enough. I think at this point reading a good novel is equal in the average person's mind to reading poetry. Why be bothered with it? It's too difficult. Too tricky. To what end?

. . . On the Existential Edge

Something can be wonderful and splendid and still be insane. Insanity is at the edge of all splendid ventures. If they fail, then the person who led them was usually insane. There's that wonderful story about Fidel Castro—he landed in Cuba with something like 86 men and lost all but 12 of them the night he landed because he'd been betrayed. He wandered around in the hills for five days, turned to one of his people one dawn, and said, "The days of the dictatorship are numbered. We will triumph." At that point, the man who writes the story says, "I thought our leader was mad." Well, if Castro had been hit by a sniper's bullet in the next moment, everyone would have said, "Of course he was mad." The fact of the matter is that he then went on and he was right. He saw something. He saw something going on in Cuba. Whatever it was, maybe some peasant took them in. He saw a peasant who wouldn't have taken them in a year or two before. He saw something that gave him the idea that the days of the dictatorship were numbered. He was a genius. So he won. He triumphed. If he had failed, then he would have been a fool. He would have been insane. There are a great many people who live in this embattled relation to existence. They are taking such enormous chances that if they succeed they're one thing, if they fail, they are another. That's what it means to be on the existential edge. It means that you can't write your own obituary. —1986

Howard Fast on the American Communist Party
Journalist, author of memoir Being Red

... My beliefs never changed, my ideals never changed, these were the ideas that I held, that the people who were in the party with me held, and now, at last, the truth about the American Communist Party must come out. Now, for example, the lexicon of great names in publishing, in writing, in art, in music, who were members of the Communist Party is a cross-section of the very best in the United States during the '30s and the '40s. These were people of talent, of high principle, of great dreams and great ideals. These people were not apostits when they left the Party. The Party which had given them, or at least pretended to give them a great dream of a brotherhood of man, became something else and what it became was illustrated on a worldwide scale in the Soviet Union. I think that if the Party here had come to power, they would not have done well, they would perhaps have done as badly as in the Soviet Union. The structure was flawed, it was terribly flawed. . . . They spread out on man's old dream of the brotherhood of man, called socialism in the Industrial Age . . . they implanted on this a rigid, terrible structure, which they called the dictatorship of the proletariat. It's not the dictatorship of the proletariat, it became the dictatorship of the handful of people who led the party. And as with all dictatorships, it could not work, it brought only doom and destruction, and we see the last stages of this horror in the Soviet Union. . . .

In the '30s Ronald Reagan, who I must say was a person of good will—there was not much there, and not enough inside, but this man had good will. And in the '30s he saw all around him people he loved and respected, people whom he admired. as the best in the Hollywood community, as members of the Communist Party. So he decided he wanted to join the Party. So this was passed on to the man who was then in a position to decide, as far as the Hollywood community was concerned, the playwright, John Howard Lawson, and Lawson was very uneasy with it. He said, "Look, this man is a flake. You, you never know what he'll do tomorrow." And he asked a very famous actor, who I will not name, still alive, to talk Reagan out of it. And this actor and his wife sat until the small hours of the morning and convinced Reagan that he could be more use to the Party as a nonmember of the Party. Now, I don't think this reduces Reagan. I think this, this helps Reagan, it helps the image of the . . . as a man of compassion, certainly at that time. But, it's an angle on the Communist Party that we do not hear. —1991

Ralph Reed on the Right and the Mainstream

Director of the Christian Coalition

Heffner: Why do you think the Christian Coalition has not been accepted as mainstream in this country?

I think part of it has been our own fault. After the Scopes Trial of 1925, evangelicals and those who hold to those very basic Christian beliefs largely withdrew from the culture and from the political square. And as a result we did not have the kind of involvement or prominence in American public life until we began to get back involved again in the late seventies. Part of it is, I think, a cultural estrangement and a cultural divide that separates middle America from opinion leaders and cultural elites. There was a survey, for example, conducted in 1981, that I think is instructive along these lines. It was conducted by Stu Rothenberg and another sociologist who interviewed editors and other prominent journalists. And 86 percent of them said they attended church either not at all or almost not at all. And only 14 percent attended church on a regular basis, meaning a couple of times a month. By contrast, when we survey the American people, according to Gallup, 57 percent of the American people say they pray every single day, and about half of America's population is in church every Sunday. There are more people in church on Sunday morning than there are watching *60 Minutes* on Sunday night. But there's a sense in which there's that divide between the churchgoing, mainstream public and those who write our books and teach our students and run our universities. And I don't mean that in any way to question their values—a lot of these people have very strong values. But I'm just saying, you know, a lot of times I will get asked, as Dan Quayle would, or other conservatives, "What would you do if your daughter had an abortion," or "What would you do if your son came in and he said he was gay?" Sometimes you almost want to turn that question on its head and ask the editor of one of America's top three or four metropolitan dailies, "What would you do if your child came in and said, 'Dad, I'm born again'?" Probably be a sense of horror in some of these, and I just don't think that they understand. I don't think they have very many friends who are deeply committed Christians. I don't think they have a social circle that encompasses those kinds of people. And I think when you don't have friends who come out of that milieu, I think oftentimes it's easy to misunderstand and misapprehend, and have stereotyped views. —1993

Allan Bloom on Great Books and American Education
Author of The Closing of the American Mind

Well, I'm a boy . . . or I once was a boy, that comes from a family that's not well-to-do. Whose grandparents were immigrants. And within this society I got a chance for a marvelous education. It wasn't part of the reigning idolatry, but it was distinctly possible. And it was that America that I grew up with, from 1946, after the Second World War, you know when we all felt we had fought a just war and the GI Bill. I started at the University of Chicago at the age of 15. That was the Hutchins plan. I started off the second year of high school with veterans who were in their late twenties, thirties, who had been war heroes, but who had never had a chance to go to college, and who came to the University of Chicago and were reading Aristotle and thrilled by it. That seemed to me an attempt to mix the best things that tradition has brought with a certain egalitarianism. I precisely think that Henry Adams and T. S. Eliot—in trying to attach themselves to places and times which no longer exist, to attach themselves in their whole being—denied part of their own existence. As Saul Bellow says: even if you're going to make the trip to eternity, you have to get . . . at least in Chicago . . . on the train at Randolph Street. You have to pass through the experiences of your own time and place. And I think I have a higher sense of the possible independence of the mind than Adams and Eliot do. Or did. . . . What I mean to say is that anybody, at any time, can with the proper resources touch what is highest humanly and that it is not in the reconstitution of other imperfect societies or in the longing or nostalgia for them that one becomes educated. —1987

Howard Gardner on American Education

Professor of Education at Harvard University and author of
The Disciplined Mind

I would say that probably all over the world we're not nearly as successful as we could be. But I think we have a particular disease in this country which I pin to some extent on the television quiz shows, the *Jeopardy, Wheel of Fortune* way of thinking that we believe that a person is educated if they have lots and lots of information. It's what you might call the idiot-savant notion . . . a person who's read the encyclopedia and memorized it, is the person who's seen as being the most erudite and the most educated. A very interesting comparison has been done across 20 or 30 countries . . . it's called the Third International Math and Science Comparisons . . . kids all over the world, East Asia and Europe and the Americas take a bunch of tests about math and science. Not only do American kids not do well in those comparisons, but deeper study has shown that in fact the United States . . . we've tried to cover two or three times as much stuff in our math and science. So needless to say, it's very superficial, we're a mile wide and an inch deep. And in these other countries, they cover fewer topics, they go into them in more depth . . . there's a better chance of the students really understanding something like evolution or the laws of mechanics. And amazingly, sometimes the students in these other countries actually do better in questions which they haven't studied because, so to speak they've learned how to think about things, they've learned vocabulary, and they can say, "Gee, I really didn't know that much about light, but if they're asking the question this way, this must be the right one out of four choices." The American kids, if they were sick the day that they did light, it's all over . . . there's no way they're going to get the right answer to the question. So, while disciplined thinking is not as well developed anywhere as it should be, I think our fetish about covering stuff . . . as I often say, "getting from Plato to NATO in 36 weeks" is a money-back guarantee that there may be a lot of stuff there at the end of the year, but there isn't much understanding. And, of course, the stuff disappears pretty quickly. We all know enough not to give kids an exam two or three years after the course is over. —1999

Arthur Levine on Helping American Children out of Poverty
President of Columbia University's Teacher's College

Heffner: . . . When I read *Beating the Odds: How the Poor Get to College,* I didn't read about devices; I read about human beings, about the impact upon a person, of mentors. How do you factor that into this whole question of educational technology? What you wrote about here are human beings acting upon human beings.

I've never, ever thought that technology was the answer to poverty. . . . The difficulty I see now is that it's going to leave kids in poverty further behind if they don't know technology. It's a human being that makes the difference. Kids move, kids succeed. The poverty-breaker isn't new technology; the poverty-breaker is people who care about kids.

Heffner: So how do you break those bonds?

. . . One of the surprises was I ended up doing this study of kids almost by accident. . . . I had moved into a housing project. I spent some time talking to moms, I spent some time talking with kids. I had asked the kids, "If you could go as far as you want in school, how far would you go?" The most common answer was, "Tenth grade," followed distantly by "Twelfth." I asked them, "Do you know anybody who has ever completed college? Who's ever gone to college?" The answer was, "No." I asked them, "Do you know anybody who's ever finished high school?" And they had friends of relatives, or relatives of friends, but nobody in their immediate lives. I talked to their moms, and I said, "Tell me about college." I guess first I asked them, "What do you want for your kids?" And they said, "Well, I want my kid to be successful. I want my kid to be happy. I don't want my kid to get into trouble." They want the same thing any other parent does. And I'd say, "Tell me about college." And the answer was glazed eyes, wide expressions. They're not college people. I asked them the same question as, "Do you expect your kid to go to Mars?" The surprise in the study that we did was finding anybody to be a mentor. Anybody. The person who really stood out for me was one who had had a fourth-grade education, spoke no English, had a child out of wedlock, worked in a hospital as an orderly, saw the doctors, concluded the doctors weren't smarter than she was, they were just better educated, and said, "My daughter is going to have what they have." Her daughter ended up being an undergraduate at

Harvard and is now doing her medical work at Yale. Anybody can be a mentor. We have the capacity to turn anybody in the United States into a mentor. They only need four characteristics in common. What we found was that there were people who really believed that hard work paid off, they really believed they could make a difference through education, they felt that they could make a difference in kids' lives personally, and finally, they were bicultural. They understood poverty, and they understood middle-class life, and they understood what it took to get from one to the other. What we need to do is train a nation of mentors.

Heffner: And? How do you go about that?

Well, there are lots of ways to do that. One of the things that colleges and universities are forever talking about is making a difference in schools. And we watch lots of colleges and universities now step into a school, adopt a school, participate in a school. One of the most useful things they could do is begin offering classes for parents, issues of mentoring, issues on schooling, teaching the kinds of very basic skills that are necessary for a kid to make it. Those classes are possible. In colleges, they're possible. In industry, they're possible. Community organizations. It doesn't take a lot to convince a parent they can make a difference in their kids' lives, and that's really where the effort needs to go. I think it would be far better to do this on a local basis than it would be to start a federal program. I think it would be more worthwhile to try this in our cities and our communities than it would be to try this in Washington, DC. —1996

Henry Grunwald on Defining America
Former Editor-in-Chief of Time, Inc.

One of our great virtues is that we really think we can do anything we set our minds to. And that, I think, has driven America to tremendous heights and to tremendous accomplishments. And I wouldn't necessarily want it any other way. But we also sometimes have a very unrealistic perception of what we can do, what human nature can accomplish. And when we fail, we become very disillusioned and very disaffected, and in a sense, blame everybody in sight: politicians, journalists. And both of these categories certainly deserve a share of blame. We blame foreigners. We blame conspiracies. We're particularly eager to blame conspiracies. And we do not, often enough, it seems to me, blame ourselves for perhaps lack of effort or lack of realism. And I think this sets up these two opposite poles, as it were, sets up a certain tension, which, more often than not, but not always, is creative. —2003

Daniel Patrick Moynihan on Why the War on Poverty Was Never Won

U.S. Senator, former American Ambassador to the United Nations

Heffner: Did we not go far enough in the war on poverty?

I can tell you the answer, and I can describe the moment it happened. I think it was March 2nd or something like that, about 10:30 in the morning. It was a Cabinet meeting. Sargent Shriver is head of the task force on poverty, and Adam Yarmolinsky and I went to the Cabinet meeting. And President Johnson was there. Shriver was asked to sit at the table opposite the President. We sat behind him and described this new program . . . Our main proposal was a major employment program which we wanted to finance by a five-cent increase in the tobacco tax. Lyndon Johnson looked across at Sargent Shriver and says, "You don't understand. This is an election year. We are cutting taxes. We are not raising taxes.". . . It was over before it began. —1985

DATE DUE			
DEC 1 9 2009			